IS THERE LIFE AFTER DEATH?

THE EXTRAORDINARY SCIENCE OF
WHAT HAPPENS WHEN WE DIE

ANTHONY PEAKE

ARCTURUS

ARCTURUS

Arcturus Publishing Limited
26/27 Bickels Yard
151–153 Bermondsey Street
London SE1 3HA

Published in association with
foulsham
W. Foulsham & Co. Ltd,
The Publishing House, Bennetts Close, Cippenham,
Slough, Berkshire SL1 5AP, England

ISBN: 978-0-572-03227-2

This edition printed in 2007
Copyright © 2006 Anthony Peake/Arcturus Publishing Limited

British Library Cataloguing-in-Publication Data: a catalogue record for this
book is available from the British Library

Printed in Finland

Contents

Foreword

This book presents a most astounding and provocative model for understanding the one inescapable event in your life: your death. You might expect a book entitled *Is There Life After Death?* to discuss your afterlife in another realm, or perhaps reincarnated into a different body. But in fact Tony Peake does not think that we survive the death of our bodies; he argues instead that we do not die at all, that bodily death as we usually think of it is in fact not possible. Presenting insights from contemporary neuroscience and quantum physics as well as ancient cosmologies and mystical traditions, Peake presents a coherent picture of a universe that literally requires you to be immortal.

What Peake suggests is that when we appear to others to die, we in fact begin our lives all over again – and again and again and again in seemingly endless succession. As preposterous as this assertion may seem, Peake finds persuasive evidence to support it from a wide variety of sources – but most of all from our common, everyday experiences. How often have you had a sensation that you were re-living an event for a second time? How often have you had a correct 'hunch' about something that was about to happen? Are these mere illusions? Peake suggests that they are glimpses of what is really going on: that you are in fact re-living a life you have already lived – perhaps many, many times.

But why is it, then, that we do not remember living this life before? Here Peake draws on ancient teachings that, at the approach of death, our consciousness 'splits' into a 'lower self' that will re-live the life without any memory of it, and a 'higher self' that retains the memory but remains in the background. How many times have you had the feeling that you have been guided by a force that knows everything about you? How many times have you 'heard a voice' guiding you in your daily life? Are these mere illusions? Peake suggests something much simpler: that they are brief intuitions of your 'higher self' breaking through.

Does all this sound like science fiction or like religious babble? Peake argues persuasively that all of this is not only compatible with contemporary science, but indeed prescribed by it. You will read in this book about Schrödinger's cat-in-a-box thought experiment, about the Copenhagen and Many Worlds Interpretations of quantum physics, about Minkowski time-lines, and about the 'quantum Zeno effect'. From these concepts, accepted by physicists for most of the past century, Peake shows how the physical world around you is completely dependent on your perception of it. If your consciousness ceased to exist, so would your universe, along with any record of its existence. Thus, this understanding of quantum physics demands that you never die.

You may protest now that this is absurd, that you have certainly known people who died. In your universe, other people can die; but in their universes they continue to live. And likewise you will surely die in other people's universes; but just as surely, you cannot die in your own universe. A corollary to this model is that your life is not a brief and meaningless hiccup in the course of eternity. In fact, Peake argues that you yourself are the very centre of your universe – and for you, that is the only universe there is.

How then do we explain your illusion that you live for one finite lifetime? Here Peake examines what happens in the brain as death approaches. You will read about the common features of near-death experiences: the slowing of time, the encounter with an apparently omniscient entity, and a review of your entire life; about brain stimulation studies, evolution, 'Freudian slips' and déjà vu, epilepsy and schizophrenia. Peake shows that the slowing of your sense of time dictated by chemical changes in your dying brain allows you to re-experience your life all over again – in seconds, in someone else's universe, but in another full life-time in yours. While an observer may fix the time of your death in his or her world, the passage of time in your universe is changing, so that you never actually reach the point of death, but instead you re-live your life in what for you is real time. Each time you approach the end of your life, your time slows down and your 'higher' self guides you into a re-experience of your entire life, but this time with the ability to make changes, allowing for your evolution over the course of your lifetimes.

You may be asking yourself at this point who Tony Peake is to expect you to accept such outlandish ideas. In fact, none of these ideas are his: what he has done is to pull together in a most creative way the puzzle pieces that were there all along. You will find in this book evidence from a wide range of sources, from quantum physics to neurophysiology, from clinical psychiatry to various mystical traditions. But Peake does not appeal to the authority of these sources; they are merely the frameworks to help you understand your own experience. The ultimate authority to which Peake appeals is your own personal experience. He challenges you to think about those 'coincidences' in life that may in fact be the fingerprints of something else.

Your own consciousness is at once the most complex problem in the universe and also the simplest, most self-evident fact. Likewise, the picture that Peake draws in this book of what happens at death is at once incredibly complex and also incredibly simple and self-evident. Peake's explanation of your immortality is the most innovative and provocative argument I have seen. The question is whether that is the way your universe really works. And as this book shows, that answer is up to you.

BRUCE GREYSON, M.D.
Charlottesville, Virginia
January 31, 2006

Prologue

We are the music makers

And we are the dreamers of dreams

Wandering by lone sea-breakers

And sitting by desolate streams;

World-losers and world forsakers,

On whom the pale moon gleams;

Yet we are the movers and shakers

Of the world forever, it seems.

Arthur O'Shaughnessy

What made you pick up this book? What series of events brought about the circumstances whereby you are reading these words? And why this book and not the dozens of others that you could have chosen? It is possible that you were guided by a power that you are, at present, only vaguely aware of – a power that has guided your life to this point, to have you looking down on this page and wondering what these words mean.

It's all to do with the one certainty that your life holds – that you will, one day, die. Death is not something that only happens to other people. As sure as you are breathing now, you will, at some indeterminate time in the future, cease to exist. Whatever is doing the self-reflection at this moment in time, whatever it is that is processing these black lines on white paper into concepts and ideas, it will suddenly cease to be. No memories, no feelings, no thoughts, just blank. A whole lifetime of learning and decision-making snuffed out in the blink of an eye. To exist no more from that moment forth until the last dying embers of the universe. You did not exist for billions of years and you will not exist again for billions of years. In relative terms, you existed for a ridiculously short amount of time and then you are gone.

So what is the point of your life and what can be the reason for conscious matter to come about only to disappear? For some philosophers and psychologists you are not really conscious at all. You are fooling yourself into believing that you exist – it is a giant self-deception. However, we know that we are conscious and we also know that we are, in some way, not part of the physical world with which we interact. We also see as a tragic waste the fact that we spend our lives striving to acquire knowledge, gaining wisdom, loving and being loved and learning from our mistakes only to disappear as if we never existed. Surely it would be better if human beings were not conscious because to be not conscious is to not be aware of one's own mortality? However, all may not be what it seems. There may after all be a plan for you and a reason for your existence. There is strong evidence to show that your life is for a reason and that you, as a conscious entity, do not die but will go on learning and growing.

If we reflect on the term 'to learn by one's mistakes', at first glance its meaning is transparent, but a moment's thought will show this to be an impossible situation. Every mistake is made just the once. A similar mistake is exactly that – similar; it is not the same. In order to learn by a mistake one must have the opportunity to put it right. One must feel in the deepest way the trauma, pain and anguish that a wrong decision can bring about not only for oneself, but also, more importantly, for others. But in the world as we perceive it there is only one life and as such we only make each mistake once. We see the error but can never put it right. We miss out on the perfect learning experience. In management training courses this method of learning is used widely – it is termed 'role playing'. You are allowed to make the error and then you are given the chance to go back and do it again the 'right' way.

In the film *Groundhog Day*, a hardened TV weatherman, Phil

Conners, is sent to Pennsylvania to cover a story about an annual event that takes place in the small town of Punksatawny. The circumstances of him being there are irrelevant but what happens to him during his 'time' covering 'Groundhog Day' is disturbingly prescient. He stays in a small hotel and checks in the day before the annual event. He wakes up the next morning and follows through a series of events, all of which show him to be a self-centred, bitter and shallow individual. Because of a snowstorm he and his film team have to stay over an additional night in the hotel. When he wakes up the next morning he discovers that he is living the previous day again. All around him are unaware of this. After his initial shock he realizes that he knows what is about to happen throughout the day and consequently finds that he can, by his previous experience, influence events to bring about a different outcome. Puzzled, he goes to bed to awake to another repeat of the same day. This time he is even more in touch with his powers to bring about change. The day then repeats over and over again with Conners using his knowledge to his own advantage. But as he continues to live the day over and over again he sees how he can influence other people's lives for the good. Slowly he becomes more caring and less self-centred until he is rushing around the small town saving lives and making small gestures of kindness that, by cause and effect, bring about great change. Conners has ceased being a selfish arrogant individual and has become a much more 'developed' human being. Although not stated in the film, he moves into a mind state that the Buddhists term 'Nirvana' – loss of selfhood. He sees himself as part of a greater whole and does good without looking for reward. Once he reaches this state he is, by some implied and unseen divine intervention, allowed to move on. The next morning becomes just that, he wakes up and it is the next day. Was it a dream or some form of time flux? *Groundhog Day* is a fiction, a parable created to entertain and possibly edify, but it may be that the writers had, in some subconscious way, tripped upon a deeper reality than mere fact and fiction. What if *Groundhog Day* is a small clue as to what reality is really about? Believe it or not, this life you are living is equivalent to a Groundhog *Life*.

Like most of us, it is likely you get the occasional sensation that you are perceiving an event for a second time. This sensation, termed *déjà vu*, (French for 'already seen') is more accurately *déjà vécu* ('already lived'). The phenomenon is the single most common psychic state that human beings perceive and is still to be adequately explained. Many attempts have been made, including convoluted theories about the brain perceiving a single event twice with a slight delay in the presentation of the two events to consciousness; another is that it is proof of reincarnation. The real explanation is far more obvious than that. It is exactly what it seems to be – the literal re-living of something that has been experienced some time in the past.

Further evidence of previous lives is when we experience 'hunches' that doing something is either right or wrong, an ill-at-ease or positive feeling that one particular course of action will have a positive or negative outcome. Related to this is an even stronger indicator that involves pre-cognitive abilities, an ability to 'know' what is about to happen before it takes place.

A final and perhaps disturbing clue to those who do not understand what is happening to them is the 'voices'. These individuals 'hear' voices in their head that literally advise and suggest actions to be taken. In many cases these are mistakenly seen as being what have now become known as 'spirit guides' and, in extreme cases, the voice of God.

At first sight all these clues can be seen as evidence for the supernatural – pointers towards a world beyond the senses. The reality is far more interesting in that all the phenomena outlined are explicable within the boundaries of known scientific knowledge, particularly the realms of quantum physics and neurology.

The truth of the matter is (for the moment you are going to find this very hard to accept), the quantum physics and neurology that explain these events are *your* quantum physics as this book is *your* book. You are its author, not me, because I do not exist in this particular universe. This is because you, and you alone, are the only conscious being in this universe. Indeed, without you perceiving it, this universe will simply cease to exist. Within this universe you are a god, not the God who may be the architect of a far more complex cosmos, but the unsuspecting creator of all you perceive.

Mankind, with you as its representative in this particular universe, is about to enter a new era of self-awareness. In a subtle way your intellect has been prepared for the arguments in this book through recent undercurrents in the media, particularly cinema and computer games. Social scientists have a term for this upsurge of collective consciousness before a seismic change in understanding takes place. The precursors to paradigm change are presented through a phenomenon known as *zeitgeist*. This word, German for 'World Spirit' manifests itself in many ways but the mass medium of cinema is a perfect tool for the third millennium. The writers of *Groundhog Day* had unconsciously picked up the vibrations of the *zeitgeist* and without being fully aware of what they were doing wrote a deeper truth clothed in a shallower fiction. And *Groundhog Day* is but one of many films that have been influenced by this subliminal manipulation.

While it is possible that you have already been directed subconsciously to see these films, it is also possible that you have not yet received guidance. In which case may I suggest that as you make your way through this book you take the time out to watch the films and read the books mentioned below. In isolation each one illuminates one subject area that you will encounter in this book. Taken together, they act as beacons pointing the way for you to go.

While *Groundhog Day* is based in everyday reality and the individuals that Phil Conners interacts with are, in some senses, real people who react with their own motivations, for Neo in *The Matrix* there is no such comfort. He discovers that reality itself is an inwardly created illusion brought about by alien life-forms. A similar thing happens to David Aames in *Vanilla Sky*, but his illusion involves him re-living his life while he 'exists' in a state of suspended animation hovering in the Netherworld between life and death. In order to help him realize this fact he is shown how he can, by force of mind, manipulate his environment and make time stop. A similar topic permeates the films *Bladerunner*, *Total Recall* and *Minority Report*. Here the issue is more to do with the truthfulness of memory; specifically can memories be implanted in such a way that the consciousness in question has no way of objectively knowing that they did not really 'experience' those events first hand?

The curious thing about all these films is that they can be linked. At first sight they are productions with different directors and different scriptwriters. However, a deeper review brings up some interesting facts. Tom Cruise stars in both *Vanilla Sky* and *Minority Report* and *Minority Report*, *Bladerunner* and *Total Recall* are all based upon short stories by the same writer, the cult science fiction author Philip K Dick. Dick in turn heavily influenced the writers of *The Matrix*; the clue lies in the choice of title. Dick firmly believed that reality was a total illusion; a fabrication that keeps human beings from knowing what reality really consists of. He termed this hidden reality 'the matrix'. For Dick we are, like Neo at the start of the film, trapped in a super-sensory illusion, a charade that Dick called 'The Black-Eyed Prison'.

Dick's beliefs were based on the teachings of the 1st-century schismatic Christian sect known as the Gnostics. Since that time Gnosticism has been a secretive and often persecuted minority within the greater Christian fold. Central to their beliefs is not only that reality is an illusion created by an evil lesser god called the Demiurge but also that all human beings have a dual nature. Everyday human consciousness exists in the 'lower' nature and is denied knowledge of its own superior 'higher' nature because it remains trapped within Dick's 'Black-Eyed Prison', the illusion that we all perceive as reality. By realizing our own higher nature we can escape this trap and access the realm of the true God, Dick's 'Matrix'.

The Gnostics believed in a higher self they called the 'Daemon'. Once the lower self (termed 'The Eidolon') realizes the reality of its own Daemon, he or she breaks out of the 'Mind-Forged Manacles', as our illusory reality was termed by another Gnostic, the poet and mystic William Blake.

Tom Cruise was keen to buy the international rights of an obscure Spanish movie called *Open Your Eyes*. Written and directed by Alejandro Amenábar, this film deals with the Gnostic idea that reality is inwardly generated. Cruise was keen to re-make the film with the assistance of director Cameron Crowe. In his own way Crowe then added his own fascination with memory and how it influences the way we build up our personal versions of reality. In scene after scene the Cruise character, David Aames, populates his version of reality with images from his own past. In one scene the cover from an early Bob Dylan album is reproduced with Cruise and Penelope Cruz doubling up as copies of Bob Dylan and his then girlfriend. This ongoing memory imagery was a subtle but revealing change made by Crowe over the original version. It comes therefore as no surprise that when released the film, renamed *Vanilla Sky*, was seen as a complex and deeply esoteric work. Many audiences failed to see the point and some critics were likewise confused. The ideas presented were simply too 'out there' for mass consumption. However, I am of the opinion that Cruise and Crowe knew exactly what they were trying to present: Gnosticism for the masses.

And so the *zeitgeist* works its magic in films as it has done in recent years in the world of publishing. Books such as the massively successful *Celestine Prophesy* touch upon the subject matter central to the book you have in front of you. Put simply, *Celestine Prophesy* and its sequels say 'Watch out for the coincidences'. Life itself consists of chance meetings, fortuitous events and weird synchronicities. What the author, James Redfern, fails to do is adequately explain what is really taking place. As with many others who show interest in the subject matter he fails to make the intuitive leap needed to catch the truth. Coincidences happen because the observer makes them happen. If it is your reality then surely coincidences will happen all the time.

It is the task of *Is There Life After Death?* to demonstrate that you are the master of all you survey, that you exist within your own 'Black Eyed Prison'. This book can provide the key whereby you can open those Mind-Forged Manacles and see the *Vanilla Sky* for what it really is, a very ornate and complex illusion.

In *The Matrix*, the hero Neo has to choose between a red or blue pill. If he takes the blue pill he will stay ignorant of what lies behind the illusion. If he takes the red pill he goes 'down the rabbit hole' to discover the reality outside of the construct called 'the Matrix'. This is another myth, a modern version.

What you now know of yourself and your relationship with the universe is the blue pill.

This book is the red pill...

CHAPTER 1

In a Mind's Mirror Reflected

Gracious one play, your head is an empty shell,

Wherein your mind frolics infinitely.

Old Sanskrit proverb

By your own bootstraps

There is something very wrong with what we term 'reality'. Indeed, if the results of the latest research into the nature of matter are to be believed then the world outside of ourselves, the world that is presented to us by our senses, is made up of... nothing.

Physicists, in their never-ending search for the building blocks of matter have, nearly a century after Einstein's discovery of relativity, come up with little more than ripples in a sea of probability. Everything you perceive, if broken down into its constituent parts, is made up of particles that zip in and out of existence as they are observed. When they are not observed they do not exist. The act of observation forces them into an unstable and begrudging solidity. Look away and they go back to insubstantial shadows. The frightening thing is that trillions upon trillions of these unstable 'things' make up a physical object, an object that depends upon its fragile existence by being perceived by an observer. In this particular universe that observer is you. However, you and your brain are also made up of electrons, quarks and the other elemental particles. Like the man who lifted himself off the ground by pulling on his own bootstraps, so it is that you bring yourself and this whole universe into existence.

And what about you – the being reading this book? Where do you start and end in this mystery? Are you your body? The logical answer is no because parts of your body may be cut away and as long as you remain alive you will exist in what is left. So, for instance, to say that a photograph is 'of you' is an error of labelling. You are not your face anymore than you are your fingernail. So just what are you? The location of the major sense organs such as the eyes and the ears give the illusion that 'you' are located in your head. As such you assume that you are your brain. But what if your eyes, ears and tongue were to be found on your knee? Would you not have the sensation that you are located somewhere just behind your kneecap?

Modern neurology has located thought as being in the brain. Certain sensations and emotions can be seen firing neurons (brain cells) in specific parts of the brain. Might this be evidence that 'you' are inside your head? Logically yes, but could not the thoughts themselves be stimulated by activity elsewhere in time and space? A television set receives radio waves and describes a picture on a TV screen. The TV studio that is seen on the TV screen does not 'exist' in the television. It is consciousness that causes the neurons to fire, not the neurons firing that brings about the sensation of consciousness.

You are 'you' because you believe that you are. You know this through your memories. You know who you are because you remember your past life. You can recall what happened to you five minutes ago. Indeed, you can remember with clarity picking up this book and starting to read the paragraph four or so inches above. However, how do you know that that is what actually happened? What if those memories, all your memories, were implanted into your consciousness a split second ago? How could you tell? You have no actual 'proof' other than your own remembrance of the events. The only thing that you know with any certainty is that 'you' are perceiving at this particular moment in time. As soon as that moment passes so your consciousness moves along to another moment. In this way you pass through time in a series of unrelated moments that exist at the junction point between what has just been perceived – termed 'the past' – and what is about to be perceived – termed 'the future'.

You are travelling along a time line of perceptions. This journey started when you first began to perceive the universe outside of you at your moment of birth and it will continue until you cease to perceive at your moment of death. Therefore, what you really are is a series of perceptions that exist between the non-existence of your pre-birth state to the non-existence of your post-death state. For billions of years you did not exist and for billions of years you will not exist. For a pointlessly small amount of time something perceived something and then disappeared again.

For religious people this is not a problem. For them the time that a conscious being spends in the physical universe is because a deity – supreme or otherwise – decides it to be so. That deity then takes the non-physical personality of that being back to the timeless and spaceless realm of eternity. The time spent in the physical universe is but a small part of the potential existence that a consciousness can experience. To understand the logic and motivation of such a deity is, quite naturally, impossible for a human being. It is simply accepted.

For those who do not have the comfort of religion, the idea of death may seem a disturbing and frightening inevitability. It simply does not make sense. Even for those with faith the simple truth is that 'being' is the only state of consciousness that we know. The idea that at some time in the future you, as a conscious entity, will cease to exist whilst the rest of the universe will continue without you is impossible to comprehend. For all of your life you have been located somewhere. In a split second you will fall through into a void; a neverwhen contained in a vast echoing nothingness. The idea that you will not be anywhere in space or time is literally unthinkable.

However, things may not be what they seem. Consciousness may survive the death of the physical body and in a way that does not invalidate any religious belief system. In a very real sense all religions may be right. The solution lies in a radical redefinition of the problem. The answer lies not in theology or philosophy but in a most unexpected source – physics.

Two slit or not to slit? A curious question

The solution lies with atoms or, more specifically, the things that atoms are made of. As you may recall from your school physics, all matter is made up of molecules. If you take any physical thing and divide it again and again until it cannot be divided any more you end up with the smallest possible 'bit' of that object, an indivisible bit. For most things this will be a molecule, although for certain more pure substances the molecule can be broken down into its constituent atoms.

The substances that can be broken down to the atomic level are called elements. As of October 2005, science had discovered 115. When the atoms of these elements are joined together we can 'create' other substances. Water, for example, can only be broken down to its molecule, which is made up of two atoms of hydrogen and one of oxygen. If you break water down beyond its molecule it ceases to be water and becomes oxygen and hydrogen. Molecules, and to a certain extent atoms, behave in a logical and sensible way. They follow the rules of normal science, the science of the 19th century and the science of 'common sense'. However, scientists wanted to know what atoms themselves were made of. This is where problems started and this is where 'hard' science and common sense parted company. Once we start looking at the behaviour of objects smaller than the atom things start to get very strange.

When physicists started experimenting with the objects that make up an atom they had to come up with a whole new way of approaching physics. They termed this variation 'quantum' physics because the results of their experiments bore no resemblance to what was expected from the laws of what has become known as 'classical' physics. This new physics has become phenomenally successful in predicting behaviour and has become the framework behind a good deal of modern technology. However weird it seems, it does appear to be an accurate reflection of what is going on.

The word 'quantum' is Latin for 'package'. The building blocks of matter are not small solid 'points' of matter, but quanta – small packages of energy, waves of probability causing ripples in the fabric of reality. In themselves they have no real solidity. They do not occupy space in the way we in the macro-world understand the term. Furthermore, one of the weirdest discoveries of quantum physics is that these 'particles' can be in two places at the same time. Not only that, but they disappear from one location and re-appear in another without travelling through the intervening space.

This is more than theory. The bilocation of subatomic particles such as electrons has been shown and repeated experimentally.[1] It may not seem to make sense but nevertheless it is true. And the weirdness does not stop there.

Particles of light – photons – when fired like bullets at a wall with two closely spaced vertical slits cut into it do the same thing – each particle passes through both slits simultaneously. To understand how such a seemingly impossible thing takes place, imagine dropping a pebble into a pond. The waves form a series of ripples moving out from the point where the pebble entered the water. Now imagine what would happen if a barrier was placed across the pond. As the waves hit the barrier they bounce back in the direction they came. If then two holes are placed in the barrier, both much smaller than the wavelength of the ripples, on the other side of the barrier two sets of waves, starting at each hole, spread out as if two new pebbles were dropped in the water at the same place as each hole. As the two new sets of ripples move out they begin to 'interfere' with each other, disrupting the flow of the two sets of semicircles. In some places the two sets of ripples add up to make extra-large ripples; in other places the two sets of ripples cancel out leaving little or no wave motion in the water.

The same exercise can be carried out with light. Light is shone through a single slit in a barrier. As the light flows out it encounters a second barrier, this time with two slits. The light acts as a wave in that each hole initiates another wave pattern on the other side of the second barrier. Immediately the two waves start to interfere with each other. A screen is set up after the second barrier. When the light hits this screen it shows a pattern of light and dark stripes. These stripes are called interference fringes. They correspond to where the light waves add together (constructive interference) and where the waves cancel each other out (destructive interference).

In 1800, the scientist Thomas Young used this experiment to prove that light is not made up of solid particles but is a wave travelling through the air like a disturbance wave travels through water. There was one significant problem with this idea and that was how does light travel through a vacuum? Without any medium of transmission a wave cannot even be said to exist. However, it was shown that light, and its variations such as heat, could 'radiate' through a vacuum. To explain how heat and light could get across the 96 million miles of empty space to arrive at the Earth from the Sun it was supposed that a yet to be discovered substance, termed 'ether', permeated space. It was this mysterious substance that was thought to carry the waves across a vacuum.

Light was found to do other things that contradicted the wave theory. One particular problem was known as the photoelectric effect. It was noted that when light was shone onto a solid object it seemed to 'kick out' electrons from the surface. In 1905, Albert Einstein was to write a paper on this subject, a paper that was to gain him the Nobel Prize for physics. His explanation of the photoelectric effect was a simple one; if light was made of solid particles then it was the impact of these particles that caused the dislodging of the electrons. Einstein called these particles of light 'photons'. Particles do not need a medium to travel within. They can easily cross a vacuum, and in doing so do away with the need for the proposed ether. Einstein's theory was subsequently proven by experimentation. Light is indeed made up of photons. Science soon advanced to the point whereby single photons could be isolated and used in experiments. However, the wave-like behaviour of light also continued to be observed. Light seemed to consist of both solid points of matter and as a smeared-out wave. Something was not quite right. To sort out this paradox science had to re-visit the two-slit experiment whilst using the most advanced measurement and detection equipment available. This has now been done on many occasions and the results have shown that reality itself is a far stranger place than anybody can ever imagine.

Suppose that a single photon is fired at a barrier containing two slits. The photon, in order to get to the other side, has to go through *one or other* of the two holes. Recording such a small particle of light needs a super-sensitive photographic plate and this is set up at the other side of the barrier. Each photon, as it arrives, registers on the photographic plate as a single white spot. As thousands, then millions, of photons arrive at the plate a pattern begins to emerge. Common sense would lead one to assume that there would be two circles of white light coinciding with the trajectory of each photon through whichever hole it selected. In fact what we do get is the interference pattern again. Each particle goes through one hole on its own, but something seems to interfere with it as it goes through to form the unexpected interference pattern. This leaves physicists with only one conclusion: the photon starts out as a particle, and arrives as a particle, but en route it seems to go through both holes. In doing so it interferes with itself as it comes through the holes, and then places itself on the photographic plate together with its fellow photons to form a perfect pattern of light and dark stripes. The mystery of this first option is how does the photon manage to go through both holes at the same time, and having done that how does it 'know' where to place itself on the photographic plate? The physics writer Ralph Baierlein attempted to answer the first part of this question by saying:

Light travels in a wave but departs and arrives as a particle.[2]

But light has no mass and, strangely enough, no location. Light particles (or waves) always travel at the speed of light and so they must exist outside of time and space. In order to be 'in space' an object must have mass. Light does not. In order to be in time an object must travel through time. However, at the speed of light time dilates to such an extent that at the speed of light it actually stops. This means that light exists in a timeless state. This becomes more disturbing when it is realized that light is just that part of the electromagnetic spectrum that is visible to the naked eye. Electromagnetic radiation is not physically anywhere, it just is. In fact, you are 'seeing' this page because this ephemeral 'something' is bouncing off the page into your retina.

So light is odd, but at least atoms, however empty they may be, are, in the final analysis, solid and do not suffer the wave-particle schizophrenia of light. Or do they? Confusingly, electrons and atoms have now been shown to be the same as light in that they are sometimes solid particles and sometimes non-physical waves. In 1987, teams from Hitachi research laboratories and the Gakushuin University in Tokyo found that electrons have the same duality. Problematic yes, but electrons are incredibly small and nobody has ever seen or photographed one. Atoms are different. We can photograph the larger types so they are 'solid' in a very real sense. The first rip in the fabric of reality began in the early 1990s when a team from the University of Konstanz, in Germany, proved that atoms also travel as a wave and arrive as a particle. And then the seemingly impossible was discovered in 1999 when Anton Zeilinger at the University of Vienna showed that a 'buckyball' – a spherical cage built of 60 carbon atoms – could travel through two parallel slits at the same time.[3]

So what does this all mean? Well, the chair you are possibly sitting on at this moment is not only made up of vast areas of empty space, but what solidity it has depends upon whether the atoms choose to be solid particles or non-solid waves. The question is what makes them make this choice? The answer is simple but hair-raising. The factor that pulls the atom from a non-physical wave to a solid point of matter is your mind through its processing of nerve signals from your buttocks. The act of perception by a conscious entity brings matter into physical existence!

The really disturbing thing is that recent experiments have shown that not only atoms do this but molecules as well. Atoms and molecules are the basic building blocks of everything we perceive, from the chair you may be sitting on to the paper that these words are printed on. Indeed, you yourself are made up of trillions of these schizophrenic particles. So if they show such strange behaviour why is it that we perceive solid objects that act well within the laws of classical physics? By what magic does individual madness become collective sanity? According to the accepted viewpoint of modern physicists, it is the act of observing these particles that makes them 'behave'.

This solution is popularly known as 'The Copenhagen Interpretation', so called because the pioneers of quantum theory were based in the Danish capital. Led by the great physicist Neils Bohr, this dedicated group of researchers suggested that we, by perceiving these particles, force them into making a decision as to which place they are located. Before they are observed they are smeared out in what is termed a 'probability wave' and as such are in both locations. At the split second of observation the particles are forced to choose one location from all other potential locations.

According to the Copenhagen Interpretation the particles can go through both slits in the wall as long as they are not observed. As soon as an experimenter turns any form of measuring device upon them (an observer) the particle is forced to go through one slit or the other. In other words, as soon as the 'big' world observes them the particles are forced out of their quantum behaviour into macrocosmic 'classical' behaviour. Atoms are forced to act 'normally' as soon as they collectively become trees, chairs or books. This act of observation is termed 'collapsing the wave function' in that at the moment of observation the wave collapses and becomes a particle. Before it is observed it is both a particle and a wave. The technical term for this is 'superposition'.

Many scientists simply could not accept the implications of Copenhagen. It suggested that without an act of observation the particles will remain in a wave of probability without ever having the chance to choose one location or another. The observer collapses the wave function and in doing so brings matter into existence. No observer, no anything. One critical issue was what constitutes an 'observer'? Do they need to be conscious or can any unthinking measuring device suffice? Some have, not unreasonably, concluded that in order to observe one has to perceive and that strongly implies consciousness. So what happens to objects that are unobserved? What about a stone on the Moon? For those of a religious persuasion, Copenhagen is not a problem but a vindication of their theism. The observer of all things is God; by the act of observing God ensures that all things exist. However, for many scientists this was simply unacceptable. In an attempt to show just how ridiculous is this idea of particles being influenced by the act of observation, the Austrian physicist Erwin Schrödinger came up with his famous cat-in-a-box experiment.

A hypothetical cat among the pigeons

Schrödinger asked us to imagine that a cat be placed inside a sealed box with no windows. Also inside this box is a bottle of deadly gas. Poised above this box is a small hammer being held back by a latch. In turn this latch is connected to a detector. This detector is programmed to scan a piece of radioactive material for the decay of one particular atom, an event that is known to have a 50/50 probability of taking, or not taking, place. If the atom does decay the detector will send a signal to the latch instructing it to release the hammer. Like a latter-day feline equivalent of the 'Sword of Damocles' the hammer falls upon the bottle, smashing it and thus releasing the poisonous gas. Obviously this will result in the immediate death of the poor cat. Conversely, if no decay takes place then the hammer does not fall and the cat continues to live. We cannot confirm the state of the cat until we open the box and look inside. According to Copenhagen, the wave function needs an observer to facilitate its collapse, which in turn will bring about the decay or non-decay of the atom in question. Thus, until observed, the cat is in a curious alive-and-dead situation.

Clearly Schrödinger felt that his thought-experiment had shown that the Copenhagen interpretation was seriously flawed. The problem is that however illogical it may seem, it is Copenhagen that most accurately explains the results of every experiment that has taken place since the Austrian's hypothetical feline first entered the world. One of the supporters of the Copenhagen Interpretation, John von Neumann, suggested that the hybrid state is transferred not to the cat but to the measuring device as it detects (or does not detect) the decay. Only then is it transferred to the cat, which in turn, on the box being opened, transfers the hybrid state to the observer. This 'von Neumann Chain', as it became known, just continues transferring from observer to observer. So what causes the chain to break down? Simple, said physicist Eugene Wigner, human consciousness ends the chain.

This is all well and good but Schrödinger was discussing a hypothetical experiment that has never been attempted. The reason for this is that it has long been argued that there is some form of invisible barrier between what happens at the level of quantum mechanics and that of the 'real' world of raindrops, roses and kittens. The 'microcosmic' and the 'macrocosmic' worlds have different rules. The journal *Nature* reported in 2000 that a group of researchers at the State University of New York (SUNY)[4] had reproduced what appeared to be impossible: an equivalent Schrödinger's cat experiment on the macrocosmic side of the barrier[5]. The SUNY team used superconducting quantum interference devices (SQUIDs). These are ring-shaped devices in which persistent currents, made of billions of pairs of electrons, can circulate in either a clockwise or an anti-clockwise direction without decaying. The experimenters started with a current flowing in, say, the clockwise direction. Next they illuminated the SQUID with microwaves which excited the system to a clockwise state with higher energy. The system could now tunnel from the clockwise state into the anti-clockwise state, and back. The question is essentially whether the system remembers or forgets its quantum state as it tunnels. To answer this the SUNY team measured the probability of finding the current flowing in the anti-clockwise direction as the shape of the double-well potential is changed. The results were exactly as predicted by assuming that the system is in a macroscopic superposition of states.

The implications of this experiment are simply staggering; Schrödinger was both right and wrong. He was right to show that the cat would be in two states, now termed 'superposition' by physicists, but wrong to state that the logical impossibility of such a state invalidated the Copenhagen Interpretation. Whatever conclusions scientists decide to draw from 'superposition', its existence as a real phenomenon is no longer in doubt.

But whatever conclusion one draws, there is something very strange going on and one that has huge implications for all of us and our relationship with the universe. These results imply that human consciousness is in fact the 'creator' of reality. Mind brings forth matter, not the other way round. You bring about the reality around you. If you do not observe it then it is simply not there. Suddenly the problem of whether the fridge light is on when you close the door takes on a whole new meaning.

The SUNY experiment metaphorically puts the cat amongst the pigeons. Even before its groundbreaking evidence most scientists found the implications of superposition unacceptable. Ever since Copernicus suggested that the Earth revolved round the Sun man has been forced away from the centre of all things. Over the last 100 years discoveries in astronomy have increasingly shown man to be insignificant as the universe is found to be larger and larger. For man to again be placed in a crucial role within the whole scheme of things was, if nothing else, regressive. Something else had to be taking place to stop the infinite regress implied by the von Neumann chain.

For over 25 years the argument continued. Einstein, whose two theories of relativity started the ball rolling, simply could not accept Copenhagen. His famous 'God does not play dice' was his response to the idea that the whole of the physical universe was made up of waves of probability. Many others attempted, like Schrödinger, to highlight the logical absurdities of superposition but none managed a credible alternative. Copenhagen may not have made sense but it was fantastically successful in predicting the behaviour of sub-atomic particles. What was needed was a radical reinterpretation of what takes place at the start of the von Neumann Chain. In 1957, a young PhD student named Hugh Everett III was to redefine the word 'radical'.

A leap of intuition

Everett argued that it was nonsensical to believe that the wave function was only brought into existence by observation of a conscious mind. The wave existed before observation and it continued after – it simply changed. So how did his new, rational and non-paranormal, proposal explain what takes place? Simply that the wave function itself splits into two realities. One where it collapses after the atomic decay and one where it doesn't. In effect two realities exist together. When the box is opened the observer in turn splits into two identical versions of himself, one of whom observes the cat dead and one who observes the cat alive. In this way Everett solved the horrible idea that mind was in some way different from matter.

So, instead of having a non-physical mind we have a science fiction scenario of parallel universes. Thus, if one accepts Everett's proposal, one version of the scientist goes off and writes up one report whereas in the other universe the other him writes a different report. Very rapidly a ripple of cause and effect changes each universe, initially in a small way but as each new scenario engenders its own outcome so the two mirror universes diverge into potentially very different places.

Everett's proposal, known now as the 'Many Worlds Interpretation' (MWI), does not stop there. The actual bifurcation of the universe took place not at the point of observation but at the point of the quantum event: the 'decision' made by the atom to decay or not. That event will have caused its own alternative scenarios at the quantum level, causing split compounded upon split. Indeed, Everett and his later champion Bryce DeWitt suggested that the universe splits at every quantum event and each new universe begins splitting in turn – and it has been doing this since the first millisecond of the Big Bang! Thus, taken to its logical conclusion, MWI implies that all possible scenarios have happened or will happen in this new, rapidly inflating multiverse.

To recap, initially quantum physics implied that the building blocks of matter, sub-atomic particles, are brought into existence by observation. If there is no act of observation then there is no matter. However, as we are all observers it is logical to conclude that we all create our own versions of reality, our own personal universes. Then Hugh Everett suggested that the Copenhagen Interpretation is correct, but physicists had misinterpreted the evidence and wrongly concluded that an observer brings about the collapse of the wave function. For him the probability wave doesn't exist because probability is not involved. In Everett's version of events there is not a one in six probability that a dice will fall giving a particular number but a one in one. The universe just splits into six copies of itself and in each universe a different number comes up. In trying to explain away a self-created universe, Everett has simply turned the egocentricity on its head. We all exist in our own universes not because we bring them into existence but because we all have our own private universes anyway. Not only that but there are literally trillions of versions of each of us all living all possible versions of our lives.

The Many Worlds Interpretation of quantum physics is an enlightening, if not disturbing, revelation. However, in the same way that the Copenhagen Interpretation has been seen to be possible through the SUNY experiment so it is that evidence of these other universes has been implied by the work of Oxford University physicist David Deutsch. Deutsch sensationally believes that the presence of these universes can be detected by experimentation.

Deutsch takes us yet again back to the two-slit experiment. He argues that although only a single photon is being fired through the slits at any one time they behave as if *something* has gone through both holes. This mysterious other entity then interferes with the path of the real photon and causes it to follow the path expected if more than one photon were travelling through the slits.

Deutsch considers that these interfering entities do not only behave like photons but they actually are photons, 'shadow' photons as he terms them. These seem to interact with the 'tangible' photons, the ones that we can see and detect with instruments. What is even more curious is that the evidence implies that there are many more of these shadow photons than tangible photons. He postulates that at a *minimum* there are one trillion shadow photons for every tangible photon! In addition, each of these shadow photons exists in its own universe, a universe so close that it can affect the trajectory of a single photon.

Here we have evidence of other worlds encroaching upon our own. Each of the trillions of shadow photons is part of a parallel universe inhabiting exactly the same space as our universe. This implies that there are trillions of universes at our fingertips.

For both Everett and Deutsch, Schrödinger's cat can be both alive and dead at the same time. All one has to do is realize that there is more than one version of the cat. At the point that the cat became either alive or dead the universe split into two copies, one containing a dead feline and the other an alive version of the same animal. Indeed, Everett proposed that the universe splits at every quantum event. In this scenario all possible events can and will happen in one of these alternative realities. This idea, initially ridiculed as pure science fiction, is rapidly becoming accepted by a growing number of theoretical physicists. DeWitt summed up the implications of the Many Worlds Interpretation when he wrote:

> *Every quantum transition taking place on every star, in every galaxy, in every remote corner of the universe is splitting our local world on earth into myriads of copies of itself... Here is schizophrenia with a vengeance.*

If all this is true then it seems a most profligate waste of matter. Why does nature allow countless numbers of universes? Maybe there is a reason for these universes, and the existence of these universes has a direct bearing on you as the reader of this book? Perhaps this universe is indeed *your* universe.

The heroes of Tegmark

In 1997, Max Tegmark, a physicist at the University of Pennsylvania, took the implications of Schrödinger's cat, and the Copenhagen and the Many Worlds Interpretations and used them to imply that death may be something that only ever happens to other people.[6]

Tegmark proposed a thought experiment similar to Schrödinger's cat. He asked us to imagine that a machine gun is attached to a device that measures the z-spin of a sub-atomic particle. All sub-atomic particles have this, and this can be either 'up' or 'down'. However, the direction of spin is entirely random and as such cannot be predicted for any single particle. If the device 'senses' a particle that has 'down' spin then it instructs the machine gun to load a single live bullet into the stock. If the particle spin is detected as being 'up' the gunstock remains empty with the weapon just making an audible click.

In order to test the gun an experimenter stands in front of the gun and asks her assistant to pull the trigger. The assistant nervously follows the instruction and presses the trigger. The device detects that the spin of the particle is up and so does not load a bullet into the stock. The gun makes an audible click and the experimenter remains alive.

The experimenter suggests that they now go through a further nine repeats of the experiment. She stands in front of the gun and on each occasion the stock remains empty. After the tenth repeat she tells her assistant that it is time to end the test and go home for the evening. The experimenter feels satisfied that she has proven to herself that the Many Worlds Interpretation has been proven correct and invites her relieved assistant out for a quick celebratory drink.

Now let's go back to the start of the experiment and experience it from the worldview of the assistant. He follows the instructions as given by his boss. He presses the trigger three times and on each occasion the gun clicks. However, on the fourth attempt the sub-atomic particle has down spin, a bullet falls into the stock and the trigger engages. A bullet flies out of the barrel and crashes through the skull of the experimenter, killing her instantly. In a blind panic he telephones the police and is arrested for murder.

What has happened here? Is the experimenter alive or dead, did they go for a drink or did the assistant face a murder charge? The answer is that in the same way that Schrödinger's cat is both alive and dead in different universes so is the experimenter. In her universe she did not die but in the universe of her assistant she did. The crucial point here is that the only reality that the experimenter can possibly perceive is the one in which she survives.

Tegmark himself acknowledges that for most of us life and death do not come about through random quantum events, but through accidents, disease or a myriad of other reasons. But it may be that Tegmark fails to realize that the human brain itself may work along quantum lines. We all make decisions based upon quantum interactions.

If one takes a section of brain material and views it through a powerful microscope, what is seen is a dense network of cells. Most of these will be what are called *glial* cells. It seems that the role of these is simply to 'glue' the brain structure together and ensure it keeps its shape. However, dotted among these glial cells at a ratio of approximately one in ten are neurons. These are cells that are adapted to send, receive and carry electrical impulses. Each neuron has a central, usually star-shaped section where the cell nucleus is located. Spreading out from this central body are long, thin tendrils that can vary from between 1 millimetre and 1 metre in length. These tendrils reach out and can receive or send electro-chemical signals from as many as 10,000 other neurons. These cells are designed to both give and receive electro-chemical messages from their fellow neurons. When a nerve cell is activated or 'fired', an electrical current runs along the nerve fibre and releases a chemical substance called a neurotransmitter.

Neurotransmitters are the chemical agents that are released by the neurons to stimulate other neurons and in the process transmit impulses from one cell to the other. In turn this facilitates the transfer of messages throughout the whole nervous system. The site where neurons meet is called the synapse, which consists of the axon terminal (transmitting end) of one cell and the dendrite (receiving end) of the next. A microscopic gap called a synaptic cleft exists between the two neurons. The size of this gap is extremely small. In dealing with such small sizes scientists use a measurement termed an angstrom. An angstrom is equal to one hundred millionth of a centimetre. Synaptic gaps range between 200 to 300 angstroms across.

When a nerve impulse arrives at the axon terminal of one cell a chemical substance is released through the membrane close to the synapse. This substance then travels across the gap in a matter of milliseconds to arrive at the postsynaptic membrane of the adjoining neuron. This chemical release is stimulated by the electrical activity of the cell. Across the other side of the cleft, at the end of the receiving dendrite, are specialized receptors that act as docking areas for particular neurotransmitters. The newly received neurotransmitters then 'instruct' the dendrite to send a particular signal along to its nucleus and then out to its own axons. When it does this it is said to be excitatory. Sometimes the effect of the neurotransmitter(s) released by the pre-synaptic axon is to inhibit rather than excite the post-synaptic dendrite. In this case it is said to be inhibitory.

This process all takes place at the scale of atomic particles. As such it is clear that quantum events can have an influence on what takes place. It is therefore possible that a synapse, teetering on the edge of its 'firing threshold', could be influenced by an event at the quantum level. In other words, the firing or non-firing of a neuron may depend upon a similar quantum event as that outlined in the Schrödinger experiment. For instance, a calcium ion has a 50 percent probability, according to Schrödinger's equations, of activating its target receptor. This receptor may make the difference between two possible states of mind. Imagine one of those split second decisions being influenced by this. For example, you are in your car approaching a set of traffic lights. You notice that they are on amber. You make a decision whether to accelerate and go through the lights or hold back and stop. The result of this decision is transferred across the synapse by neurotransmitters.

This neurotransmitter tells your leg to press on the accelerator or the brake. At that point we have a quantum event taking place. You press the accelerator, cross the lights and get hit side on by a juggernaut. You die instantly. However, your death is only one outcome. In another you may have decided to stop. At that point we have two alternate realities: you dead and you alive. As with the experimenter in Tegmark's theory, you follow your own world line and remain alive. In the world line of any bystanders you die. Your perceived universe will always split in such a way to ensure your personal survival. You may die in my universe but you will go on and on in your own.

But is there any objective proof to show that this takes place? Unfortunately, since conscious experience is the most subjective of all phenomena, as such it is impossible to have anything other than subjective and therefore non-provable examples.

We are the dreamers of dreams

Frederick Myers was a founder member of the Society for Psychic Research, a group of scientists and like-minded individuals who, in the late 19th century, wished to apply scientific method to phenomena such as ghosts, mediumship, precognition and other anomalous happenings. At the time orthodox science was happy to simply ignore the claims made by individuals experiencing such phenomena. In 1895 Myers published an article entitled 'The Subliminal Self' in the society's *Proceedings*. In this he discussed in some detail the evidence that certain individuals had an ability to have an abnormal knowledge of events in the past (termed 'retrocognition'). Later in the article he highlighted how dreams can sometimes warn about future events. He gives a few examples but it is one in particular that, when interpreted with knowledge of the Many Worlds Interpretation of quantum physics, can be explained.

Myers tells of a lady who had an especially vivid dream. In this dream she went on a coach ride to London. The coach stopped in a certain street and the coach driver began to disembark. As he did so he fell from his perch and badly smashed his skull on the roadside below.

She was of the opinion that the dream had been stimulated by the fact that the next day she had planned to go to London by coach. Undeterred by her dream she went ahead with the journey. The day went well with no unfortunate events. However, on the way back home the coach turned into the very street of her dream:

My dream flashed back upon me. I called him to stop, jumped out ... and called a policeman to catch the coachman. Just as he did so the coachman swayed and fell off the box.[7]

The policeman was there to catch him and a serious injury was thus avoided. She continued her account saying:

... my premonitory dream differed from reality in two points. In my dream we approached Down Street from the west; in reality we came from the east. In my dream the coachman actually fell on his head ... in reality this was just averted by the prompt action, which my anxious memory of the dream inspired.

In commenting upon this incident, the Switzerland-based American psychotherapist and authority on such phenomena, Dr Arthur Funkhouser, makes the following comment:

It is as if the action of the lady created a split in the flow of time, a fork on the way, where the dream-seen future was one possibility and she got things to go another.[8]

It is possible that Dr Funkhouser is unaware of the Many Worlds concept, as this would neatly explain the bifurcation at the moment that the lady in question called out. It turned out that the coachman had suffered a severe bout of diarrhoea the preceding night and had misjudged his strength - he fainted and that caused his fall. Had the woman not had the dream she would not have called out and he would not have been caught by the policeman.

Tegmark's idea is an interesting one but ultimately unsatisfactory because he fails to explain the mechanism by which individual immortality may be facilitated. He has no evidence, reported or otherwise, that leads us to conclude that he may be right. Indeed, at this point you may well be far from convinced that the Quantum Machine Gun is anything other than a very clever but totally fictional account of reality.

In my opinion, though, Tegmark is absolutely right. He has, possibly inadvertently, discovered something that is not only true but can be proven to be true. Not only that, but there is evidence that this alternative solution to the mystery of death has long been known but kept secret for hundreds of years. The answer, as with everything in this book, lies within your head.

CHAPTER 2

The Echo of Eternity

For one of those Gnostics the visible universe was an illusion or (more precisely) a sophism. Mirrors and fatherhood are abominable because they multiply and disseminate the universe.

Jorge Luis Borges, (from: Tlön, Uqbar, Orbis Tertius).

Existence or existentialism?

If Tegmark is right then this implies that we are all alone, existing in ever-refining versions of the universe that we were born into. You are just one version of the trillions of you that exist in different parts of the Macroverse. In untold millions of these universes you did not pick up this book, in other countless universes you gave up after the first paragraph, in others you got as far as the second paragraph, in others the third – and so it goes on. To be alone in your own version of reality, a reality created by your every decision, is terrifying in the extreme. It is exactly the state described by the French philosopher Jean-Paul Sartre in his masterwork *Being and Nothingness*. We all exist in a state of existentialist isolation.

If this is the case, how can we explain the seemingly independent actions of others? Those you share your life with seem very real, with motivations of their own. These motivations have a cause and effect that must be outside of your control. However, these other consciousnesses may still be unthinking spectres acting out an elaborate stage show for your version of reality. In the movie *Vanilla Sky* there is a scene in which the hero, David Aames, is forced to realize that all those seemingly real people he interacts with are projections of his own inner world. During the course of the film Aames builds up a close relationship with his psychiatrist, Curtis McCabe (Kurt Russell). On being challenged about his non-reality McCabe begs Aames not to believe the irrational information that he has been given. The psychiatrist stresses he is a real person and for Aames to think otherwise is crazy. But by now Aames is convinced that he is living within a three-dimensional illusion, and he manages to stop Russell in mid flow. The look on McCabe's face is of total astonishment. This spectre simply cannot accept the truth but truth it is nevertheless.

So do we all exist in an existentialist nightmare? Can it really be true that all those you love and hold dear are merely shadows and sprites? The answer, you will be happy to hear, is no, although the process by which we can all share our individual universes is complex and difficult to understand. In order to appreciate how it all works we have to return to quantum physics, to the only viable alternative to Many Worlds and Copenhagen – the truly wonderful and ultimately uplifting Hidden Variables/Implicate Order.

God does not play dice

Albert Einstein could never accept the theories that developed from his ideas. He was particularly concerned with the probabilistic aspects as suggested by the Copenhagen Interpretation. It is from a letter that Einstein wrote in 1926 that the oft-quoted phrase about God and dice is taken. What he actually said was:

> Quantum mechanics is very impressive. But an inner voice tells me that it is not yet the real thing. The theory produces a good deal but hardly brings us any closer to the secret of the Old One. I am at all events convinced that He does not play dice.[9]

In this letter it is clear that the 'dice' comment is a direct allusion to the probability elements of the Copenhagen proposal.

Einstein simply could not accept that the whole of the physical world was made up of non-physical 'waves of probability'. For him there had to be an objective physical world underlying the probabilistic behaviour of quantum systems, a lower 'level' of reality in which the observed non-rational behaviour was just a part. This lower level would show behaviour more akin to classical physics. It was Einstein's successors, in particular David Bohm, who would argue that this level, a level of 'hidden-variables', did in fact exist.

At the same time that Schrödinger was attempting to disprove Copenhagen with his cats in boxes, so Einstein, teaming up with his associates Boris Podolsky and Nathan Rosen, tried a similar attack. In 1935 they published a paper outlining another thought-experiment. You will recall that according to the Copenhagen Interpretation sub-atomic particles only come into existence at the point of observation by a conscious mind. Before this observation the particle is but a wave of probability. Bearing this in mind, the three asked, quite simply, what would happen if a particle consisting of two protons decayed, sending each proton off in a different direction. Like snooker balls each one would carry an imprint of the other in the form of angular momentum. One spins in one direction, the other in the opposite direction. However, it is only by observing one of the particles that we can tell in which direction it is spinning. In doing so one can immediately deduce the direction of spin of the other. Put another way, imagine that the two particles have a specific colour: one is blue and one is red. The decay takes place and they both fly off into the darkness. The observer does not know which one has gone in which direction. However, by observing one of the particles he, or she, 'collapses' the wave function and brings the first particle into existence. On discovering the newly formed particle to be red, it then becomes obvious to the observer that the other particle will be blue. Across the vast void of space a message is sent to the other wave function, which, at that moment of observation, also collapses, to reveal a blue particle.

This communication, argues Einstein, Podolsky and Rosen, will take place even if the particles are light years apart at the point of observation. Einstein then pointed out that this communication, 'spooky action at a distance'[10] as he termed it, is logically and scientifically impossible. In order for communication to take place in an instant across light years of space implies that the medium by which the message is sent is travelling infinitely faster than light. This is known to be impossible.

As far as Einstein was concerned, this thought experiment, known to posterity as the EPR paradox after the initials of its creators, showed how ridiculous the implications of Copenhagen Interpretation were. It was self-evident, stated Einstein, that the two particles had been in existence at all times of their journeys and had had their individual properties (spin or colour) from the moment of departure. There was no spooky action at a distance. Just a straightforward, logical proposition that if one is observed to be red then the other is blue, and has always been blue.

By this stage we are as far away from 'common sense' as it is possible to be. We have all lived in a world where things behave sensibly. Objects fall to the ground as predicted by Newtonian physics. Objects do not disappear and re-appear again in another location and there is no such thing as spooky action at a distance. To accept such nonsense is to let go of everything about reality that we believe to be true. But as we have seen there is something distinctly wrong with reality as we perceive it. At the quantum level it stubbornly refuses to behave as we wish it to. But those who study in depth the building blocks that make up our universe know that 'common sense' simply does not work at the quantum level. Indeed, many students of physics when first encountering these issues simply cannot accept them. Richard Feynman, one of the greatest theoretical physicists of the late 20th century, felt the need to say the following to new students approaching quantum phenomena for the first time. Feynman advises:

Do not keep saying to yourself, if you can possibly avoid it, 'But how can it be like that?' because you will 'go down the drain' into a blind alley from which nobody has yet escaped. Nobody knows how it can be like that.[11,12]

Bell rings in a new aspect on reality

There is good reason for the inclusion of a cautionary quote at this point. A real life experiment, similar to EPR, has taken place and it is the Copenhagen Interpretation, not Einstein and common sense, which is proven right by the empirical evidence. Unfortunately for common sense and relativity, we do seem to have 'spooky action at a distance'.

In 1964, the Irish mathematician John Bell published a paper showing that it was the quantum mechanics of the Copenhagen Interpretation that predicted stronger statistical correlations between the two photons of EPR than Einstein's commonsense approach. Bell's theorem, as it has become known, takes three Einsteinian assumptions; that particles are always real, that no faster-than-light travel can take place and that the usual rules of logic can be found in the quantum world. Bell's theorem can calculate mathematically the actual degree of co-operation between EPR-type particles. In experimental conditions if it can be shown that the degree of co-operation exceeds the value laid down by Bell, then Einstein would be proven wrong. This paper was greeted with great interest and stimulated a number of theoretical physicists to attempt a live version of EPR to see if the value would, indeed, be exceeded.

In 1981, a team of physicists based in Paris proved Bell's proposal. Alain Aspect, Jean Dalibard and Gérard Roger of the Institute of Optics at the University of Paris[13] produced a series of twin photons by heating calcium atoms with lasers. Each photon then travelled 6.5 metres in opposite directions down two pipes. At the end of the pipe the French team had placed a special filter.

This directed the individual photons to one of two possible polarization analyzers. In a staggering piece of engineering each filter could switch between allowing access to one or the other analyzer in 10 billionths of a second. This was about 30 billionths of a second less than it took for light to travel the entire 13 metres separating each set of photons. In this way, Aspect and his team were able to rule out any possibility of communication between the two photons.

On completion of the experiment they discovered that, as quantum theory predicted, each photon was still able to correlate its angle of polarization with that of its twin. This meant that either Einstein's ban against faster-than-light communication was violated, or the two photons were, in some curious way, connected. By Bell's theorem one of these two assumptions had to go. The evidence was conclusive; Neils Bohr and his Copenhagen Interpretation were right and Einstein was wrong. However, this result begged an additional choice for physicists. Either uncertainty is a central 'law' of the quantum world or the particles communicated in another way that violated the speed of light. One way they could do this would be if they were connected in some deeper way than modern science can discover.

Just watch the fish Wanda

So what can this connection be? David Bohm, an American by birth but British by exile (he fell foul of the McCarthy 'witch hunts' of the 1950s), initially followed the received wisdom of Bohr and the Copenhagen Interpretation. However, after completing a book in support of this position he began to have serious doubts about the seemingly irrational behaviour of the quantum world. He found himself agreeing with Einstein that there must be some form of reality underneath the seemingly random behaviour of particles. In the same way that the swirls and eddies of a swollen river seem random in their movement when viewed from a bridge, those same random swirls are joined together as part of the flow beneath the surface. Bohm wanted to look below the 'surface' of quantum behaviour, find the 'hidden variables', as he termed them, and show that classical mechanics remain consistent.

One huge obstacle he faced in this regard was a mathematical formula of John von Neumann called, surprisingly enough, the 'von Neumann Proof'. This first appeared in 1931 and seemed to prove categorically that nothing could possibly underlie the quantum interpretation. In order to get to his 'hidden variables', Bohm had to disprove the famed equation. In 1952 he did just that, uprooting this 'proof' by constructing a model of the electron with classical attributes whose behaviour matched the predictions of the quantum theory. In this model, the electron is viewed as an ordinary particle, with one key difference: the electron has access to information about its environment.

The way in which the particle communicates with the rest of its environment Bohm termed the 'quantum potential'. It is through this that all the seemingly strange distant communications implied by EPR and proven by Aspect take place. Rather as two waves may seem like individual towers of water, if you look below you will see that the ocean links them. So how 'low' is it necessary to look to find the 'ocean surface' for our quantum waves?

For Bohm, where the hidden variables sit is to be found between the smallest distance that science can detect and the smallest possible distance that physics can allow. When this is first encountered it is an extremely strange concept. It seems that at a distance of 10^{-33} cm space just breaks down. 10^{-33} is a distance so small that it simply cannot be imagined. Bohm argued that the smallest distance that physics can detect is 10^{-17} centimetres. This leaves an unknown realm that spans sixteen orders of magnitude in relative size, which is comparable to the size difference between our ordinary macroscopic world and the smallest detectable physical distance [10^{-17} cm]. Having no empirical knowledge of this realm, we cannot dismiss the possibility that causal factors could be operative in this place. It is within this realm that the 'quantum potential' functions.

Bohm's 'quantum potential' is a wave-like information system that guides the electron via the medium of the 'hidden variable'. He uses the analogy of an aircraft guidance system in support of his theory. Airliners change course in response to radio wave instructions. However the radio wave does not provide the power to change course, purely the active information. The airliner itself supplies the energy to make the required course revisions. In the same way the quantum potential instructs the electron to make certain changes to its condition. This could explain the notorious mystery of the 'collapse' of the wave function discussed above. This occurs as a seemingly random event in the laboratory and is taken by the Copenhagen Interpretation to mean that reality does not exist until observed. Before information is received by the particle it has infinite potentials, but once instructions are received from the quantum variable the particle 'collapses' into one particular potential state.

In Bohm's concept of quantum mechanics all particles are linked by this quantum potential within a huge interconnected web. Rather as a spider can tell movement anywhere within its web so is it for the particles in the quantum potential. This is the way the particles communicate in the Aspect experiment. According to Bohm, special relativity is not violated because it simply does not function at the deeper level where the quantum potential exerts its influence.

So how can we visualize how these hidden variables act? Bohm came up with an ingenious way of showing how observers without having all the information at hand can confuse what they see and make totally wrong assumptions. He asked us to imagine creatures living on another planet who have never seen fish and have no concept of what an aquarium is. As we cannot send an aquarium or fish to them a solution is to set up two closed circuit

TV cameras pointing at real fish swimming in an aquarium. One camera is directed at the aquarium's front and one at its side. Our alien friends rig up two television sets, one to receive the signal from one camera and one to receive the signal from the other. Not knowing any better, the aliens quite rightly assume that they are looking at two separate entities, not one fish. After a time our clever aliens note that there seems to be a definite relationship between the two entities. Although they do not move in the same direction or look exactly alike at any one time they do show similarities; when one faces the front the other faces the side, for example. The aliens come to the conclusion that some form of subliminal but instantaneous communication is taking place. But this is not the case. The two fish are actually one and the same.

For Bohm this was precisely what is going on between the subatomic particles in Aspect's experiment. The apparent faster-than-light connection between sub-atomic particles is really telling us that there is a deeper level of reality we are not privy to: a more complex dimension beyond our own that is analogous to the aquarium. And, he adds, we view objects such as subatomic particles as separate from one another because we are seeing only a portion of their reality. Such particles are not separate 'parts', but facets of a deeper and more underlying unity, what Bohm was to term 'the Implicate Order'.

At first sight it seems that Bohm's ideas are based on common sense in that they show that faster-than-light communication is not actually taking place, nor is 'spooky action at a distance'. After all, as far as Bohm is concerned, there is no distance between the two particles; they are, like the fish, the same object.

Bohm formulated his ideas many years before the 1981 Aspect experiment. He realized that he needed empirical proof to support his suspicions. In 1959 he did just that. Together with a young research student, Yakir Aharonov, he found that under certain circumstances electrons are able to 'feel' the presence of a nearby magnetic field even though they are travelling in areas where the effect of that field is non-existent. Although this discovery, the Aharonov-Bohm (AB) effect, has been verified by independent experiments it is still rejected by many scientists.

Just how strongly Bohm's ideas have been ignored by the mainstream can be seen by an event that took place in the 1950s. It seems that a group of students, not willing to accept the status quo as regards Copenhagen, spent time analyzing Bohm's theory and could not fault it mathematically or theoretically. With the enthusiasm of youth they challenged their professor to find anything wrong. He in turn had to admit that he could not find fault. In desperation the great theoretical physicist and father of the atomic bomb, Robert Oppenheimer, was called in to give an opinion. Bohm was told that Oppenheimer's reaction was that it was 'well known' that there was something wrong with Bohm's ideas. In a subsequent colloquium set up to discuss the implications of Bohm's 'hidden variables' Oppenheimer was reported as having said 'Well, we cannot find anything wrong with it, so we'll just have to ignore it.'[14]

In recent years, however, there has been an increase in interest in Bohm's ideas and the rigidity of the statistical interpretation is being challenged. So what is it that Bohm says that is so revolutionary? Surely the idea of a hidden, implicate order where causality and classical mechanics again rule is arch conservatism, not revolutionary iconoclasm? If Bohm had left it at that it is probable that his theories would have been accepted. However, being the independent thinker he was, he took his concept of the implicate order to its logical extreme – and what an extreme!

Bohm's revolutionary concept of the universe was stimulated by a particular mundane event – watching television. While at home one evening he happened to watch a BBC TV programme that discussed a peculiar new device that had been invented. It consisted of a jar containing a large rotating cylinder. The narrow space between the cylinder and the jar was filled with glycerine – a thick, clear liquid – and floating motionlessly in the glycerine was a drop of ink. As the handle of the cylinder is turned so the drop of ink is spread out through the glycerine. It slowly becomes more and more thinly spread until it disappears altogether. But as soon as the handle is turned the other way so the faint tracing of ink slowly collapses on itself and goes back to the form of the droplet. Bohm said:

> *This immediately struck me as very relevant to the question of order, since, when the ink drop was spread out it still had a hidden (i.e., non-manifest) order that was revealed when it was reconstituted. On the other hand, in our usual language, we would say that the ink was in a state of 'disorder' when it was diffused through the glycerine. This led me to see that new notions of order must be involved here.*[15]

Bohm suspected that everything is in some way contained by and contains everything else. In other words everything is, as he termed it, 'enfolded' upon itself. What we see as separate objects are things that are linked at a much lower level of reality. Just like the fish in the aquarium analogy was a single entity perceived as two entities because of the perceptual tools available to the observers so it is with our universe. The two particles in the Aspect experiment communicate at a distance because they are enfolded in each other. That is how the communication takes place. For Bohm there is an underlying order of wholeness beneath our perception of separate things. He likened this to a flowing steam:

> *On this stream, one may see an ever-changing pattern of vortices, ripples, waves, splashes, etc., which evidently have no independent existence as such. Rather, they are abstracted from the flowing movement, arising and vanishing in the total process of the flow. Such transitory subsistence as may be possessed by these abstracted forms implies only a relative independence or autonomy of behaviour, rather than absolutely independent existence as ultimate substances.*[16]

This enfolding involves everything that exists, including human consciousness itself. Bohm said:

> *In the implicate order the totality of existence is enfolded within each region of space (and time). So, whatever part, element, or aspect we may abstract in thought, this still enfolds the whole and is therefore intrinsically related to the totality from which it has been abstracted. Thus, wholeness permeates all that is being discussed, from the very outset.*[17]

Initially Bohm had difficulty in explaining his ideas because they seemed so alien to the way we perceive reality. He argued at great length that language itself brought about this inability to conceive of wholeness. European languages have a fixation with measurement, an approach in itself that leads to the division of reality into categories and classifications. Languages such as Sanskrit do not have such a structure. They describe the world as a timeless whole. Indeed, Indian culture sees the whole of reality as being an illusion. The concept of Maya is central to this. To Hindus the word *'maya'* means 'illusion' but its root is another word, *'matra'*, which means measure in the musical sense. In a telling way, this explains why measurement is not central to Eastern concepts of reality. As Bohm says,

> *... in the East measure has now come to be regarded commonly as being in some way false and deceitful.*

Going on to say:

> *In this way the entire structure and order of forms, proportions and 'ratios' that present themselves to ordinary perception and reason are regarded as a sort of veil, covering the true reality, which cannot be perceived by the senses and of which nothing can be said or thought.*[18]

Bohm was fortunate in that there is one modern invention that implies that every part of the greater object contains versions of itself. This invention is the hologram. Holograms, so much taken for granted these days, are very peculiar things. Laser light is split into two beams, one of which is reflected off the object to be recorded. This beam arrives at a photographic plate, where it interferes with the first beam. To the naked eye the pattern on the photographic plate is seen as simply meaningless swirls and patterns. However, when this plate is illuminated with laser light an amazing effect takes place; the swirls give forth a three-dimensional image of the original object. This image can be viewed from any angle. Like the dispersed ink drop the photographic plate contains a hidden, or enfolded, order. And if a holographic film is cut into pieces and again illuminated with laser light each piece does not, as one would expect, hold a part of the full image, but has a miniature copy of the whole original image. This is slightly fuzzy but nevertheless can be identified as such. This peculiar effect vindicates in a very visible way Bohm's idea that the part contains the whole. The form and structure of the entire object is encoded within each region of the photographic record.

From this Bohm suggested that the whole universe could be thought of as a kind of giant, flowing hologram, or holomovement, in which a total order is contained, in some implicit sense, in each region of space and time. The explicate order is a projection from higher dimensional levels of reality, and the apparent stability and solidity of the objects and entities composing it are generated and sustained by a ceaseless process of enfoldment and unfoldment. In this process subatomic particles are constantly dissolving into the implicate order and then recrystallizing again.

This leads us to understand that other consciousnesses do exist within the Macroverse. Each one inhabits its own universe but within the implicate order each individual time line meshes and intermeshes against all the others. In this way every possible action you may take will be mirrored in the universe of those beings you interact with. The process is understandable but involves dealing with numbers so vast as to be impossible to comprehend.

In Everett's Many Worlds Interpretation, the universe splits into initially identical copies of itself at every 'observation'. A central point of contention within quantum physics is what constitutes 'observation' or, more precisely, what particular elements are needed in order to be an 'observer'. The evidence seems to suggest that a self-referential 'conscious' observer is needed, so that observer must be a sentient being, like you and I.

Accepting that an event is brought about by an act of observation by a conscious mind, most 'events' will take place at the quantum level and numberless consequences, and therefore countless 'baby' universes, are born every microsecond. These all develop, and in doing so each one generates its own myriad of universes in the blink of an eye.

Within a very short period so many universes arise that essentially their numbers will be infinite. However, as space is seemingly infinite, there is more than enough 'space' available to accommodate such exponential expansion. *Every possible outcome* of every action by every mind in every universe *will* come to pass. Every *overlapping* event between universes will also take place. Your actions will, in one universe or another, continually affect the actions of all the other human beings that you encounter in a lifetime. This continual intermeshing of universes takes place within the Bohmian implicate order. It allows for continual and instantaneous communication of information across every universe within the ever-expanding and therefore ever-enfolding Macroverse.

Bohm came to a similar conclusion. For him both consciousness and matter are different facets of the same thing. There is no mind–matter dichotomy because at the level of enfoldment they are identical. Towards the end of his life, and in his last published work, he was to write the following:

> *Consciousness is much more of the implicate order than is matter ... Yet at a deeper level [matter and consciousness] are actually inseparable and interwoven, just as in the computer game the player and the screen are united by participation in common loops. In this view, mind and matter are two aspects of one whole and no more separable than are form and content.*[19]

In this way, quantum physics, of whatever interpretation, places consciousness at the centre of all reality. However, what is being missed is how consciousness actually 'creates' this reality. Each individual human being can expect to exist for 100 years at most. At that time his, or her, consciousness seems to simply disappear. How can we on one hand proclaim that consciousness brings the universe into existence while on the other acknowledge that that consciousness is finite. It simply does not make sense. Human personality must, in some yet unknown way, be able to effect reality before birth and after death. There is evidence that this incredible possibility may also be true.

CHAPTER 3

Only the Lonely

There was a young man who said, 'God

Must think it exceedingly odd

If he finds that this tree

Continues to be

When there is no one about in The Quad'.

REPLY:

Dear Sir,

Your astonishment's odd:

I am always about in The Quad

And that's why the tree

Continues to be,

Since observed by

Yours faithfully

God.

Ronald Knox

The dream and the dreamers

So the universe is not at all what it seems. We have seen that in some mysterious way you are crucial to its existence. Of course, by universe I mean the universe that you exist in. You have overlapping influences in other universes as yours intersects with others via the synapses of other consciousnesses. Like an eternal braid the minds of all conscious beings weave a web that holds the Macroverse together. In this way my words can influence your thoughts. This book 'appears' in your universe as a creation of your consciousness, which in turn has been in some subtle way influenced by mine.

Whether the book has some objective existence is an unknown because at the present time it exists solely as ideas that by the rules of the Implicate Order are transferring from me to you.

The evidence presented thus far has involved physics and cosmology. Subjects of great interest but divorced from your own little world. Whatever the implications of the Many Worlds Interpretation and cats in boxes, in no way can these esoteric concepts be personal to you, and after all this book is all about you. The level of analysis has to be brought down from the macrocosmic to the personal.

Solipsism, so what do you make of it?

Solipsism is a thought exercise that at one time or another most intelligent and reflective people play and it is one that normally comes to mind in those seemingly endless hours of a sleepless night. It is the simple realization that you know only one thing with absolute certitude and that is that you think.

If you are to focus in on exactly what you are, you will realize that you are a thought, not the machine doing the thinking. You are the software running on the hard drive called your brain. Even the idea of ownership of something like a brain is a weird idea when you focus in on the meaning of what you are saying.

You react with the outside world by stimulus, usually generated by your nerves. For example you feel a sharp pain in your finger. Where is the pain? Is it actually in your finger or is it in your head? Painkilling drugs can make the pain disappear, but where does the pain go when that happens? The injury is still there – it is just that by a drug being released in your brain the pain stops. However, if we take this one step further, what is pain itself? There is no machine that has been invented that can measure pain objectively because it has no independent existence outside of the perceiver. In many ways it is analogous to a wave that has no objective existence other than the effect it has on the medium it disturbs. To say 'that really hurts' means nothing to an observer. Indeed, it has been shown that different people have different tolerances to pain. Pain exists solely within the mind of the perceiver.

A similar discussion can be had as regards colour perception. Colour, like pain, is a totally subjective experience. Red does not exist outside of the perceptions of the observer. While it may not be difficult to accept that pain is a subjective experience, the notion that a colour, any colour, has no objective existence is a little more confusing. Imagine you and I sitting in a room watching the film *Schindler's List* on television. We are both moved by the fact that the only use of colour in an otherwise black and white film is a red coat worn by a little girl. This startling use of colour in a monochrome background is a very moving cinematographic device that assists in the telling of a harrowing story. After the film we both comment upon the way in which the red coat appears twice and acts as its own tragic symbol of a greater tragedy. That we both saw the red coat at the same times is solid evidence that the redness was out there in the external world.

We run the video back to confirm that we did both see the redness. You will see it as red and I will agree that it is indeed red. This corroboration of a quality external to both of us surely proves that the quality of the 'redness' exists outside of our personal worldview. Indeed, we can double-check our mutual perceptions by matching the perceived redness of the image on the TV screen against a selection of different coloured cards, one of which is red. We will both agree that the red of the coat has the same quality of redness as the red card. By any objective criteria used this will prove that the quality known as redness is out there in the external world, termed the 'phenomenal' world by philosophers as a way to differentiate it from the inner world of thought and perception.

However, this can all be seen as an illusion as soon as one simple question is asked: where is the 'red' located? Your initial response to this question is likely to be the same as that of most people: that the red is in the coat, that the coat is red because a red dye has been placed into the material that in turn makes the coat red. But is the red coat always red? What happens in the dark? Is the red coat still red although we only perceive black? What about if we look at the coat in moonlight? The red then becomes a shade of grey. Again most people believe that the coat is still red – it is the light that has changed how we see the coat. The redness is still an intrinsic quality of the coat. But this is an error. The coat is not red, green, or blue. In its natural non-illuminated state it is black, as is everything else. Objects being illuminated by light bring about colour. So what do we mean when we say something is 'illuminated'?

Pure white light, when passed through a prism, is broken down into a rainbow. This rainbow has seven colours, red, orange, yellow, green, blue, indigo and violet. In fact, there are millions of shades within the spectrum but these are the divisions that are identified and agreed by most people. Colour is brought about when white light waves (or photons) shine onto an object. So in our scene from *Schindler's List* we perceive a red coat being worn by a young actress. In a scene filmed years before, light hit the surface of coat as the actress ran across the film set. The surface of the coat absorbed all the light with the exception of the red part of the spectrum. The red light was reflected back and some entered a cine camera. The image of the young girl and all the action around her, including the red coat, are then recorded on light sensitive film. Now what is startling about the director's film technique is that the red in the red coat is the only colour in an otherwise black and white scene. In order to do this I can only assume that with the exception of the coat all the other elements of the scene were subsequently processed in black and white.

The red in the coat is now on cine film. That cine film is then copied onto videotape and sold to you. Many years after the filming of the scene, and the recording of the 'red' of the coat, the images are recreated on your TV screen. The tape in the video player sends a signal to the TV screen instructing it to fire a stream of electrons against your TV screen. It 'instructs' the TV to reproduce a black and white screen with the exception of one small area that it states has to be red. On hitting the TV screen the electrons stimulate the screen to emit red light, which crosses the room and enters your eyes.

The redness, or more accurately a stream of photons, hits the light sensitive cells in the back of your eyes. The red seems to disappear magically from the TV and re-appear as red at the back of your eye. You then perceive the sensation of red and 'see' a red coat on the TV screen. But where, in space and time, is that red colour? We know that it was not in the coat, we know that it was not in the camera, cine film, videotape, TV screen or the back of your eye. It only became 'red' when you perceived it as being red. Your inner vision, for want of a better term, interprets the re-created light waves as being 'red'. The red is your creation, your interpretation of the light wave frequency: it exists nowhere 'out there' in what we mistakenly call reality.

For philosophers and cognitive scientists such discussions are not at all unusual. They even have a term for that internal creation of sensations, be they colour, taste or sound. The technical term is 'qualia' and these qualia puzzle the hell out of everybody concerned. Put simply, 'redness' and 'pain' do not exist outside of the perceiver. They are as much mind-created illusions as dreams and hallucinations.

Philosophers also have a name for this extreme interpretation of perception. Termed solipsism, it has been a much-criticized concept but one that is curiously beguiling. For a solipsist the crucial fact is that the human mind never actually interfaces directly with the world 'out there'. We see through light waves bouncing off objects, we hear from sound waves and we feel through electrical impulses. All these stimuli are not the actual object being perceived. The British Idealist, FH Bradley summed up this position when he wrote:

I cannot transcend experience, and experience is my experience.
From this it follows that nothing beyond myself exists; for what
is experience is its (the self's) states.[20]

This world of experience, the 'phenomenal world' of the philosophers, is an internal projection of a possible external reality. However, the fact that it is processed by internally generated factors leads one to the unavoidable conclusion that these may not be presenting an accurate or true representation of that external world. This disturbing thought can be vindicated at any time by the consumption of too much alcohol.

For the philosopher Charles Pierce, this subjective world of the senses was a real psychological location, an inner world that he called the *phaneron*.

Wheeler adds to the circularity

So we all exist in our own phanerons. With our awareness of Many Worlds and the Implicate Order this is not such a curious idea as it would have been for 19th and early 20th-century philosophers. Indeed, John Wheeler, recognized as one of the greatest theoretical physicists of recent years, was stimulated to write the following in an article published in *The Intellectual Digest* of June 1973:

> *No theory of physics that deals only with physics will ever*
> *explain physics. I believe that as we go on trying to understand*
> *the universe, we are at the same time trying to understand*
> *man. Today I think we are beginning to suspect that man is*
> *not a tiny cog that doesn't really make much difference to the*
> *running of the huge machine but rather that there is a much*
> *more intimate tie between man and the universe than we*
> *heretofore suspected. Only as we recognise that tie will we be*

able to make headway into some of the most difficult issues that confront us. Nobody thinking about it from this point of view can fail to ask himself whether the particles and their properties are not somehow related to making man possible. Man, the start of the analysis, man, the end of the analysis – because the physical world is, in some deep sense, tied to the human being.

By taking the implications of the Copenhagen Interpretation to their logical extreme, Wheeler has proposed that the universe, any universe, needs an observer to come into existence. In 1983, he proposed an idea that has become known as 'Wheeler's Participatory Universe'. For Wheeler there is strong theoretical evidence to suppose that a human observer not only brings about the present universe but also the state of that universe billions of years before the observer was even born. If Wheeler is right then you, as the observer of your own 'Everett Universe', are responsible not only for its existence now but also for it coming into being billions of years ago. By observing evidence of the Big Bang you actually bring about that Big Bang. The implications of this suggestion are simply mind-blowing. This makes you very significant indeed – this universe is yours and yours alone.

In 2002, Wheeler explained just how this could occur. Quasars are probably the most mysterious objects known to astronomers. They are clearly visible in a telescope and look like normal stars. However, in recent years it has been shown that they are unbelievably distant objects, in some cases they are the most remote objects in the universe. And yet their luminosity is so great that they seem much closer. For Wheeler one of these objects can be used to update the mysterious two-slit experiment encountered earlier.

Wheeler suggested in an article in *Discover* magazine[21] that the light source for this new version of the famed experiment would be a quasar at the farthest reaches of the universe, billions of light years away. Since a light year is the amount of distance it takes light, a stream of photons (or waves), to travel in one year, when we observe a quasar we are seeing it not as it is now but as it was billions of years ago. Indeed, many cosmologists believe that quasars only existed at the start of the universe and ceased to be hundreds of millions of years ago. It is a mind-boggling thought to realize that by observing objects in space we can observe the past.

Wheeler asked us to imagine that between this quasar and the Earth are two huge galaxies. These are located parallel to each other and midway between the Earth and the quasar. Since gravity can bend light in the same way as a glass lens can, huge objects like galaxies will bring about the bending of any light waves (or photon streams) that pass by them. Therefore the two galaxies can fulfil the same role as the parallel slits in the two-slit experiment.

On Earth a group of astronomers decide to observe the quasar through a telescope. In the original experiment there was a photon detector; in this case the telescope acts as that detector. Because of the vast distances involved the light from the quasar enters the telescope one photon at a time. If the astronomers point the telescope in the direction of one of the intervening galaxies they will see photons that were deflected by that galaxy, and they will see the same result if they look at the other galaxy. By cleverly locating mirrors at certain positions they can make the two groups of photons simultaneously deflect onto a photographic plate. A pattern of light and dark bands will develop on the plates in exactly the same way as those in the less spectacular two-slit version. Now here comes the strange bit. As the photons hit the photographic plate one at a time an identical situation occurs as it does in the smaller experiment. In order to generate the striped pattern each single photon will have travelled both paths to Earth, going round both galaxies at the same time.

But it gets stranger again. As with the two-slit experiment, and its other version, Schrödinger's cat in a box, it is the act of observation that makes the photon 'decide' which galaxy it had gone round. The past tense here is crucial. The photon will have sped past the galaxy hundreds of millions of years ago and yet one observation by a conscious being changes an event that happened before life existed on Earth. It seems that we create our own universe as it is now and as it has always been.

Logic demands that this state of affairs is impossible. Time flows in one direction and it is therefore impossible to change the past. However a tabletop version of Wheeler's experiment has already taken place at the University of Maryland in 1984. This showed beyond any doubt that the paths the photons took were not fixed until the physicists made their measurements.

The implications of this are clear. An individual human consciousness not only seems to bring about the reality around it but also in some curious way it sits outside of time and space. It is interesting to note that due to the parochialism of the sciences, particularly between the 'hard' sciences such as quantum physics and astronomy and the 'soft' sciences such as psychology and sociology, no serious cross-fertilization of ideas on this theme has really taken place. This is unfortunate because the implications of such theories as Wheeler's Participatory Universe and Everett's Many Worlds have interesting echoes in experimental psychology and the sociology of religion. Wheeler's idea that human consciousness functions in a subjective and timeless way is fascinating but can it be supported by that most important arbiter, human experience?

Hypnogogic history

Surprisingly, evidence that the human mind can track backward in time has been given support by anecdotal reports regarding dreams. It seems that in certain circumstances dream scenarios are created by a stimulus that occurs after the dream has finished. A classic description of such an event was graphically illustrated by

Alfred Maury, the French science writer, who described his experience as follows:

> *I was slightly indisposed and was lying in my room; my mother*
> *was near my bed. I am dreaming of The Terror. I am present at*
> *scenes of massacre; I appear before the Revolutionary Tribunal; I*
> *see Robespierre, Marat, Forquier-Tinville, all the most villainous*
> *figures of this terrible epoch; I argue with them; at last, after*
> *many events which I remember only vaguely, I am judged,*
> *condemned to death, taken in a cart, amidst an enormous crowd,*
> *to the Square Of Revolution; I ascend the scaffold; the*
> *executioner binds me to the fatal board, he pushes it, the knife*
> *falls; I feel my head being severed from my body; I awake seized*
> *by the most violent terror, and I feel on my neck the rod of my*
> *bed which had become detached and had fallen on my neck as*
> *would the knife of the guillotine. This happened in one instant,*
> *as my mother confirmed to me, and yet it was the external*
> *sensation that was taken by me for the starting point of the*
> *dream with a whole series of successive incidents. At the moment*
> *that I was struck the memory of this terrible machine, the effect*
> *of which was so well produced by the rod of the bed's canopy, had*
> *awakened in me all the images of that epoch of which the*
> *guillotine was the symbol.*[22]

It seems that the young Maury's subconscious had created a whole dream to account for the impact of the canopy onto the back of his head. Indeed, either the dream was fabricated in the split second between the sensation of the impact and his conscious mind registering the blow, or else the dream itself was perceived 'back to front' – that is, that the dream started with the blow and worked backwards to the trial. Either option ensures that time was warped in one way or another. Maury concluded from this that dreams arose from external stimuli, instantaneously accompanying such impressions as they acted upon the sleeping person. In other words, the subconscious mind has the ability to immediately process outside sounds or events and create from them a complete, and subjective, incorporation into a dream. This is all done in a microsecond.[23]

Maury was writing in the 1870s. Times and fashions may change but certain psychological states do not. In the 1980s, at the request of the research organization, the Koestler Institute, members of the public sent in examples of curious coincidences that had occurred to them. Brian Inglis recorded many of these in his book *Coincidence: A Matter of Chance or Synchronicity.* One of these responses, however, did not involve coincidence, but time. The correspondent, Rian Hughes, wrote:

I dug out an old alarm clock – it had always been faultless in the past, but had not been in use for some years – to wake me up for a morning appointment.

My dreams, early that morning, concerned boxing. Despite my protestations, I was to go several rounds with an enormous bruiser who looked ready to settle the business without bothering about my puny frame. Forced into the ring, I took a deep breath – then the bell went.

I woke up. The bell was the alarm clock – ringing once and once only (a 'ding'), at exactly the right time in my dream (or my dream had led up to the time the clock went off exactly). It had never rung only once before.[24]

For both Maury and Hughes, something very strange was taking place. These dream events seem to suggest that under certain conditions human consciousness can perceive what is yet to happen. Maury's subconscious was somehow aware of an event that was yet to take place – the falling of the headboard – and created a dream to explain the impact on the back of his head. For Hughes it was the bell of the alarm clock that he was about to hear that brought about his boxing match dream.

To science fiction writer Philip K Dick such curious temporal anomalies were his bread and butter. In his novel *Minority Report*, subsequently filmed by Stephen Spielberg, Dick describes a special group of people who could, under certain circumstances, become aware of what is about to happen in the very near future. The film has one particularly fascinating scene in which the hero, with the aid of a 'precog', hides from his pursuers in a crowded shopping centre. Because the precog can predict the location and viewpoint of the 'bad guys' she can tell the hero where and when to move in order to be permanently out of sight of those who wished to do him harm. For Dick this 'skill' was a day-to-day fact that he had disguised as fiction. Dick viewed not only time but reality itself as a total illusion: a fabrication that keeps human beings from knowing what the universe really consists of. This belief is not as bizarre as it first seems – modern physics implies as much – but Dick believed that he had personal revelation that this was the case. In his autobiographical novel *Valis* he describes a series of experiences that happened to him in the 1960s. These lead him to the conclusion that our everyday reality of the senses is a charade, a charade Dick called the 'Black-Eyed Prison'. Outside of this super-sensory illusion is the real universe, a reality Dick called the 'Matrix'. And this is not a coincidence. The writers of the *Matrix* films have readily acknowledged their debt to Dick; however, the Wachowski brothers inverse the terminology in that their machine-controlled illusionary reality is termed *The Matrix*. If Dick was right then it is possible that we all may have this ability to see through the illusion.

Many of us have experienced a strange sensation when we have heard an unexpected loud noise. It seems that you jump before you actually hear the noise. It is as if you are already subconsciously aware of the sound and your body reacts before you become aware. This effect has long fascinated cognitive scientists as it implies that conscious awareness lags behind what is actually happening. If this was shown to be the case then the dreams of Maury and Hughes could be explained, as could any short-term precognitive abilities. If we are all creating the sensory world around us then it is not surprising that we unconsciously know what is about to take place next. However, the truth may be even stranger. Could it be that we are viewing a recording of this self-created *phaneron?* In which case what is actually taking place is a recollection of something that has already happened rather than a prediction of something that is about to take place – as Dick's precogs do in *Minority Report.*

The Bohmian IMAX plays in the Cartesian Theatre

On 22 May 2002, one of the most significant presentations in modern psychology took place. The location was the Slovak Academy of Sciences at Tatranská Lomnica in the Slovak Republic. The presentation was part of a three-day conference set up by NATO to look into the implications of the issue of non-locality in quantum physics and its implications as regards human consciousness. (Evidence, if it was ever needed, that while this subject matter may be relatively unknown to the general public, it is far from marginal and is of profound interest within certain influential sections of the scientific community.) The presentation in question took place late in the afternoon. Its title was a somewhat esoteric 'Empirical Evidence for an Apparent Biological Time Anomaly: a Functional MRI Study on Pre-sentiment'. However, its content was to 'shake a few foundations', as the seminar notes were to comment.[25]

The presenter was Dick J Bierman of the University of Amsterdam. He discussed the findings of a series of experiments he and an associate, Dean Radin, had devised in the late 1990s. Dr Bierman explained that the experiments involved a group of subjects who were placed in front of a computer screen. The left index and middle finger of each subject were connected to a skin conduction measuring device. (It has been shown that skin conductance is a good measure of emotional arousal.)

Each subject started the experiment by pressing a key on the keyboard. After 7.5 seconds a randomly chosen picture was displayed on the screen for a specific exposure period. The pictures were either calm or highly emotional. Before, during and after exposure the subject's skin conductance was measured at 5 samples per second.

The results clearly demonstrated that there was a significant difference in skin conductance response between emotionally calm and emotionally arousing stimuli. Indeed, this is what one would expect. What was astonishing was that the skin conductivity responded to the picture *before* it was shown on the screen. Bierman explained that only one conclusion was possible; that the human mind is somehow able to scan the emotional content of its immediate future.

A science writer, Mark Anderson, commenting upon these curious discoveries was motivated to make the following allusion:

> *Bierman's work may have revealed a crude ability to sense the future, much like the 'precogs' in the forthcoming Stephen Spielberg movie Minority Report, even if the skill only spans a few heartbeats.*[26]

There is another, equally intriguing conclusion, and that is that all conscious beings perceive external events after they have taken place. In other words, there is some form of delay mechanism that holds back sensory data until all the information is available. It is then, and only then, that 'out there' is presented to the observing consciousness.

As we have seen, there is strong evidence that the universe you perceive as out there may be brought into being by you observing it. No you, no outside world. As such, your universe is unique to you and you are possibly the only conscious inhabitant of your phaneron. It is logical to conclude that this phaneron is a creation of your brain and that 'out there', if 'out there' really exists, is nothing like the comfortable illusion created by your brain. This belief runs totally contrary to the common sense which tells you that what you are perceiving now is not only really there – 'out there' in the physical world that exists outside of your body – but also that you are perceiving it as it happens in real time.

You can test this. If you close your eyes and then open them it is all still there. All the objects that were around you are located in the same places, are made of the same substances and are the same colour. It is both real and immediate. For cognitive scientists this belief is termed Naïve or Direct Realism (DR).

DR is common sense. According to this theory 'out there' is exactly as we see it and feel it. Our senses, in particular vision, allow us direct contact with the object being perceived. What we see is what is there. However, another school of thought argues that common sense, although intuitively satisfying, is, as has happened with particle physics, incorrect. The alternative, termed Indirect Realism or the Representative Theory (RT), suggests that our perceptions of reality are recorded in some process analogous to the process whereby computers 'buffer' in-coming digital information (for example, when downloading media files from the web). In doing so the computer gives the 'observer' the illusion of seamless processing. When the brain's 'buffer' is full the sensory information is then presented to conscious awareness.

For the followers of DR, the only conclusion that can be drawn from the Bierman/Radin experiments is that some, if not all, sentient beings have short-term precognitive abilities. For those in the RT camp the solution is far more prosaic – we are all 'viewing' an internally generated facsimile of whatever is really 'out there'. What may be surprising is that the results of experimentation and empirical research imply that Representation Theory is correct and 'common sense' is, again, wrong.

It was in 1972 that common sense first lost out. An experiment, popularly known by the curious term of the 'cutaneous rabbit'[27], was to cause both interest and consternation. The two psychologists involved, Frank Geldard and Carl Sherrick, had individual subjects sit at a table. The subject was then asked to rest their arm on the table with a cushion placed underneath the limb in question. Mechanical tappers were then placed at three equidistant locations along the arm. A series of taps in rhythm were delivered to the tappers and these respond by tapping the subject's arm. The usual sequence was five taps at the wrist followed by two near the elbow and then three more on the upper arm. Each set of taps had an interval between them. Thus, there were five taps on the wrist then an interval of 50 to 200 milliseconds before the next set of two taps on the elbow. The same delay then took place between the elbow taps and the three on the upper arm. A complete sequence of taps would therefore take under a second to complete one full series. The astonishing thing was that the subject, instead of feeling three discreet groups of taps at specific locations on the arm, experienced the sensation of a group of taps travelling in regular sequence over a series of equidistant points up the arm. This sensation was likened to that of having a small animal, like a rabbit, hopping along the arm. In describing this experiment, the eminent science writer Professor Daniel C Dennett asks:

> *Now, at first one feels like asking how did the brain know that after the five taps at the wrist there was going to be some taps near the elbow? The subjects experience the 'departure' of the taps from the wrist beginning with the second tap, yet in catch trials in which the latter elbow taps are never delivered, subjects feel all five wrist taps at the wrist in the expected place. The brain obviously cannot 'know' about a tap on the elbow until after it happens.[28]*

Can it be that the brain waits until all the taps are received before 'informing' consciousness that the event is taking place? Until the final tap is received, all the sensations are stored at some way-station between the arm and the seat of consciousness.

Four years later, in 1976, a supporting experiment was reported by a group of German psychologists.[29] A number of human volunteers agreed to have an EEG record the electrical signals at a certain position on their skull. While this was picking up any electrical activity in the brain the subjects were asked to flex the index finger of their right hand. The decision of when this movement was to occur was left totally to the subject. What Kornhuber and his associates were trying to do was to isolate what sort of mental activity was generated when a decision to make a movement was made. What was discovered was another facet of the curious way the human mind functions. It seems that there was a delay of between a second and a second and a half from when the decision to move was made and the actual movement took place. Yet the subjects perceived that the decision to move and the actual movement were simultaneous. This in itself was interesting but it was then discovered that a response to an external signal to engender a particular movement was much faster than the body's ability to cause the physical action. As mathematician Roger Penrose comments:

> For example, instead of it being 'freely willed', the finger
> flexing might be in response to the flash of a light signal. In
> that case a reaction time of about one-fifth of a second is
> normal, which is about five times faster than the 'willed' action
> that is tested in Kornhuber's data.[30]

A graph of the results of the experiment shows the point at which the decision to flex was made. Penrose says that this suggests a 'foreknowledge of the intention to flex'.[31]

In 1979, a little known but revolutionary experiment was to

take place that gave further support for the belief that we are all watching a recording of events rather than experiencing them first hand.

In the scene from *Schindler's List* we both saw a little girl in a red coat run down a street. You looked at a TV screen and your eyes perceived a seemingly natural event. However, what you were actually seeing was a series of static images on the TV screen. It was your mind that created the movement, the movement exists nowhere else in the process.

Motion pictures are made possible because we perceive continuous movement in response to a rapid succession of static views. This phenomenon is called apparent (or stroboscopic) movement. To the non-specialist this concept of 'visual persistence' is sufficient to explain why you see the illusion of movement. This involves the belief that the eye holds an 'after image' and because the next image is presented so quickly the new image is superimposed over the other. However, this persistence, although real enough, simply cannot explain apparent movement. What it cannot explain is why you fail to perceive the blank sections between the actual frames. These are flashed onto the cinema screen for 1/80th of a second each time and during these small periods the screen is not just blank, but also dark. Added to this is the curiosity that you do not blur the images. As one image superimposes on the other, the retina, like the film in a camera, will confuse, not segregate the images. It is therefore evident that we do not 'see' a movie with our eyes. There is another, more subtle, mental process going on.

The first psychologist to think in this way was the Czech Max Wertheimer. While on a train journey in 1910 he became fascinated by how his mind was processing the visual information coming to him through the train window. The train stopped long enough in Frankfurt for him to leap off the train, find a toyshop, buy a stroboscope, and get back on to continue his journey.

On his arrival back home he immediately set to work. He noted that two lights flashed through small apertures in a darkened room at short intervals would appear to be one light in motion; this perception of movement in a stationary object he termed 'the PHI phenomenon' and this in turn became the basis of a whole school of psychology, Gestalt. Together with two assistants, Wolfgang Köhler and Kurt Koffka, he began to study the PHI phenomenon in earnest. Although they spent many years looking into the subject it was to become something of an oddity within human perception. That did not mean that the phenomenon did not continue to intrigue and beguile all that encountered it.

In 1977, the philosopher Nelson Goodman asked psychologists Paul Kolers and Michael von Grunau what would happen if, in the PHI phenomenon, the two illuminated spots were of different colours. This was so simple but revolutionary that the two psychologists immediately set up an experiment. They had a good idea of what to expect; either that two flashing spots would replace the single spot, or an illusory spot would change from one colour to another working its way through all the hues between. What actually happened was astounding. Two different coloured spots were illuminated for 150 milliseconds each (with a 50-millisecond interval); the first spot seemed to begin moving and then change colour abruptly in the middle of its illusory passage toward the second location. Goodman wondered:

> How are we able to fill in the spot at the intervening place-times along a path running from the first and second flash before the second flash occurs?[32]

For Daniel Dennett the mind somehow holds back the full perception of this experience until it is fully understood. The colour change is experienced by consciousness after the exercise has been completed. Dennett says:

Suppose the first spot is red and the second, displaced, spot is green. Unless there is 'precognition' in the brain (an extravagant hypothesis we will postpone indefinitely), the illusory content, red switching to-green-in-midcourse cannot be created until after some identification of the second, green spot occurs in the brain. But if the second spot is already 'in conscious experience' would it not be too late to interpose the illusory content between the conscious experience of the red spot and the conscious experience of the green spot? How does the brain accommodate this sleight of hand?

In 1979, yet more empirical evidence was found for this delay in perception when Benjamin Libet of the University of California and Bertram Feinstein of the Zion Neurological Institute in San Francisco pooled their knowledge to experiment directly on an exposed human brain. This allows the neurosurgeon to receive immediate feedback on what the patient is experiencing. Running along the top of the brain is a strip known as the somatosensory cortex. It has been long known that individual points in the body can be made to feel sensations by the direct stimulation of this strip. For example, a stimulation of a point on the left somatosensory cortex can produce the sensation of a brief tingle in the subject's right hand. Libet was keen to compare the time course of such sensations to those more normally induced by direct stimulation by applying a brief electric pulse to the hand itself. He then asked the conscious patient what had come first, the hand tingle that started right in the cortex, or the hand signal sent to the brain from the hand. Logic says the cortex message, because it does not have to travel so far, would arrive first.

The work of Libet, Kornhuber, Geldard/Sherrick and Kolers/von Grunau all imply that the brain uses a buffering process similar to a computer. It waits until all the data is received before it presents them to consciousness. This internally generated facsimile of reality is termed the 'Cartesian Theatre' by Dennett. By this Dennett means the point in the brain where 'it all comes together', or as he says

> *... there is a crucial finish line or boundary somewhere in the brain where the order of arrival equals the order of 'presentment' in experience because what happens there is what you are conscious of.*[33]

If there is a single point in the brain where it all comes together it is reasonable to conclude that that must be the point where consciousness can be found. The idea that consciousness is located in one place in the brain is based on one simple logical observation; neuronal signals engendered by external stimuli need time to get from the sense organs to the point of consciousness. In other words, if consciousness is located in various places in the brain how is it that you and I perceive 'reality' in terms of time intervals? Everything we perceive has two states, 'not yet observed' and 'already observed'. The point of observation is the nexus between these two states. It happens at a specific point in time. If the 'observer' in your brain is spread across that, brain signals will arrive at different times to different locations. That you perceive all incoming data (sight, sound and touch) at exactly the same point implies that 'you' as the observer are located at a central point; the geometric termination point of all those inbound processes.

Although this argument is persuasive, the location of the 'Ghost in the Machine' as English philosopher Gilbert Ryle sarcastically termed it[34] has never been found. Indeed, there is strong evidence that brain processes such as memory seem to occur across the brain rather than at specific locations.[35] In his attack on Cartesian Dualism[36] Dennett argues very effectively that this belief is wrong and that there is no central point of consciousness. For Dennett consciousness is located all over the brain.

If all the incoming stimuli are held back until they are assimilated, digitized and 'hologramed' then the problem of consciousness being located across the brain disappears. The 'Cartesian Theatre' is played to consciousness some time after it is initially received. The major implication of Representative Theory is that your brain works somewhat like a programmed video recorder. Imagine that you wish to record a film on television. Let us say that we agree to go out for a meal to discuss the finer points of Everett's Many Worlds Interpretation. You look through the TV listings and notice that *Schindler's List* will be on television while we are out. I say that there is a section in that film that is of importance for our next area of discussion. We therefore agree to programme the VCR to record the film while we are out. In our absence the VCR switches itself on at the allotted time, starts recording the signal coming in from the TV station and then, when the film finishes the timer switches the VCR off. We come back three hours later, your head still finding it difficult to accept that billions of versions of us are also returning to watch the film in a myriad of alternative universes. We settle down, wind back the videotape and watch the film. Now what has happened is that the VCR has recorded the film to be presented later. Up until the moment the recording lights up the TV screen the images have not been perceived by a sentient mind, they have simply been recorded on tape, but as soon as the TV screen receives the images the opening credits appear on the screen and are presented to our consciousnesses.

And so it is with Dennett's 'Cartesian Theatre'. The brain processes incoming sensory data without any involvement of consciousness. Like the VCR recording without the television itself 'perceiving' the signal, so it is with the brain. All the incoming sensory data are automatically recorded in order for them to be presented to consciousness at a later date. Dennett's choice of the image of a theatre is particularly interesting in that a theatre involves a stage where the action takes place. The stage, like the TV in my analogy, exists 'out there', inhabiting a three-dimensional world that also contains other 'real' (ie, not part of the recording) objects such as the television itself. I feel that the word 'theatre' simply fails to convey the totality of the experience presented to consciousness. The brain generates a three-dimensional event that involves all the senses, not just sight and hearing. The observer 'feels' the re-created world around them. They can sense their body in space and can feel the pressure of objects in contact with their body. This is not simply a theatre, more a virtual reality IMAX cinema that immerses the observer to the extent that he or she cannot tell the difference between the recreation and the original. This inwardly generated IMAX re-creates reality using the holographic processes suggested by David Bohm. So my version of Dennett's 'Cartesian Theatre' is the possibly more accurate 'Bohmian IMAX'.

In *The Matrix*, there is an incident where Neo experiences what is commonly known as a *déjà vu*. He sees a cat walk past a door and then sees what he takes to be a second cat do exactly the same thing a second later. His companions tell him that it was indeed a replay of the first incident and that all *déjà vu* experiences are caused by 'reality' being reprogrammed. This is, of course, fiction. This kind of thing does not happen in the real world because if it did it would lead us to doubt what external reality really is. It would be well to bear this prejudice in mind as you read the following account taken from JB Priestley's masterwork, *Man and Time*:

> *The only time that time became misplaced for me happened when I was working as a maid in a place called Dunraven Castle in South West Wales. There were three of us in the servery just after Saturday luncheon – Hans, the odd-job boy, Renate, the senior maid and me. The floor of the room was a terra cotta orange colour. I saw Renate pick up a jug, a white jug, of chocolate sauce. As she turned to hand it to Hans she*

dropped it. It smashed and the pastel-brown sauce formed a
very definite pattern on the floor, something like an amoeba as
shown in a school biology textbook. As I looked the whole scene
melted and, like a loop of film, started again. It was terrifying!
I remember shouting to Renate, as she picked up the jug, not to
touch it, and screaming in horror as I watched the sauce make
its pre-destined shape on the orange floor. I tried to explain to
them how I had watched the scene take place a couple of
seconds before it had – and, of course, they said that if I had
not shouted the whole thing wouldn't have happened.[37]

While *The Matrix* contains some disturbingly accurate reflections on reality for a film that is supposedly fiction, the woman in question wrote these words at least 40 years ago and had the experience many years before and yet she outlines the event as if she was describing a scene from the film. I would also like to draw your attention to her comment that 'the whole scene melted and it was like a loop of film'. With our knowledge of holographic imagery and memory recall we can easily explain what was taking place in that kitchen all those years ago. The lady's internal imaging 'skipped' for some reason. As we will discover later, this is not only entirely possible but may happen on a regular, if less spectacular, basis. Our young kitchen maid had, for a few seconds, accidentally upgraded her ticket in her internal IMAX cinema.

The startling implication of this scenario is that there is no way that you, as the perceiver, can tell if this three-dimensional presentation is a recording of events that happened a few milliseconds or a thousand years ago. In this way Dualism is updated to reflect the latest in cognitive science and neurological research. This is proof, if it were needed, that what you are perceiving at this moment in time, this book, its words and ideas and everything around you is an internally generated version of reality, a copy projected in front of you like an unbelievably complex sensurround, virtual reality computer game. This is generated by the manipulation of hologram-like images and using the processing power of the greatest computer in the universe – your brain.

Here you are reading this book, or should I say perceiving an image that contains this book. Look up and take in what is around you. It's all an illusion, a series of inwardly generated holographic images. You are not here at all, you are being fooled into thinking you are. You are somewhere else entirely. From this place you are generating the world around you, re-creating it piece by piece and second by second. We already know this from the evidence of quantum physics. As Hugh Everett proposed, there are literally trillions of universes; you exist in just one, a version of John Wheeler's 'participatory universe' creating it as you go along, each micro-decision that you make causing ever-increasing new timelines, like the branches of some magical tree.

But there is one huge problem with this personal universe. If you have always only existed within your own self-created version of reality, how have you created such a rich and varied environment? If this universe is all you have known, how have you created giraffes, quasars and rap music? In order to create such concepts you must, at some time or other, have known of these things and projected them into your version of reality. How can it be otherwise? You are like a baby who is abandoned on a desert island. As the baby grows up he has no knowledge of anything external to the island. How could that baby mentally visualize anything outside of his direct experience, a glacier for example? So it is for you. It is likely that within your universe exists the Eiffel Tower. You may even visit Paris and take in the view from the top. Now here is the weird thing; I am writing these words at my home in Harrogate, England, on a beautiful June morning. This is my version of Harrogate and my idea of what a beautiful June morning should look like. I have chosen the Eiffel Tower as an example of a well-known man-made feature. You now read these words in your version of the universe, surrounded by objects and weather conditions of your own creation. But strangely you immediately visualize Paris with the Tower dominating all around it. How can we both have a similar vision in our heads? How can we both have inwardly created an object that we both can agree on in terms of size, shape and location when we have never met and exist in totally different versions of reality? Sometime in both our pasts there must have been a real world populated by real objects, animals and buildings. Indeed this original 'objective' universe may be analogous to the biblical Garden of Eden, a place where we all perceived the original blueprint of objective reality, a place where the original Eiffel Tower stood in all its glory. This internally generated world is a facsimile, a copy, but as with all facsimiles and copies there must be an original – a first edition if you like.

And so there is. There was a time in both our distant pasts where we first perceived not only the Eiffel Tower but also all the wonderful objects, concepts and structures that we now populate our illusory world with. This very fact is one of the major clues as to what is really going on.

The question you have to ask yourself is how do you know about the Eiffel Tower, or indeed any event, incident or place that has taken place in your life? By what mechanism can you instantly recall an image of Paris in the spring or Maine in the autumn? This mechanism we term our 'memory'. Everything that you know about yourself and the world comes from your ability to recollect. The only non-memory element of your perception of 'reality' is that transitory concept we call 'now', that small sliver of time that links the 'was' with the 'will be'. The rest is purely memory. The question is, what exactly do we mean when we talk about memory? As you may have guessed, memory, like everything else, is not quite what it seems.

CHAPTER 4

A Reflection on Memory

The light of memory, or rather the light that memory lends to things,
is the palest light of all. I am not quite sure whether I am dreaming
or remembering, whether I have lived my life or dreamed it.

Just as dreams do, memory makes me profoundly aware of the
unreality, the evanescence of the world, a fleeting image in the
moving water.

Eugene Ionesco

That's a flash back you have there

We have just finished watching our video recording of *Schindler's
List*. We have discussed in some detail the issue of the little girl in
the red coat. You turn to me and ask if it is possible to see the
sequence again. I agree and I wind the tape back to that particular
point. We watch the scene again. As if by magic the images are
identical to the last viewing. The videotape has not only recorded
the film from the TV but it has recorded it for as long as the tape
exists. The videotape 'remembers' the images and can recreate
them at our request. Isn't technology wonderful!

Reality is recorded in a similar process, its images being
presented to us some time after the event. It is logical to conclude
that something that is once recorded and viewed can be reviewed
at a later time. Is it possible that experiences in our life are stored
somewhere in the brain like vast ranks of videotapes? Can the
Bohmian IMAX be played more than once? If that were seen to be
the case it would add more weight to the idea that you are living
inside a simulation. Well, let's see what you make of the following
anecdotes from the world of literature (I am sure that you would
like a break from all the hard science).

The first involves the Swedish playwright August Strindberg. In his book *Legends*, he describes a strange incident that happened to him while he was sitting in a wine shop. He was trying to talk a young friend out of giving up his military career. In an attempt to lend support to his position he began to describe a past incident that had involved them both. They had been in a tavern. As he began to describe the scene Strindberg suddenly 'lost consciousness' and found himself actually back in the tavern in question. He found himself sitting at the table talking to his friend. Although the vision only lasted a few seconds it was extremely vivid.[38] In his own words this is how Strindberg described the incident:

> After arguments and endless appeals, I wished to call up in
> his memory a past event that might have influenced his
> resolve. He had forgotten the occurrence in question, and in
> order to stimulate his memory I began to describe it to him:
> 'You remember that evening in the Augustiner tavern. I
> continued to describe the table where we had eaten our meal,
> the position of the bar, the door through which people
> entered, the furniture, the pictures ... All of a sudden, I
> stopped. I had half lost consciousness without fainting, and
> still sat in my chair. I was in the Augustiner tavern, and had
> forgotten to whom I spoke, when I recommenced as follows:
> 'Wait a minute. I am now in the Augustiner tavern, but I
> know very well that I am in some other place. Don't say
> anything ... I don't know you anymore, yet I know that I do.
> Where am I? Don't say anything. This is interesting.' I made
> an effort to raise my eyes – I don't know if they were closed –
> and I saw a cloud, a background of indistinct colour, and
> from the ceiling descended something like a theatre curtain;
> it was the dividing wall with shelves and bottles.

'Oh yes!' I said, after feeling a pang pass through me. 'I am in F's wine shop'.

The officer's face was distorted with alarm, and he wept.

'What is the matter?' I said to him.

'That was dreadful,' he answered.[39]

Strindberg has no reason to make this story up. It is simply too strange. So what did happen? If my theory is correct then the playwright inadvertently set in motion a short section of his Bohmian IMAX. It seems that for a few seconds he had dual consciousness, as if one image (the past) was overlain on another (the present) like a temporal double exposure.

Flashbacks are but part of the evidence for the existence of my Bohmian IMAX. A flashback tends to be unexpected and is not called forth by the conscious mind. It seems to just appear in the mind's eye. However, there is another much recorded phenomenon that implies that at certain times the medium by which the brain records memories is super-effective. Termed 'Charged Memories', these images are usually stimulated by a particular set of circumstances and occur more than once. On each occasion the stimulus and recollection are identical. Marcel Proust's *À la Recherché du Temps Perdu* uses charged memories as its main subject matter. The title is usually translated into English as *Remembrance of Things Past*, but this translation fails to convey the central point of the book. The literal translation from the French is 'In Search of Lost Time' and is thus a far more accurate reflection of the content. By finding involuntary memories stimulated by some object or circumstance the hero discovers the true meaning of a past experience. Proust described the process by which these charged memories collide with the present:

And at the same time in the context of a distant moment, so

*that the past was made to encroach upon the present and I was
made to doubt whether I was in one or the other, the truth
surely was that the being within me which had enjoyed these
impressions had enjoyed them because they had in them
something that was common to a day long past and to the
present, because in some way they were extra-temporal, and
this being made its appearance only when, through one of these
identifications of the present with the past, it was likely to find
itself in the one and only medium in which it could exist and
enjoy the essence of things. That is to say, outside time.*

Again we have a description of an overlapping of two parallel
perceptions, one in the present and one in the past but both being
equally vivid. As Proust says: 'I was made to doubt whether I was
in one or the other.'

The weakness with these particular examples is that they were
experienced by somewhat sensitive literary types. These writers
and poets depend on their fertile imagination for their fame.
However, the phenomenon has also been recorded under
controlled circumstances with qualified scientific witnesses. Here
is an example:

*Her attacks were characterised by sudden fright and screaming.
She then held onto the people about her for protection. This
was followed by falling and, occasionally, by a major
convulsion. On careful questioning it was learned that during
the preliminary period of fright she invariably saw herself in a
scene that she remembered to have occurred at the age of
seven. The scene was as follows: a little girl was walking
through a field where the grass was high. It was a lovely day
and her brothers were walking along ahead of her. A man
came up behind her and said, 'How would you like to get in
this bag with the snakes?' She was very frightened and*

screamed to her brothers, and they all ran home where she told her mother about the event. The mother remembers the fright and the story and the brothers still recall the occasion and remember seeing the man. After that she occasionally has nightmares during her sleep and in the dream the scene was re-enacted. Three or four years later ... it was recognised that she had attacks by day in which she habitually complained that she saw the scene of her fright. There was a little girl, whom she identified with herself, in the now familiar surroundings. During the attack she was conscious of the actual environment and called the names, and yet she saw herself, as the little girl, with such distinctiveness that she was filled with terror that she should be struck from behind. She seems to be thinking in two minds.[40]

Again we have the situation of a charged memory in which the 'observer' is both watching and experiencing an event at the same time. The young girl in question found her consciousness in two places, but this time the circumstances by which this event took place was not a random and uncontrolled event but had been artificially stimulated by the application of an electrode onto the exposed temporal lobes of the 14-year old. It took place in the 1930s in an operating theatre in Canada. The young lady's memory recall was far from unusual.

The evidence gets Wilder

Wilder Penfield was born in Spokane, Washington and educated at Princeton and Oxford, where he was a Rhodes scholar. He specialized in neurosurgery both in New York and Baltimore, but it was in Montreal that he was to make his name. Here he set up the Montreal Neurological Institute and became its first director. Under his leadership it became a world centre of advanced neurosurgical techniques, particularly applied to epilepsy.

Penfield's interest in epilepsy was brought about through personal tragedy. His older sister, Ruth, had suffered from brief alterations in consciousness that worsened in her forties. By this time she was undergoing full *grand mal* seizures that demanded medical attention. Penfield used an ophthalmoscope to look at the back of his sister's eyes where the swollen veins and optic nerve suggested the presence of a brain tumour. Penfield knew that only one person was qualified to attempt the removal of the tumour, himself. He managed to remove most, but not all of the cancer and she died a year later. This incident was to focus his attention on a surgical approach to the control or elimination of epilepsy.

It may come as a surprise to learn that the human brain does not feel pain. All that is needed is local anaesthetic to deaden the pain in the skull for a surgeon to open up the cranium and look inside. While this takes place it is essential for certain operations that the conscious patient can report any sensations taking place. In this way Penfield was able to both treat a disorder and also, in the process, experiment on a live brain, something that under ordinary circumstances would have been ethically unthinkable.

He could do this because in 1929, at the same time that Penfield was opening his Institute in Montreal, a German psychiatrist by the name of Hans Berger had invented a machine that could measure the electrical currents in the brain. In 1930, Penfield managed to acquire one of these machines, called an electroencephalograph, together with a doctor who was an expert in its applications. Penfield and his new associate, Herbert Jaspers, quickly saw the opportunity that was available to them.

After some thought Penfield designed a pencil-shaped electrode that could stimulate the surface of the brain, so allowing the conscious patient to report any sensations brought about by the application of the electrical current. Very soon he made a curious discovery. During the application of the charge to the exposed cortex, one of his patients claimed that she had perceived a strong memory recall. Penfield was to consider this a coincidence, and continued to do so even when it happened again with another patient some time later. However, an operation on a 26-year-old woman a few years later was to change totally our understanding of human consciousness. Before cutting out brain matter Penfield would use the electrode to isolate carefully the areas that should not be removed. On applying a two-volt charge to the exposed brain Penfield asked the young woman what she experienced. When she reported a tingling in her thumb he knew that that section controlled sensation; when she momentarily lost her ability to speak he knew that he had found the section that controlled speech. He then moved his probe to another section and a totally unexpected response occurred. 'I hear something', the woman said. 'I don't know what it is'. Penfield re-applied the probe. 'Yes sir', the woman replied, 'I think I heard a mother calling her little boy somewhere. It seemed to be something that happened years ago. It was somebody in the neighbourhood where I live, and I was close enough to hear.'[41]

She explained later that the memory was so vivid that it could have been a present experience. It was more than just a memory, she insisted that she had actually re-lived a long-forgotten moment in her past. Trying to control his excitement, Penfield told her that he was going to re-apply the current, but instead he pressed the electrode to another spot close by. This time her memory was both visual as well as auditory. She said: 'Yes, I heard voices down a river – a man's voice and a woman's voice calling ... I think I saw the river.'

The second the brain was given the electrical stimulation the patient was taken back to a point in their own past. This was not simply the stimulation of a memory; it was a total recall of past events. In his book *Mystery of Mind*, published just before his death, Penfield was quite categorical about the nature of these recollections. He wrote:

It was evident at once that these were not dreams. They were
electrical activations of the sequential record of consciousness; a
record that had been laid down during the patient's earlier
experience. The patient 're-lived' all that he had been aware of
in that earlier period of time in a moving picture 'flash-back'.[42]

Thus he believed these to be actual memory traces that were being automatically called forth from the subconscious. It was not as if the patients decided to remember a particular event. They had no control over what the memory was or indeed at what point the memory started or ended. In one classic incident a woman recalled being back in her house of many years before with her son, Frankie, playing outside in the garden. She stated that she could hear all the neighbourhood sounds around her. She was not remembering, she was re-living a particular moment from her past. Ten days after the operation she was asked if this was a memory. 'Oh no,' she replied, 'it seemed more real than that.'

This response to stimulation was a single experience. Her memory of such occasions was a generalization. Without the aid of the electrode she could not recall any one of the specific instances nor hear the honking of automobiles that might mean danger to Frankie, or cries of other children or the barking of dogs that would have made up the neighbourhood 'sounds' on each occasion. These memories were not available to her normal consciousness. Penfield's electrode was probing into an unknown area of human experience.

What was particularly puzzling to Penfield was that if the stimulation was interrupted for any reason and then restarted the whole recall would start again. It was as if it was some form of recording that was being played back.

Penfield reported many other examples, all of which reinforce the suspicion that these are actual recordings. These include one man who suddenly recalled a conversation with friends in South

Africa and a boy who heard his mother talking on the telephone (and who, after several touches from Penfield's electrode was able to repeat the entire conversation). He then describes the incident of the woman in her kitchen. In each case it was the same part of the brain (the temporal lobe) that brought about these responses.

In his book *Speech and Brain Mechanism*, Penfield, together with his co-author Lamar Roberts, made the following telling comments:

> *Time is a strip of film run forward, never backward, even when resurrected from the past. It seems to proceed again at time's own unchanged pace. It would seem, once one section of the strip has come alive, that the response is protected by a functional all-or-nothing principle. A regulating inhibitory mechanism must guard against activation of other portions of the film: as long as the electrode is held in place, the experience of a former day goes forward. There is no holding still, no turning back, no crossing to other periods. When an electrode is withdrawn, it stops as suddenly as it began.*

> *A particular strip can sometimes be repeated by interrupting the stimulation and then shortly re-applying it at the same or a nearby point. In that case it begins at the same moment of time on each occasion.*

They concluded:

> *Every individual forms a neuronal record of his own stream of consciousness. Since artificial re-activation of the record, later in life, seems to re-create all those things formally included within the focus of his attention, one must assume that the re-activated recording pattern of neuronal activity*

may be considered much more than a record, for it was once used as the final stage of integration to make consciousness what it was.

The evidence seems clear: the recall brought about by Penfield's probe was a recording of past events that was being replayed. The salient point here is that the human mind has two elements, termed the 'screen' and the 'viewmaster' by Professor Richard Gregory of Bristol University. While this conclusion concerns Gregory in that it implies an infinite regress, it is important to acknowledge the fact, commented on by Penfield and Jaspers, that everyday consciousness is like a television without a video recorder. The television 'views' the events as a stream of information that flows from past to future. The conscious mind does the same. There is also a second, parallel process, taking place at the subconscious or automatic level, whereby the data is recorded and held. This section is analogous to the video recorder which exists autonomous to, but in a relationship with, the television. This video recorder is continually on and continually recording information. The implication is clear; the brain records every perception it receives during a lifetime of processing – in other words we forget nothing, with one small exception, and that is the crucial fact that we have an ability to access all this information. It is like having a safe containing all the secrets of the world, with the key to the safe locked inside.

So there you have it. My seemingly crazy idea of the Bohmian IMAX is supported by scientific evidence. Not only that but the recording remains intact once laid down. It can be re-awakened by a stimulus such as Penfield's electrodes. However, if my Bohmian IMAX theory is to stand up it is necessary to find evidence that such a process exists within the brain.

The holographic mind field

Each of the examples of flashbacks and 'charged memories' mentioned so far seems to imply that they are all recordings. The subject is acting as an observer of a three-dimensional, fully sensory, virtual reality experience. They are viewing the events in a linear format. The experience runs its course as a film runs through a projector. The same can be said for Penfield's patients – they are observers, not participants. So what does this mean? The answer lies in a physical effect that we have already encountered in the last chapter: holograms.

Penfield's experiments show strong evidence that memory is located in one place in the brain. Memories were stimulated when the electrode was placed on a specific spot and those same memories could be re-stimulated by applying the current at the same spot some time later. Other scientists have shown that learning, and by implication memory, can be 'hard wired' into particular brain cells. By repeated use a form of feedback loop is developed and the memory is stored for future recall, a little like the grooves on a gramophone record or the digital code on a DVD.

However, these cases do not 'prove' that memory is not to be found all over the brain as well. Memory is stored right across the brain. The question is how. The American psychologist Karl Pribram believes he has the answer: the brain is not a storage device at all, it is a tuning system, and it works on the principle of holography.[43]

Again I would like to return to the little girl in the red coat in *Schindler's List*. The mystery of vision, and particularly how your brain converts photon stimulation of your rods and cones at the back of your eye into the sensation of redness has yet to be solved. Pribram was fascinated by this mystery. After many years' study he suggested a revolutionary theory not only about memory but also about human consciousness itself. He wrote:

How are images reconstructed? Where are these images

located? What is the physical property that makes superposition
of the functions of neighbouring elements mandatory? How
can a pattern, the encoded information, be transmitted without
transmission of the substance or medium in which the
communication occurs?[44]

Pribram began his quest in 1966 when he proposed that the brain might interpret information in a similar way to how a hologram records an image. He suggested that the fine fibres in the nerve cells digitize incoming information and store the data in this format. The brain then decodes these stored memory traces in the way a hologram decodes, or more accurately de-blurs, its original image.

Hooray for the homunculus

In 1971, a distressing yet vital question began troubling Pribram. If the brain indeed perceives by putting together holograms – by mathematically transforming frequencies from 'out there' – who in the brain is interpreting the holograms? The idea of dualism is of great concern to orthodox science. The concept of a little man in the head viewing the reconstituted images may cause what is termed an 'infinite regression'. Put simply, if the little man is viewing the images he in turn must be using some form of visual apparatus. The images will in turn be processed inside his 'brain'. In order to do this he must himself have a little man in his head ... And so we end up with endless little men. This simply does not answer the question. For this reason Pribram felt that he had to find an alternative scenario.

Like Archimedes in his bath, inspiration was to come unbeckoned. He was giving a lecture at the University of Minnesota when a question was asked about the dualism issue. In a flash Pribram blurted out, 'Maybe the world is a hologram!' After thinking about this for a time he realized that this indeed would solve his problem. He concluded that all of reality is a projection.

Pribram's son, a physicist in his own right, was obviously concerned about his father, but in one of those defining moments of the human search after truth, he suggested to his father that he read some of the writings of David Bohm. On doing so Pribram realized that his suspicions may be correct. Holography was the answer.

David Bohm was of the opinion that the whole Universe worked as a joint holographic image. He was working inwards from Outer Space, coming in the reverse direction to Pribram. who saw holograms as the answer to the problems of Inner Space, the human mind. A crucial part of Bohm's theory was the idea that we never perceive visual 'reality' at first hand. We can only encounter the world of images through lenses. We view the universe through telescopes, we view the inner world of particles though microscopes, we identify the make-up of matter through spectrometry, and we view all this through the most important lens of all, the human eye.

Lens us some reality

Pribram took this idea into the realms of human perception. He suggested that the brain itself acted as a form of lens. A lens that brought the blurred potential of a holographic universe into sight, sound, colour and all the other sensory inputs that make the 'outside' become 'inside'. In the same way that the image on a holographic photographic plate is a swirl of blurs and fuzziness, so it is with the universe 'out there'. It is only when the lens of the brain, acting as a laser light on a holographic plate, brings out the three-dimensional image that the universe comes into being. As Pribram says:

> Maybe reality isn't what we see with our eyes. If we did not
> have that lens – the mathematics performed by our brain –
> maybe we would know a world organized in the frequency

domain. No space, no time, just events. Can reality be read out
of that domain?

The commonsense viewpoint, termed the 'ecological model' by Pribram – that reality is perceived as it happens – is, for him, inadequate in explaining perception. He feels that his 'Holographic Model' successfully addresses these issues. In this model, images are constructed when input from the inferior temporal cortex activates and organizes the holographic store. Images are then produced and:

> *... are therefore as much a product of the 'information residing in' the organism as they are of 'information' contained in the environment. Philosophically speaking, the holonomic model is Kantian and Piagetian; the ecological model partakes of a critical realism'.*[45]

In other words, the internal projection of the external world is mixed with internally generated subjective thoughts, feelings and interpretations. We take external 'reality' and we make it into our own subjective internal world. In a psychological reflection of the Copenhagen Interpretation and my Bohmian IMAX we do indeed create our own reality.

Pribram justifies this in a simple and straightforward way. He cites examples of people who suffer from severe perceptual problems such as macropsia and micropsia. This is where a person perceives objects as being much bigger or much smaller than other people do. It has been shown that these individuals see these objects in much more detail (in terms of macropsia) than 'normal' people. He gives an example of one of his own patients who, after a blow on the head, suffered bouts of severe vertigo. At the end of an attack he would see the world upside down. His visual system was interpreting the input from the retina in totally the wrong way. This would persist until another vertigo attack placed his vision the right way round. This man's visual system was acting like a television that was confusing the signal, not as a person who was directly interfacing with 'out there'.

In this way Pribram was also able to explain the problem of the infinite regression implied by the observer in the mind. For him the external hologram and the internal hologram are aspects of the same construct. Bohm argued, in his ideas regarding the holomovement, that everything is enfolded into itself. The perceiver and the perceived are but two aspects of one unity.

That we process our perception of reality rather than perceive it first hand can be dramatically illustrated by the case of a Swiss woman who suffered a most peculiar perceptual problem: motion blindness. The woman, called 'Ingrid' by the neuroscientist Dr VS Ramachandran, suffered bilateral damage to an area of her brain called the middle temporal (MT) area. Her eyesight was normal as long as she was looking at a stationary object, but if she looked at a person running or a car driving past then strange things took place. Instead of seeing motion she saw a succession of static, strobelike snapshots. Ramachandran describes her perceptions:

> She said that talking to someone in person felt like talking on
> the phone because she couldn't see the changing facial
> expressions associated with normal conversation. Even pouring
> a cup of coffee was an ordeal because the liquid would
> inevitably overflow and spill on the floor. She never knew when
> to slow down, changing the angle of the coffeepot, because she
> couldn't estimate how fast the liquid was rising in the cup.[46]

For this unfortunate woman reality was perceived in 'chunks' rather than in a wave-flow. It is almost analogous to the 'quantum' rather than 'wave function' behaviour of sub-atomic particles.[47] One also has to ask what is happening to her concept of temporal flow, of time itself. If she sees movement in 'snapshots', what has happened in relation to her perception, of the time between the snapshots? Again it seems that the moving car that she sees as a series of static images is, like the electron when it changes orbit, disappearing from one position in space and reappearing at another. The car is, as Bohr would have described it, moving in a series of 'quantum leaps'. It is interesting to note that this perceiving of 'reality' in quanta is echoed in the words of Penfield and his associate Jaspers when they say that perception is:

> ... originally like a strip of film. Its meaning was projected on the screen of man's awareness, and somehow it was held in place there for a brief time of consideration before it was replaced by subsequent experience and consequent neuronal patterns ... Consciousness, 'forever flowing' past us, makes no record of itself, and yet the recording of its counterpart within the brain is astonishingly complex.

It is not just movement that can be manipulated by internal processing of our perceptions of 'out there'. In his book *An Anthropologist on Mars*, Oliver Sacks describes the case of an artist who suffered such a small stroke that he did not notice it. As it took place in the evening he failed to realize that the brain damage brought about by the stroke had changed his perception of colour to simple black and white. But although he had lost all ability to see colour, we have to assume that the 'colour' was still 'out there'.[48]

Both these curious cases can be explained using Pribram's internal hologram theory. The neurological damage was to the internal projector, not to external reality. In one case the 'videotape' was jumping 'frames' and in the other the colour signal had been lost. In this purely mechanistic way many on-going puzzles of visual, aural and tactile perception can be explained.

If this is correct, and the evidence does seem reasonably strong, memories function in exactly the same way as David Bohm's holographic universe. To say that it is all done with mirrors is somewhat flippant, but in a strange way it is quite accurate. The mechanism both in terms of process and output has now been explained. For some reason as yet to be explained, all human beings have the ability to record every single event that takes place in their lives. Not only that but it seems that under certain circumstances they are able to access this information and re-live, in three-dimensional recall, events from their own past.

This belief has been a long-held suspicion. In the mid-18th century, the French philosopher Denis Diderot wrote:

> *I am led to believe that everything we have seen, known, perceived, heard – even the trees of the deep forest – nay, even the disposition of the branches, the form of the leaves and the variety of the colours, the green tints and the light; the look of grains of sand at the edge of the sea, the unevenness of the crests of waves, whether agitated by a light breeze, or churned to foam by a storm; the multitude of human voices, of animal cries, and physical sounds, the melody and harmony of all songs, of all pieces of music, of all the concerts we have listened to, all of it, unknown to us, exists within us.*[49]

To be followed two and a half centuries later by the 21st-century neuroscientist Stephen Pinker:

> *People live for a paltry 2 billion seconds so there is no known reason why the brain could not record every object and every event it experienced if it had to.*[50]

These two quotations are separated by 250 years of progress in man's understanding of the world around him. However, they both echo a long-held suspicion that our mind is like a huge library where the librarian has forgotten the reference system. Volumes of information lie stored away, serried rank upon serried rank, waiting to be accessed. But for what purpose do these vast stores of information exist? This may seem like a curious question but it is a very important one. What possible evolutionary advantage can be gained by remembering every single incident and piece of information?

Welcome to the meta-mind

Survival depends on making a quick decision and sticking to it. To stand in front of a hungry sabre-toothed tiger evaluating all the options is a sure way to end up like the dodo. To be able to recall what happened on 12 October 1981, however emotionally significant that date may be, is of no use as a house fire creeps towards you – it is selective relevant information that is important. Data that can help you evaluate in an instant what your options are. That is what assists survival, both in terms of the individual and the species.

Henri Bergson, the great French philosopher of time, was also fascinated by memory, and its role within the human condition fascinated him. As we have seen, his ideas had a great effect on his relative, Marcel Proust. Bergson recognized that the human mind remembered all experiences but that the brain had a mechanism that stops the mind from being flooded.[51]

That the brain has the capacity to hold all the data needed has been suspected for many years and now, with greater understanding of digital technology, is recognised as such. As we have seen, John von Neumann made two great contributions to quantum physics, one positive and one not so. It was he who suggested the 'von Neumann chain' – that the uncertainty brought about by the dual nature of quantum particles transfers itself from particle to observer. This proposition led to the Many Worlds

Interpretation. His other contribution was his famous 'Proof' that turned out to be exactly the opposite in that nothing lies below quantum uncertainty. However, the human brain also fascinated him. As an exercise he once calculated that over a normal lifetime the human brain stores something in the order of 2.8×10^{20} (280,000,000,000,000,000,000) bits of information. He came to this huge figure because he was sure that it remembered everything that it experienced.

The human brain is the most complex form of matter in the universe. If you look at a section of brain matter you will discover that it is composed of neurons, or nerve cells. At birth the brain contains around 100 billion of these cells. Each neuron has a cell body and tens of thousands of tiny branches called dendrites. These dendrites receive information from other neurons. Each neuron also has what is called a primary axon. This is a projection that can reach great distances across the brain. Neurons make contact with each other at the synapse. Each neuron has between 1000 and 10,000 of these contact points. These can be either on or off, excitatory or inhibitory. A piece of your brain the size of a grain of sand would contain 100,000 neurons, 2,000,000 axons and 1,000,000,000 synapses, all 'talking' to each other. From this it has been calculated that the number of possible brain states – the number of permutations and combinations of activity that are theoretically possible – exceeds the number of elementary particles in the universe. For you to have a memory of every event, thought, feeling and sensory input that takes place during your meagre 2 billion seconds of life would take up only a tiny percentage of the storage potential of this amazing organ. The question is not whether we have the capacity to record everything, but why it is that even after doing so we still have such a massive excess capacity. It simply does not make logical sense.

Under certain circumstances memory of particular events in the past can be stimulated by means other than Penfield's electrode. Hypnotism can do the trick. In 1973, a bus was destroyed by a bomb that had been planted earlier by a terrorist. While fortunately the bus was parked at the terminus and there was no one on board, it was important for the authorities to apprehend the culprit as soon as possible. The driver could not be expected to recall all of the passengers who had boarded during the day, so it was suggested that he be hypnotized. Not only did the driver describe the passengers in such detail that the police were able to arrest the terrorist within a few days but also he described the bomber's companion, who was subsequently chased out of the country. Both these descriptions came from no more than a glance of a couple of seconds.[52,53]

This was by no means the earliest, or indeed most impressive, case of hypnotic recall. In a series of controlled experiments that took place in the early 1950s, hypnotherapist Bernard Gindes reports:

> *A (hypnotised) soldier with only grade school education was able to memorise an entire page of Shakespeare's Hamlet after hearing the passage read to him seven times. Upon reawakening he could not recall any of the lines, and even more startling was the fact that he had no remembrance of the hypnotic experience. A week later he was hypnotised again. In this state he was able to repeat the entire passage without a single error.*

> *In another experiment to test the validity of increased memory retention five soldiers were hypnotised en masse and given a jumbled 'code' consisting of twenty-five words without phonetic consistency. They were allowed sixty seconds to commit the list to memory. In the waking state, each man was asked to repeat the code; this none of them could. One man hazily remembered having had some association with a code but could not remember more than that. The other four soldiers were allowed to study the code for another sixty seconds but all*

denied previous acquaintance with it. During re-hypnotism
they were individually able to recall the exact content of the
coded message.[54]

Here again we have evidence that somewhere deep within our subconscious we do remember everything. For reasons of informational overload this information is not available to everyday consciousness. However, for one man at least this 'gift' was available and it was a gift that was to make his life almost impossible.

The real Johnny Mnemonic

While we have evidence that we do have the memories available and it is simply that some protection mechanism acts as a filter, in the history of psychology there has been at least one possible example of total memory recall. That unfortunate individual was a Russian by the name of Solomon V Shereshevski, who was studied over a period of 30 years by the Russian psychologist Aleksandr R Luria.[55] Shereshevski's abilities were so repeatable that for many years he earned a living as a theatre performer. Day in and day out he would enthral audiences with his phenomenal feats of memory. Unfortunately, every time he did a show the lists and numbers he had memorized stayed in his memory. In desperation he even tried writing the lists down and burning them. This did not work. He was paralyzed in conversation because each word heard or said would bring forth dozens of images, ideas and memories. His life was a nightmare. In a final effort to rid himself of his 'gift' he went to see Luria.

To test Shereshevski's ability, Luria gave him a list of 30 words to remember which he was able to do on hearing them just once. It was found that he could also do the same with numbers or nonsense words. Luria was interested in the fact that there did not seem to be a process of memorizing the information. It was as if it just sat in his memory as soon as it had been heard. Luria then found to his amazement that there was no limit to the numbers of names or objects that Shereshevski could recall – and never forgot. Many years later he would mention a time in the past when he had a list to remember and would recall the list faultlessly. One case was 15 years later when Shereshevski was given a list, and he said, with his eyes closed:

Yes, yes ... this was a series you gave me once when we were at your apartment. You were sitting at the table and I in the rocking chair ... you were wearing a grey suit and you looked at me like this ... now, then, I can see you saying ...

And with that he reeled off the series precisely. What is even more remarkable is that as a famous mnemonist Shereshevski would have been given thousands of series to memorize. The process that Shereshevski used was to convert the words or numbers into images. This is a standard technique for memory training and is used by most mnenomists, but it seems that Shereshevski had come by this technique because of the way his mind worked. He had what is called 'synaesthesia'. This is a confusion of the senses; for example, some musicians experience colours for certain notes. In Shereshevski's case words, names, sounds all had colours or textures or feelings associated with them. In a fascinating proof of Pribram's Ecological Model of Perception (*see* page 91), Luria traced these synaesthetic reactions to a very early age. As Shereshevski described it:

When I was about two or three years old I was taught the words of a Hebrew prayer. I didn't understand them, and what happened was that the words settled in my mind as puffs of steam or splashes ... Even now I see these puffs or splashes when I hear certain sounds.

According to Luria this is not as uncommon as one might believe. For him a particularly interesting example was the composer Aleksandr Scriabin. Scriabin worked to incorporate his synaesthesia into his concerts. In 1911, he wrote a symphony entitled 'Prometheus, the Poem of Fire'. This symphony was to incorporate the usual orchestra, piano, organ, and choir. However, this score also included orchestrations for a 'clavier à lumières', or colour organ, which would play coloured light during the symphony. The light would be in the shape of clouds, beams, and other shapes which would flood the concert hall. The climax would include a white light so strong as to be painful to the eyes.

For Shereshevski, people's voices had colours associated with them, while others had physical shapes. He described the Russian film director Sergei Eisenstein's voice as being a 'flame with fibres protruding from it'. Simple speech took this form – vowels appeared as simple figures, consonants as splashes; for example, to him 'A' was 'white and long'. It was as if Shereshevski's internal holographic processing of external 'reality' had become confused in some way.

It was similar with numbers. Shereshevski perceived the number 2 as whitish grey, while 8 was milky blue, like lime. So for him there was no distinction between seeing and hearing and taste. According to Luria this 'ability' was central to his memory.[56] It seems that Shereshevski could remember events in his past with the same clarity. His childhood memories were rich in detail. His recollections went back to when he was only a year old. He says:

> I was very young then, not even a year old perhaps. What comes to mind most clearly is the furniture in the room, not all of it, I can't remember that, but the corner of the room where my mother's bed and cradle were. A cradle is a small bed with bars on both sides with curved wickerwork on the underpart, and it rocks. I remember the wallpaper in the room was brown and the bed white. I can see my mother taking me in her arms,

then she puts me down again. I can sense movement, a feeling
of warmth, then an unpleasant sensation of cold.

What is particularly interesting is his recall of the sensations of warmth and cold and his sense of movement. It is reminiscent of the memories stimulated by Penfield with his epileptic patients. It appears that it is these types of memories, memories that Shereshevski could recall at will, that can be effected by an electric stimulus to the exposed temporal lobe. He seems to recall even earlier memories when his eyes had not developed the muscles to focus. He says:

> *This is the sense I have of my mother: up to the time I began*
> *to recognise her, it was simply a feeling – 'This is good.' No*
> *form, no face, just something bending over me from which*
> *good would come ... Pleasant ... Seeing my mother was like*
> *looking at something through the lens of a camera. At first you*
> *can't make anything out, just a round cloudy spot ... then a*
> *face appears and its features become sharper.*

The way in which Shereshevski describes how his infant self saw his mother is very interesting and may be indirect proof of the accuracy of his recall. In the 1930s the structure of a baby's eye was known and it was assumed that they could see as well as an adult. The mechanism of sight and focus are fully functional, so this conclusion was a reasonable one. However, research over the last 30 years has shown that although after only two months of age infants begin to be able to focus clear images on the retina, their vision is still not clear. It is now known that although the optics of the eye are mature, the areas of the brain responsible for sight are not. To use a camera analogy, the reason that an infant's vision is blurry is because of the 'film' not the lens. The retina (the film of the eye), in addition to the other visual parts of the brain, is incompletely developed in infants. It is reasonable to conclude that Shereshevski was describing a real memory rather than making it up from information he had read or heard.

This ability to 'recall' events was a particular talent of Shereshevski, but the evidence seems to be that we all have this information stored away: it is a question of access. It is as if we have a huge library of books available to us but because we do not understand the filing system we come by books at random. Certain individuals such as Shereshevski have the ability to use the filing system and therefore can reclaim memories at will.

The most relevant part of Luria's account is late on, when he is discussing the personality of the mnemonist. It is here that we discover that Shereshevski has signs of multiple personality. What can we make of this amazing comment?

> *I had to go to school ... I saw myself here, while 'he' was to go off to school. I'm angry with 'him' – why is he taking so long to get ready?*

And then another incident he recalls from childhood:

> *I'm eight years old. We're moving to a new apartment. I don't want to go. My brother takes me by the hand and leads me to the cab waiting outside. I see the driver there munching a carrot. But I don't want to go ... I stay behind in the house – that is, I see how 'he' stands at the window of my old room. He is not going anywhere.*

According to Luria, this split between the 'I' who issues orders and the 'he' who carries them out persisted throughout Shereshevski's life. Luria refers to 'split personalities' but feels that this is simply some form of coping mechanism. I am of the opinion that the curious mental abilities may have come about because in some way the Russian was accessing information that was not his to access. In the record of October 1934, Shereshevski says the following:

> *Take the situation here. I'm sitting in your apartment*
> *preoccupied with my own thoughts. You, being a good host,*
> *ask: 'How do you like these cigarettes?' 'So-so, fair ...' That is,*
> *I'd never say that, but 'he' might. It's not tactful, but I can't*
> *explain the slip to him. For 'I' understand things but 'he'*
> *doesn't. If I'm distracted, 'he' says things he oughtn't to.*

The implication given by Shereshevski is that both personalities communicate verbally. The comment, 'I can't explain the slip to him' is a telling one. He has two distinct personalities; a 'lower' self that seems to live in a world of normality, of restricted memory and perceptions. The second or 'higher' self, inhabits a psychological state of heightened awareness, a state where all memories are recalled, however small and insignificant. Most of us inhabit the world of Shereshevski's 'he'. We see the world in this limited way. However, it seems that certain human beings can either access (as in the case of schizophrenics) or 'become' this higher self. Shereshevski was functioning as his own 'higher' self as part of his day-to-day consciousness.

How your senses 'matrix' you

For Pribram the world as we perceive it is an internal holographic projection of external reality. This external reality is not as our internal senses perceive it. When illuminated in normal light a holographic plate is seen as a jumbled mess of lines and squiggles. It is only when laser light is shined on the plate that the three-dimensional image can be seen. So it is with reality. 'Out there' is a jumble of electromagnetic energy. This 'mess' is converted into a three-dimensional sensual 'reality' by consciousness taking the role of the laser light. This version of 'out there' is then projected onto our 'internal' IMAX screen and 'viewed' by the 'person'. In this way we all have our own private versions of reality although we never actually interact with 'out there'. We see it all from the centre of our own personal 'phaneron'.

And it seems that there are two classes of ticket for this Bohmian IMAX. The standard ticket gives the observer a one-way, linear trip through life. He or she progresses through his or her lifetime in a logical sequence. The 'show' is projected in such a way that none of the future 'plot' is revealed. In the same way, events that have already been screened are lost, with only important recollections made available in order that the plot is not lost. This is the standard version, analogous to a video recording with no facilities for fast-forward or re-wind.

The first-class ticket is very different. The 'show' is the same but the format is analogous to DVD rather than simple television signal. Fast-forward and re-wind are available to the observer, as is random access. Access to other useful areas of data is also available. The observer can control what is viewed. It seems that Shereshevski walked into the wrong screening. He was perceiving the show intended for somebody else. Fortunately for his sanity he only had limited access to the multi-media extravaganza. As we shall see later, chemical imbalances in the brain can give accidental access to the full show. In doing so it can drive the unfortunate individuals affected into a temporary insanity usually diagnosed as schizophrenia.

Aldous Huxley, the English writer and philosopher, was preoccupied with higher levels of consciousness. He was convinced that man was living his life as a sleepwalker, unaware of the potential knowledge that was available to him. In his book *Doors of Perception*, Huxley quotes the Cambridge philosopher CD Broad, commenting upon the ideas of Bergson:

> *We should do well to consider much more seriously than we*
> *have hitherto been inclined to do the type of theory which*
> *Bergson put forward in connection with memory and sense*

*perception. The suggestion is that the function of the brain and
nervous system and sense organs is in the main eliminative
and not productive. Each person is at each moment capable of
remembering all that has ever happened to him and of
perceiving everything that is happening everywhere in the
universe. The function of the brain and nervous system is to
protect us from being overwhelmed and confused by this mass
of largely useless and irrelevant knowledge, by shutting out
most of what we should otherwise perceive or remember at any
moment, and leaving only that very small and special selection
which is likely to be practical and useful.*[57]

This opening of Huxley's *Doors of Perception* can cause psychic
concern to those unprepared for his iconoclastic opinions on
consciousness and perception. Huxley says that like the light
perceived in heavenly 'trips', so a bad trip has its own light.[58] He
likens this to the 'smoky light' of the Tibetan *Book of the Dead* and
the 'darkness visible' of Milton. He is, again, interested in the role
schizophrenia has in this sensation, pointing out that in *Journal
d'un Schizophrènel*[59], the autobiographical record of a young girl's
passage through madness, the world of the schizophrenic is called
'le pays d'éclairment' – the country of lit-upness. For Renée, the
schizophrenic in question, this illumination is not wonderful as it
would be to a mystic, but infernal – an intense glare without a
shadow, ubiquitous and implacable. Huxley says:

*Everything that, for healthy visionaries, is a source of bliss
brings to Renée only fear and a nightmarish sense of unreality.
The summer sunshine is malignant; the gleam of polished
surfaces is suggestive, not of gems, but of machinery and
enamelled tin; the intensity of existence which animates every
object, when seen at close range and out of its utilitarian
context, is felt as a menace.*

*And then there is the horror of infinity. For the healthy
visionary, the perception of the infinite in a finite particular is
a revelation of divine immanence; for Renée it is what she calls
'the System,' the vast cosmic mechanism which exists only to
grind out guilt and punishment, solitude and unreality.*[60]

Later Huxley makes the very interesting observation that:

*The shadow world inhabited by some schizophrenics and
neurotics closely resembles the world of the dead as described in
some of the earlier religious traditions. Like the wraiths in
Sheol and in Homer's Hades, these mentally disturbed persons
have lost touch with matter, language and their fellow beings.*

There is therefore strong evidence that the reality that you and I
perceive is not exactly an accurate copy of what exists 'out there',
the phenomenal world behind what our senses tell us is there. It
also seems clear that we receive from our brain an internally
created and totally subjective facsimile of the external world. If
this is the case then everything we perceive is an illusion, an
illusion that exists outside of space and time.

CHAPTER 5
Zeno's Universe

Time flies like an arrow but fruit flies like a banana.

Groucho Marx

Too many forking universes

The work of Bierman and Radin we encountered earlier seemed to imply that some part of the human mind can predict what is about to occur, and with total accuracy. The problem is, what future awaits you? If we are to accept Everett's Many Worlds proposal then there are literally trillions of alternative time lines that your consciousness can follow. Each one of them exists out there, exists 'now', just waiting for you to discover it.

This idea has long fascinated writers and artists, none more so than the great Argentinian writer and philosopher Jorge Luis Borges. In his short story *The Garden of the Forking Paths*, one of his characters makes the following statement:

> Your ancestor ... believed in an infinite series of times, in a growing,
> dizzying net of divergent, convergent and parallel times. This network
> of times which approached one another, forked, broke off, or were
> unaware of one another for centuries, embraces all possibilities of time.
> We do not exist in the majority of these times; in some you exist, and
> not I; in others I, and not you; in others, both of us. In the present one,
> which a favourable fate has granted me, you have arrived at my house;
> in another, while crossing the garden, you found me dead; in still
> another, I utter these same words, but I am a mistake, a ghost ...

And so it is with all of us. We are each following one lonely pre-recorded timeline. Like Max Tegmark's scientist, we will invariably decide upon the right route through the garden because rather like watching a film we are but passive observers. En route we will encounter many ghosts – indeed, all those conscious beings we meet are ghosts, illusions, sprites.

This predestination is not as rigid as it first may seem. In Everett's universe there are literally trillions of universes all containing a version of you; there are also trillions of recordings of your life. Therefore you can, given certain circumstances, swap the videotape or DVD for another one, one containing an alternative future. The question is how one 'future' becomes actual whereas all the other trillions of options do not. There is one argument that states that you are one of trillions of you. For each possible version of the future, for each of the paths through Borges' garden, there is a copy of you treading boldly onwards.

From this evidence we have to conclude that time only exists as part of our own personal perception of reality; it has no objective external existence. We therefore measure time in terms of its duration from the evidence given to us by our own conscious perception. It is 'common sense' to conclude that although we may sense that time passes more slowly in dreams this is a mental state that can in no way be effected by measurable or quantifiable factors. But as we know, common sense is so often wrong.

The keys of time

We use the word 'time' as if it was a measurable and quantifiable reality. It has long been argued by philosophers that this is not the case. Temporal flow is simply a construct of the mind. In the same way that subatomic particles need consciousness to come into existence, so it is with time. Without a perceiver time has no objective reality. This is not a new idea. Henri Bergson, who saw time as an error of perception, wrote the following in 1889:

*Time, conceived under the form of a homogeneous medium, is
some spurious concept, due to the trespassing of the idea of
space upon the field of pure consciousness.*[61]

For Bergson this 'spurious concept' leads to the error of supposing time to be a quantity or commodity, something that can be divided up and parcelled out like a piece of material. Bergson considered that the major culprit responsible for this error was the clock, the machine that dissects time into lumps, units and numbers. Bergson suggested that the term *durée* (duration) should be used to describe this true, mental time. He explains:

> *When I follow with my eyes on the dial of a clock the
> movement of the hands ... I do not measure duration ...
> Outside of me, in space, there is never more than a single
> position of the hand ... Within myself a process of organisation
> or interpretation of conscious states is going on, which
> constitutes true duration ... States of consciousness, even when
> successive, permeate one another, and in the simplest of them
> the whole soul can be reflected.*[62]

In September 1962, a young French geologist named Michel Siffre spent 63 days in a cavern deep in the Alps. Although he had absolutely no contact with the outside world his waking and sleeping patterns maintained their normal 24-hour rhythm. His world consisted of the light from his torch and the food he had to eat. Indeed, he had no way of knowing how long he had been underground or even if it was night or day. When he did eventually emerge he was convinced that he had been underground for 36, not 63 days. The interesting fact is that although his internal clock had kept time his mind had failed to put this into days and weeks. So our concept of time, when denied access to either clocks or the rising and setting of the sun becomes confused and is ultimately of no benefit. He described his feelings thus:

> *Most curious of all, time seemed to pass very quickly ... Time*
> *passed without me being aware of it in the darkness and*
> *silence. I felt I was on another planet; for the most part I dwelt*
> *neither in the past or the future, but in the hostile present. In*
> *that environment everything was against me; the rocks that*
> *crashed down from time to time; the damp, chill atmosphere;*
> *the darkness.*[63]

Siffre's experience has interesting similarities with events that took place in Northern France in 1906. In that year one of the worst mining disasters of all time took place. The male population of the small town of Courrières was virtually wiped out by the deaths of over a thousand miners killed in an explosion in the local mine. Out of this horror were a few small miracles where pockets of men survived. When eventually brought to the surface, they all believed that they had been trapped underground for four or five days. In actual fact it was three weeks.

Sometimes the loss of time can be stimulated by stress and sometimes it can be during a period of spiritual and personal peace, an effect that is so common that we all seem to take it for granted. However, it is always of interest if a famous person tells it, and doubly so if it involves two well-known individuals. In his book *Powers of Darkness, Powers of Light,* John Cornwall tells of a meeting he had with the novelist Graham Greene.[64] Cornwall and Greene were discussing the fact that although the latter had no real belief in God, heaven, hell or an afterlife, he still had faith. When challenged on this, Greene replied that he supposed that he had been lucky to 'doubt my disbelief'. He then explained why this was so:

> *... because I once had a very slight mystical experience. In 1949*
> *I travelled out to Italy to see a famous mystic known as Padre*

Pio. He lived in a remote monastery in the Gargano Peninsula at a place called San Giovanni Rotundo. He had the stigmata, displaying the wounds of Christ in his hands, feet and side. At this time my belief in God had been on the ebb; I think I was losing my faith. I went out of curiosity. I was wondering whether this man, whom I had heard so much of, would impress me. I stopped in Rome on the way and a monsignor from the Vatican came to have a drink with me. 'Oh!' he said, 'that holy fraud! You're wasting your time. He's bogus.'

But Padre Pio had been examined by doctors of every faith and no faith. He'd been examined by Jewish, Protestant, Catholic and atheist specialists, and baffled them all. He had wounds on his hands and feet, the size of twenty-pence pieces, and because he was not allowed to wear gloves saying Mass he pulled his sleeves down to try and hide them. He'd got a very nice, peasant-like face, a little bit on the heavy side. I was warned that his was a very long Mass; so I went with my woman friend of that period to the Mass at 5:30 in the morning. He said it in Latin, and I thought that thirty-five minutes had passed. Then when I got outside the church I looked at my watch and it had been two hours.[65]

We all live our lives by the clock, by the measured circle of time. Time gives structure to our lives, it pulls together the fractured, fleeting, sensory inputs that collectively define what and who we are. And yet curiously time is also the most overlooked dimension in human nature. Astronomers can calculate with fine precision the pulses of a distant galaxy but we know very little about the internal pulses that tune our bodies to the cycles of nature. Time is so central to how we live; indeed, without some form of inner time how does the body take care of the myriad of processes that it has to follow just to keep us alive? You are not conscious of the metronome-like beatings of your heart, or the fact that your brain-wave rhythms displayed by an encephalograph show changes of the polarity of your brain cells which occur in micro-seconds. This all takes place without any reference to external time. You carry your own internal clock, and it is that that you use to measure the passing of time. Michel Siffre's experience shows that what we term inner or 'psychological' time is not clock or external time. It is something personal to you and it changes as you become older and, for short periods, due to emotional feelings or drug influence.

You will recall the curious dream of Alfred Maury – how his dream was somehow 'back created' in order to accommodate the fact that the bed's headboard fell onto the back of his neck. Either the dream was fabricated in the split second between the sensation of the impact and his conscious mind registering the blow, or else the dream itself was perceived 'back to front'. That is, the dream started with the blow and worked backwards to the trial. Either option ensures that time was warped in one way or another. Maury concluded from this that dreams arose from external stimuli, instantaneously accompanying such impressions as they acted upon the sleeping person. In other words, the subconscious mind has the ability to immediately process outside sounds or events and create around them a complete, and subjective, incorporation into a dream. This is all done in a microsecond.

We all have two temporal existences, external and internal. Psychological time is not the same as objective time. This has been long recognized by other cultures. In India, the Hindu religion has a concept that conveys this very well. This is called 'Maya'.

Maya it now become more clear

Maya is commonly but not altogether accurately translated as 'illusion'. It is more the idea that reality and time are but part of Brahman, the ultimate reality. Life and perception are all part of this greater reality. Human beings confuse reality with the dreams of Brahman. The concept can best be explained by the retelling of the Indian myth of Narada and Vishnu.

Narada was an Indian holy man who was a great seeker after knowledge. One day he meets Vishnu, the major Hindu deity, and asks him to be shown the magical powers of 'Maya'. Vishnu consents and asks Narada to follow. Narada does so. After walking for some time the two of them find themselves out in the desert. The sun is hot, so that Vishnu suggests they stop for a few moments to rest. He then turns to Narada and says that there is a village nearby and would Narada be kind enough to walk on to the village, get some water and bring it back to him. Narada agrees and leaves Vishnu. He calls at a house in the village. The most beautiful girl Narada has ever seen opens the door. It is love at first sight and she feels the same way. He spends a great deal of time with her and decides that he wishes to marry her. He discusses this with her parents, who agree that they are happy for this great ascetic to give up his search for truth and settle down with their daughter. A great marriage feast is arranged and people come from all around to join in the celebrations. Narada and the girl are given a small house on the outskirts of the village and soon she becomes pregnant. She gives birth to a beautiful baby daughter. So enchanted are Narada and his wife with the child that they soon have two more, another girl and then a son. All is happy. The children grow strong and joyful and the crops grow well. Then one terrible day the storms come. There is a huge flood, the waters rise higher and higher and Narada watches as each of his children are taken by the torrent. Finally, his wife also slips from his grasp and drowns in front of his eyes. He has to swim for it and eventually becomes stranded on a rock. He feels the sun on his head and slowly drifts into unconsciousness. As he does so he hears a voice asking him 'Where is the water you were to bring me? I have been waiting for more than half an hour.' The voice belongs to Vishnu. Narada opens his eyes and looks around. The flood has gone. He looks with surprised eyes. The god smiles, bows his head and says, 'And now do you understand the secret of Maya'?

This description of events reflects the concept of temporal flow for many Eastern peoples. This static concept of time is strongly reflected in the Sanskrit of ancient Indian manuscripts. The very grammar of Sanskrit engineers in the speaker a very different concept of time from that of a speaker of European languages. Sanskrit uses few descriptive verbs to denote action – 'John ran down the street', for example, becomes 'John did running down the street' in which 'running down the street' is regarded as a state in which John happened to be rather than an action he chose to perform. Similarly, 'Because of the rain, the crops flourish' becomes 'Because of the rain, flourishing of the crops'.[66] Indian culture and its perception of time is based on the grammatical structures of its language in the same way as the West sees time in a linear fashion. This difference is best shown by a famous quotation by Heraclitus, a line that defines in a simple but powerful way the concept of time flowing in Western philosophy. Heraclitus wrote:

All things flow, nothing stays still: Nothing endures but
change.

An attempt to translate the first section of this quote, 'all things flow' into Sanskrit results in the words *sarvam anityam*, which mean, 'all existences are impermanent'. This attitude to time carries on to the present day. In modern Hindustani *kal* means both 'yesterday' and 'tomorrow'; *parsan* means both 'the day after tomorrow' and 'the day before yesterday'. The real meaning of these words can only be determined by analyzing the context in which they occur.[67]

As a final point on language, and one that really helps to highlight how language structures our concept of time, it is helpful to consider this question – 'In your mind's eye where is the past located, to your right or to your left?' The vast majority of European language speakers will, without hesitation, say that the past is to the left and the future lies to the right.[68] The reason for this is simple but enlightening. We write and read from left to right: therefore what we see to the left of a sentence has already been written or read and as such is perceived to be in the past. Our construction of time really is language-based.

It has been long known from experimentation that animals have no concept of time. This issue was considered carefully by Wolfgang Koehler in the course of a study that he undertook on the higher apes – in particular, chimpanzees.[69] It seems that the higher primates live in a continual present with no concept of past or future. More recently this has been reinforced by the work of Stephen Walker, who has concluded that it is surprisingly difficult to produce convincing experimental proof that any animal has any memory or foresight at all.[70] However, is the conclusion that a sense of time is peculiar to mankind valid? There is certainly evidence that some members of the human family get by very well with no concept of time.

The classic study of this is that of Benjamin Lee Whorf.[71] Whorf studied the language of the Hopi people of Arizona. The language of these Native Americans has a very peculiar grammatical structure. It is, according to Whorf, devoid of any forms, constructions or expressions that refer to time or any of its aspects. Instead of space and time the Hopi use two other basic states that Whorf refers to as 'objective' and 'subjective' respectively. Everything that exists outside of the person – the external world – is included in the 'objective'. The inner, or mental world of thought and dreams is included in the 'subjective'. These two categories have no past, present or future states. Although the Hopi language, unlike English, prefers verbs to nouns, its verbs have no tenses such as past, present and future forms. It is as if the Hopi exist in a continual present.

Have we time to explain?

So what exactly is time? In order to make sense of it we need to start at the most basic of all concepts – what time actually is. Initially this may seem a strange question but in reality we never really think of time in itself, we measure it against other things. For example, we all use the term 'now'. Now is the present moment, the point in which the future turns into the past, but how long is 'now' in terms of time? How 'thick' is it? Is it a tenth of a second, or a nanosecond (one thousand millionth of a second) or a picosecond (one thousandth of a nanosecond – equivalent to one second in 30,000 years)? Put this way, does 'now' really exist or are we, as I suspect, trying to bring into existence something that does not exist in the way our senses or our philosophy tells us. There is only a continual 'now', not an imaginary point moving at a second per second from the past into the future.

In this way one has to assume that the point that constitutes 'now' must consist of the smallest possible piece of time available, an amount of time that cannot be divisible. In practical terms this must be the smallest amount of time that is actually physically measurable. As such this will be one cycle (or one frequency) of the transition in the caesium atom of an atomic clock. This is measured at 1/9192631770 of a second. This is about a nanosecond. That is not to say that in theory time cannot be measured smaller amounts. The American physicist John Wheeler semi-seriously proposed a unit that he termed a 'jiffy'. This is the time it takes light to travel a million billion billionth of a second. Although impossible to measure, this amazingly small interval is calculated as 1/(1 then 43 zeros) of a second. At this minute size is it possible that the ultimate 'particle' of time can be encountered?

As we have seen, scientists have carried out a similar exercise for energy. It has been 'quantized', that is, reduced to a basic packet size or particle of quantum of energy. This smallest amount of energy is called the 'Planck's Constant' and is named after the great 19th-century German scientist, Max Planck. Scientists now believe that Planck's Constant is the smallest possible amount of space that can exist. In other words, space has limits, and that limit, the Planck length, is 10^{-25} metres. In the film *Honey I Shrunk The Kids*, Ricky Moranis invents a machine that can shrink people and objects. At one stage the machine shrinks a couch down to about three centimetres across (in fact it did, as the title implies, shrink the kids as well, but wishing to avoid potential charges of cruelty to children I am going to use the couch in my analogy). That is as far as the shrinking goes. However, let us assume that the shrinking continued unabated. The couch would get smaller and smaller, shrinking even tinier than its own constituent atoms, electrons and quarks. However at 0.000000000000000000000 0001 metres it stops. It simply has no smaller space to fit into. At this point everything seems to stop, including reality itself. After all, everything that exists, exists in space. Without space available there cannot be anything. What then happens to time itself at this size? Are there particles of time?

The physicist David Finklestein has coined the term 'chronon' for such a particle. It is here that the whole philosophical and subjectivity of time comes into focus. If chronons did exist as individual 'bits' of time, how could they be measured? How would a scientist isolate their duration? In order to decide on its size the scientist would have to use a time interval shorter than a chronon, which is logically impossible. It now becomes clear that time is like nothing else in the physical universe. It is the only perceived 'something or other' (I cannot come up with a word that actually describes time in an adequate way) that is measured by itself. You can have a pound of apples or a litre of petrol but you can only ever have a second per second or sixty seconds per minute. Time has no external point of measurement except in the mind of the observer.

But do we not all share the same concept of 'now'? We are all moving along this time line at the same moment. Unfortunately, even this small comfort is denied us. According to relativity there is no concept of 'now'. The closest we get to such an idea is an observer's 'simultaneous space' in spacetime, but even this depends on the motion of the observer. The 'now' according to one observer will not agree with the 'now' for another.

It was one of Albert Einstein's old teachers, Hermann Minkowski, who coined the term 'spacetime' in an attempt to make Einstein's Special Theory more palatable to the general public. In a lecture given in 1908, he said:

> The views of space and time which I wish to lay before you
> have sprung from the soil of experimental physics, and therein
> lies their strength. They are radical. Henceforth space, by itself,
> and time, by itself, are doomed to fade away into mere
> shadows, and only a kind of union of the two will preserve as
> an independent reality.[72]

This union of space and time is where the term spacetime originated. What Minkowski did was introduce the concept of a fourth dimension, time. We live in a world of three dimensions, breadth, height and length. By introducing time as a dimension Minkowski radically changed the way scientists perceive reality. So what do scientists actually mean when they talk about four dimensions? Let us look at a pencil and the shadow it casts onto a flat surface. In our three-dimensional world the pencil has a defined length that you can measure with a ruler. This length is consistent at all times. However, if you twist the pencil and watch the shadow, the shape and length of the pencil's shadow on the two-dimensional flat surface changes. And by changing the angle of the pencil you can make the shadow zero, as long as the pencil itself, or any length in between.[73] The length of the shadow in two dimensions depends upon the orientation of the shadow in three dimensions.

Minkowski said that the pencil also has a fourth dimensional length, which he termed its 'extension'. This extension, however, is not in space but in time. This is the pencil as it exists in time.

As it progresses through time it follows what is termed its 'worldline'. For example, if I choose to take a photograph of the pencil using a slow shutter speed of, say a tenth of a second, and I move the pencil backwards and forwards the pencil, when photographed, will cease to be a pencil shape but will be an oblong with a length corresponding to how far I moved the pencil from side to side. It will have a depth equivalent to the width of the pencil and it will be seen as a solid object. The photograph will show the timeline of the pencil in four dimensions. Imagine that you can actually hold this four-dimensional pencil. You could cut it laterally at any point and end up with a slice of the pencil as it was at any point in that tenth of a second period. According to Minkowski all things really exist in this four dimensional state, including you and me. We move through spacetime perceiving reality as a slice of this fourth dimension. It is us that do the moving, not time. Until this revolutionary view of the universe, time was seen to be flowing from the future, into the present, then into the past. Time flowed around us as around rocks in a river. Minkowski and Einstein changed all this. Past, present and future do not exist; they are introduced by human consciousness. It is us that do the moving, not time. The slice of spacetime consciously perceived defines the present moment for the observer.

Each individual consciousness travels, like a spotlight moving over a dark landscape. Those bits of the landscape that the spotlight has already picked out, the observer terms as the past; those that are yet to appear in the spotlight are termed as the future. The four-dimensional block universe is static and unchanging. However, consciousness is under the illusion that things 'happen' in the same way that a traveller on a night train sees an illuminated station platform rush past and disappear. To the traveller the station was somewhere in the future, 'happened' and then disappeared into the past. In reality the station was static and has an ongoing and unchanging existence that will be 'perceived' by another train as it travels along its own timeline.

So for Minkowski, and his student, Einstein, space and time are not separate entities. They are a continuum or different aspects of the same fundamental 'something'. Their ultimate interchangeability is like that of matter and energy. We move in our own little bubble of consciousness, perceiving time in our own subjective way. We can never 'share' somebody else's perception of time. The 'flow' is relative to what we feel it to be. According to Minkowski, your future exists now; it is just that you have yet to reach it.

The idea that your future is already out there waiting for you to arrive is a disconcerting concept. And this idea can be expanded to assume that your own past, although experienced, is also still here. The German mathematician Herman Weyl proposed this curious idea when he wrote:

> *Every world-point (as suggested by Minkowski) is the origin of*
> *the double-cone of the active future and the passive past.*
> *Whereas in the special theory of relativity these two points are*
> *separated by an intervening region, it is certainly possible in*
> *the present case for the cone of the active future to overlap with*
> *the passive past; so that, in principle, it is possible to experience*
> *events now that will be in effect part of my future resolves and*
> *actions. Moreover, it is not impossible for a world line*
> *(particularly that of my body), although it has a time-like*
> *direction at every point, to return to the neighbourhood of a*
> *point that it has already passed through. The result would be a*
> *spectral image of the world far more fearful than anything the*
> *weird fantasy of ETA Hoffman has ever conjured up.*[74]

If it is to be accepted that psychological time is a completely personal construct what then about objective time? In the US Naval Observatory in Washington DC there is a building identified simply by a number – 78. There, external time is measured not by watching the moon and the sun, or with a sundial, or even a quartz crystal, but with a tiny mass of the element caesium. In this building are 50 individual atomic clocks all feeding a bank of computers and in the middle of all these flashing lights is a digital read-out with bright red numbers. These show hours, minutes and seconds and it is by this display that the world keeps its time. This set-up is accurate to a billionth of a second a year. In 1967, the regular pulse by which caesium absorbs and emits energy was calibrated to 9,192,631,770 oscillations per second. This is now the official measurement of world time, replacing the old standard of the Earth's rotation and orbit. This old method used as its base number a second, which was equal to 1/31556925.9747 of a year. The change means that the official year, as measured by caesium, is no longer officially measured as 365.242199 days, but as 290,091,200,500,000,000 oscillations of the caesium atom.

All the same, the atomic clock is not too accurate. Because the Earth wobbles in its orbit this master clock has to be re-calibrated to get it back in line with Earth-time. Since 1972, leap seconds have been added almost every year. At this level of the nano-second even objective, external time starts to wobble; or to be more accurate, it warps.

JC Hafele of Washington University in St Louis and Richard Keating first successfully achieved this effect in 1971. They borrowed four atomic clocks from the US Naval Observatory where Keating worked, placing them on commercial airlines and had them flown round the world, first towards the east and then towards the west. Commercial aircraft fly quite slowly, less than one millionth of the speed of light. As such, any time dilation effect on board would have been very small, but the clocks were of such accuracy that any level of change could be detected, even the predicted one millionth of a second (a microsecond) per day. It was found that on the eastward journey the four clocks returned to America an average of 59 nanoseconds (billionths of a second) slow relative to a set of atomic clocks kept at the Observatory. On the westward journey the average had the clocks 273 nanoseconds fast. This difference between the east and west figures is due, as Einstein predicted, to the rotation of the Earth itself which produces time dilation.

A similar experiment was organized by Dr Carrol Alley of the University of Maryland. In this exercise he showed that time is not only affected by human perception but also by gravity. The closer you are to the Earth, the quicker time passes. The experiments that took place in the winter of 1975 involved the calibration of two atomic clocks. One group of experimenters took their atomic clock to 9,000 metres above Chesapeake Bay in a balloon. The other group stayed on the ground. The clock in the air lost a few billionths of a second every hour in relation to the one on the ground.[75]

This raises further questions about the accuracy of time. If time runs faster the nearer you are to Earth, and we can calculate time to incredibly small periods, then it is not in any way a facetious comment to say that time runs faster for shorter people (always assuming that it is the brain that does the processing). Indeed the gravitational pull of a larger object such as the sun will mean that time runs differently there than it does on Earth. A second on the sun runs at 1.000002 Earth seconds. This makes the time difference on the surface of the sun in relation to the surface of the earth one second every six days or, roughly, a minute a year. This calculates at, again roughly, 2 years for every million years. So during the existence of the Earth the Sun will have 'lost' over 9,000 years in relation to the Earth. As each of the planets have different masses, and therefore gravitational pulls, it is logical to conclude that each planet is running on a different time scale.

The fact that the nearer a particle approaches the speed of light the more time becomes distorted can be demonstrated much closer to home than the sun. Photons are the fastest known ordinary particles. Most gamma ray primary particles are photons.

These have amazing levels of energy. Particle energies are measured in a unit called an 'electron volt'. The typical energy of an electron circling within an atom is just a few electron volts. The typical energy of a cosmic ray primary particle is a trillion electron volts. These primary particle photons carry so much energy that they can travel at 99.999999 percent of the speed of light. For a ten trillion volt photon the difference between its speed and that of light itself is three metres per second – walking speed. At a hundred trillion volts the difference is 3 centimetres and at a thousand trillion it is a mere 0.3 millimetres per second. In 1993, a primary cosmic ray (almost certainly a photon) with an energy of 300 million trillion electron volts was spotted. Even at 100 million trillion volts the time dilation factor is a staggering one hundred billion. A clock moving alongside this particle would tick at one hundred billionth of the rate of a clock on Earth. A tick of this clock would occur once every 3,000 Earth years. But even this is nothing to the problems caused by an object called Cygnus X-3.

Cygnus X-3, an X-ray source consisting of an imploding star, is located about 35,000 light years away. The cosmic ray particles arriving from this object were seen to be travelling in a straight line, showing no signs of having been deflected off course at any time. Usually, charged objects such as photons will be deflected by our galaxy's magnetic field. The only way that these particles could avoid deflection was that they must be uncharged. What were they? A potential solution was that they were neutrinos, since neutrinos are uncharged particles, but the half-life for a neutrino is about 15 minutes, and they cannot travel far in that time. This is where the concept of time warps comes into its own. If the neutrinos were travelling fast enough then, in our frame of reference, their lifetime could become greatly increased. At a million trillion electron volts, and a warp factor of a billion, 15 minutes translates into 30,000 years across space before decaying. So if it were possible to hitch a ride with one of these neutrinos it would take me 15 of my minutes to travel 30,000 light years.

This information adds to the suspicion that time, as we customarily understand it, is completely in error. If time can dilate for these cosmic rays to the extent it does and if the universe is 15 billion years old, whose 15 billion is this? To a super-charged particle the universe is only a year old. To this add the fact that some galaxies are travelling away from Earth at speeds approaching that of light; then time becomes totally confused and confusing. Put simply, time is a construct of man's mind – it does not exist 'out there'.

But even for cosmic rays time runs in only one direction, the past is the past and the future is the future. This is a universal constant that we can cling to. Well, not quite. Muons are heavy relatives of electrons – in fact, they are about 200 times heavier than an electron. When the energetic particles of cosmic radiation strike the nuclei of atoms in the upper atmosphere they produce showers of sub-atomic particles. Most of these promptly decay into electrons but among the longer-lived ones are those that go by the name of muons. Since they have a longer life, most of them make it to ground level. If a Geiger counter is placed anywhere on Earth it will click fairly frequently and it is likely that some of these clicks will be caused by muons.

The interesting thing is that muons are inherently unstable and decay with a half-life of about two microseconds. Assuming that they are travelling at virtually the speed of light, the fastest a muon could travel in two microseconds is less than a kilometre. Light travels this distance in a few microseconds and as we know, it is impossible to travel at faster than the speed of light. In order for the muons to get from the upper atmosphere to the surface of the Earth they have to be travelling many times faster than light. How can this be possible? The answer is that for the muon time dilates relative to our time.

It works like this. According to Einstein's theory of relativity, when a muon moves close to the speed of light its time becomes highly warped. In our time reference on Earth the moving-muon time becomes considerably stretched out (dilated) – perhaps by a thousand times. Instead of decaying in a few Earth-time microseconds the muon can live a lot longer. Long enough to reach the ground. The direct test to show this time dilation effect took place in 1941 and was performed by Bruno Rossi and David Hall of the University of Chicago. Paul Davies describes the experiment:

> They wanted to show that faster muons live longer (as observed by us in the Earth reference frame). To accomplish this they deployed metal shields of various stopping powers to filter out the slow muons, and then detected the survivors at two different altitudes, using a bank of connected Geiger counters. They were able to show that the slow particles – which they quaintly referred to as 'mesotrons' – decayed about three times quicker than the fast ones.[76]

Evidence of time dilation is even closer than travelling on an airline, in a balloon or being bombarded by muons. Many of us wear proof of time dilation close to our bodies. As Davies explains:

> A typical electron orbits a hydrogen atom at about 200 kilometres per second, one per cent of the speed of light. However the speed is much greater for heavier atoms on account of the greater electric charges on the nucleus. The inner electron within atoms such as gold, lead or uranium can whirl around the nucleus at an appreciable fraction of the speed of light. Consequently, the influence of time dilation and other relativity effects will modify the behaviour of these electrons in important ways.[77]

And it is because of time dilation that gold has its colour. Most metals have a silvery appearance, but not gold. Its distinctive glitter and colour can be traced to the effects of relativity on the motion of the electrons inside the metal, the ones that reflect the light. Muons are certainly strange particles, but the strangest of all are the hypothetical, and as of yet, undiscovered, tachyons.

And back we go

In 1974, the world of theoretical physics collectively held its breath. Two researchers, Roger Clay and Philip Crouch, reported that they had recorded a precuser 'blip' from cosmic ray collisions. This result seemed to show evidence for the existence of tachyons.[78] Although the results still stand, subsequent experiments have failed to repeat the discovery, but this does show that particle physicists take the concept of tachyons very seriously.

A tachyon is a conceived particle whose slowest speed is that of light. It is termed a 'superluminal' particle because of this – the word *tachyon* is taken from the Greek word for 'speed'. A tachyon requires energy to slow down. Although in order to travel faster than light an object needs infinite mass, it is postulated that tachyons could have 'imaginary rest mass' if imaginary numbers are included in the calculation. Relativity does actually not say that objects cannot travel faster than light, even in a vacuum, but only that such objects can never travel slower than light. In other words, nothing can cross the light barrier by going either up or down in speed. What Einstein said was that the mass of a particle becomes indefinitely large as it approaches the speed of light. And it has been pointed out by theoretical physicists Olexa-Myron Bilaniuk and EC George Sudershan[79] that tachyons are not being accelerated up to the speed of light; they are travelling at faster than the speed of light at the moment they are created. In a similar fashion, it is known that photons and neutrinos travel with a velocity equal to the speed of light as soon as they come into existence. There is no such thing as a slow photon or neutrino.

So what did Clay and Crouch discover? We have seen that when an energetic cosmic ray particle collides with an ordinary atomic particle at the top of the atmosphere it produces a shower of lesser particles that can be detected on the ground. If some of the particles created in this way are tachyons, they will travel backwards in time and arrive in the detectors on the ground not only before most of the other particles in the shower but even before the original cosmic ray (the Primary) hits the top of the atmosphere. The experiment outlined above discovered such a blip.

That particles cannot travel faster than the speed of light is not technically true. Einstein's speed of light refers to its speed in a vacuum. This is the famous constant 'C' for which no particle moving slower than 'C' can be given enough energy to get to the speed of light. But light itself moves slower than 'C' when it passes through a transparent material such as a sheet of glass or a tank of water. Ordinary particles can thus travel faster than the speed of light in water without exceeding 'C'. When a charged particle such as an electron does this it radiates light. This is similar to the sonic 'boom' of a plane as it goes through the sound barrier; the particle creates an 'optical boom'. In 1934, this effect was first noticed by the Russian physicist Pavel Cherenkov. Consequently, this light is known as Cherenkov Radiation. A charged particle moving faster than light, even in a vacuum, would have to emit light. Calculations show that such a particle would lose all its energy in a flash, ending up with zero energy and travelling at infinite speed, so in a sense it would be everywhere in the universe at the same time!

The American particle physicist Richard Feynman took this idea to its logical limit and proposed that there is only one electron in the universe. He suggested that this particle moves backwards and forwards in time with such an elaborate trajectory that at any moment we think we see many of them. This trajectory involves the particle bouncing backwards and forwards in time. In other words, as Paul Davies says:

You and I, the Earth, the Sun, the Milky Way and all other
galaxies are composed of just one electron (and one photon and
one neutron too) seen squillions of times over. This offers a
neat explanation as to why all electrons appear to be identical.

This will also predict that the universe must be made up of equal amounts of matter and anti-matter, because every 'zig' must have a 'zag'. To expand on this idea, if these particles came into existence milliseconds after the 'Big Bang' they would immediately travel to the edge of the available universe. There is then nowhere for them to go but back where they came from. They then make the same journey again and indeed continue doing so today, making the journey an infinite number of times a second. As space is curved, one can argue that they in fact come back in two ways: backwards in time (arriving back the instant they leave) and in space (as space is curved they also arrive the moment they leave). As these objects are literally everywhere at the same time, is it reasonable to believe that they are the particles that make up the very fabric of reality, the backdrop of everything that is? For these objects there literally is no time; they are outside of the concept. To them there is just the present with everything that was, is and will be, all contained in an ongoing 'now'. The concept of time dilation, speeding up, and indeed stopping are subjective realities because time itself is a psychological construct of the perceiver; we make our own 'time'.

The science writer Jack Sarfatti believes that each continuous worldline or space-time history is just a probability. In an interesting amalgamation of Everett's Many Worlds Interpretation and Bohm's Implicate Order, Sarfatti proposes that all possible histories of the universe occur and interfere with each other. The overlap or constructive interference of these 'interpenetrating universes' is the universe we perceive during normal states of consciousness.[80] This is a proposition that we will review in greater detail in a later chapter.

It helps to realize that scientists at the leading edge of physics, and mathematicians who are pushing the boundaries of human knowledge further and further, do not cling on to the concept of time held so dear by the wider public. To them time is a psychological, not physical, state. After Minkowski, one of the greatest mathematicians of the last century was the Austrian Kurt Godel. He was an eccentric and reclusive logician who worked alongside Einstein at the Institute for Advanced Study in Princeton. This following is taken from his 'A Remark about the Relationship between Relativity Theory and Idealistic Philosophy':

The assertion that events A and B are simultaneous (and for a large class of pairs of events, also the assertion that A happened before B) loses its objective meaning, in so far as another observer, with the same claim to correctness, can assert that A and B are not simultaneous (or that B happened before A).

Following up on the consequences of this strange state of affairs one is led to conclusions about the nature of time which are far reaching. In short, it seems that one obtains an unequivocal proof for the view of those philosophers who, like Parmenides,[81] Kant and the modern idealists, deny the objectivity of change, considering it to be an illusion or an appearance due to our special mode of perception. The argument runs as follows. Change becomes possible only through the lapse of time. The existence of an objective lapse of time means (or, at least, is equivalent to the fact) that reality consists of an infinite number of layers of 'now' which come into existence successively. But, if simultaneity is something relative in the sense just explained, reality cannot be split up into such layers in an objectively determined way. Each observer has his own set of 'nows' and none of these various systems and layers can claim the prerogative of representing the objective lapse of time.[82]

Theoretical physicist Julian Barbour has taken this position to its logical conclusion. In his book *The End of Time*, he argues that there is sufficient evidence to conclude that the problem is not with perception but with time itself. For Barbour time is an illusion.

Barbour cuts time out of the equation

Barbour argues that time is an illusion and that the universe is, in reality, timeless. His theory is complex but in essence he suggests a universe similar to Hugh Everett's Many Worlds but with one important difference; for Barbour the universe splits not into an identical copy of itself at each quantum event but only into a probability, in the same way that Schrödinger's cat has an equal probability of being alive or dead. He says:

> ... in that scheme (the Many Worlds Interpretation) time still exists: history is a path that branches whenever some quantum decision has to be made. In my picture there are no paths. Each point of Platonia (Barbour's mythical universe that he uses to explain his theory) has a probability, and that is the end of the story.[83]

In the same way that we saw particles existing in a mist of probability so it is for Barbour's idea of outcomes. Actual events are more likely to take place where the 'probability mist' is at its densest. Some 'nows' have a higher probability of taking place in the same way that the chance of finding a sub-atomic particle in a particular place is higher if the probability of that particle being found in that location is higher. In Platonia, the 'nows' that are experienced are the ones with the higher probabilities. Barbour recognizes that this theory causes profound problems with how time is understood:

> All this seems like a far cry from the reality of our lives. Where is the history we read about? Where are our memories? Where is the

bustling, changing world of our experience? These configurations
of the Universe for which the probability mist has a high density,
and so are likely to be experienced must have within them an
appearance of history – a set of mutually consistent records that
suggest we have a past. I call these configurations 'time capsules'[84]

Barbour argues that these 'time capsules' exist within our own minds and have no objective reality. These records exist now, not in the past. We all live in an ongoing present. On first encountering Barbour's proposition it appears easy to disprove by simple observation. If time does not exist then how is it that we perceive motion? After all, motion can only exist in time. At one point in time an object is in one position and then it moves to be found in another position at a later point in time. However, he shows in a reasonably convincing way that motion may not exist external to our perception.[85]

It is important to realize that we 'see' reality as a light-stimulated image on our retina. The important term here is 'image' – a singular image like a photograph. We perceive motion in exactly the same way that cinema film gives the illusion of motion, through the PHI effect (*see* page 70). A series of static images is flashed across the field of vision at such a speed that they 'fuse' into a single image. This single image has a duration in time that gives an illusion of motion. A series of static images is perceived as a single moving image. The retina works in the same way. The preceding images are held in the brain and superimposed upon the next image.[86] As Barbour explains:

> *Suppose we could freeze the atoms of our brain at some*
> *instant. We might be watching gymnastics. What would brain*
> *specialists find in the frozen pattern of the atoms? They will*
> *surely find that the pattern encodes the position of the*
> *gymnasts at that instant. But it may also encode the positions*
> *of the gymnasts at preceding instants. Indeed it is virtually*

certain that it will, because the brain cannot process data instantaneously, and it is known that the processing involves transmission of data backwards and forwards in the brain.[87] *Information about positions of the gymnasts over a certain span of time is therefore present in the brain at any one instant.*

I suggest that the brain in any instant always contains, as it were, several stills of a movie. They correspond to different positions of objects we think we see moving. The idea is that it is this collection of 'stills', all present in any one instant, that stands in psychophysical parallel with the motion we actually see. The brain 'plays' the movie for us, rather as an orchestra plays notes on the score.[88]

Earlier we looked at the case of the neurologist VS Ramachandran, who worked with a patient called 'Ingrid', who suffered bilateral damage to an area of her brain, the middle temporal area. Her eyesight was fine as long as the object she was looking at remained stationary, but as soon as the object began to move she would perceive it as if it was being illuminated by a strobe light. She was, as Ramachandran describes it, 'motion blind'. To re-quote him:

She said that talking to someone in person felt like talking on the phone because she couldn't see the changing facial expressions associated with normal conversation. Even pouring a cup of coffee was an ordeal because the liquid would inevitably overflow and spill on the floor. She never knew when to slow down, changing the angle of the coffee-pot, because she couldn't estimate how fast the liquid was rising in the cup.[89]

This example certainly supports Barbour's theory. However, Wilder Penfield discovered that full, synaesthetic, memories could be stimulated by placing an electrode on certain points in the human cortex (*see* page 84). This was recognized as being similar to a movie recording in that it could be paused when the electrode was taken away, only to be started again at the same point when the electrical current was reapplied. This is a perfect echo of Barbour's movie analogy. If Barbour's theory is correct then Penfield's patients' stimulated 'memories' were not actual memories at all because a memory is a recall of a past event. If our concept of time is incorrect and we all live in an ongoing present then those 'memories' were not memories but a re-living of the actual events!

And if we accept Barbour's theory then we have to conclude that time only exists as part of our own mind; it has no objective existence. We therefore measure time in terms of its duration from the evidence given to us by our own mind. In fact, evidence that the subjective perception of time flow can be changed by experimentation exists in the François-Hoagland Theory.

From metaphysics to metabolics

In the early 1930s, a concerned physician was ministering to his sick wife. On discovering that her temperature had soared to 104 degrees he decided that he needed to get her some drugs. Although the fever had placed her in a semi-conscious state, she agreed to be left alone for a few minutes while he went out to the drugstore. He told her that he would be back as quickly as possible.

He returned less than 20 minutes later to find his wife in some distress. In her fevered state she had thought that he had been away for many hours. Realizing that something interesting was taking place, the doctor went back downstairs and picked up a stopwatch, and brought it back into the bedroom. Without explaining why, he asked his wife to count to 60, requesting that she counted each number as a second of time. As a trained musician, the woman had a perfect time sense and, although confused, she went along with her husband's bizarre request. Much to his surprise she counted to 60 in much less than a minute. He repeated the exercise 25 times, with the same result. Over the next few hours he repeated the experiment as her body temperature came down. As it did so, he discovered that her internal clock moved slowly back to normal. It was evident that her body temperature directly affected her perception of time duration.

On his return to his teaching post at the University the doctor set up experiments to support his suspicions. Using a technique known as 'diathermy', where high frequency electric currents are used to produce heat in the deeper tissues of the body, he was able to duplicate the fever that his wife suffered that day. In this way he tested out his ideas on many student volunteers. In almost all cases his subjects counted faster when their body temperature was higher.[90]

The physician in question was Dr Hudson Hoagland of the Worcester Foundation for Experimental Biology. His fascination as regards the effects of body temperature and metabolic rate on the subject's perception of time was shared by the Frenchman M François, who had, using different methods, drawn similar conclusions.[91] On hearing of each other's work, the American and the Frenchman decided to pool resources. Working together, they came to believe that a metabolic-chemical pacemaker in the brain may modulate the perception of short time intervals. Hoagland postulated that longer intervals were judged in terms of other master reactors, the ones that attuned to daily changes in the external environment.

Put simply, the François-Hoagland Theory states that we all have an internal chemical clock that can be speeded up by a rise in body temperature. This causes objective time to appear to go more slowly since clock time would pass in the same interval of objective time. These conclusions have some fascinating implications when reviewed in the light of the discoveries of Wilder Penfield. Penfield presented strong evidence that the brain physically records all incoming sensory data in a similar process to DVD or video. The François-Hoagland Theory implies that the higher the temperature or metabolic rate of the observer the more rapidly the 'frames' are recorded – there are more frames per time period. As body temperature drops, so the recording speed moves from long play, through standard play and then to a much slower rate. May this be what happens to animals when they hibernate? Does their perception of time slow down to the extent that the recording process stops altogether? If this is the case then from the viewpoint of the hibernating animal the winter never happened. It is simply not recorded. The analogy of a video recorder is again useful here. Hibernation is as if the VCR had been programmed to record two programmes, one in the start of autumn and one at the start of spring. When replayed, the videotape will present to the receiving television a seamless cut between the autumn 'programme' and the spring 'programme'. Consciousness is equivalent to the TV set. As regards how the TV/consciousness perceives the train of events, the winter didn't happen – it disappeared.

There are significant implications of this viewpoint. It suggests that your metabolic rate influences what you experience and what you remember. You can have totally blank areas of temporal perception. For you, and one assumes for all conscious creatures, whole periods of time can simply disappear.

On 13 June 2003, Terry Wallis, who had been in a very deep coma since 1984, existing in what is termed a 'persistent vegetative state', suddenly became conscious again. For him time had not passed whilst he was in the coma – he had lost 19 years of his life. Where had his personality been in the intervening years? If the evidence presented above is true then he was nowhere. For him those years never existed – he had fallen out of time.

It can be reasonably concluded that your metabolism affects how you perceive the passage of time. As your metabolic rate increases and your body temperature gets higher, so it is that you perceive time slowing down. The higher the rate, the slower time flows past your consciousness. But this slowing down of time only occurs within your perception. To an observer watching, you simply seem to be slowing down. This may be evident from your movement, speech patterns or just a general malaise. Generally we all know these to be the usual symptoms of fever or illness, but there are two other states in which our behaviour can seem strange and lethargic: when we are under the influence of drugs and when we are in the other well-known manipulator of mental states, hypnotism.

Into the realm of Chronos

Hypnotism is a subject about which a fair degree of confusion still reigns. Stage shows in which members of the public are placed in a trance by mesmerists and are seen to do strange things and act in ways totally contrary to their usual behaviour are extremely popular. Although this is a form of entertainment, it has long been believed by experimental psychologists that within the deep trance states brought about by hypnotism can be found clues to man's real nature. One of the most interesting areas of study is how our perception of time can be totally thrown while in these states.

Dr Milton Erickson, the American psychologist, has made a lifelong study of how and why the human mind can, when distracted, slip outside of normal 'clock-time'. In 1954, he, together with an associate, Linn Cooper, realized that this curious subjectivity can be reproduced during hypnotically induced trance states. In one session they placed a college student into a light trance. In her mind she perceived that she was sitting at a table and gazing out of a window. She had shown a great interest in dress design as a future career, so Erickson and Cooper suggested that she let her mind idly mull over some potential designs. After about an hour of quiet reflection she decided to sketch her ideas onto a drawing pad on the table in front of her. She was pleased that she had completed a full design, particularly as in a normal fully conscious state it could take her four to ten sessions of two or three hours each to get to this stage. The real shock was not only that it had taken her just an hour to do this but also that in actual clock time the session had actually been ten seconds.

Cooper was keen to have some objective and measurable proof that time perception can be manipulated during deep trance states. In 1956, he had a patient hypnotized to believe that a metronome was beating at one click per clock second. She was then told that the metronome was slowing down to one click every two seconds, then one click every five seconds and finally one click a minute. The passage of only a few minutes of clock-time was experienced by the subject as an interval of many hours. Cooper then attached electrodes to the scalp of the patient. This allowed him to monitor the actual brain-wave activity while she was in dream state. In this way he was able to objectively measure the duration of a dream. One dream was measured as three seconds whereas within her perception of the dream the subject imagined that 4,800 seconds had passed and during that time her dream self was able to pick up and count 862 bolls of cotton. In her altered time scale this was perfectly reasonable – she was taking five seconds for each boll – but in reality it is simply impossible to count 862 of anything in three seconds.[92]

If Cooper had left this woman in her dream state for a few days, for every second of real time she was experiencing, it would, in effect, be nearly half a minute. So in 2 days in hypnosis she would experience 60 days of subjective time. Within a very short period of clock-time the subject and the experimenter are existing in totally different time scales. They are in mutually exclusive worlds.

It is clear that the brain itself is manipulating how the passage of time is presented to consciousness. We are again drawn to the conclusion that our perception of 'reality' – be it physical or temporal – can be manipulated because it has no objective existence outside of the phaneron of the perceiver. This suspicion is reinforced by the fact that there is another way that time perception can be disrupted, and that is by the application of drugs.

Examples of drug-induced temporal flow disruption are many. In one recorded case a songwriter, while in a drug-induced trance, found herself walking down a street in a large town. She spotted a cabaret and decided to go in and take in the show. She sat down, ordered a beer and a sandwich and settled down to watch the show. On to the stage walked a singer who began to sing a very interesting song. The subject decided to stay and hear more. The singer then performed two more songs. All three songs were new to the subject and she decided in her trance state that they were very good. She then awoke from the dream state to discover that only two minutes of clock-time had passed. What is particularly interesting about this incident was that the songwriter could recall all three songs in their entirety and could sing them word and tune perfect.[93] It is reasonable to conclude that in order to recall the songs in such detail she must have heard them in normal time within her own temporal time-bubble.

Just how long time can be extended within dream states, drug-induced or otherwise, is of great interest. Is it possible that days or even years can be subjectively experienced within a few seconds of clock-time? Certain researchers think this to be so. In 1968, the psychiatrist JR Smythies observed that under the influence of hallucinogenic drugs, particularly mescaline, time elongates to the point that one second can seem like a hundred years.[94] In effect, somebody could, in their own mind, live a whole lifetime while within the timescale of an observer only a second has passed. Each of the two protagonists, observer and subject, exist in totally divergent Everett Universes.

The invisible guide

Of all the experiments that Milton Erickson was involved with, one in particular stands out. It is so curious that even Erickson had no explanation for it. It involved a 26-year old student who was interested in controlling his own thought patterns. He requested that Erickson place him in a trance state for exactly two hours. During this period the young man intended to observe quietly and note his experiences.

As events turned out, Erickson was the one to be woken up. His work was disturbed by exclamations of surprise emanating from the corner of the laboratory. Not only had the student come to but he was also in a state of extreme excitement. Erickson, after a second or two, realized that the young man had brought himself out of the trance state; unusual in itself, but what his subject was to tell him had occurred under hypnosis was simply incredible. The student had been given a glimpse of a world of reality that affects us all, proof that we are most definitely not what we think we are.

As he drifted into the trance-state, the subject saw the laboratory melt away to be replaced by an intense blue sky with small clouds drifting across its vast expanse. The sun was warm and he could feel its warmth on his face. He was lying on his back looking up at the firmament. He could smell the scents of summer all around him, the deep green smell of grass and the pollen-laden breezes of August. The feeling of reality was total. This was somewhat puzzling to him because he had never felt such intensity of sense stimulation in his other trance exercises. The overall feeling was so intensely pleasurable that he was happy to just enjoy the feeling. After a few moments he decided to sit up. It was at this point that he realized that this hallucination was synaesthetic in its intensity. He could feel his body in space. There was most definitely a hillside underneath him, not an old armchair in a psychology laboratory. He sat up and took in the view. He was, as he sensed, sitting on a hillside in midsummer. This was some dream. However, a shiver went through him when he saw, out the corner of his eye, a movement – a movement that belonged to somebody, or something else. For a split second fear of the unknown welled up in him. This was all too real. He slowly turned his eyes towards the movement. To his utter amazement he saw, a few yards away, a child facing away from him. He had a most peculiar feeling of familiarity. He knew that the child was six years old. This information was pulled out from his deep subconscious in a way that he simply could not understand. He picked himself up and began to walk towards the little one. As he got closer the child turned and immediately the young man knew why he was so sure that he was six. He was looking at himself at that age. As he walked towards the boy he was confused. The boy was looking straight through him. For some reason he was invisible. However, it was not his invisibility that caused his feelings of strangeness; it was something far more peculiar. He was aware that the child was hungry. Not only that, but he could sense that the child craved a specific type of brown cookie.

His mind exploded with memories. This was an actual event in his own past. He remembered now the incident on the hillside. He remembered what he wore and recalled with mounting amazement his own hunger 20 years before. He was witnessing an incident from his own past; but as an observer, not a participant. Some form of time-slip had taken place. He waited for something to happen, a change of scene, to be carried forward to another incident. But nothing happened. It slowly dawned on him that he was living, or more accurately, observing, in the same time-scale as his younger self. Each minute was equal for both of them. He found himself to be the boy's unspeaking and invisible companion. The minutes turned to hours, which turned into days. He followed the boy to school and lived his whole childhood again, in real time. He was aware who he was but it seemed that he had developed amnesia regarding all the events that had taken place, or more accurately, were about to take place, between the ages of 6 and 26. As such, each new experience was as new to the 'hidden observer' as it was to the boy. Time moved on. The little boy grew up, moved on to high school. All the time his older self viewed events. This older self had a 'double consciousness' in that he shared the boy's hopes and fears, pains and disappointments. He was, in effect, two beings.

Eventually time came for 'them' to decide on whether to go to college or not. This was not an easy decision but the 'hidden observer' knew that it was of great importance. If the now teenage boy did not go to college then the observer would not have been hypnotized and the regression would not have taken place! Much to the observer's relief, the decision was made and a college was decided upon. The observer had spent many years with his younger self but suddenly there was an overwhelming urge to go back from whence he came. With great concentration he hauled himself back into consciousness; the world melted around him and a laboratory came into view. This new world felt as real as the world he had just left. He could feel an armchair surrounding him and he caught, in the corner of his eye, somebody moving around. His confusion slowly dissipated and he recalled who he actually was. He realized that the person he could see was Dr Erickson; he called out to him in great excitement. He was back from the most amazing experience.

Erickson was to describe the event, saying that his subject:

> ... explained that the experience was literally a moment by moment reliving of his life with only the same awareness he had then and that the highly limited, restricted awareness of himself at 26 was that of being an invisible man watching his own growth and development from childhood on, with no more knowledge of the child's future than the child possessed at any particular age.[95]

Imagine now that situation from the viewpoint of the child. We have to assume that at no time was the little boy aware of the subject accompanying him through his life, but we do not know this for sure. Could it be that under certain circumstances the little boy could sense the presence or even 'attune' into what his older self was thinking? If the older 'observer' was concerned about a turn of events it is natural to assume that he would try to assist by making an effort to communicate advice. If limited communication was possible it is logical to conclude it would be through the more 'intuitive' non-dominant hemisphere of the little boy's brain. He would probably 'hear', or more accurately sense, a communication that would manifest itself as an external voice. The little boy's 'hidden observer' – his older self – may, under certain conditions, manifest himself in visual form. Now we have no way of knowing what the future person, as the hidden observer, would look like, but it is feasible that any visible manifestation would take the form of the hidden observer as he was at the time of the incident – the same age as his younger self. As such he would look exactly like his younger self: his double or *doppelgänger*.

This event is much more than a case of time dilation while in a 'twilight state'. Here we have a subject who has actually gone back in time and viewed himself as a younger person. Not only that, but he concurrently existed in two versions of himself. Can it really be that he went back and re-experienced his own past again, that time not only slows down but also repeats itself?

The wry cycle of Oroburus

So where does this leave us as regards time? We have reviewed evidence from physiology, psychology and neurology, all of which point to the same conclusion, that time is an illusion. It is an internally generated perception that is misinterpreted as an external reality. I have proposed that you are totally alone in your own Everett universe, isolated from all other human beings who in turn inhabit their own universes. This may seem worrying, as most likely does the fact that you also exist outside of time. You are in effect an observer 'travelling' through your own life, a life whose future events are out there waiting for you to encounter.

They do not exist in any objective future. They exist now, embedded in the block universe, just waiting for you.

The fact that your future already exists waiting for you to experience it within your own personal universe has interesting implications in that although your future and mine may be similar as regards events that we personally have no influence upon – events such as presidential elections and wars in far-flung areas of the globe – any situations in which our actions directly affect outcomes cause our mutual universes to diverge. In this way you create your own personal reality. And this all comes down to that often reported and always controversial phenomenon, precognition.

CHAPTER 6

Echoes of the Future

If you want my opinion of the mystery of life and all that, I can give it to you in a nutshell. The universe is like a safe to which there is a combination. But the combination is locked in the safe.

Peter De Vries, Let Me Count the Ways

De La Harpe remained sharp to the end of his class

If you read your horoscope, I am sure you find that the predictions made for you rarely come true. When astrologers do seem to get something right we are so amazed that we tell our friends about it. In this way a degree of credibility is awarded to an 'ability' that has absolutely no foundation in science and one that regularly fails objective testing. For example, I find it extraordinary that, to my knowledge, not one newspaper or magazine astrologer predicted the death of Princess Diana or the events of 11 September 2001. If astrologers and clairvoyants have an ability to see the future, how could they possibly miss such massive news items?

This is not to say that people cannot predict the future, far from it – after all, the future already exists and as such should, under certain conditions, be 'perceived'. Indeed, there is considerable evidence that this is the case. Take, for example, the famous case of the Marquis of Cazotte.

In the spring of 1788, Jean-François de La Harpe, a critic and dramatist attended a dinner in Paris. This was no ordinary dinner because attending it were some very famous and influential individuals. Among the guests were the Marquis de Condorcet, a mathematician and politician; Jean Sylvain Bailly, France's leading astronomer; Chrétien de Malesherbes, a politician; Félix

Vicq-d'Azyr, the queen's doctor; and Sébastien de Chamfort, a fashionable writer. But it was the comments of another guest, the Marquis of Cazotte, that were to be recorded for posterity in the journal of La Harpe.

Jacques Cazotte was a novelist and a fellow of the Society of French Academicians. He was also known to dabble in the occult and had developed a reputation for clairvoyance. On that particular night, it was his unusual seriousness that evoked the curiosity of his fellow guests. After the meal the conversation had turned to the present condition of French society. The mood was of satisfied optimism. All the guests, with the noticeable exception of Cazotte, agreed that a new Age of Reason was just around the corner. The novelist cut the frivolity short by announcing, in a portentous and direct tone, that the revolution that they all hoped for was, indeed, about to take place but, he added, this new 'reign of reason' would bode ill for all present. The guests were dumbfounded. After a few seconds the questions started to fly and Cazotte systematically predicted the fate of each one present. He informed Condorcet that he would cheat the executioner by poisoning himself in his prison cell; Chamfort would slash his wrists in despair; Vicq-d'Azyr would also die by having his veins opened; and Malesherbes and Bailly would be guillotined. As he went round the table the guests reacted with a mixture of horror and amusement, unsure as to whether the novelist was playing a game with them. When Cazotte arrived at de La Harpe he forecast that the confirmed atheist would die a Christian. This was the point that the dinner guests relaxed. This was evidence, for them, that this was an elaborate joke. At this point one of the guests said, 'All my fears are now gone, for if we have to wait until La Harpe becomes a Christian then we shall live forever.' For a few moments the mood improved. The Duchess de Gramont pointed out that the women present seemed safe, as women do not get involved in revolutionary matters. This was the opportunity for Cazotte to imply even greater levels of disruption and death. He said that women would suffer as much as men – princesses and 'even greater.' The dinner guests took this to mean the Queen, Marie Antoinette.

La Harpe was so disturbed by these predictions that he made notes about them when he got home. These notes were not to be published until after most of Cazotte's predictions had come to pass. The French Revolution broke out in 1789. In an act of anti-clericalism an actress, taking the role of the Goddess of Reason, was enthroned in Notre Dame Cathedral. As Cazotte had said, a new reign of Reason had indeed begun. Within five years Bailly and Malesherbes had gone to the scaffold, Condorcet had taken his poison and Chamfort had slashed his wrists. Vicq-d'Azyr was to die, not by being bled, but in fever. However, had he not died sooner the 'cure' for fever in those days was to have the veins opened. Cazotte himself was to die – he was implicated in a plot to rescue the King and paid for this with his head.

La Harpe did convert to Christianity. While in jail he found God. On his release he became deeply religious, dying in a monastery in 1803. His account of these events was not published until 1806 but there are sworn statements attesting that the events did take place and were not written up afterwards. In fact, there is strong evidence that the story was circulating many years before the actual publication.[96]

While this is an interesting and fascinating story, when placed within its particular historical context it is not at all unusual. Time after time we read of people making accurate predictions as regards future events. What is of particular interest in the Cazotte case is that the person making the prognostication is making predictions in relation to events that will come to pass during that person's own lifetime. As we shall see later there is a theory that suggests that we are all travelling through a personal and already existent time line. If this is the case then it is not surprising that some of us can see what is about to occur. Some writes have compared travelling through time as analogous to a train journey where the future is the next station along the line. In theory all sensitive people need to do is look towards the horizon and record what they see. The skill is knowing how to look forwards rather than sideways.

At this point a crucial observation has to be made; as with the train analogy the future can only be seen as far as the terminus. The train is on a set route that starts at the observer's birth and ends at their death. It is impossible for an observer to see any further than the final station, for the line ends at that point. Those who have the gift of seeing the future can only accurately predict events that they will become aware of in their own future.

In order to look at the evidence for 'lifetime' accuracy, I have selected three of the greatest recorded clairvoyants of the last 600 years; Mother Shipton, Robert Nixon and Nostradamus.

The best yorkie bar none

Ursula Southiel, or Mother Shipton as she became known, was born near Knaresborough in North Yorkshire. There is a good deal of uncertainty of the year of her birth but it is thought to be around 1488. Her fame lies in the predictions she made regarding many public figures of the time, most specifically Cardinal Wolsey. For example it is said that she prophesied that Wolsey would never enter York but that he would see it:

> *The Mitred Peacock (Wolsey) shall now begin to plume*
> *himself, and his train shall make great show in the world ...*
> *He shall want to live in York, and shall see it, but shall never*
> *come thither.*

In this she was correct. En route to the city the Cardinal stayed at Cawood Castle eight miles away. York is clearly visible from the castle towers. However, Wolsey was never to travel those eight miles because he was called back to London by the King. Predictions such as these would have given her a local reputation as a prophet, but the important point is that these predictions took place during her lifetime. She may have indeed 'foreseen' these events but she would, in time, have known about them during the normal course of events.

Her reputation was such that in 1641 some alleged predictions by her were published. These found their way into a work by the astrologer William Lilly published five years later. Of the eighteen prognostications cited, the majority were after the event. In 1677 Richard Head was to publish a book dealing solely with her life and prophecies. Head claimed that she had foretold the Spanish Armada in 1588 and the Great Fire of London in 1666.

The Great Fire of London seems to be one of the most predicted events in history. If the supporters of future predictions are to be believed then it seems that this event has echoed up and down time. So what exactly did Mother Shipton say about this event? Using Head's original structure, a later writer, John Tyrrel, has the great lady say:

> Time shall happen a ship shall sail upon the River Thames, till
> it reach the City of London, the Master shall weep, and cry
> out, Ah! What a flourishing City was this when I left it!
> Unequalled throughout the World! But now scarce a house is
> left to entertain with a flagon.[97]

But how can this be interpreted as the Great Fire when the main cause of the disaster, fire, is not mentioned? With all of future time available any vaguely similar set of circumstances involving London can be used in support of this prediction.

It again must be noted that both these events had already occurred before either Head's or Tyrell's books had been published. In fact, there is a suspicion that Head fabricated the predictions. As with many events of a psychic nature, subsequent writers build on the assumptions of earlier ones. In this case it was the reprint of Head's book, published in 1862 by Charles Hindley that was to make Mother Shipton's reputation. Hindley updated Head by adding some other predictions from a long-lost manuscript, although it has long been believed by many that these 19th-century additions were to be found in the original 1641 document. In describing these 'predictions' even Colin Wilson, writing in 1983, falls into this trap. He says:

> To Mother Shipton is attributed a piece of doggerel, published in 1641, beginning: 'Carriages without horses shall go,/And accidents fill the world with woe./Around the Earth thoughts shall fly./In the twinkling of an eye ...' and prophesying that iron would one day float on the water 'as easily as a wooden boat' (steamships) and that men would fly in the air.[98]

Yet, in 1873, Hindley admitted that he had written the verses himself and it is for this particular piece of verse that Mother Shipton's fame lies, even though it contains a massive error. At the end of the verse he has Southiel predict the end of the World in 1881. An event that is more a reflection of 19th-century apocalyptic religious beliefs than the confined world of 16th-century Yorkshire.

Later forgeries do not invalidate Mother Shipton's precognitive abilities. Reputations such as hers do not come about spontaneously. Contemporaries must have had some reason for believing that she could indeed see the future, the evidence of the Wolsey incident being a case in question. It is fair to assume that she was consistently accurate in more parochial circumstances and on a shorter time scale, a time scale of within her own future lifetime.

The Nixon without precedent

Robert Nixon was even more parochial and it was moving away from the small world he knew that was to lead to his self-predicted death. Nixon was a classic 'idiot savant', an individual that, although retarded, shows superhuman abilities in a particular aptitude or skill. In Nixon's case it was foretelling future events.

Nixon was born in 1467 in Over Delamere in Cheshire. When he correctly predicted the death of an ox belonging to a local farmer named Crowton, he attracted the attention of the local squire, Lord Cholmondeley. Cholmondeley gave him a job as a ploughboy. As with everything else, he showed little skill in this role. Although it seemed that the ox prediction was a fluke, one day Nixon fell into a trance while ploughing. He claimed that he had seen things that man had never seen before. He informed his contemporaries of many future events in European history. But this was just the start. On 22 August 1485, he was ploughing as usual when he suddenly stopped in his tracks. He then started dancing round the field, screaming and foaming at the mouth. Brandishing his whip like a sword, he shouted, 'There, Richard! There! Now! Up, Henry! Up with all arms! Over the ditch, Henry ... over the ditch and the battle is won!' He then turned to the group around him and said, 'The battle is over, Henry has won.' With this he went back to his plough. A week or so later news reached Cheshire that England had a new king. A great battle had taken place at Bosworth Field in Leicestershire on 22 August. In this showdown the old king, Richard III, had been killed. The victor, Henry Tudor, became King Henry VII.

The new King's messengers recorded that the people of Vale Royal in Cheshire knew already of the victory. When word of this curiosity came to the ear of Henry he ordered that Nixon be brought down to London to work in the royal household. Nixon knew of this before the King's men came for him. One day he became extremely agitated. He ran round Cholmondeley Hall asking to be hidden from the men who were coming for him. If he were taken to the royal palace, Nixon insisted, he would end up 'clammed' or starved to death. This was totally confusing to all on two counts; firstly why would the king send for the village idiot, and secondly, even if he did it was highly unlikely that Nixon would starve surrounded by the largesse of a royal palace. A few days later another Nixon prediction was proven correct. The King's men did turn up and, after giving him assurances about food, took him to London.

Nixon quickly became one of the King's favourites. He was given complete run of the palace and, of course, was allowed to have food anytime he wished. The King had a scribe follow him to note any predictions that he made. However, Nixon could not get over his fear of starvation. Always hungry, he often annoyed the cooks by stealing food that had been prepared for the King himself. One day, while Henry was away on a hunting trip, the cooks reached the end of their tether. Annoyed by his continual demands for food, they locked Nixon in a closet and forgot about him. Two weeks later Henry returned and asked for his court prophet. Nixon was found in the closet. He had died of starvation and dehydration.

So Nixon proved his ability to predict events in his own life, but how good was he with events outside of his own time? Not at all impressive, it seems. One particular prediction noted by Henry's scribe stated:

> *Foreign nations shall invade England with snow on their helmets and shall bring plague, famine and murder in the skirts of their garments.*

As of today, this has singularly not come to pass. As to his 'trance predictions', which included the English Civil War, the defeat and beheading of Charles I, the Restoration, and the French Revolution, there is no provable documentation. It has been pointed out that it is strange that Nixon was successful in predictions in his own lifetime but then had a gap of over 150 years before his next foreseen event. It is suspected that the later predictions are wrongly attributed. The first published account of Nixon's predictions, similar to Mother Shipton's, were published after many of the events predicted had taken place. This was in 1714, when John Oldmixon had them published. Again it seems that Nixon, like Mother Shipton, did have an ability to predict the future, but only one that he would subsequently experience or live through.

Our Lady of the quatrains

We now turn to the Prophet whose reputation, until September 1999, was virtually unassailable, Michel de Nostredame, or Nostradamus. Born in St Rémy, Southern France, on 13 December 1503, Nostradamus was to study medicine at Montpellier, where he gained a nationwide reputation when he assisted in dealing with the Black Death that ravaged the area. He saved many lives but not those of his wife and two infant sons. For many years he drifted aimlessly from city to city, but in 1547 he settled in the small town of Salon in his native Provence. In 1550 he began publishing astrological almanacs with no great success, but after this date he started composing long-term prophecies. It was from these that his fame became assured.

The first edition of his 'Centuries', published in 1555, was a book of predictions set in verse. In it he deliberately wrote in cryptic phrases and used puns, anagrams and scientific jargon to obscure his meaning. This was supposedly to avoid conflict with the Church authorities. This first series caught the attention of many influential people, including Queen Catherine de Medici, but it was an event that took place on 1 July 1559 that was to ensure his fame.

To celebrate two royal weddings a three-day tournament was held. Catherine's husband, Henry II, was involved in a mock joust with a young captain of the Scottish Guard, Gabriel de Lorges, Comte de Montgomery. As the two charged towards each other, Montgomery was late in lowering his lance. Before he realized his mistake the lance had hit the King in the face. The point of the lance crashed through Henry's golden helmet and pierced his head behind an eye. Henry did not die immediately. He was to linger in agony until the 10 July, when he passed away.

Attention was immediately drawn to the 35th quatrain (four-line verse) in Nostradamus' first *Century*. In translation this stated:

The young lion will overcome the old one.

On the field of battle in single combat

He will put out his eyes in a cage of gold;

Two wounds one, then to die a cruel death

The accuracy of this prediction is startling. Henry wore a golden helmet (cage of gold) and took two wounds, not one. One was in the eye, the other in the throat. As can be imagined, this caused a sensation not only at the royal court but also in the streets of Paris. The mobs were convinced that Nostradamus was a sorcerer and they burned his effigy. Catherine had no such reservations. She invited the provincial doctor to the Court, Nostradamus accepted the offer and his predictions were then to influence politics, diplomacy and national affairs for many years. With increasing infirmity, Nostradamus returned to Salon, where he died on 1 July 1566. By this time all but the final few *Centuries* had been published. A final edition containing all his predictions was published in 1568.

In an echo of Nixon's prior knowledge of his own death,

Nostradamus also showed this knowledge. On the night he died his pupil, Chavigny, bid his master goodnight. The old man was to reply, 'Tomorrow at sunrise I shall not be here'. The next morning he was found dead at his workbench.

It is clear that Nostradamus was accurate in terms of events in his own lifetime. But what of his overall accuracy? In a fascinating survey, Geoffrey Ashe, in his book *The Book of Prophesy*, reviews all 942 quatrains for what he terms 'Class A Predictions'. In order to be Class A the quatrain must make at least one prediction that is open to only a single interpretation. There must be no ambiguities. He terms 'Class B' as those that seem accurate but are open to dispute because of rival interpretations.

As far as Ashe is concerned there are 26 'Class A' predictions and 24 'Class B'. This gives an accuracy of around 5 percent.[99] Although Ashe considers that 5 percent is reasonable, I find it somewhat disappointing. It implies that 95 percent of his predictions are wrong, or have yet to take place. Indeed, 'Class A' predictions are only 2.5 percent of the total. How many people would follow a racing tipster who was wrong 39 times out of 40? And I cannot, with post-millennium hindsight, avoid reminding the reader of quatrain X.72, a verse that was unavoidable in June and July 1999:

L'an mil neuf cens nonate neuf sept mois,

Du ciel viendra un grand Roi deffraieur.

Rescusciter le grande Roi d'Angolmois.

Avant que Mars regner par bonheur.

Translated by the Nostradamus scholar Erika Cheetham, this reads:

In the year 1999 and seven months from the sky will come the Great King of Terror. He will bring back the Great King of the Mongols. Both before and after this, war reigns unrestrained.[100]

So what went wrong? Of all 942 quatrains this is the only one that gives an absolute year and month of an event. This is unusually unambiguous. In a curious echo of both Mother Shipton and Robert Nixon much is made of his prediction of the Great Fire of London for 1666. However, in his *Century II*, quatrain 51, what he actually wrote was:

Le sang de juste à Londres sera faulte

Brulés par fouldres de vingt trois les six:

La dame antique cherra de place haute,

De mesme secte plusieurs seront occis.

Cheetham translates this as:

The blood of the just will be demanded of London,

Burned by fire in three times twenty plus six.

The ancient lady will fall from her high position

And many of the same denomination will be killed.

To begin with, the word *fouldres* does not translate as 'fire' but as 'lightning fire': immediately there is a crucial change in meaning. Burned by lightning fire clearly implies multiple strikes during a thunderstorm. There is also a major translation issue as regards the year. *De vingt trois* is 'the twenty three' not 'three times twenty'. Thus 'twenty-three (and) the six' would be 29 not 66. As the Great Fire evidently did not take place in 1629, nor have there been multiple thunderbolts hitting London in the 23rd year of any century to date one can only assume that this commonly accepted 'Class A' prediction is far from accurate.

Further scrutiny causes the whole prediction to fall down in flames. For example, St Paul's Cathedral has never been known as 'the Old Lady'. Why would a cathedral named after a male saint be given a female appellation? Finally, in old French *antique* meant eccentric, not ancient, the derivation being the same as the English word 'antic'.

The arch debunker of all things irrational, James Randi[102] argues that there is a much more straightforward interpretation of quatrain 51 of *Century II*; that Nostradamus was referring to events that took place in 1555, not 1666. Randi says that during that year Mary I of England began her quest to turn England back to the Church of Rome. On 22 January Mary's supporters began the burning of Protestant heretics. These unfortunates were burned in groups of six. In order to ease their agony packets of gunpowder were tied between their legs and around their neck. When the fire reached a certain heat the gunpowder exploded like 'a thunderbolt'. While these things were taking place in her name, Mary was to become more and more eccentric. She was deeply in love with her husband, Philip of Spain, but in 1555 he had returned to Spain, never to return. This added to her mental problems. She died three years later, incoherent and probably insane.

And so we have another, far more reasoned interpretation of the quatrain. The 'sixes' are the numbers of each group burned; the 'thunderbolts' that Nostradamus mentions are the gunpowder packets; the 'eccentric lady' who loses her high position is Queen Mary I and the many of the same denomination that die are those

Protestants who were put to the stake.

This does not prove that Nostradamus did not foresee these events. The first edition of the *Centuries* was actually published in 1555, the year that the reign of Mary Tudor took a nasty turn. It may be that he wrote the quatrain in question before the news of the events in London reached Paris. His level of accuracy implies intimate knowledge of what took place. This could be an example of a stunningly accurate short-term precognition. If this is the case then the misinterpreted *Century II*, 51 could be a 'Class A' in Ashe's categorization.

Nostradamus was a prophet who gained a massive reputation during his life, deservedly so as some of the predictions are accurate and testable; in each case it is beyond doubt that the prediction was made before the event prophesied. A reasonable conclusion is that prophecy depends in some way upon memory – even if it is a memory of an event that is about to happen.

The evidence seems to show that an ability to see future events is indeed a possibility, at least for certain individuals. Predictive ability only really seems effective as regards future events that are due to take place within the lifetime of the prophet. It is as if they carry a form of future memory within their subconscious. Analysis of predictions involving events after the death of the seer shows that accuracy becomes at best erratic, and at worst simply wrong. Clearly, with tortuous logic and an open mind, the predictions can be forced to fit a particular event, but this exercise is always done from the position of hindsight.

What actually takes place in the mind of these people when they 'see' what is about to take place? Nixon, it seems, went into some form of trance state or seizure. As regards Mother Shipton, we have no information. Nostradamus, on the other hand, was quite clear on this score; he had assistance from what he termed his *Splendeur Divine* or Divine Splendour. In *Century 1*, quatrain 2 he says:

La verge en main mise au milieu des BRANCHES

De L'onde il moulle et le limbe et le pied:

Un puer et voix fremissant par les manches:

Splendeur divine. Le divin prés s'assied

In translation:

> *The wand in hand is placed in the middle of the legs of the tripod.*
>
> *He sprinkles both the hem of his garment and his foot with water.*
>
> *A voice: Fear: he trembles in his robes.*
>
> *Divine Splendour. The God sits beside him.*

Nostradamus is crystal clear that he is given his predictions by 'a voice'. He does not 'see' the future. It is described to him by another personality within his mind, a personality that seems to know the future. We will meet this person later.

A pattern seems to be emerging in all this – the future that is predicted by these prognosticators is their own future. They predict, or recall, the events as they were received by themselves in their own future. This is a very important point to stress. In other words, Robert Nixon did not 'see' the battle of Bosworth Field, he play-acted the events as they were to be told to him in his own future. I know it sounds strange but he was remembering the remembering.

This idea that precognition is the recollection of a memory was first suggested in 1927 by a British aircraft designer by the name of JW Dunne. In his book *An Experiment with Time*, Dunne suggested that the age-old mystery of precognition could be explained quite easily: precognitions are quite the reverse of what we believe them to be. They are memories not predictions. Dunne based this idea not upon the reports of others but through personal experience involving a most peculiar incident.

What you will do rather than what you actually Dunne

In 1902, Dunne was in Lindley in the Orange Free State, supporting the British Army's involvement in what was to become known as the Boer War. One night he had a particularly vivid dream. He saw an island about to blow up because of a volcano. In the dream he was aware that the explosion was going to put the 4,000 inhabitants in grave danger. He was desperate to save these people and in the dream he was involved in pleading with the authorities on a nearby island to send boats and ships to get the inhabitants off the island and to safety. In the dream he was aware that the authorities on the safe island were French. A few days after the dream he received a copy of the *Daily Telegraph*. The paper's headlines announced the disaster in Martinique. It reported that 40,000 people had died. What is interesting is that Dunne's dream did not actually foresee the disaster. What his dream foresaw and then created a dream around it was his reading of the newspaper headline. The reason that Dunne felt this way was that at the time he misread the headline, seeing 4,000 instead of 40,000.[103]

It was only 15 years later that he realized his error. From this Dunne came to the conclusion that many dreams actually predict the future in a confused way. By this he meant that a dream is created by the subconscious with information about events that are about to happen to the dreamer in the future. The dream creation process is exactly the same as for normal 'in time' dreams. They are twisted and re-worked by the subconscious. His dream of

Martinique was stimulated by the newspaper headline and wove a tale around the number 4,000 because that is what he actually read the next day. The prediction was not of the disaster itself but of Dunne reading, and therefore subconsciously processing, the headline in the newspaper.

Dunne decided to apply his engineer's mind to this conundrum. He believed that we all have predictive dreams; it is a question of remembering them. He looked for statistical evidence, so he approached 23 students at Oxford University. He asked them to examine their dreams very closely. He suggested that they have a notebook by their bedside so that on awaking they could immediately write down what they remembered. He argued that the images would be deeply symbolic and related directly to the individual's subconscious. He found that 12 percent of the dreams had elements of prediction within them. In all these involved 165 dreams, 148 from the students and 17 of his own.

In a classical example of his technique Dunne tells of a dream that he had while on holiday in Austria with his brother. In the dream a horse had gone mad but he was protected from it because it was in a field enclosed by high railings. In his dream he was concerned that the horse might escape. He checked the railings to convince himself that the horse could not escape, but as he walked away he heard the sound of hooves behind him. The horse had escaped and so he ran away from the wild beast and saw in front of him a flight of stairs. It was then that he woke up. Next day he was fishing with his brother down a little river that runs into the Aachensee Lake. His brother called out 'Look at that horse'. Glancing across the river he saw the scene in his dream. Dunne says:

> But though right in essentials, it was absolutely unlike in
> minor details. The two fields with the fenced off pathway
> running between them were there. The horse was there,

behaving just as it had done in the dream. The wooden steps
were there. But the fences were wooden and small – not more
than four or five feet high. The horse was also far smaller.
However in the same way as in the dream the horse did,
inexplicably, get out and just as in the dream it thundered
down towards the wooden steps.[104]

What is particularly interesting is that the incorrect details again support Dunne's idea that the dream had been based upon the future events, not that the dream was predicting the actual events. Dunne comments on this:

They were the ordinary, appropriate, expectable dreams; but
they were occurring on the wrong nights.

He then adds the comment that they were 'displaced in time'. For Dunne this seemingly impossible set of circumstances could be shown to be scientifically possible by the application of the theories of Herman Minkowski (*see* page 118).

Dunne suggested that the person who perceives the slice of spacetime that we call 'now' is 'Observer 1'. As time passes by in successive slices of the universe, this Observer 1 experiences time as a flow. However, in the same way that relativity needs something to gauge velocity against, so it is with time. The 'something' that sees Observer 1 moving through time is another observer whom Dunne called 'Observer 2'. This second observer exists in another time frame that allows it to observe all Observer 1's past, present and future. Observer 2 manifests itself in the consciousness of Observer 1 in the form of dreams. Might this be Nostradamus' 'Divine Splendour'?

In the early 1970s, a series of experiments took place at the Maimonides Medical Center in New York. This hospital has a department that involves itself solely in the research of dream states. Under the leadership of Dr Montague Ullman this team have made some fascinating discoveries, including evidence that Dunne was correct – dreams can predict short-term future events. Working with his associate Stanley Krippner and researcher Charles Honorton, Ullman had subjects spend eight consecutive nights at the centre. Each night they were told to try and dream about a picture that would be chosen at random the next day. The best Ullman hoped for was a 'hit rate' of one out of eight. To his utter amazement some subjects hit five out of eight. One volunteer dreamed of 'a large concrete building' from which a 'patient' was trying to escape. The subject said that the patient was wearing a white coat like those worn by doctors and had only managed to get as far as 'the archway'. The painting chosen at random was Van Gogh's *Hospital Corridor at St Rémy*. This watercolour shows a patient standing at the end of a massive hallway about to escape through a door beneath an archway.[105]

The implications are that somebody, or something, communicates with the conscious mind in dreams. And this entity knows what is about to happen. We will consider the possible identity of this being later. For now the question is: how far in the future can this being see?

Certain psychologists consider this phenomenon to be of great importance and a good deal of research has taken place as regards the 'time lag' of dream precognition. Dr Arthur Funkhouser, the Zurich-based Jungian psychoanalyst, has made a study of this research. He reports that in 1953 an article was published that reviewed 47 precognitive dreams.[106] It was found that 15 were fulfilled in 1 day or less, 11 were with 2 to 3 days, with the remaining 21 spread over a period of 4 days to 8½ years. Funkhouser goes on to say:

> *Kooey, a professor of theoretical physics at Breda, Holland,*
> *discovered 193 'Dunne effects' in 2½ years of dream diary*
> *entries and found that most occurred in reality within 24 hours*

of the dreams.[107] More recently, Sondow discovered that most future-determined elements in her dreams came from the day following the dream, while a lot fewer were from days later on.[108] Orme plotted the logarithm of the incidence against the logarithm of the fulfilment time intervals and showed that the relationship is a nearly linear, negative slope, indicating that the relationship is probably inversely exponential.[109] While not specifically concerned with dreams, Radin's research on presentiment[110] may also bear mentioning in this connection in that it seems to show that the unconscious has access to the immediate future, especially when it holds emotionally strong events.[111]

This evidence supports the contention that predictive ability is only accurate when the predicted event is 'experienced' in the future of the person making the prediction. Full conscious communication by Dunne's Observer 2, by whatever means, is restricted to the lifetime of Observer 1. It seems that whatever this entity may be, its ability to predict events depends upon the future knowledge of its lower self. However, there is strong evidence that this entity uses its precognitive skills to warn its ignorant partner of future dangers. It may be that taking on the role of a psychic protector becomes the main *raison d'être* of this mystery consciousness.

The dream protector

On 20 October 1966, Eryl Mai Jones woke up in tears. The 9-year-old told her mother of a particularly vivid dream that she had had regarding her school. In her dream she had gone to school as usual, only to find that the building had disappeared. She told her mother that 'something black' had come down all over it. Her mother calmed her down. The next day little Eryl Mai joined her school friends at Aberfan Primary School. She was never to return. On that fateful day half a million tons of coal waste slithered down the hillside and engulfed the school. This black mass killed Eryl Mai and 139 others – most of them children.

Eryl Mai Jones was not alone in foreseeing this tragedy. Although not directly involved in the impending tragedy, many claimed that they too had had dreams outlining the horror. Dr JC Barker of Shelton Hospital in Shrewsbury decided to make a systematic study of these forewarnings and he made an appeal to the general public. Of the 76 letters he received, he managed, through investigation, to confirm 24 cases. When pieced together, the details provided a complete picture of the disaster – including the name of the village, the collapse of the coal tip, and that it would kill many children by suffocation. Barker termed this phenomenon the 'Disaster Early Warning System'.[112]

So here we have two sorts of predictions. The one involves people 'recalling' reading the newspaper reports on Aberfan or seeing the harrowing pictures on television. They were not directly involved and therefore were not affected nor could they effect any change on the events. The second sort is far more disturbing. Here we have a little girl whose Observer 2 is only too aware that if its Observer 1 goes to school that bleak October morning then they both will die. In desperation the entity communicates with its lower self through the medium of a dream. Tragically, it fails and a little life is snuffed out.

Stimulated by this report, researcher WG Cox carried out a remarkable study. He suggested that we all receive these dream-based warnings and in the majority of cases we are saved by our protecting partner. Cox argued that although the premonition of a future disaster may never reach the conscious mind in a recognizable form, it may be strong enough to influence a person's behaviour. Cox selected a number of railway trains involved in major accidents, and obtained data regarding the number of passengers on each train and the total number on the same train on the same run on previous occasions. Analysis of Cox's data suggests that some precognitions of misfortunes may be sufficiently strong to cause changes of mind or cancellation without crossing the threshold of consciousness as a full-blown premonition. Could it be that in the case of little Eryl Mai the entity was so desperate to get the message across that it forced the images into waking consciousness?

There are many cases in which vivid dreams have not only predicted a series of events but have actually brought about a different outcome. For instance, here is a tale told by the American parapsychologist Dr Louisa Rhine:

> *My father was a manufacturer of washing machines and twice a year he would make a trip to the wholesalers and sell them a car load or two of washing machines. He saw dealers in Koekuk and was to take the 10pm train for Davenport. He went to the depot, bought his ticket and then had a feeling that he should not go. It was so strong that he went back to the hotel and stayed in Koekuk overnight. In the morning when eating his breakfast he looked over the paper and found that the train he was supposed to have taken had been wrecked and nearly all the passengers in the smoker had been killed. Dad was an inveterate smoker.*

This feeling that something was against him travelling on that particular train is probably a manifestation of the phenomenon statistically isolated by Cox. If Rhine's subject's father had travelled on that train he may have died or been seriously injured. As such, a potential future ceased to be, but what if a dream manages to avert an accident, or even a death? These next two cases are quite clear in their implications: the message from Dunne's Observer 2 was to save a life!

The first involves another case recorded by Dr Rhine. It tells of a mother who had a particularly vivid dream. In this dream she found herself on a camping holiday with friends. They had decided to pitch their tent next to a river creek. Her dream had her deciding to go and wash some clothes in the water. Taking her baby with her, she made her way down to the water's edge. On arrival she realized that she had left the soap back in the tent. Without thinking, she made her way back to the camp, leaving the child throwing stones into the water. On her return she found her baby floating face down in the waters of the creek. When she pulled him to the shore she found that he was dead. The dream was commented on at the time but was then forgotten. The following summer she went camping with friends. She decided to do some washing, so took her baby down to the nearby creek. She realized that she had forgotten her soap. As she began to walk back she saw the child throwing stones in the water. As she did so, the dream crashed through into her consciousness. Suddenly she could recall the dream in vivid clarity, even to the clothes that her son was wearing. With a shudder she picked up the child and took him back to the tent with her.[113]

The second case is taken from JB Priestley's book *Man and Time*. Priestley, although famous as a playwright and author, also had a fascination with man's relationship with time, particularly in relation to the theories of Dunne. He used his fame by making a request on the radio that if any listeners had a peculiar incident regarding time dilation, precognition or any other related phenomenon, they should write to him. One of the most interesting was sent to him by a lady living in Ireland. The lady in question described the incident in this way:

> In my dream I was driving my car along a road near my home, and quite suddenly, out of nowhere it seemed to me, a little girl of about three years of age appeared right in front of the car. I did all I could but found it impossible to avoid hitting her. On getting out, I was told that she was dead. I looked at her as she lay in the road, and felt completely

shattered, though I never had a chance to save her from what seemed to be her inevitable fate. I must stress that feeling I had of inevitability. When I awoke I realised with horror that I had to drive down that road that very morning on my way to lunch with my youngest daughter, and I decided to be more than usually careful. On approaching the spot, I looked round most carefully for any sign of children. There were none in sight, only five women standing at a bus stop. Relieved beyond words, I glanced down at my speedometer to check and, on lifting my eyes, was completely horrified to see, standing still in the middle of the road, the little girl of my dream, correct in every detail, even to the dark curly hair and the bright blue cardigan she was wearing. I was afraid to use my horn in case I startled her and precipitated what I felt was going to be a fatal accident, so I slowly brought the car to a halt, just beside her. She never moved, but stood staring at me.

Meanwhile the women in the bus queue made no sign of interest, and no one tried to get such a young child off the busy road. In fact they seemed more interested in the fact that I had stopped. Feeling very shaky, I continued on my way, and looking in the mirror, I saw that the child was still standing there and nobody was bothering about her. By the time I got to my daughter's flat I was over half an hour late. When she opened the door she was looking very worried and upset, and said how glad she was to see me safe and sound.

I asked why she had been so worried, as I have been driving for over thirty years, and she looked at me and said 'O I know that Mummie, but you see, last night I had a terribly vivid dream. In this dream you ran over and killed a lovely little girl dressed in a bright blue cardigan and with lovely dark curly hair.'[114]

Priestley was, quite naturally, suspicious of this story with its neat twist at the end, but he had confirmation not only from the writer but also from her husband, to whom she told the story that morning, and the daughter.

Both these cases ensured that the future foreseen in the dream did not come to pass. On both occasions children who were to die were saved by the intervention of the hidden guide. This throws up many questions about causality and fate. Indeed, the whole issue concerned Priestley greatly. As regards the saving of the baby described by Dr Rhine, he wrote:

> *The future can be seen, and because it can be seen it can be changed. But if it can be changed, it is neither solidly there, laid out for us to experience moment by moment, nor is it non-existent, something we help to create moment after moment. If it does exist it cannot be seen; if it is solidly set and fixed, then it cannot be changed. What is this future that is sufficiently established to be observed and perhaps experienced, and yet allow itself to be altered?*[115]

Of course, Priestley was not fully conversant with modern developments in quantum physics. If he were he would have had his answer – Everett's Many Worlds Interpretation. It will be recalled that Hugh Everett proposed that the universe splits into identical copies of itself at each quantum event. Every logical possibility that can happen will happen in one of the universes. Therefore it is reasonable to conclude that the baby boy lived in one universe and died in another. The same goes for the curly-haired little girl. What happened was that the dream precognition changed the future not for either child, but for the observers. It was the future of the mother and the Irish lady that changed. Neither observer can ever know what *actually* happened to the child *from the child's point of view*. This echoes the Tegmark experiment in that the experimenter only dies in the world line of the assistant, but in her world the experimenter survives and writes up her report.

Priestley cites one case in which the dream itself brought about its own fulfilment. In a story that would not be out of place in *The Outer Limits*, Priestley takes the story from a book called *Foreknowledge* by HF Saltmarsh, who in turn took the report from Frederick Myers, one of the founders of the Society for Psychical Research. Myers tells of a woman with a particular dislike of monkeys who, in 1867, had a vivid dream involving a monkey following her. On waking she was quite distressed. The husband, presumably exasperated at his wife's harping on about the dream, suggested that she take the children out for a walk. He said to her that this would take her mind off monkeys and vivid dreams. As this was a rare event, the chance of what then occurred was unlikely in the extreme.

As she was walking along the Grand Union Canal in Regent's Park she noticed a movement on the roof of a nearby coach house. To her absolute horror it was a monkey, as predicted in her dream. She said:

> *In my surprise and terror, I clasped my hands and exclaimed ... 'My dream! My dream!' This I suppose attracted the attention of the monkey and he began to come after us, he on top of the wall, and we beneath, every minute I was expecting he would jump upon me and having precisely the same terror I experienced in my dream.* [116]

She rushed back home and informed her husband of the disturbing encounter. It was subsequently discovered that the monkey was a pet of the eccentric Duchess of Argyll. It had escaped from her lodge that was located nearby. The woman in question, identified simply as 'Mrs C' by Myers, was to wait 21 years before she wrote to Myers in 1888. While Myers was concerned about the time lag, he received independent corroboration of the story from both Mrs C's husband and her nurse. He also found that there had indeed been a monkey at Argyll lodge.

If the woman had not had the dream her husband would not have suggested that she take the children out for a walk. She would have stayed at home and done whatever Victorian ladies of leisure did to pass the time. It was while on the walk that she was followed by the monkey and therefore the dream itself caused the incident it predicted! Again we can argue a case for three alternative futures: a future when the dream did not occur; a future where the dream occurred and she stayed in; and the future that actually happened. One can see, without knowledge of Everett's Many Worlds, how events such as these can cause such confusion.

Sometimes fate simply cannot be avoided. In her book *Beyond Explanation*, researcher Jenny Randles describes a most fascinating case. In 1981, British Rail received a telephone call from a woman who claimed to have had a vision of a fatal crash in which a freight train had been involved. The vision had been so clear that the woman not only described that the diesel engine was blue but also that its number was 47 216. Two years later the described accident did take place. It was exact in every detail but with one small, but crucial difference; the train number was 47 299 not 47 216. In a really bizarre twist it was pointed out by a train spotter that 47 299 was not the original number. He said that it had been renumbered a few years before from 47 216. It seems that British rail, in an effort to ward off the inevitable had had the engine's number changed. Their ruse obviously failed.[117] What is of particular interest is that the woman in question had had an incorrect 'vision'. If she had indeed 'seen' the crash in her mind's eye as it actually took place she would have seen the revised, not original, number. What she saw in her vision was a 'memory' of the information available to her two years in the future. Her 'vision' was of the original number because that is how she recalled the 'memory' of her own future.

So it does seem that this other consciousness, when it can, will use its power to try and ensure that tragedy is avoided, but sometimes it fails. We have already seen the tragic tale of the little Welsh girl who foresaw the Aberfan disaster. There is also evidence that the Observer 2 knows the method and timing of the death of its partner. A particularly fascinating example of this is the tale of Robert Morris.

Robert Morris senior was an American agent for a Liverpool shipping company. His son, Robert junior, was to become one of those responsible for the American Constitution and it is from the son's biography that we learn of the events.

As was his responsibility, Morris senior was awaiting the arrival of a ship at the harbour of Oxford, Maryland. The night before its expected arrival he had a vivid dream in which he was being honoured by a salvo being fired by the ship in question. Unfortunately, he saw himself being mortally wounded from it. He woke up convinced that the dream had been a warning. The next day the ship, the *Liverpool*, docked on time. The master of the ship, Captain Matthews, sent a request ashore that he would like to invite Morris on board. Morris replied explaining about the dream and made the point that his family had a reputation for precognition. The cynical sea dog accused Morris of superstition but agreed that he would not allow any salute to be fired. After some thought Morris agreed to attend a reception in his honour on board the ship. The party went well and Morris was seen to visibly relax. The captain took his opportunity to inform Morris that the crew were disappointed that they could not honour their guest by firing the salute, as was the custom. Morris replied, 'Very well, but do not fire until I or someone else gives the signal.' In due course the time came for Morris to leave. Captain Matthews joined him in the boat that was to row him ashore. As he sat in the boat a fly landed on his nose. Matthews brushed this away with irritation. The gunner assumed that this was the signal to fire the salvo, which he did. As the salute erupted from the gun some wadding flew off, striking Morris on the elbow. He reacted in pain, only to discover that his elbow had been broken. He managed to get ashore but was to die a few days later from an infection.

So it seems that you share your mind with another being, a being that knows everything about you, including what is about to happen to you. It is as if this being has lived your life before and therefore knows in advance any problems, difficulties, or opportunities that may come your way. For some of us this being is communicative, using dreams to warn us of dangers and in doing so changes the future it predicts. It is as if this entity fulfils a similar role in your Everett Universe, as does genetic mutation within evolution. By forewarning you it gives you the chance to change your plans or to be aware of a danger in advance. In doing so you take a different timeline – in effect, the universe splits and your future changes. No doubt another version of you did not heed the warning and the events still took place.

But this gets even stranger. There is not only experimental proof that this entity exists but also that under certain circumstances it can be communicated with using hypnotism. It seems that at a certain level of trance state the hypnotist encounters another consciousness. Called the 'Hidden Observer' by Sanford University's Professor Ernest Hilgard, this being seems identical to Dunne's Observer 2.

The hidden observer

Hilgard has written extensively on the subject of trance states and is convinced that the Hidden Observer really does exist as another aspect of our personality that watches and evaluates our lives.

Hilgard describes a classic test of how this hidden entity is part of our consciousness.[118] He tells of a blind student who was hypnotized and while in a trance state was told that he would become deaf. The suggestion was so strong that he failed to react to any form of noise, even large sounds next to his ear. Of course, he also failed to respond to any questions he was asked while in the trance state. The hypnotist was keen to discover if 'anybody' else was able to hear. He quietly said to the student: 'Perhaps there is some part of you that is hearing my voice and processing this information.' He added, 'If there is, I should like the index finger of your right hand to rise as a sign that this is the case.' The finger rose. At this the student requested that he be brought out of the hypnotically induced period of deafness. On being 'awoken', the student said that he had requested to come out of the trance state because: 'I felt my finger rise in a way that was not a spontaneous twitch, so you must have done something to make it rise, and I want to know what you did.' The hypnotist then asked him what he remembered. Because the trance was light the student never actually lost consciousness: all that occurred was that his hearing ceased. In order to deal with the boredom of being deprived of both sight and sound he decided to work on some statistical problems in his head. It was while he was doing this that he suddenly felt his finger lift. This was obviously strange to him because under normal circumstances he was, like all of us, the 'person' who decides on how the body moves. In this case he was not. Not only that but somebody else in his head was responding to an external request that he had not heard. As far as Hilgard was concerned, the person who responded was the Hidden Observer.

Hilgard then re-hypnotized his subject and spoke directly to the Hidden Observer that had made the man's finger rise. This is what it said:

> *After you counted to make me deaf you made noises with some*
> *blocks behind my head. Members of the class asked me*
> *questions to which I responded. Then one of them asked if I*
> *might not really be hearing, and you told me to raise my*
> *finger, so it is all clear now.*[119]

This is clear evidence that the Hidden Observer is conscious at all times. Hilgard went on to do many other experiments in this area, all of which added weight to his belief. Indeed, there is evidence that this other being is aware of all sensory input to the brain. A classic example of this was when a hypnotized woman had her hand immersed in icy water. Her hypnotized self steadily reported that she felt no pain. The experimenters asked her to grade the pain from 0 to 10. The hypnotized 'self' continued to report a level of 0. But her other hand, with an access to a pencil, reported an increase in pain '0, 1, 2, 4, 7'. Thus the Hidden Observer was not only feeling the pain but evidently became concerned that the hand was about to be ice-burned. On discussing the results of the experiment the subject made the following statement about what she had experienced, making particular reference to what she sensed was her higher self:

> *The hidden observer is cognisant of everything that is going on ... the hidden observer sees more, he questions more, he is aware of what is going on all of the time but getting in touch is totally unnecessary ... He is like a guardian angel that guards you from doing anything that will mess you up ... the hidden observer is looking through the tunnel, and sees everything in the tunnel ... Unless someone tells me to get in touch with the hidden observer I'm not in contact. It's just there.* [120]

Note that she calls her hidden observer a 'guardian angel'. As we have seen, there is evidence that this entity manifests itself in dreams to protect its 'partner'. The subject's curious description of the entity looking down 'a tunnel' is also worth noting.

It appears that the deeper the trance the more chance there is of encountering this being, or so it seems from the work of the American psychologist Charles Tart. In the 1960s and 1970s, Tart was keen to see just how deep a trance state could be brought about by hypnotism. Depth cannot be described solely by the responsiveness to suggestion. In fact, at greater depths responsiveness can disappear. In experiments the subjects were required to assign self-consistent numerical values to the depth they subjectively feel. Tart had a particularly good subject called William who was in the highest 1 percent or 2 percent of hypnotic responsiveness. He had been hypnotized 18 times previously, often with an emphasis on depth. William usually gave reports of 40 or 50, with amnesia experienced at 30. He had never gone beyond 60.

It was agreed that an attempt would be made to take him much deeper than he had gone before. He was instructed that at each 10-point interval on a depth continuum he should remain at that depth while the experimenter had him describe what he was experiencing. As he went through the levels he experienced the normal effects; early relaxation followed by a sensation of distance, an increase in peacefulness and a gradual withdrawal from the environment. Beginning at a level of about 50 on this scale, he began to have distortions of consciousness. These distortions are similar to those reported in mystical experiences. At this stage the passage of time becomes meaningless and the body seems to be left behind and a new sense of infinite potentiality emerges. At a level of 50 another consciousness is experienced, an individual that William described as being him but not him. This 'other' William showed that he was fully aware of the experiment and what was going on. What is strange was that this other being was amused by the attempts of the psychologists to understand the human mind. This event is described as an 'intrusion' by Tart. The other entity accompanied William from level 50 to level 90, where it totally disappeared. It was at its strongest at level 70.[121]

What is of interest here is that the intrusion at the early stages of the now deeper hypnosis of the experience is amused by William's participation in these experiments. Amusement is not something one would expect of the non-dominant hemisphere of the brain.

This seems to be a being that knows exactly what is going on and is observing from a position of superiority not inferiority.

It seems that this being has access to information denied to everyday consciousness, and has great knowledge including, apparently, the future of its own lower partner. In most cases it goes out of its way to warn and protect its charge, although there is evidence that sometimes it simply goes along with fate. Such was the case of the French actress Irene Murza. This deep trance encounter with the Hidden Observer showed, in the clearest terms, its precognitive abilities.

Murza was hypnotized by an associate in order to see if a trance state could assist her in predicting the future. What the hypnotist discovered was both disturbing and ultimately fascinating. When asked what the future held, the actress, or more accurately her Observer 2, was clear and precise. It replied:

My career will be short. I dare not say what my end will be: It will be terrible.

This disturbed the witnesses so much that they agreed that when Murza came out of the trance they would not tell her what had been said. On awaking, the unsuspecting actress was informed that the hypnotic session had been inconclusive. Murza had absolutely no idea of what was to befall her. Her end was indeed terrible; a few months later her hairdresser accidentally spilled some mineral spirits on a lighted stove, causing Murza's hair and clothing to catch fire. Within seconds she was engulfed in flames and died in hospital a few hours later.[122]

Was the communication an attempt by Murza's Hidden Observer to avoid the inevitable? If so, it could have been far more precise in its description of her horrific death. On the other hand, it could be that it, too, was unsure as to what exactly did take place. She was badly burned and took a few hours to die. Could it be that the entity shares not only the mind of its lower self but also its sensory inputs? If so, this higher being would lose all communication with 'reality' whilst its partner slowly died. All it would be aware of would be severe pain and heat and then a loss of signal analogous to a close circuit television camera ceasing to work. It could also be that some entities are more effective at communicating than others. These 'higher entities' encountered during hypnotism seem to be the least communicative, followed by those in dreams. The evidence is that both these types have only short-term precognitive abilities and cannot communicate directly with their 'lower self'. A third sort, however, Socrates 'Divine Sign', and Nostradamus' 'Divine Splendour', seem to be more advanced. They can choose their method of communication and, on occasions, manifest themselves as an image or as a voice.

But who or what is this entity? It seems to exist deep in the subconscious, so it is part of the body it shares with its host. Indeed 'host' is a very misleading term because it implies some form of parasitism. In fact, the relationship is far closer; the entity is an aspect of the everyday person that inhabits consciousness. The relationship is even closer than this because the two beings are the same being: it is just that one has a much wider viewpoint. Indeed, we have already encountered a description of what it is like to be a Hidden Observer.

There are certain logical problems with the predictive abilities of this entity. If it is simply remembering the future, does this not imply that it has lived your life before, Block Universe or otherwise? You may reasonably wonder how it can be aware of the moment of death of its lower self, since presumably the one memory that it is impossible to have is the memory of your own death because consciousness must cease before we know with absolute certainty that we are dead.

When Erickson described the experience of the young man who shared the life of a younger version of himself, he wrote that the subject:

... explained that the experience was literally a moment by moment reliving of his life with only the same awareness he had then and that the highly limited, restricted awareness of himself at 26 was that of being an invisible man watching his own growth and development from childhood on, with no more knowledge of the child's future than the child possessed at any particular age.[123]

Although Erickson says that the 'observer' had no more knowledge than his younger self, he was aware that going to college was of great importance. He did have awareness over and above his 'lower' self; not only that, but it was an awareness of a future event that saw him actually go to college.

Earlier I suggested that you are alone within your own Everett universe, a universe created by your own consciousness. Well, this might not strictly be the case. There is an entity that shares your every thought, sees all that you see and knows exactly what you are going to do today, tomorrow, and the rest of your life. This entity has a purpose. It is the facilitator of changes within your Minkowskian timeline.

You will recall the description of you sitting in the train carriage looking out of the window at the passing scenery, and the possibility that by pressing your nose up against the compartment window you may just be able to glimpse a small part of the future. Imagine how the view would seem from the viewpoint of an entity sitting on the roof of the train, or inside one of those viewing sections found on the Trans-Canadian trains that travel through the Rockies. For that being the future and past can all be viewed as an ongoing present. They can perceive this because they are literally higher than you are. This is what your hidden partner does. It is your 'higher' self and it is here to help. It gives you occasional subconscious guidance and in doing so presents you with an opportunity to change your own future, and places you in another Everett Universe.

This is the biggest secret of all time, a truth that has been known since the time of the ancient Greeks. It may be the single most amazing thing you will come across in your life. May I introduce to you your greatest friend, the Daemon!

CHAPTER 7

Clues from History

Each human being is the dwelling place of an infinite power, the root of the universe.

Mani

The hidden associate

You and I and every Multiverse-based human being consists of two, not one, consciousness. This additional hidden consciousness shares your life and experiences. It revels in your successes and feels the pain of your rejections. From its position in the shadows it tries to help you but cannot, except under unusual circumstances, communicate with you. It gives you guidance through dreams or 'hunches'. It can, on occasions, talk to you and, if your mind is correctly attuned, it can appear to you. All cultures recognize its existence and have done since the dawn of time. It has been termed many things: your Guardian Angel, your Divine Sign, your Hidden Observer, your *Doppelgänger*. But it was the ancient Greeks that first gave it a name. They called it the *Daemon*. To understand the background to both this name and why its existence is virtually unknown, a swift lesson in theological history will be useful, as it is only through the past that the present can be understood.

The idea that a human being consists of mutually independent internal entities is as old as humanity itself. The ancient Chinese called them *hun* and *p'o* and the ancient Egyptians the *ka* and the *ba*. For the builders of the pyramids the equivalent of the consciousness that is reading this book would be the *ba*. This entity calls itself 'I' and is responsible for the animation of the body (termed the *khat*). As such, the *ba* is the everyday personality that interfaces with the outside world, ensuring that the *khat* is fed and watered and communicates with other *bas*. Motivating the *ba* and working closely with it is the *khu*. The *khu* is the holder of the thoughts, emotions, motivations and ambitions of the *ba* – as such it had no real independence of the *ba*. However, the *ka* was a totally independent being that shared the *khat* with its less perceptive compatriots. For the ancient Egyptians this being was a semi-physical presence that although sharing the same physical location as the *khat*, sometimes could be seen poking out around the edges in a slight haze. This is of great interest later when we discuss the concept of *doppelgängers*, because on occasions the *ka* could manifest itself outside of the *khat* and be seen by its own *ba*.

The *ka* was usually depicted in tomb paintings as a small bird with a human face hovering over the body of the deceased. The *ka* was considered to be a form of guardian spirit but an entity that was also an element of the individual, not a discarnate spirit. This is an important concept: the *ka* and the *ba* are in effect the same being, but existing in different locations of time and space.

It is impossible to say whether the Greeks took these ideas of the Egyptians and incorporated them into their own theology, but the similarities cannot be ignored. For them the *ba* and the *khu* were aspects of the same entity, a being that they termed an *eidolon*. The *ka* continued as a totally independent entity called a *daemon*. In echoes that cannot be mere coincidence, the Greeks also saw the *daemon* as being a form of guardian spirit that looked after and, on occasions, assisted its *eidolon*. The *daemon* also had other similar skills to its Egyptian equivalent. It had a habit of poking out of the body, being perceived as what the Greeks termed an *aura*[124] and on occasions it, too, would go walkabout. An example of this belief can be found in Homer's *Iliad*. The Trojan prince, Aeneas, has his hip smashed by a rock. The god Apollo decides that he needs to take the stricken Aeneas back to Troy for medical help. However, the god does not wish the Trojans to know that their hero is no longer on the battlefield and so he:

> *Created a phantom which looked exactly like Aeneas and was armed as he was. Round the phantom,*[125] *the Trojans and the brave Achaeans hacked at each other's leather shields.*[126]

The idea of this *daemon-eidolon* duality was to fascinate the ancient Greeks and soon a whole philosophy of universal structure was to be built around this relationship. The earliest-known writer on the subject was Empedocles. For him the *daemon*, although semi-imprisoned in the body, is a divine being exiled from its rightful place among the gods. It exists independently of its lower self, or *eidolon*, and has great knowledge and power.[127] Our knowledge of this belief really comes from the writings of Plato and his descriptions of the teachings of his master, Socrates.

Plato tells that throughout his life his great teacher had assistance from a 'guide'. Socrates called this discarnate voice his Divine Sign. From childhood this voice had communicated to him its opinions on what he was doing – or intended to do. According to Plato this 'voice' forbade Socrates to do things and regularly gave prognostications on whether good or bad luck would follow a certain action. It is as if Socrates' Divine Sign was directly aware of the philosopher's potential future. Plato was at great pains to point out that many of these predictions were marked by extreme triviality, as if this spirit was tied very closely to the minutiae of Socrates' life.[128] Socrates explained this in the following speech to the jury who were about to condemn him to death:

> *I have had a remarkable experience. In the past the prophetic voice to which I have become accustomed has always been my constant companion, opposing me even in quite trivial things if I was going to take the wrong course.*

In this final act, Socrates was to find that his Divine Sign did not oppose him. It was as if his lifelong guide and mentor was resigned to the inevitable; Socrates had to die as decreed both by fate and the jury. The hemlock goblet could not be avoided. The voice remained silent.

Even so, the idea that all human beings have two independent elements continued. The theology proposed by Empedocles and refined by Socrates was to find many followers in the ancient Greek world and was to become a central tenet of the school of philosophy that was to become known as Stoicism. Founded by Zeno of Citium in around 300 BCE, this philosophy was to carry through to the later Roman Empire and also have a great influence on certain Christian groups. It acquired its curious name from the fact that its original adherents used to meet under the *Stoa Poikile* (Painted Colonnade) in Athens. Its major attraction was that its teachings transcended the boundaries of race, status or sex and stated that all men and women were equal. Equality existed because for Stoics all mankind had a dual nature and that divinity could be found in each individual. This belief can be found in the teachings of one of its most influential philosophers, Epictetus. As with Socrates and Empedocles, nothing remains of his original writings, although his pupil Arrian wrote down his teachings, recording them in two works: *Discourses* and the *Encheiridion* (or *Manual*). In these works it is clear that he had taken the evidence of Socrates' Divine Sign and the old belief of human duality and created a cogent philosophy. He wrote:

> God has placed at every man's side a guardian, the Daemon of
> each man, who is charged to watch over him; a Daemon that
> cannot sleep, nor be deceived. What greater and more watchful
> guardian could have been committed to us? So, when you have
> shut the doors, and made darkness in the house, remember,
> never to say that you are alone; for you are not alone. But God
> is there, and your Daemon is there.[129]

Here we see the idea that this other entity, the *daemon*, is more than simply another facet of human nature. It is an independent being that watches over its lower self. That it has an ongoing consciousness is stated by the phrase 'cannot sleep'. Indeed, the implication is that the *daemon* perceives even when the *eidolon* sleeps.

This belief was not unique to Epictetus or even the Stoics. According to the noted historian of the late classical and early Christian period, Robin Lane-Fox, the Romans had an ancient but popular belief that each man had his own attendant 'spirit' that followed him throughout his life. This being, termed his *genius*, was born with him and as such was honoured by each individual, on his birthday.[130]

Some find the word 'daemon' (or 'daimone' as it is sometimes written) disturbing because it is similar to the word 'demon' and indeed this was exactly the intention of the early Christians who first used the term. The concept of the *daemon* was a potential heresy that had to be suppressed and denigrated. The most simple and effective device for doing this is semantics; take the word and apply it to another concept and given enough time, people will make one association only: d(a)emon equals an evil incarnate spirit that has been spawned by the devil to tempt man away from the true God. However, this is not how the ancient Greeks saw the meaning of the word. The ancient Greek word was *daimön*, meaning deity, or god, and as such they saw the word in a very positive, or at least ambivalent, way. The Romans latinized the Greek word, turning it into *daemon*.

Even at this time, as supported by its usage by Epictetus, the concept remained positive. To the Romans a *daemon* was an inner or attendant spirit that sometimes gave humble man a touch of genius (hence the term 'the demon of creativity'). This semantic playfulness was not unusual within religions during ancient times. *Baal* was the chief fertility god of the Semitic peoples who had not followed Judaism. Indeed, the word *bà'al* is Hebrew for 'lord' or 'master'. Baal as a God was literally demonized by the Israelites and was to become, within later Christianity, an attendant to Satan. To show just how effective this semantic manipulation can be, one can cite the example of the Assyrian version of Baal, *Baal-Peor*. In time the name became corrupted to that of *Belphegor*. In medieval times the demon Belphegor was a busy denizen of the hordes of hell. His job was to test rumours concerning the happiness of married life on earth. And so a great fertility god of ancient times had been demoted to that of some form of infernal gossipmonger.

It is understandable that non-Judeo-Christian gods were put down in such a way, but less clear as to why a much less threatening concept of the *daemon* should be so treated. On the face of it, the *daemon* seems little more than a pagan version of a guardian angel. The problem seems to have begun when this pagan concept was refined and Christianized by a heretical sect, the Gnostics.

As is widely known, Christianity did not come fully formed from the teachings of Jesus. The historical Jesus never wrote a single word, and the description of his life and work was carried forward as an oral tradition to be later transcribed by others. The Gospels of Matthew, Mark, Luke and John were all written many years after Christ's death and by unknown individuals who never actually met him. These men used secondary sources such as the stories circulating within the nascent Christian community. With the exception of John, it is clear that the three Synoptic Gospels were copied from each other, although the debate is still raging as to which is the oldest. Biblical scholars consider that there is another source, yet undiscovered, that each synoptic writer used. This is called 'Q' (from the German word *Quelle*, which means 'source'). The earliest known actual writings are the letters of Paul, a known historical figure, but he readily admitted that he never actually knew Jesus, receiving his knowledge of the

Lord in a vision on the road to Damascus. Notwithstanding, it is Paul's version of the theology of Christ that was to move Christianity away from being a small Jewish sect to become the religion of an empire.

Those who gnu about the two

By the 2nd century CE, Christianity was in a fair degree of disarray. The lack of any writings by Jesus had led to a proliferation of documents, gospels, tracts and other assorted pieces of writings, all of which could be considered as indirect revelation from the incarnate Son of God. This led to many conflicting ideas and interpretations. These differing groups can be broadly categorized into two different schools. The main school was what can be loosely termed the 'literalists'. They believed that Jesus was an actual man who had lived and died in Palestine and that he was God made flesh. They also took his teachings at face value. It was this school that became successful across the Roman Empire and was adopted as the state religion in the 4th century CE. From this position of strength the literalist school eventually became the Catholic Church. The offshoots of this monolith, Orthodox Christianity and Protestantism, followed the same line. The other school, termed the Gnostics, disappeared from history and, with certain notable exceptions such as the Cathars and Bogomils (*see* pages 198-201), their ideas largely died out. Unlike the literalists, the Gnostics took a far more radical position, one that could not be tolerated by the more conservative literalists.

The word 'Gnostic' gives a clue to their approach. The designation, which was never used by the Gnostics themselves, is derived from the Greek word *gnöstikos* (one who has *gnösis* or 'hidden knowledge'). However, because the school was persecuted out of existence by the triumphant Roman Church, very little Gnostic teaching was available for study. Moreover, until recently that evidence was highly biased and unreliable. The only information available on Gnosticism came from the writings of the early church fathers, the bulk of which was the work of Irenaeus. In his volume, *Against the Heresies*, Irenaeus attacks with great venom such representatives of Gnostic Christianity as Cerinthus, Valentinus, Basilides and Marcion. Before he attacks the teachings of the Gnostics, Irenaeus gives a description of their beliefs, the only description available until 1945, when a chance discovery was to rejuvenate interest in this sect.

In December of that year some Egyptian villagers from the township of Nag Hammadi had made their way to a spot beneath the cliffs of the Jabal al-Tarif. They were looking for *sabakh*, birdlime, and the foot of cliffs is an ideal place to seek deposits – for obvious reasons. One of the group spotted an earthenware jar near a large boulder. The jar contained a whole library of ancient manuscripts, none of them later than the 4th century CE, and the oldest were judged to be from the 1st and 2nd centuries. Most of the texts were Coptic (Egyptian) translations of Gnostic texts originally written in Greek. Although Irenaeus and other hostile church fathers such as Justin Martyr had referred to many of them in their writings, some were completely unknown. The careful burial of the scrolls demonstrated the love and respect those responsible had for them. It is believed that the process had been executed by Gnostics, possibly monks, in response to the harder line been taken by the authorities as to what was, and what was not, to be believed. To those caught in possession of them they were a potential death sentence.

Had the jar's discoverer, Ali al-Sammān, been able to read and understand Coptic his eyes would have alighted on the following words:

> *I shall give you what no hand has seen and what no ear has heard and what no hand has touched and what has never occurred to human mind.*[131]

It was to be many years before any eyes would read these powerful words since it was not until 1966 that the Colloquium on the Origins of Gnosticism, meeting in Sicily, decided that a full translation of the *Nag Hammadi* texts should be published. Conflicts in the Middle East were to lead to a further delay. In 1972, the first photographic edition was published, followed by nine other volumes. The complete set was available in 1977.[132] Scholars could at last read what the Gnostics themselves considered to be their world view.[133] No longer did researchers have to depend on the biased accounts of their adversaries – here was a literal treasure trove of information. This was a collection of original texts that were most certainly in circulation within the Christian World, texts that had been deliberately excluded from the canon of the New Testament. These included gospels attributed to Thomas and Philip, texts recording the acts of Peter and the Twelve disciples, apocalypses attributed to Paul and James and many other smaller texts.

So why were these people hounded to extinction, and why were their ideas considered so dangerous that their texts suffered from extreme censorship and exclusion from the present New Testament? And, more importantly, why is it that even now, some 60 years after their discovery and over 30 years after they were translated into English, these documents remain unknown to the vast majority of Christians?

The texts portray a religious movement that arose during the 1st century CE. At that time it seems to have had a following among the Hellenized Greek-speaking Jews of the Diaspora (those Jews living outside of the Holy Land). Their intellectual centre was Alexandria in Egypt, a city open to both new ideas and ancient ones filtering up from the upper reaches of the Nile. They did not term themselves Gnostics. Their self-designation varied: the Saints, the Children of Light, the Perfect Ones – terms also used by the early Christians and that other interesting group, the Essenes.

The realm of the Demiurge

According to the documents, the Gnostics believed that the universe was under the influence of two conflicting forces: the Light and the Darkness. Human beings are in turn a reflection of this duality. Our soul is a spark that comes from the Light; it is a part of the positive side. However, our bodies are made up of matter and matter is part of the Darkness. As such, there is this ongoing conflict within the human condition. The soul is imprisoned in this body of darkness but it retains memories of its divine origin. God, the source of the Light, sends out his angels, who have the power to lead the soul back to its real home, the abode of Light or Paradise. The Gnostics believed, and this is one of the major areas of conflict with Roman Christianity, that the true God did not make the world. They came to this conclusion by questioning the fact that if God is good, why does he allow evil to exist in a world that he himself created? How can a good God not only tolerate, but also create evil as part of his universe? Christians and Jews answer this question by saying that man causes evil. For the Gnostics this was not good enough. They argued that God created man and therefore he cannot avoid the ultimate responsibility. Consequently, they concluded that the God who created the World in the Old Testament erroneously believed himself to be the ultimate God. For the Gnostics there is a greater God, a supreme creature of pure Goodness and Light, a God that is not tainted by matter in any way. This supreme God has no human features and men can only reach him through the divine spark in themselves. The God that calls himself Yahweh is not this ultimate being – he is simply too human. He has temper tantrums and fits of jealousy. In the Old Testament, Yahweh proclaims: 'I am a jealous God, and there is no other God besides me'.[134] In response to this, the Gnostic *Secret Book of John* calls this 'madness' and comments:

> *By announcing this he indicated to the angels that another*
> *God does exist; for if there were no other one, of whom is he*
> *jealous?*[135]

This is a God that is all too human; he also has a physical side. Moses sees him and his voice is heard many times. To the Gnostics this is simply impossible unless this God is not all he believes himself to be.

The basic Gnostic myth has many variations, but all of these refer to Aeons, intermediate deific beings who exist between the ultimate, True God and ourselves. They, together with the True God, comprise the realm of Fullness (*Pleroma*) wherein the potency of divinity operates fully. The Fullness stands in contrast to our existential state, which in comparison may be called emptiness.

One of the aeonial beings, Sophia ('Wisdom'), is of great importance to the Gnostic world-view. In the course of her journeying, Sophia came to emanate from her own being a flawed consciousness, a being who became the creator of the material and psychic cosmos, all of which he created in the image of his own flaw. This being, unaware of his origins, imagined himself to be the ultimate and absolute God, and he took the already existing divine essence and fashioned it into various forms. The Gnostic writer Valentinus, adopting a term used by Plato in *Timaeus*, called this lesser god, Yahweh, 'The Demiurge' or 'half-maker'. Valentinus derogatorily termed Yahweh as 'The Builder', meaning that Yahweh had created the material, sensory world from material supplied by somebody else, as a builder creates a house from stones and wood. However, he is unaware that deep within his greatest creation, man, lies the spark of the true God.

As far as the Gnostics were concerned, the whole of the physical world, the creation of the Demiurge, was part of the Darkness. The only way that the inner soul of man could reach the True Light was by avoiding the powers of evil. He could only do this by inner knowledge gained by study and understanding of closely guarded secrets, 'the mysteries' conveyed by angels to the select few, those who had the Knowledge or *Gnōsis*.

In general terms, this viewpoint of Yahweh, although not in keeping with received wisdom, was probably not an insurmountable issue to their fellow Christians. But it was of great concern to the Jewish community who must have been unimpressed by being told that their God was an insane demagogue. What was of much greater concern was the overall status of Jesus in this dualist world-view. Jesus was God made flesh and as such had a physical, and therefore implicitly evil, corporal presence. If he was the Son of God, which God?

A major problem we have in understanding the Gnostic position on the divinity of Jesus is that we mainly have the negative comments of Irenaeus to go by. The earliest Nag Hammadi texts seem to be from around 100 CE. By this time it is likely that the influence of mainstream Christian thought had imposed itself upon Gnostic beliefs. It is likely that those who buried the texts in the 4th or 5th century CE would have carefully selected which texts to bury and which to destroy. One can only assume that they were Christians who were living in a time when Roman Christianity was fully in the ascendancy, and as such they may have exercised their own censorship. It is interesting to note that although Jesus is given some prominence in many of the texts, he is portrayed primarily as a teacher and preacher. Very little is said about Jesus' life on Earth.

The descriptions in the texts are very much in keeping with those outlined by Irenaeus: that in the beliefs of the Gnostics Jesus was not really a human being. He was a divine person who only 'seemed' like a man. This was the downfall of the Gnostics. In the eyes of mainstream Christians this was, and one assumes still is, heresy. That Jesus was born of woman, lived, and died on the Cross is central to Christian belief. To accept that he only 'seemingly' was a man implies that he did not suffer on the Cross and, more importantly, as a non-human being he could not have atoned for man's sins. This belief was termed the 'docetic' heresy, a word derived from the Greek verb *dokein* ('to seem'). This could not be tolerated and it is these beliefs that ensured that their version of Christianity was censored and quietly incorporated into the main body of the Christian Church.

Some modern scholarship considers that the 'Christianity' of the Gnostics was in fact a later development and that the original beliefs of the Gnostics were based upon the much older, pagan mystery cults. In reality it is almost certain that Gnosticism was based upon something far more enigmatic than Christianity, something that has direct relevance to our world, a bridge between us and the great unknown.

If one takes away the Christian additions within the Nag Hammadi texts, it is possible to have glimpses of what these greater mysteries involved – the mysteries that allowed the spark to reach up to the realm of light. Many cryptic statements are made, an example of which is the advice that the Gnostic sage Silvanus gives. He advises that the seeker should:

> *Knock on yourself as upon a door and walk upon yourself as a straight road. For if you walk on the road, it is impossible for you to go astray. Open the door for yourself so that you may know what is.* [136]

It appears that Gnosticism was about looking into yourself to seek enlightenment from within; discovering the spark of the eternal Light within your soul. This is again an application of the overall dualism of Gnosticism, a belief that has its roots far deeper in human memory than the 1st century CE. Gnosticism was simply an adapted form of these ancient beliefs, the 'mystery religions'.

Two into one does go

Central to the beliefs of these mystery cults was the duality of man, the concept intimated earlier in this chapter in the ideas of Epictetus. It is here that we come back to our concept of the Daemon. This entity was part of the pagan duality but was easily incorporated into the philosophy of Gnosticism. The Daemon is the spark, that part of you and me that is also a part of the Realm of Light. However, the Daemon is only part of a duality within each person. There is a part of the human consciousness that is rooted in the world of Darkness. It is here that we reintroduce the concept of the Eidolon, a word that had been originally used to describe an image or statue of a god. In turn it became associated with a copy of something divine. This copy looked like the original but lacked all the qualities. For the pagan sages this was a perfect description for the part of the human duality that was trapped in the Realm of Darkness – the Eidolon. This is the embodied self, the physical body and the personality; this is the person. This 'lower self' is mortal and is totally unaware, unless initiated into the mysteries, of its higher self. It is very much part of this world of darkness and is a slave to emotion and all the other ills that beset the physical being. The Daemon, on the other hand, is the immortal self. This Daemon is always with the Eidolon and where possible, tries to assist and guide, although it is dangerous for the Eidolon to know of the existence of its other self without gnosis.

There are times when the Daemon has to make itself seen or heard. Usually this takes place with the semi-initiated individual. In these circumstances the Eidolon will perceive the Daemon to be some form of guardian angel or spirit guide. As Plato teaches:

> *We should think of the most authoritative part of the soul as the Guardian Spirit given by God which lifts us to our heavenly home.*[137]

The Gnostic sages carried this belief forward in its entirety. Valentinus taught that a person receives gnosis from their Guardian Angel but in reality that being is simply that person's own higher self.[138] This implies that the angels that communicate between the World of Light and the World of Darkness are not independent beings at all; they are Daemons from this world. We are our own teachers.

Once this link is made, the evidence for duality within Gnosticism is compelling. Mani, the founder of an eastern Gnostic religion in northern Babylonia, melded sections of traditional Iranian religion to create a new version, Manichaeism. Mani was born near Baghdad in 216 CE into a family related to the Persian royal house. He had been brought up as a member of a sect known as the *almughtasila* ('those who wash themselves'). As a boy he received a revelation in 228 CE from a spirit that he described as 'a twin'. Around 240 CE, the 'twin' appeared again and urged him to preach what he had learned. This visitation involved an interaction with a more focused and knowing version of himself. Mani explained that this 'twin' taught him:

> *Who I am and what my body is, and how my arrival at this*
> *world occurred ... Who is my father on high and what order*
> *and commission he gave me before I put on this material body*
> *and before I was led astray in this abominable flesh ... Who is*
> *my inseparable twin ... He revealed it to me to, the boundless*
> *heights and the unfathomable depths.*[139]

According to Robin Lane-Fox, this twin concept was not unique to the teachings of Mani. The idea of the duality of the world being reflected within the human mind was also to be found in various heretical sects in Syria. In keeping with these dualist beliefs, Mani taught that there was a primeval conflict between the realms of light and darkness, in which the material world represents the invasion of the realm of light by the realm of darkness. For Mani, the purpose of religion was to release the particles of light imprisoned in matter. This is an amazing belief, taking into account what we now know about matter. The mathematician Sir James Jeans suggested in the early 1930s that what we call light is really matter moving at its fastest possible speed, and that to move matter at this speed requires *infinite* power. As he pictured it, the moment this infinite energy is reduced and the speed of matter slows down, it ceases to be light and becomes 'matter'. He termed matter 'bottled light' and he termed light 'unbottled matter'.[140] Can it be that Mani, writing over 1,700 years ago, had awareness of the ultimate nature of matter? If this is so then his teachings on the possible dual nature of human consciousness should be taken very seriously.

Manichaeism and Gnostic Christianity also share a great deal, not only in terms of their philosophies but also in the fact that both fell foul of the religion that they were closest to. In terms of Manichaeism, the religion concerned was Zoroastrianism, a religion with an even greater idea of dualism than Christianity. However, it is how Mani describes his spirit guide that reinforces the concept of the Daemon. Mani said that his heavenly twin was 'the most beautiful and largest mirror image of his own person'.[141]

The concept of the twin is to be found in many of the Nag Hammadi documents. What is even more curious is that some of these refer to Jesus himself as having a twin. The *Acts of John* has a particularly interesting passage. John writes:

> *When all of his disciples were sleeping in one house at Gennesaret, I Alone, having wrapped myself up, watched from under my garment what he did; and first I heard him say,'John, go thou to sleep', and thereupon I feigned to be asleep; and I saw another like into him come down, whom I also heard saying to my Lord, 'Jesus, do they whom thou hast chosen still not believe in thee?' And my Lord said, 'Thou sayest well for they are men'.*[142]

Gnostic teaching, as a mystery religion, was oblique in its symbolism. For them Jesus symbolized the Daemon in that he was a transposed being from the Realm of Light. Within the controversy of docetism, Jesus was a visible Daemon who by his very nature could not have a body. By contrast, according to Gnostic belief he did have an Eidolon, represented in the role of his twin brother Thomas. In *The Book of Thomas* the Contender Jesus (Daemon) teaches Thomas (Eidolon):

> *Brother Thomas, while you have time in the world, listen to me, and I will reveal to you the things you have pondered in your mind. Now since it has been said that you are my twin and true companion, examine yourself and learn who you are, in what way you exist, and how you will come to be. Since you will be called my brother, it is not fitting that you be ignorant of yourself. And I know that you have understood, because you have already understood that I am the knowledge of the truth.*
> *So while you accompany me, although you are uncomprehending, you have in fact already come to know, and you will be called 'the one who knows himself.[143]*

The allegorical content is thinly disguised here. The name Thomas is Aramaic for 'Twin'. There is a further potential play on words that may contain a hidden Gnostic message, and this can be found in the Authorized Version of the Bible. It revolves around the incident where Pilate offers the crowd the choice between Jesus and Barabbas. The name Barabbas is generally agreed to mean 'son of the father' (Aramaic *Bar Abba*), and in Matthew's version of the incident, the name appears in some ancient manuscripts as 'Jesus Barabbas'. This was the reading of Matthew 22:16 that was accepted by the early Church, and attested by one of the church fathers, Origen, in the 3rd century. He distrusted its origin on grounds that he knew of no sinful man with the name Jesus! Even so, it is considered by many Biblical scholars to be the original reading of the name. If this is to be accepted then the crowd was given the option of choosing, Jesus, son of the father, or Jesus, son of the father. With a choice like that, Pilate was in the position of having to crucify whichever one of the two men he saw fit. However, if this was a subtle Gnostic insertion that was missed by the censors then what we have is a very clever re-working of the twin myth: Jesus symbolizing the Daemon, and Barabbas the Eidolon.

Gnosticism was a structured and intellectually attractive view of the world. It explained the existence of evil and gave man hope for future perfection. Nevertheless, it had within it the seeds of its own destruction. The evidence shows that it was an inclusive, not exclusive religion. Individuals had to choose to join. Initiates to the mysteries had a far from passive role, and since the central concept of Gnostic philosophy was knowledge, they had to study and follow rigorous intellectual exercises. As an alternative, Roman Christianity was a much easier route to salvation. Followers could literally be followers; the elite clergy of Popes, archbishops, bishops and priests did the thinking for the masses. Attend church and receive the sacraments, live a life within the rules laid down and you will go to heaven. As the Roman Empire disintegrated and the Mongols, Vandals and Visigoths murdered their way across the remnants of Pax Romana, people did not have time for aesthetic pursuits. Religion needed to be received, and that was it. Simple survival was the order of the times. Thus Gnosticism died out, not just as a consequence of attacks by the Church but from a myriad of sociological and cultural factors.

So the two parallel, but unrelated, forms of Dualism died out. An interesting last vestige of classical civilization appeared to have ended.

The not so Languedoc

In July 1209, the tranquil and beautiful part of what is now southern France was visited by a vortex of bloodletting the like of which would not be seen again in Europe until the dark days of the 'Final Solution'. The peaceful hills of the Languedoc were to ring with screams and its mountain air to be adulterated by the stench of burning flesh. An army of 30,000 knights and foot soldiers moved into this area. They destroyed crops, towns and cities were rased to the ground, and a whole population put to the sword. This horror continued unabated until March 1244, when it came to a painful end in the barren, windswept mountain citadel of Montségur.

In 1208, Pope Innocent III had declared a Crusade against a group of heretics called Albigensians. This name had been given to them after an ecclesiastical council in the Languedoc town of Albi condemned them as heretics in 1165. The initiates of this sect called themselves Cathari, or the 'purified ones', and because they stressed the Christian values of humility and charity they attracted many followers. The Church, in condemning them at Albi, had given a strong message that this schism would not be tolerated and strong measures were to be taken to stamp it out. This met with a fair degree of success but in the Languedoc, under the protection of the Counts of Toulouse, Catharism flourished. This was all to change in 1209, when the first major town to fall to the invaders was Béziers, where at least 15,000 men, women and children were slaughtered wholesale. The fanatical zeal by which these atrocities were perpetrated caused the papal representative, in a letter to Innocent, to announce proudly that 'neither age nor sex nor status was spared'.

After Béziers, Perpignan, Narbonne, Carcassonne and Toulouse were all to be visited with the same savagery. For 35 years Languedoc became the place in Europe where men could do all kinds of evil and receive God's blessing. As the Pope had declared this venture to be a crusade, the rewards were the same as those available by fighting in the Holy Land, and it did not involve a sea journey. Individuals could pull on a red-crossed tunic and literally walk to salvation and, more importantly, potential riches. For the reward of the remission of all sins, an expiation of penances and an assured place in heaven, all they had to do was fight for no more than 40 days. Another incentive was the automatic ownership of all the booty that they could lay their hands on.

By 1243, all major Cathar towns and bastions had fallen to the invaders, except for a handful of remote and isolated strongholds. Major among these was the majestic mountain citadel of Montségur. For 10 months the invaders besieged Montségur: standing upon an almost sheer rock rising some 500 feet from the surrounding plain, the citadel stood firm. In the end, time took its toll and on 2 March, 1244 Pierre-Roger of Mirepoix, the leader of the defenders, was compelled to sue for a 15-day truce. On 16 March, the Cathars finally surrendered the castle to the Archbishop of Narbonne and the Seneschal of Carcassonne. On that day 225 people, male and female, were taken to a stake below the rock and summarily burned alive. This was the effective end of Catharism, although there is evidence that small groups survived, living in caves and mounting a sporadic, but bitter, guerrilla war against their persecutors.

So how did this outburst of bloodletting and religious intolerance erupt in such an obscure part of France, and what had the inhabitants of this area done to reap such a whirlwind? The reason was quite simple: Gnosticism had not died out as the Church had hoped. The belief had held true in small communities in the Balkans and had survived through the Dark Ages as a secret church, an esoteric belief system at odds with, yet uncomfortably similar to, official Christianity. It was to come out of the shadows in the 10th century when a humble Bulgarian priest named Bogomil established a church openly espousing dualist beliefs. During the 11th and 12th centuries it spread rapidly through many European and Asian provinces of the Byzantine Empire. Such was the concern of the Orthodox authorities that in 1100 many prominent Bogomils were tried and imprisoned. This culminated in the public burning of their leader, Basil.

There is evidence that many crusaders returning from the Second Crusade (1147–9) had become exposed to Manichaeism. To the more open-minded of them this belief was attractive, as it rationalized why evil exists in a world created by a good god. The Cathars accepted the dualist philosophy as advocated by Mani, the Bogomils and the Gnostic sages. To them the physical world was intrinsically evil, created by the Demiurge. They re-named the Demiurge 'Rex Mundi', the 'King of the World'. They also accepted the dualism of the human personality and so continued the belief in the Daemon and the Eidolon. The belief that salvation was available through personal growth and inward knowledge was as antithetical to Church teaching in the 12th century as it was in the 3rd.

Knowledge of God could only be gained through the intercession of intermediaries, be they priests or popes. This 'do it yourself' religion, if it became too popular, would do away with the need for a 'professional' clergy, which was not a situation that the princes of the Church would look on kindly from their palaces.

Catharism had proven itself popular and in the face of continued hostility from both ecclesiastical and civil authorities, the Cathari had still managed to form themselves into an organized church. Bogomil missionaries had been active since the early years of the century and had sown the seeds well. In about 1149, the first Cathari bishop established himself in the north of France; a few years later he established colleagues in Albi and in Lombardy. Their status was recognized in 1167 when the Bogomil bishop Nicetas visited Albi. By this time the ecclesiastical conference at Albi, chosen because of the strength of the Cathar presence in that town, had condemned the sect as heretical (1149). Even so, this failed to stop the spread of the heresy. By the turn of the century there were 11 bishoprics in all, 1 in the north of France, 4 in the south, and 6 in Italy.

The action by Innocent III was not just against a small group of heretics in the South of France. It was a message to all of Christendom that neo-Manichean dualism would not be tolerated. After the disaster at Montségur, the remaining Cathari had to go underground. While some stayed to fight a small-scale guerrilla war, many others sought sanctuary in Italy, where persecution, although evident, was less common. By the 1270s, the hierarchy had faded out and by the 15th century Catharism had disappeared from view.

The way in which Gnosticism, Manichaeanism, the Bogomils and Cathari all seemed just to fade away seems peculiar. All suffered great persecution but so have many other religions – most notably, Christianity itself. It is unclear why a belief that has such a degree of rationalism attached to it erupted with such power on the historical stage, only to disappear again with equal rapidity. Some scholars argue that the Bogomils and the Cathari were forerunners of certain Protestant groups such as the Anabaptists and the Hussite Brethren. However, these groups are extreme fundamentalists, accepting totally the literal truth of the Old Testament. In the face of this it is clear that the Cathari and Bogomil belief that the God of the Israelites was a god of Evil would be totally unacceptable to them. It may be that the answer is far more intriguing – these groups did not die away at all but continue among us even to this day.

The answer lies in the reason why these dualistic religions, churches of extreme asceticism, became so popular. As we have seen, the central belief of all these neo-Gnostic groups is that matter is evil. It is only by the total ascetic renunciation of the world that purity can be regained and the soul commune with the true God of light. Accordingly, strict rules had to be followed: fasting, including the total prohibition of meat, total sexual abstinence, and avoidance of all alcohol. But would this be the way to attract the masses? The faithful were divided into two groups, the 'believers' and the 'perfect', or *parfaits*. The perfect were set apart from the mass of believers by a ceremony of initiation known as the *consolamentum*. These individuals then pursued a life of extreme asceticism given over to study and contemplation. This was in keeping with the Gnostic belief that religious or mystical experience must be apprehended at first hand, not through priests or received wisdom. The believers, on the other hand, were not expected to attain the standards of the *parfaits*. Thus when disaster strikes and persecution takes place it is the believers that usually fade away; the *parfaits* do not. They go underground and seek out others to carry forward their beliefs. These individuals become initiates into what is, in effect, a secret society. When circumstances are right and the wider culture is open to such beliefs, dualism again becomes popular.

The view from inside

Here we have consistent evidence that human beings consist of two, quite separate, personalities, the Daemon and the Eidolon. One, the everyday personality, called the *Ba* by the Ancient Egyptians, lives its life in a linear fashion. It travels along its Minkowskian time line minute by minute. It has no knowledge of the future and focuses the majority of its attention on ensuring the survival of its body. The other, termed the *Ka* by the Egyptians, is an entity that perceives reality and the world in a totally different way. It shares the senses of its *Ba* but has a much greater awareness of other things. For example, it knows all that is going to be perceived by its lower self. In effect, it can see the future.

We now have new terms for these two aspects of the mind. Instead of using such terms as Observer 1 and Observer 2 or the Hidden Observer, Gnosticism and the Ancient Greeks have presented us with the far more accurate terms of 'eidolon' and 'daemon'. I feel that these terms should be personalized and capitalized – from now on we will use the idea of the Eidolon and the Daemon.

You are the Eidolon within your own universe, but you are no longer alone because watching over your every move is the Daemon. It knows your past and your future and, if you listen, it will guide you.

The anecdotes we have read in this book suddenly make sense when reviewed in the light of this discovery. We now know why it is that Mother Shipton and Robert Nixon could only predict the future that was likely to take place in their own respective lifetimes. They both attuned to the 'memories' of their respective Daemons. Evidently, even a being such as the Daemon cannot know of events that take place after its death, but it knows in detail the things that it knows of whilst alive.

Nostradamus is more interesting. You will recall that he was quite specific about the source of his predictive abilities. He wrote:

> *The wand in hand is placed in the middle of the legs of the tripod.*

> *He sprinkles both the hem of his garment and his foot with water.*

> *A voice: Fear: he trembles in his robes.*

> *Divine Splendour. The God sits beside him.*

In this quatrain, Nostradamus attempts to explain the source of his predictions. It seems that a 'voice' talks to him and he senses the presence of another being. Can this voice be that of Nostradamus' Daemon? If so, it is a curious coincidence. Nostradamus calls this being Divine Splendour. Earlier in this chapter we discussed Socrates and his life-long guiding spirit. Socrates, who insisted that this being had predictive abilities and had assisted him on many occasions, called this entity his Divine Sign.

These 'voices' have been heard throughout history. For instance, Joan of Arc's 'voices' told her when, where and how she would be wounded. These were noted down at the time and their accuracy later confirmed. It may be that these entities assisted in the precognition of Mother Shipton, Robert Nixon and Nostradamus. Perhaps the researchers into clairvoyance and precognition have been simply looking in the wrong place.

Human duality has been a theological concept since ancient times and has carried through the ages in a constant and consistent format, but religion is by its nature a subjective and, in most cases, non-rational system. It deals with unknown and non-measurable facets of human understanding. This in no way detracts from the veracity of those who claim a religious experience but is simply a statement of fact. That individuals subjectively believe that they are a dual rather singular being cannot be scientifically proven. The following chapter approaches this same topic from the scientific side. Can the Eidolon-Daemon dialectic be 'proven' via neurology, psychology and anatomy?

CHAPTER 8

Evidence of Cohabitation

Mind Has Mountains

Cliffs of fall

Frightful, sheer, no-man fathomed.

Gerard Manley Hopkins

Wigan's chosen few

In the late 1830s a peculiar discovery was made, a discovery that was to be the first clue to the existence of the secret squatter living in our personal attic. Dr AL Wigan was involved in what should have been a fairly routine *post mortem* examination. The body in question was that of a man who had no history of mental illness or indeed any behavioural traits that made him in any way unusual. However, on opening the skull Wigan found he was a good deal more than unusual – bizarre would be a more accurate term – because on looking into the cranium Wigan discovered only one hemisphere when he was naturally expecting two. The Victorian pioneer had no option but to conclude that this man had lived a perfectly normal life with only half a brain! What Wigan had found was the first recorded instance of extreme one-hemisphere dominance.

The implications of this discovery suggest that if somebody can live a perfectly normal life with only half a brain then it is reasonable to conclude, as Wigan did, that the being we call 'I' exists in only half the brain. If this is the case – and it does not matter which hemisphere of the brain is missing for a person to function normally –then one has to conclude that there are two 'people' in your head: you, and the person that lives in the other hemisphere.

The significance of this event was not lost on Wigan. He immediately began researching and reading all he could on the dual nature of the human brain and in 1845 he published his findings. His book, *The Duality of Mind*, was to become a classic of its type. In this work Wigan proposed that the twin hemispheres of the brain functioned as totally separate units and in this way all human beings are literally in 'two minds'. As we shall see later, Wigan was to use this theory to explain many psychological peculiarities such as schizophrenia and that most important of all psychic states, *déjà vu*.

It must have been a great frustration to Wigan that surgery on a live brain was not possible at the time. All he could do was observe the behaviour of people with damage to one side or other of the brain. It is only in the last 50 years or so that surgical techniques have advanced sufficiently for live observations, and even now this work is considered by some to be morally questionable.

A behavioural observation was to open up the debate again, and it was an event that took place nearly a century after Wigan's book. It all began with a perfectly normal-looking middle-aged woman seeking the assistance of a neurologist by the name of Kurt Goldstein. As she sat down to discuss her problem, the problem manifested itself: her left hand flew up to her throat and tried to strangle her! In a wrestling match straight out of *Dr Strangelove* her right hand came up to protect her. After a few seconds the murderous limb gave up and returned to its normal role. She explained to the stunned Goldstein that this was an ongoing and totally unpredictable occurrence. She tearfully described that sometimes the only way she could protect herself from assault by the rogue limb was by sitting on it.

After examining her Goldstein came to the conclusion that she was neither mentally disturbed nor neurotic. The problem with her arm was being caused by something far stranger; he concluded that her right hemisphere had developed suicidal tendencies. Usually any form of irrational behaviour stimulated by either hemisphere could be controlled by inhibitory messages sent across the corpus callosum, the bridge of nerves that acts as a communication channel between the two hemispheres. Goldstein suspected that these 'brakes' were failing to be transmitted. He believed that a stroke had damaged the callosum in some way. Her murderous left hand was thus free to attack her.

Tragic events were to prove Goldstein correct. Soon after visiting him the lady died of a second stroke. An autopsy confirmed that prior to the manifestation of the errant arm the lady had indeed suffered a massive stroke in the corpus callosum. In this way it was 'proven' that there is, as suspected by Wigan, a dual nature to human consciousness.

The bridge of sighs

The reason why the corpus callosum is so crucial in proving the theory of human duality lies in the curious structure of the brain itself. The two hemispherical sections of the brain are virtual mirror images of each other. Neatly bisecting down the middle of the head from front to back, each hemisphere contains not only identical cerebral cortexes (the grey matter that most non-physicians would readily identify as a 'brain') but also one each of all the other smaller structures that make up what is termed the limbic system. Neuroanatomists cannot agree as to what exactly constitutes this area of the brain but it is generally accepted that the formation is responsible for visceral processes, particularly those associated with the emotional state of the organism.

So when anatomists talk about the hippocampus or the hypothalamus they are, more correctly, discussing two organs, one found in each hemisphere. This peculiarity had been noted by even Greek and Roman physicians and because of this the pineal gland, the only organ in the brain of which there is only one, has long been believed to be the location of the soul.

Linking these two hemispheres are two nerve masses, the corpus callosum and the anterior commissure. The latter connects the unconscious limbic structures and carries emotions and basic instincts across the hemispheres. The former is of crucial importance; this mass of about 200 million nerve fibres acts as a bridge linking the two hemispheres. Its name comes from the Latin for 'thick-skinned body' and in many ways that is how it looks. Its location led to the supposition that it was crucial to the totality of the brain, but neurologists could not test this by the ideal method: cutting through the corpus callosum. This does not mean that they did not experiment with animals – far from it; many cats and monkeys were experimented on but for the neurologists continuing disappointment was encountered. With the exception of a slight change in conscious responses there were no lapses in voluntary coordination. The results of these operations led the psychologist Karl Lashley to suggest that the role of the corpus callosum was simply to hold the two hemispheres together. Another neurologist, Warren McCulloch, made an interesting link when he proposed that the corpus callosum's only function was to spread epilepsy across the brain. It seems that this link had become more of a Bridge of Sighs than a Golden Gate.

An all-over Tan

Until the mid-19th century it had been assumed that the two hemispheres of the brain had exactly the same functions. Then the work of two neurological pioneers, Paul Broca and Carl Wernicke, was to show that although very similar in structure, the two hemispheres had different roles to play in both behaviour and function. Broca had discovered that damage to a particular part of the brain, Broca's Area, led to the subject being unable to speak. From his work with a patient called Tan, he was able to show for the first time that a small set of muscles as well as a mental function – the expression of ideas through words – could be localized to a specific area of the brain. This stimulated Broca's interest in the physical location of the speech centres of the brain and by 1863 he had examined eight additional patients, all of whom were unable to verbalize their thoughts.

In fact, Broca had discovered one of the two areas of the brain that are responsible for speech. Also found in the left hemisphere, further back and lower in the brain, is an area that is responsible for how the patient *understands* speech, as opposed to Broca's Area, which is to do with the ability to *produce* speech. This area was discovered by Carl Wernicke, a German neurologist, who published his findings in 1874 at the tender age of 26. The title of his paper was *'Der Aphasische Symtomencomplex'* (the Aphasic Syndrome). By this time the syndrome discovered by Broca had been termed 'motor aphasia', but the form of aphasia described by Wernicke is marked by a severe defect in the understanding of speech. For this reason it was termed 'sensory aphasia'. In due course, Wernicke was able to isolate the precise location of the brain area responsible. Damage to this area, Wernicke's Area, is in many ways more interesting than the effects of trauma to Broca's Area. It results in disturbances in the patient's ability to understand the speech of others. Such patients can produce words and sounds but these words and sounds are not comprehensible to the receiver. It is as if the subject's thoughts become garbled as they are transformed into speech.

What was now known was that specific areas are responsible for specific skills, and there are no equivalents of Broca's Area or Wernicke's Area in the right temporal lobe. From this it was logical to conclude that speech is not a skill of the right hemisphere. Together with the discoveries of Wigan, scientists were faced with an interesting problem: why do we have two hemispheres and just how different are they?

In a world made up of classes – upper, middle and working – of armed forces with rigid hierarchies of rank, and a religion that had an 'elect' looking down on the damned, it was inevitable that one side of the brain would be considered dominant to the other's subordination. The notion of cerebral dominance probably came out of the ideas of John Hughlings Jackson, a pioneer in the study of epilepsy. Jackson, writing towards the end of the 19th century, proposed the idea of a 'leading' or dominant hemisphere. He wrote:

The two brains cannot be mere duplicates... for these processes
(of speech), of which there are none higher, there must surely
be one side which is leading.

... in most people the left side of the brain is the leading side –
the side of the so-called will, and that on the right is the
automatic side.

It is significant to note that this conclusion was not based on empirical research or observation but was merely a belief. As the concept of 'will' is by its very nature a person's major motivation factor, one can only conclude that in Jackson's opinion the seat of consciousness was the left brain.

Neurosurgeons were aware that the only way to finally solve the puzzle was by cutting the link in an operation called a 'commissurotomy'. Some psychologists, who were aware of the potentiality of this operation, wondered if the sectioning of the corpus callosum would, in fact, produce two minds.

The cutting edge of surgery

It had long been suggested that an operation to cut the link between the right and left hemispheres could be the catalyst that would bring the two schools, the neurologists and psychologists, together. Such was the enthusiasm for knowing the outcome of such an operation that William McDougall, the wonderfully – if somewhat disturbingly – titled Wilde Reader of the Mind at Oxford University volunteered himself for the operation. He even tried to persuade the physiologist CS Sherrington to undertake to divide his corpus callosum should he become incurably ill. The reason for McDougall's willingness to undergo this ordeal was to see if his theory of human personality could be proven by such an operation. McDougall believed that human personality was not a single consciousness but was made up of various entities that he termed 'monads', after the work of the German philosopher Leibniz. To him, cases of multiple personality disorder were clear evidence of breakdowns in the telepathic communication between these monads. In *An Outline of Abnormal Psychology*, McDougall explains his ideas thus:

> *I am only the dominant member of a society ... There are many purposive activities within my organism of which I am not aware, which are not my activities but are those of my associates ... I consciously control and adjust only a few of the executive processes of my organism, those only which are of primary importance for my purposes. But I and my associates are all members of one body; and, as long as the whole organism is healthy we work harmoniously together... But, when I relax my control, in states of sleep, hypnosis, relaxation, and abstraction, my subordinates, or some of them, may continue to work and then are apt to manifest their activities in the forms we have learned to call sensory and motor automatisms ... And in extreme cases such a revolted subordinate, escaped from the control of the dominant member or monad, may continue his career of insubordination indefinitely, acquiring increased influence over other members of the society and becoming a serious rival to the normal ruler or dominant.*

By the mid-1940s, knowledge of surgery and surgical techniques had advanced sufficiently for cerebral commissurotomies to take place. It had been supposed that epilepsy could be checked if doctors could somehow stop the discharges reverberating between the hemispheres causing severe damage to the cortical tissue.

These operations were of limited success and what follow-up psychological tests were performed on the patients showed only trivial and uninformative consequences. Consciousness appeared to be slightly depressed and there were transitory lapses in voluntary co-ordination but that was all. From 1954 onwards, the American neurologist Roger Sperry and his co-workers at the California Institute of Technology had been involved in split-brain experiments involving cats and monkeys (*see* page 208). Sperry was keen to discover why it was that such a drastic operation seemed to have only minor effects on the subjects. What Sperry discovered was of great importance and totally supported the ideas of McDougall. The split-brain animals were found to have totally divided perceptions and learning. However, these changes were not at all obvious from their general behaviour.

In Los Angeles, the neurosurgeons Philip Vogel and Joseph Bogen concluded that certain epileptic patients would gain from surgery and suffer no serious mental loss. Between 1962 and 1968 nine operations took place. Overall, the effects of the operation were beneficial. All of the patients showed some short-term memory loss, problems of orientation and mental fatigue immediately after the operation and some of them were unable to speak for two months after the operation. But in all cases there was gradual recovery. Within a few months none of them felt any different from how they had before the operation. Indeed, the post-operation states were very similar, if not identical to, those of the monkeys and cats. The difference this time was that these patients could explain how they felt and what they experienced. Sperry, Bogen and another psychologist, Michael Gazzaniga, set up a series of tests to discover what changes had actually taken place in the patients. These tests were to change forever our understanding of how the human mind works. In short, Sperry and his co-workers unknowingly confirmed the beliefs of the Gnostics, that each and every one of us has two, separate, conscious minds in our head. Sperry, in his article, sums up the findings:

> *In our split-brain studies of the past two decades, the surgically separated hemispheres of animals and man have been shown to perceive, learn, and remember independently, each hemisphere evidently cut off from the conscious experience of the other. In man the language dominant hemisphere further reports verbally that it is not consciously aware of the concomitant or immediately preceding mental performances of the disconnected partner hemisphere. These test performances of which the speaking hemisphere remains unaware obviously involve perception, comprehension, and in some cases non-verbal memory, reasoning and concept formation of different kinds depending on the nature of the test task. In these and many other respects, the split-brain animal and man behave as if each of the separated hemispheres had a mind of its own.*[144]

Still in two minds?

I would like you to ponder for a few seconds on the final sentence of Sperry's quotation. Here is one of the world's leading experimental neurologists stating quite clearly that indeed we do have two individuals in our brain. Could it be that here can be found the existence of the *Daemon* and the *Eidolon*? Can human duality be experimentally proven? It takes the cutting of the central connection between the two hemispheres to show this in normal people, but nevertheless the evidence seems to show that this is a universal trait.

In order to understand the method of testing and interviewing each half of the brain separately, two points of functional anatomy must be kept in mind. The first is that language functions such as speech and writing are, as Broca discovered, the responsibility of the left hemisphere in most people (virtually all right-handed people and 60 percent of left-handers), and the disconnected right hemisphere cannot express itself verbally. The second point is that the neural pathways that carry information from one side of the body and one-half of the visual field, cross over and connect *only* with the opposite side of the brain. This means that all sensations in the right hand are transmitted to the left hemisphere. The visual field is more complex. Each eye has two visual fields, right and left. Each eye sends its left-side images to the right brain and its right-side images to the left brain. This ensures that both hemispheres have binocular vision and therefore a concept of space and depth. Therefore a patient who has had the two hemispheres disconnected can describe or answer only questions about objects placed in their right hand, or pictures flashed to the right visual field. They can give no verbal response when the information is presented to the left hand, or the left visual field. However, the non-verbal right hemisphere can point to the correct object if it is given a selection of drawings to choose from.

A striking example of this was demonstrated during tests when the word 'heart' was flashed across the centre of a patient's visual field, with 'he' to the left of centre and 'art' to the right of centre. Since language and speech are largely left hemisphere functions, the patient said they could see the word 'art' when it was presented to the right and projected to the left hemisphere. But when they were asked to point with the left hand to one of two cards ('art' or 'he') to identify the word they had seen they invariably pointed to 'he'. The reason, again, is that the right hemisphere controls the movement of the left hand and 'he' had been presented to the right hemisphere.

Sperry also found that visual material projected to the left hemisphere could be described by the patients in speech and writing in an essentially normal manner. But when the same material was presented to the right hemisphere, the patient would insist that he had not seen anything, or that there had only been a flash of light. Yet if the patient was then asked to use his left hand to point to a matching picture or object, he had no trouble in indicating the very item that he had just insisted he had not seen.

Many of the experiments were filmed and one in particular was an amusing variation. Among a series of neutral geometrical figures which were being presented to the right and left fields of vision, a photograph of a nude woman was flashed to the right hemisphere. The patient blushed and giggled. Sperry asked, 'What did you see?' The patient said that she had seen only a flash of light. Sperry then asked what she was laughing at. She insisted that she had not seen anything, but a sly smile spread over her face and she began to laugh. When asked again, she replied: 'I don't know ... nothing... oh, that funny machine.'

It is clear that these experiments were crucial to the understanding of the human mind. But what was it that they told us? One line of reasoning was that each hemisphere of the brain must have a mind of its own, not only after surgery but also in its intact state. The normal individual is a compound of two persons, one based in each hemisphere. This was the position taken by the surgeon, Joseph Bogen, who undertook the first operations, in an article he wrote in 1969. This analysis was reinforced by the work of the English psychologist Roland Puccetti. In 1973 Puccetti had an article published in *The British Journal of the Philosophy of Science*.[145] In this article, 'Brain Bisection and Personal Identity', Puccetti came to the conclusion that even without commissurotomy (the cutting of the corpus callosum) there are always two independent centres of consciousness in the human brain. He draws on the cases where a complete hemisphere is removed. In this event, and whichever hemisphere is left, there remains a person. He argues that if people were unitary then these operations or circumstances would leave only half a person. Puccetti concludes that the only way he can explain the completeness of the remaining person is by supposing that before the operation there was not a unitary person.

A contrasting interpretation, proposed by Sir John Eccles, a philosopher and neurologist who specialized in the mysteries of consciousness, suggested that only one, the language dominant hemisphere, remains conscious. This implies that the non-dominant hemisphere operates like an automaton. But if this is the case, it is unclear what happens to a person who damages or injures his dominant hemisphere. If one follows the position of Eccles, then that person ceases to be a conscious being.

To some a load of PS

Until the mid-1970s, all split-brain patients showed only one consciousness that of the dominant hemisphere. The non-verbal side may have been aware but was not in a position to comment. In 1977, a researcher named Donald Wilson and a group of co-workers, including Michael Gazzaniga, published a paper in the periodical *Neurology* that was to move the debate onto another plane. The article, 'Cerebral Commissurotomy for the Control of Intractable Seizures,' described the case of a patient known as 'PS'. After the brain of PS was split, only the left hemisphere could speak but both hemispheres could comprehend speech. Evidently both hemispheres were conscious, separately conscious. The problem for Gazzaniga, and his co-worker LeDoux, was how to communicate with PS's right brain without the dominant left brain also being aware and, in effect, pushing into the conversation with its opinions. They came up with an extremely ingenious strategy. They would ask a question verbally so that both hemispheres would hear it, but they would leave out the crucial word that would make the question answerable. An example of this is the question: 'Please would you spell ...?' The dominant hemisphere cannot answer this question because it does not know the full question. Gazzaniga and LeDoux would then flash the image of a card with the word 'car' on it to the right hemisphere via the left visual field. This ensured that only the right hemisphere had all the information. Although the right hemisphere could not speak, it could, by using PS's left hand, select scrabble letters to answer the question. In this way the researchers could communicate directly with PS's right brain. And what a surprise they received! This is what occurred as described by one of the other co-workers:

> 'What do you want to do when ...?' – this time the word 'graduate' was flashed on a screen to PS's left. The boy's left hand reached for the scrabble letters. To the amazement of all in the laboratory, including, presumably PS himself, the hand arranged the letters A-U-T-O-M-O-B-I-L-E R-A-C-E (R).[146]

The reason for the collective astonishment about this answer was that earlier the same question had been asked to PS's left (dominant) hemisphere by normal verbal methods. The boy's everyday conscious self answered, 'I want to be a draftsman, I'm already trained for it'. The response from the mute side of the brain was a complete contradiction: the safety of a drawing office and the dangerous excitement of a racing circuit are quite different environments. This response is still one of the longest and most complex verbal messages ever to emanate from a non-dominant hemisphere. The implications are quite disturbing. The evidence seems to be that we all have another personality trapped inside our own heads, a second consciousness that is a prisoner that has his (or her) own opinions, motivations and objectives as regards how the whole person should live their lives. The tragedy is that however much PS's non-dominant personality wanted to be a racing driver, he would have to stand by helplessly and watch PS become a draftsman. Puccetti puts this very well when he describes the way we (dominant personality) take control of 'our' lives without giving a second thought to:

> ... the untalkative right-brained person I have been verbosely overruling most of our lives.

Commenting on this case, Roger Penrose says:

> If we accept that PS does have two independent minds then we are presented with a remarkable situation. Presumably, before the operation each split brain subject possessed but a single consciousness; but afterwards there are two! In some way, the original single consciousness has bifurcated.

Penrose then goes on to ask:

> Which of PS's consciousness 'is' the PS of before the operation?
> ... The puzzle would be further exacerbated if somehow the two consciousnesses could later be brought back together again. Reattaching the individual severed nerves of the corpus callosum would seem out of the question with present technology, but one might envisage something milder than actual severance of the nerve fibres in the first place... Presumably, after the corpus callosum has been re-activated, only one consciousness would result. Imagine this consciousness is you! How would it feel to have been two separate people with distinct 'selves' at some time in the past?[147]

This case also intrigues the Australian biologist Daryl Reanney in his book *The Death of Forever*. Reanney is more open to 'new age' interpretations of the evidences than Penrose, but he still cites information taken directly from the research. Reanney explains that PS was presented with two pictures on a screen, separately shown to each hemisphere: the right was shown a sequence of pictures including a chicken's head and a snow shovel. When asked to indicate which picture in the sequence related to the image on the screen, PS picked the chicken head picture with his right hand and the snow shovel picture with his left. But when asked to explain his choice PS produced a give-away answer:

> *That's easy, the chicken claw goes with the chicken and you need a shovel to clean out the chicken's shed.*

This showed that PS's left hemisphere used its facility for language to construct a logical but incorrect explanation for what had happened. The dominant left-side brain solved the puzzle of its own right-side partner's choice by creating a fictional story to link two unconnected sections. From the evidence it does seem that the more radical interpretation – that we are really two people – is in keeping. In the view of Michael Gazzaniga:

> *All the evidence indicates that separation of the hemispheres creates two independent spheres of consciousness within a single cranium, that is to say, within a single organism. This conclusion is disturbing to some people who view consciousness as an indivisible property of the human brain ... it is entirely possible that if a human brain were divided in a very young person, both hemispheres could as a result separately and independently develop mental functions of a high order at the level attained only in the left hemisphere of normal individuals.*[148]

The question is, are there alternative methods of communication? Indeed, it seems that there may be, and these are through hypnotism.

Mesmerizing magnetic metaphysics

As we have seen, hypnotism is a tool by which the other entity that shares our subconscious can be isolated. What is interesting about hypnotism is that even in the 21st century psychologists and neurologists are at a loss to explain how it works, although duality of consciousness is one of the explanations put forward to explain the enigma.

During a hypnotic trance, the conscious ego, the part of your brain that calls itself 'I', falls asleep. Although on awakening the subject recalls nothing of the events that take place during the hypnosis session, somebody responds to the words of the hypnotist in that the suggestions made are responded to and carried out. Many psychologists conclude that the 'person' who is speaking during a hypnotic session is in fact the non-dominant hemisphere of the brain. Thus by hypnotizing a person we can communicate directly with their hidden self.

In the late 19th century, the great French psychologist Pierre Janet came up with conclusive evidence that the second self does have a continuous existence parallel to that of normal waking consciousness. In order to communicate with this second self while the subject was fully awake Janet, together with another French psychologist, Alfred Binet, used a technique that he called the 'method of distraction'. This involved the experimenter getting the subject involved in an activity that distracted them totally from what was going on around them; for instance, this could be a lively conversation with a third party. At that point, and while the subject was pre-occupied, the experimenter would whisper a command. With those suffering from hysteria it was found that they would obey the instruction even though their waking self was totally unaware why they had done something. For Janet this proved that the second self is always present, lurking just below the surface of normal consciousness but aware of everything that is taking place.

In 1898, the American psychologist Boris Sidis, in his book *The Psychology of Suggestion*, described an example of how this was done:

P, a man of forty, was received at the hospital at Havre for
delirium tremens. He improved and became quite rational
during the daytime. The hospital doctor observed that the patient
was highly suggestible, and invited M. Janet to experiment on
him. 'While the doctor was talking to the patient on some
interesting subject,' writes M. Janet, 'I placed myself behind P.,
and told him to raise his arm. On the first trial I had to touch
his arm in order to provoke the desired act; afterwards his
unconscious obedience followed my order without difficulty. I
made him walk, sit down, kneel – all without him knowing it. I
even told him to lie down on his stomach and he fell down at
once, but his head still raised itself to answer at once the doctor's
questions. The doctor asked him, 'In what position are you while
I am talking to you?' 'Why, I am standing by my bed; I am not
moving.' The secondary self accepted motor suggestions of which
the primary self was totally unaware.

In experiments eerily reminiscent of the split-brain work carried
out by Gazzaniga on PS, Janet was able to communicate directly
with the second self and, on asking a question, she was able to
receive a direct answer. Adam Crabtree describes this in his book
Multiple Man:

In this case he had presented the subject with a number of
blank white cards and induced the hallucination of a portrait
of one of them. He (Janet) then mixed them up and asked the
subject to pick out the one with the 'portrait.' She was always
able to do so, no matter how well they were shuffled.

By using this technique of distraction, Janet then placed
himself in contact with the subject's second self and asked what
it saw on the card in question. It pointed out a small black spot
on the card, which enabled it to distinguish that one from the

others. So while the waking personality believed it was able to
pick out the card because of the portrait on it, the second self
revealed the real means of distinguishing.[149]

Thus the 'second self' or, as we now know it, the Daemon, can be communicated with during normal, waking consciousness. It is present sensing all that is going on. In fact, its position seems to be superior to the primary self in that the Daemon cannot, unlike the primary self, be hypnotized. It is conscious at all times, even during sleep.

The 'superior' position of the Daemon was hinted at in a fascinating series of experiments that Alfred Binet carried out involving an ability to not see an object. For example, a hypnotic subject can be instructed, on awaking, that they will cease to see all the furniture in the room. This will include the table between the subject and the experimenter. When the subject is awoken, careful questioning is used to confirm that they cannot see any furniture. The experimenter then asks the subject to get up and walk across the room to the experimenter. In reality the table is in the way, but the subject is unaware of it and you would think they would try to walk through the table. The interesting thing is that they do not. They still walk round the unseen table. When asked why he walked such a peculiar route, the subject will either say that they do not know or else come up with some weak excuse.

As Crabtree says, in order that the subject does *not see* something, something inside him *had to see* the object and act upon that perception. Binet describes this problem:

> *... In order to cease to see an object – to have that alone*
> *excluded from sight – a person must begin by perceiving and*
> *recognising it, however that may be done, and the rejection of*
> *the perception can only take place after it has been established*
> *... Now, who does this supervising? What is the intelligence*

that always decides that the subject shall perceive this and not
that? It is not the normal ego, for that is not conscious of
anything. It only accepts what it gets. It must be, therefore, a
personality capable of seeing the object... As to what this
personality may be, I for one am completely in the dark.[150]

In his book *The Holographic Universe*, Michael Talbot cites a modern case of this ability to not see an object. Talbot's father had hired a professional hypnotist to entertain a group of friends. One of the group, Tom, proved to be a particularly strong subject. After the usual 'tricks' the hypnotist informed the entranced Tom that on awaking from the trance his daughter, Laura, would be completely invisible to him. Talbot describes what happened when on awaking the hypnotist asked Tom if he could see his daughter:

Tom looked around the room and his gaze seemed to pass
straight through his giggling daughter. 'No', he replied. The
hypnotist asked Tom if he was certain, and again, despite
Laura's rising giggles, he answered no. Then the hypnotist went
behind Laura so he was hidden from Tom's view and pulled an
object out of his pocket. He kept the object carefully concealed
so that no one in the room could see it, and pressed it in the
small of Laura's back. He asked Tom to identify the object.
Tom leaned forward as if staring directly through Laura's
stomach and said it was a watch. The hypnotist nodded and
asked if Tom could read the watch's inscription. Tom squinted
as if struggling to make out the writing and recited both the
name of the watch's owner (which happened to be a person
unknown to any of us in room) and the message. The hypnotist
revealed that the object was indeed a watch and passed it
round the room so that everyone could see that Tom had read
its inscription correctly.[151]

Talbot took the opportunity to speak to Tom afterwards. Tom confirmed that he simply did not see his daughter. All he had seen was the hypnotist standing with the watch in his hand. Had the hypnotist not informed Tom of what had happened he would have considered the reading of the inscription to be part of normal reality.

This has huge implications. It means that the Daemon can decide what is, and what is not, perceived by the senses of the subject. We may all be living our lives with Daemon-induced censorship, but if reality is only an inwardly generated illusion, then it is very easy for such censorship to take place. The Daemon simply allows a few 'frames' of the recording to be omitted. Strangely, for some people the Daemon seems to do the opposite – instead of restricting the external in-puts it increases them, and in doing so contributes to those people mentally collapsing under the pressure.

Schizophrenia as a clue

In *Consciousness, Brain, States of Awareness and Mysticism* (edited by Daniel Goleman and Richard J Davidson), a schizophrenic named Norma McDonald describes the sensations and feelings that schizophrenics experience. What she talks about in particular is the exaggerated state of awareness that she had during her illness. She says that at the onset of the condition it was as if parts of her brain 'awoke' after being dormant for many years. She became deeply aware of events around her and the motivations of people. Looking back she says that she can:

> *... appreciate what had happened. Each of us is capable of coping with a large number of stimuli, invading our being through any one of the senses. We could hear every sound within earshot and see every object, line and colour within the field of vision, and so on. It's obvious that we would be*

incapable of carrying on any of our daily activities if even one-hundredth of all the available stimuli invaded us at once. So the mind must have a filter which functions without our conscious thought, sorting stimuli and allowing only those which are relevant to the situation in hand to disturb consciousness.[152]

It seems as if she had become super-attuned to all the sensory inputs invading her consciousness. As she says, her 'filter' had somehow been taken away. Could it be that what actually happens in schizophrenia is that the dominant hemisphere suddenly becomes aware of the processing going on in the non-dominant side; that these individuals sense the world as the Daemon does without the abilities that that being has to process and categorize? One can draw parallels here with the amazing memory abilities of Shereshevski as described by Luria (*see* page 99). Shereshevski suffered not only from 'sensory overload' but also the additional problem of not forgetting any of the stimuli. It seems reasonable to conclude, particularly when taking into account Shereshevski's obviously split consciousness, that these things are somehow related.

Schizophrenia is a very peculiar illness. Towards the end of the 19th century, Emil Kraepelin, a German psychiatrist, suggested that many forms of insanity could be categorized as one of two major disorders. He termed these 'manic-depressive insanity' and 'dementia praecox'. He considered that the former was an illness that hit the individual in phases during their lifetime. Although this may involve periods in hospital in many cases the patient recovers and reverts back to their old personality.

Dementia praecox, however, was a progressive illness that started in adolescence or early adulthood and followed an inexorable downhill course. Recovery, if it ever occurred, was usually short-term and the patient would continue their decline.

This idea was expanded and elaborated by Eugen Bleuler, the medical director of the Burgholzli Hospital in Zurich. It was Bleuler who coined the term 'schizophrenia', meaning 'split mind'. By this Bleuler meant that there was a splitting or loss of co-ordination between different psychic functions, particularly between the cognitive (intellectual) and connative (emotional) aspects of the personality. The monograph he published in 1911[153] defined this illness so well that Kraepelin's original terminology was forgotten. Schizophrenia is now recognized throughout the world as being the most important cause of chronic psychiatric disability. In general terms, the sufferer of schizophrenia has the following symptoms:

> *The subject ceases to experience his mental processes and his will as under his own control; he may insist that thoughts are being put into his mind or removed from it by an alien force, or suspect that he is being hypnotized. He hears voices telling him what to do, commenting on or repeating his thoughts, discussing him between themselves, or threatening to kill him.*[154]

So what do the neurologists and psychiatrists believe causes this illness? Surprisingly, despite a great deal of research, the cause or causes remain elusive. What is of great interest is that *post mortem* examinations show that the number of dopamine receptors in parts of the basal ganglia of the brain is increased in chronic schizophrenia. The importance of this discovery will be discussed later, but for now it is important to note that there is a chemical link here.

Whatever the cause, sufferers of the illness show some very curious side effects that fail to fit any easy explanation. An example of this is the result of a survey of profoundly deaf schizophrenics: it was discovered that 16 out of the 22 individuals questioned 'heard' the voice of the hidden observer.[155] The question is: how can a person who has never heard another human voice somehow hear a voice inside their head? One 32-year-old woman who had been born deaf was continually being told off by her voice about having a therapeutic abortion a few years previously. But even these curiosities pale into insignificance when we learn that schizophrenics also show pre-cognitive abilities.

Julian Jaynes, whose work on human duality will be discussed in the following chapter, describes a peculiar event that was experienced and noted by Bleuler, who tells of a patient whose voices showed an ability to foretell events about to happen. Jaynes paraphrases Bleuler:

> *A janitor coming down the hall makes a slight noise of which the patient is not conscious. But the patient hears his hallucinated voice cry out 'Now someone is coming down the hall with a bucket of water'. The door opens and the prophecy is fulfilled.* [156]

Jaynes cannot accept the facts as they present themselves. Obviously an ability to predict the future is 'impossible' so another explanation has to be found. He says:

> *The nervous system of a patient makes simple perceptual judgements that the patient's 'self' is not aware and these may be transposed into voices that seem prophetic.*

In researching for this book I frequently came across this kind of logical gymnastics. Occam's Razor states that the simpler explanation is usually the correct one. Here we have a case that seems to be fairly clear evidence of short-term precognition. A scientist, particularly one such as Jaynes who, we shall see later, finds nothing peculiar about disembodied voices shouting at him, should deal solely with the facts as they present themselves. As far as science is concerned 'precognition' is impossible and therefore there have to be other reasons. It is worth taking a look at these alternatives and, presumably in Jaynes' mind, more rational reasons. 'A janitor comes down the hall and makes a slight noise that the patient is not aware of'. Perhaps Jaynes means that the patient did not hear this slight sound, but it seems that the 'hallucination' manifesting itself as an internal 'voice' has acute hearing. The trouble with this is that the 'hallucination' is brought about by the patient's own subconscious. From this the only conclusion can be that the patient himself has super-hearing that he is not aware of. If for the sake of argument we accept this unknown ability to be a fact, even so Jaynes fails to explain how the patient extrapolates a 'slight sound' into the fact that it is the janitor with a pail of water. To me the explanation is clear; the patient had, for some reason, developed an ability to know what was to happen in the short-term future. Here is an additional clue to the peculiar mental states of schizophrenics:

> *A chronic schizophrenic woman who had an exacerbation of her illness seemed to have lengthy episodes of déjà vu, which she used in a psychotic way to indicate she knew everything that was going to happen next. For example, she began an interview by stating 'I know all about this. I've been through this same thing many times before. I know what is going to happen'. She continued by describing the situation in minute detail to prove her foreknowledge.* [157]

As we have seen, there is strong evidence that the Daemon exists in a sensory world very different from its Eidolon. It exists outside of time and, presumably, space. It perceives 'reality' as it really is, a confusing mass of signals and images illuminated by the whole electromagnetic spectrum. To a being not ready for such an explosion of inputs such as an Eidolon, this would drive them insane. It may be that the chemical imbalances that cause schizophrenia bring about aberrant behaviour in the subject, not in themselves, but because they change the 'frequency' by which their brain receives incoming data. The 'tuning' moves into the frequency normally reserved for our Hidden Observer and the sensory floodgates are flung open to drown the unsuspecting Eidolon. How this can seem to a schizophrenic Eidolon is wonderfully described by Australian physicist Raynor Johnson in his tower analogy:

> *We are each rather like a prisoner in a round tower permitted to look out through five slits in the wall at the landscape outside. It is presumptuous to suppose that we can perceive the whole of the landscape through these slits – although I think there is good evidence that the prisoner can sometimes have a glimpse out the top!*[158]

The problem is that the escaped prisoner, without protection, can be blinded by the light of the 'real world', a world that he has been denied for good reason. We simply cannot cope with the intellectual and emotional stimuli brought about by full awareness. Schizophrenics, through no fault of their own, have lost touch with matter, language and their fellow human beings because they are in touch with the perceptions of their own higher selves and in doing so they realize that matter itself is an illusion.

C H A P T E R 9

The Guardian of Forever

When all the souls had chosen their lives, they went before Lachesis.
And she sent with each, as the guardian of his life and the fulfiller of
his choice,

the daimon that he had chosen.

Plato, Republic, Book X

Julian Jaynes and the bicameral mind

You are now all alone in your living room. You look round the
room, taking in the chairs, the windows and the television set.
Your mind still finds it hard to accept that this is all an illusion –
it looks too solid and real. You close your eyes and re-open them.
You are relieved to see that everything remains in the same place.
Surely this is proof that reality is out there and consistent – this is
not *Alice In Wonderland*.

Even so, the argument about the location of the red in the red
coat scene in *Schindler's List* keeps playing on your mind, so you
decide to check out one more time the process of perception. You
find your video of the film, wind it back to the scene in question,
and watch the scene unfold on the screen. As you do so your
thoughts focus in on the idea that you are not alone in your mind,
that you have another self, another you that uses your sensory
apparatus to view your phaneron.

You realize that in fact you have no way of knowing if
somebody else is also looking out of your eyes, using your ears
and enjoying that gin and tonic that you are sipping. You ask
yourself how you would know whether there was another person
watching the selfsame television from a location behind you. After
all, you cannot see them or sense them in any way because the

only stimulus you are receiving is from the screen in front of you. This 'other', however, can see both the television and you illuminated in the glow of the TV screen. This analogy is not as strange as it seems. As we know, 'reality' is not perceived 'first hand'. What we perceive as being 'out there' is an internally constructed model built within our mind from sensory perceptions; it is merely an interpretation of what is really 'out there'. This construct works exactly like an internally projected television image – only it involves all the senses – and another entity can also perceive this inner projection, Dennett's Cartesian Theatre or my Bohmian IMAX.

In this scenario, I have been specific about you being alone in your room because it was in identical circumstances that one of the most interesting theories about human consciousness was first conceived. The individual in question describes the event:

> *In Boston, I had for about a week been studying and*
> *autistically pondering some of the problems in this book,*
> *particularly the problem of what knowledge is and how we can*
> *know anything at all. My convictions and misgivings had been*
> *circling about through the sometimes precious fogs of*
> *epistemologies, finding nowhere to land. One afternoon I lay*
> *down in intellectual despair on a couch. Suddenly, out of an*
> *absolutely quiet, there came a firm, distinct loud voice from my*
> *upper right which said, 'Include the knower and the known'.*
> *It lugged me to my feet absurdly exclaiming 'hello?' looking for*
> *whoever was in the room. The voice had an exact location.*[159]

The writer is the psychologist Julian Jaynes, and it was from this strange event that he was stimulated to write his most famous work, *The Origin of Consciousness and the Breakdown of the Bicameral Mind*.

Jaynes suggested that the auditory hallucination he had experienced in Boston was a common occurrence. He was surprised to discover that among the Anglo-Saxon race one man in twelve experiences this form of hallucination. For women it is even more common – one in eight. Indeed, this was quite low in relation to other groups – in Russia the figure was twice as high and in Brazil almost 25 percent of the population have had, or will have, a similar experience. These are normal people, not those under mental or psychological stress. From this Jaynes concluded that under certain circumstances many, if not all individuals might experience auditory hallucinations, the differences being purely cultural.

For Jaynes this vivid form of auditory hallucination can explain the universal religious experience of communicating with the gods. He found it understandable how an individual, living in a culture or a historical period where the existence of gods is unquestioned, could naturally assume the voice to be the words of a god. The curiously portentous and somewhat obscure meaning of what the voice says then reinforces this belief.

Jaynes thought there was more to it than just this. He pointed out that for 99 percent of human evolution, men and women grouped together in tightly bonded, mutually dependent groups. Within these groups each individual had no sense of individuality, no sharp sense of 'ego-self'. The concept of selfhood came about, according to Jaynes, about the first millennium BCE. Jaynes bases his theory on studies he made on early writings such as the *Iliad* (*c.* 1000 BCE). He notes that the *Iliad* makes no reference to concepts such as thought and mind, human actions being the results of the gods willing men to do things:

> *When Agamemnon, king of men, robs Achilles of his mistress,*
> *it is a god that grasps Achilles by his yellow hair and warns*
> *him not to strike Agamemnon.*[160] *It is a god who then rises out*
> *of the grey sea and consoles him ... a god who whispers low to*
> *Helen to sweep her heart with homesick longing ... it is the*
> *gods who start quarrels among men,*[161] *that really cause the*

war,[162] and then plan its strategy.[163] It is one god who makes Achilles promise not to go into battle, another who urges him to go ... In fact, the gods take the place of consciousness.[164]

Jaynes argues that there is no evidence of introspection in any writings of that period. Motivations are not analyzed in any way, but are synonymous with what the gods want the individual to do. The voice in the head is what causes motivation and that voice was interpreted as a god's communication. For ancient man there was no inner debate about what action should be taken. The gods told him and he obeyed.

So what was it that made pre-modern man think this way? For Jaynes the solution is fairly straightforward; ancient man had a brain that was a singular unit. The 'splitting' of the brain into right and left hemispheres took place at this time, leaving just the corpus callosum as the bridge of communication. For early man the two sides worked as one unit. The right brain 'person' could talk directly to the 'I'. These words of guidance or advice were interpreted as the external voices of the divine. When the split took place; when man became 'bicameral', this communication channel ceased to be fully effective. Man developed a concept of self and began to listen to his own (left brain) thoughts. This isolated the 'hidden observer', trapping him in the non-dominant hemisphere and allowing him only occasional opportunities to communicate. These opportunities arise during periods of great stress or worry when internally created opiates flood the brain, or when the subject is placed in a deep trance state via hypnotism. It is this voice that Jaynes heard that afternoon in Boston and it is this voice that talked with Socrates.

That voice had a profound effect not only on Jaynes' book but also on his whole life. Without those words he may have not followed up on certain areas of research and his book, if he had written it at all, would have come to very different conclusions.

In the same way that Socrates was guided through his life by his Divine Sign, a discarnate voice that spoke to him, could it be that Jaynes' voice was his Daemon? With reference to Socrates, later writers were keen to link the philosopher's guiding spirit with the voices of the gods. In the 2nd century CE, Maximus of Tyre was to write:

> *What was the truth of the old mystery of Socrates' divine*
> *guidance? Surely Homer had explained it best when he wrote*
> *how the gods appear to the heroes? Just as Athena guided*
> *Odysseus, so a divine sign directed Socrates and other virtuous*
> *men. You are not so vulgar as to think that Homer meant these*
> *'gods' in a literal, physical, sense'.*[165]

Maximus went on to say that Homer had actually meant divine powers:

> *The Daimones, which accompany virtuous people, which share*
> *their lives and hold their hand above them.*

So what of modern man? If Jaynes' statistics are to be believed then many of us interact with our Daemon on a regular basis. The implication is that this 'other person' shares our life with us, unseen and unheard until he, or she, decides that intervention is needed. In his book *Coincidence*, Brian Inglis tells of various modern equivalents of Socrates' Divine Sign. An example is the tale told by the Italian opera singer Tito Gobbi. In his autobiography he tells of a time when he was driving far too fast on a precipitous mountain road. As he became more reckless he heard his brother, Bruno's voice:

> *... so distinctly that he seemed to be sitting beside me, saying*
> *'Stop – instantly'. Instinctively I obeyed, coming to a halt on a*
> *wide grass verge, practically the only spot of any width in the*

whole path. A few minutes later, round the narrow bend came
an articulated lorry out of control.[166]

In another example, the writer Philip Paul was walking to work during the Blitz when a voice told him to stop. He was, quite naturally, surprised and his rational mind decided to ignore the intruder. In *Some Unseen Power* he recalls that:

The warning persisted. So, putting a foot on a pile of rubble, I pretended to tie a shoelace. At that moment, the high wall ahead collapsed into the alleyway, filling it ten feet high and burying walkers a few yards ahead of me..

In these cases the 'voice' saved the life of its lower self and the Daemon showed an ability to see the future. Suffice to say that without the interventions it is likely that both Paul and Gobbi would not have survived to tell the tale.

It is unclear which of the two entities controls the 'I' personality. We have seen evidence that under certain circumstances an individual's everyday consciousness can communicate directly with the Daemon – a dialogue as opposed to a monologue.

The British psychic Rosalind Heywood spent most of her life in discussions with her higher self. In a telling way Heywood comments that her 'other half' seemed to have access to information denied to her everyday personality. She says:

On other occasions when I have been aware of the duality in myself, the split seemed to be because a hidden part of me wanted to act on information that the conscious part did not possess.[167]

We cannot avoid the conclusion that for all of us this other entity, the Daemon, Hidden Observer or 'the higher self', has access to information that the 'lower' personality does not. For Heywood her Daemon was such a central part of her life that she even gave it a name, 'Orders'. This voice that she hears in her head instructed her on actions she needed to take. It appeared at the oddest of times and gave instructions that seemed strange at the time. Nevertheless, Heywood always went with what Orders instructed. It is as if Heywood's inner voice forced her life down a particular route. An example of this is the way in which a chance decision (stimulated by Orders) was to change her viewpoint on psychic matters. Heywood describes the incident:

It was during the Second World War. My husband had been sent to the War Office, and when the journey to and from Sunningdale became too unreliable we took a little house in Westminster. Immediately afterwards he was moved to a distant post where I could not follow him. 'What shall I do with this place?'
I asked myself, sitting alone in the empty house. Is there any good use to which it could be put?'

'Yes,' said Orders promptly. 'Write at once and ask Mr and Mrs Tyrrell to come round and live in it.'

I found this preposterous. Mr Tyrrell was an elderly member of the S.P.R. (Society for Psychical Research) Council. I had only met him a few times at meetings and had once had supper with him and his wife. Early in the war they had been bombed out of their London flat and had gone to a quiet place in the country where he was now peacefully writing a book.

'It would help the book,' said Orders, 'for him to come to London.' That, I thought, was a tiresome attempt to rationalise an absurd impulse: what elderly man could write better in bomb-ridden London than in the country? However Orders once more defeated reason, and very apologetically I wrote. The

immediate and delighted reply was that my letter had come in the nick of time. The Tyrrells had just been told that their landlord wanted his house back.
Mr Tyrrell's book could get no further until he lived near the library of the S.P.R., and he could afford to set up in London again.[168]

The book that Tyrrell was to complete was *The Personality of Man*, a publication that was to have a profound effect on Heywood's work and writings. The suspicion cannot be avoided that Orders knew that that book had to be written. In an alternative, Everett-like, universe Tyrrell would have been forced to move out of his cottage and, without access to home or library, would have failed to complete his work. But, by intervening, Orders changed the future in this part of the Macroverse.

In each case we have seen so far, the intention of the 'other' entity has been benign or positively supportive of its host consciousness. The evidence seems to imply that the Daemon consciousness is in a deep way directly related to the host, a facet of the same personality. However, sometimes the 'other' is not at all supportive of the Eidolon and the Daemon seems more like a parasite than a flatmate; while showing these negative qualities it seems to manifest itself not as one being but as many. This psychological state, termed Multiple Personality Disorder (MPD) seems to be the negative side of the Daemon-Eidolon relationship.

More minds than one

The best-known case of MPD is probably that of the young woman reported in *The Three Faces of Eve* by Corbett H Thingpen and Hervey M Cleckley. The subject of this best-selling book was a quiet housewife and mother until she found herself overwhelmed by the personality of a coarse, seductive woman who loved the nightlife. This confusion forced her to take herself to the University of Georgia Medical School. While undergoing treatment there, a third personality manifested itself. This was a level-headed individual who seemed to act as a mediator between the two other personalities. Unfortunately, there was not to be a neat and tidy ending to this situation. The publication of the book about the three personalities brought about a divorce for the central character, now identified as a lady by the name of Christine Sizemore, and a splitting into three more personalities. She then began to produce personalities in groups of three, with the first one out acting as the communication channel with the outside world for the other two. However, one cannot escape the suspicion that this case was nothing to do with split brain and more to do with an individual who seemed to thrive on mini-dramas.

A much more disturbing case was that of Billy Milligan, a man who gained notoriety in 1977 as the 'Campus Rapist' of Ohio State University. Milligan was arrested in Columbus and charged with four counts of rape, three counts of kidnapping and three counts of aggravated robbery. His testimony was so confused that a psychiatrist was called in to assess Milligan's fitness to stand trial. Because he had shown signs of multiple personality it was agreed that the psychiatrist Cornelia Wilbur, who had treated another famous MPS individual who went under the name of 'Sibyl', was well qualified to review Milligan's psychiatric state.

Up until this point those who spoke to Milligan had been frustrated by the fact that a number of personalities had been encountered but with varying degrees of willingness to cooperate. Wilbur's experience in previous cases enabled her to get Milligan to relax to a point where he could allow his stronger personalities to recede and the original 'Billy' to emerge. Billy showed extreme concern that he was about to be punished for actions that he had no responsibility for. Quite naturally the authorities were suspicious about this turn of events, and so the prosecuting attorney was allowed to attend one of the sessions between Wilbur and Milligan. He began to believe Billy's story.

By the time the case had come to court there was no doubt that Milligan had committed the crimes. The matter in dispute was his responsibility for them. After some debate the judge found Milligan not guilty by reason of insanity. This was the first time in the history of American law that a man had been acquitted of major crimes because of insanity due to multiple personality. Milligan was also in violation of parole in a number of cases and he could still have ended up in prison but his attorneys managed to obtain his release on the agreement that he would be placed in the custody of the Athens Medical Centre in California.

Under the care of Dr David Caul and Dr Ralph Allison, a Californian psychiatrist noted for his work with cases of multiple personalities, Billy subsequently came up with 24 personalities of both sexes and of all ages. This case is particularly interesting because Billy seemed to allocate individual emotions to each character.

Up to this point, Billy's case is no more than a complex version of the other cases of this sort. It is on an analysis of the characters that some real questions arise. One of the 24 characters identified himself as Arthur and spoke with an English accent and demonstrated a wide knowledge of physics, chemistry and medicine. He could also read and write fluent Arabic. Another gave his name as Ragen, spoke with a thick Slavic accent and proved that he could read and write fluent Serbo-Croatian.[169] All of these skills were way beyond the abilities of Billy Milligan. If this can be taken at face value the case seems to throw up some fascinating questions, none more so than how a young man can speak fluent Serbo-Croatian when there is no evidence of him ever learning such a language.

It is fascinating to read why it was that Arthur and Ragen decided that the original core personality, Billy, was not allowed to control the consciousness for the six years before he was brought out by Dr Wilbur in her interview. It seems that at that earlier time Billy had been on the verge of suicide and was in danger of destroying 'the family'. Billy had been bullied at school and had decided to end it all. He had gone to the roof of his school with the intention of throwing himself off. At this point Ragen came forward, throwing Billy down to the floor. Stimulated by this turn of events, Ragen and Arthur called an emergency conference to determine the rules for the whole family of 24 personalities. The discussion that took place deserves to be repeated in detail:

> Arthur: 'He is a danger to us all. In his depressed state, he might succeed in killing himself.'

> Ragen: 'What is the solution?'

> Arthur: 'Keep him asleep.'

> Ragen: 'How?'

> Arthur: 'From this moment forward, Billy is not to hold the consciousness again.'

> Ragen: 'Who can control it?'

> Arthur: 'You and I. We'll share the responsibility. I'll spread the word to the others that no one is to allow him to take the consciousness under any circumstances. When things are ... in relative safety, I'll control things. If we find ourselves in a dangerous environment, you take over. Between us we will determine who may or may not hold the consciousness.'

Arthur then had to explain the situation to the junior personalities. These were termed 'the children'. How he describes this evokes some very peculiar images of what it is like inside of a human consciousness inhabited by multiple individuals:

> *Think of it as if all of us are in a dark room. In the centre of this room is a bright spot of light on the floor. Whoever steps into this light, onto the spot, is out in the real world and holds the consciousness. The rest of us can go about our regular interests, study or talk or play. But whoever is out must be very careful he or she does not reveal the existence of the others. It is a family secret.*

However, central to my thesis is that there are only two personalities sharing the human mind; the individual we know as 'I' and the 'Hidden Observer' or 'Daemon'.

On reading about the Billy Milligan case it is initially confusing that there appears to be no evidence of a Hidden Observer or Daemon. In fact, he was there in the shadows, waiting to pull everything together. He appeared as the sum of all 23 previous personalities and was called 'The Teacher'.

Dr Caul first learned about the Teacher's presence in a conversation with Ragen. The Serb said that as well as the 10 separate personalities and the 13 that had been banished because they caused 'disruption', there was a totally dominant personality who existed in the background. This entity was called 'The Teacher' because he was responsible for teaching the other personalities all they knew. Caul videotaped the conversation with Ragen and then called Billy to show him the videotape. It seemed that there were only two 'real' personalities; Billy and the Teacher. It was the Teacher who had created all the other sub-personalities. He was also responsible for the crimes that they had committed.

It was now that an inner transformation took place as all of the personalities took the stage at once and the Teacher emerged for the first time. Dr Caul was communicating directly with a Daemon! Together, Dr Caul and the Daemon worked to focus Billy into one personality. As it happened, a particular set of circumstances came together that ensured that Billy was accused of rape again and he was imprisoned under changed circumstances.

The implication of these cases is that the human mind has more than one consciousness inhabiting its brain. Roland Puccetti argues that this is a permanent state of affairs, not only taking place after a split-brain operation. We are all not one individual but (at least) two. This other shares your experiences but processes the incoming data in a very different way. The two sides of PS, the split-brain patient mentioned earlier (*see* pages 216-218), had lived exactly the same life and therefore shared exactly the same experiences. Their inherited traits and life events had to be identical. His dominant self brought all these together to decide that he wished to be a draftsman whereas his non-dominant Daemon wanted to be a racing driver.

So it seems that the Daemon does exist and is active in the life of its Eidolon. There is also evidence that Daemonic guidance is far more common than we think. The problem is that in a telling semantic confusion we have misinterpreted the clues. The Daemon is with us but within Western culture we call him or her by another name – our Guardian Angel.

Talk of angels

Angels are big in the USA these days. People from all walks of life seem to be tuning into the possibility that we are not alone in our lives, that there is a specific celestial being that has been charged by God to look after each and every one of us. This personal Guardian Angel is around at all times and watches our every move.

In a recent American survey it was found that 70 percent of people questioned believed in angels, and 50 percent in a personal Guardian Angel. Most 'educated' people find this all slightly silly and dismiss such stories as being wishful thinking and a misinterpretation of explicable events. However, there remain a large number who do believe and this can only imply that many have had personal dealings with disembodied entities.

The English word 'angel' is taken from the Latin *angelus* which in turn was used by Biblical translators as the Latin equivalent of the Hebrew and Greek word for 'messenger'. The belief in a personal guardian spirit can be traced back far further into history. Nabopolassar, father of Nebuchadnezzar the Great, says:

> *He (Marduk) sent a tutelary deity (cherub) of grace to go at my side; in everything that I did, he made my work to succeed.*[170]

In the Bible, angels not only act as the executors of God's wrath against cities of the plain, but they also deliver Lot from danger (Genesis 28–29). In Exodus 32:34, God tells Moses, 'my angel shall go before thee.' In the Old Testament, angels were seen as God's ministers who carried out his instructions and who were at times given special commissions regarding men and mundane affairs.

In the New Testament, angels are everywhere the intermediaries between God and man. Even little children have guardian angels, and these same angels still perceive God even when they have a mission to perform on Earth (Matthew 18:10). The early Christian Church was obliged to recognize their status within dogma and this is exactly what the bishops did at the Council of Nicaea (325 CE) although there was a degree of confusion as to whether angels are sent by God to guard over all men. This was long the accepted belief reflected by St Jerome in one of his commentaries when he says that: 'The dignity of a soul is so great, that each has a guardian angel from its birth.'

It was this comment that assisted St Thomas Aquinas in concluding that guardian angels did exist. He discussed the issue in some detail in his major work *Summa Theologica*. Aquinas came to the conclusion that as Jesus was born a man but was also a part of the Trinity that was God then he, for one, was not in need of a guardian angel. For all other men, including Adam, an angel was available. Aquinas wrote:

> *Man while in this state of life, is, as it were, on a road by which he should journey towards heaven. On this road man is threatened by many dangers both from within and from without, according to Ps. 159:4: 'In this way wherein I walked, they have hidden a snare for me.' And therefore as guardians are appointed for men who have to pass by an unsafe road, so an angel guardian is assigned to each man as long as he is a wayfarer. When, however, he arrives at the end of life he no longer has a guardian angel; but in the kingdom he will have an angel to reign with him, in hell a demon to punish him.*[171]

He also concluded that angels could act directly upon the senses of human beings[172] and also their imagination through the medium of dreams:

> *Those things which are seen in dreams are seen by imaginative vision. But the angels reveal things in dreams, as appears from Mt. 1:20; 2:13–19 in regard to the angel who appeared to Joseph in dreams. Therefore an angel can move the imagination.*[173]

This is exactly the method by which many daemons chose to influence the behaviour of their respective eidolons. Aquinas makes an interesting point when he argues that while a guardian angel may influence the intellect, our will, or faculty for choice, remains our own. An angel cannot override our God-given freedom to do right or wrong.

As a popular image angels are nowadays depicted as having wings. This was not always the case. Early images of angels showed them without wings and in many cases they were simply depicted as a dove, presumably a symbol of their hovering, light presence. It is likely that the accretion of wings was an attempt to convey the transparent, airy incorporeality of these beings. This image has since become so deeply ingrained into Western iconography that many modern cases of encounters with angels have the perceiver describing the being as having wings.

While many cynics will use this as clear evidence of fabrication on the part of the witness, there is a counter-argument. If the Guardian Angel is an incorporeal entity inhabiting, and presumably manipulating, the brain-generated projection of 'reality' then it can, presumably, decide in which image to show itself. To be presented with an alien presence in front of you is no doubt quite shocking, but if this presence can manipulate your senses to perceive a less frightening image then surely that is what it would do.

It therefore comes as no surprise that many angel encounters fulfil the stock image of what an angel should look like. This is particularly interesting as the angels of the Bible, particularly the Old Testament, seem to have been far more human in appearance. Indeed, just how human in appearance angels were perceived to be can be shown from the quote from the New Testament book of Hebrews which exhorts believers to 'entertain strangers for many have thereby entertained angels without knowing it'.

So if the Daemon projects an image that is in keeping with the beliefs of the perceiver, what does it really look like? Well, there is strong evidence, together with a certain degree of logic, that if the Daemon is part of you then it should look like you.

Earlier we learned about Rosalind Heywood's inner dialogue with the being she called Orders. This inner voice regularly guided

Heywood to make correct decisions within her life and could easily be considered an auditory Guardian Angel. At no time did Heywood consider that this entity was anything other than something external to her psychological make-up. In her autobiography she describes one event that implies that her duality was particularly well developed.

It was late one evening and Heywood was feeling particularly selfish. Her husband was fast asleep beside her but she was keen to wake him up and demand his 'attention'. As she was about to shake him into consciousness the following curious event took place:

> Before I could carry out this egoistic idea I did something very odd – I split into two. One Me in its pink nightie continued to toss self-centredly against the embroidered pillows, but another, clad in a long, very white, hooded garment, was now standing, calm, immobile and impersonally outward-looking, at the foot of the bed. This White Me seemed just as actual as Pink Me and I was equally conscious in both places at the same time. I vividly remember myself as White Me looking down and observing the carved end of the bed in front of me and also thinking what a silly fool Pink Me looked, tossing in that petulant way against the pillows. 'You're behaving disgracefully,' said White Me to Pink Me with cold contempt. 'Don't be so selfish; you know that he is dog-tired'.
>
> Pink Me was a totally self-regarding little animal, entirely composed of 'appetites', and she cared not at all whether her unfortunate husband was tired or not. 'I shall do what I like', she retorted furiously, 'and you can't stop me, you pious white prig!' She was particularly furious because she knew very well that that White Me was the stronger and could stop her.

A moment or two later – I felt no transition – White Me was once more imprisoned with Pink Me in one body. And there they have dwelt as oil and water ever since.[174]

It seems that for a moment Heywood had literally become 'in two minds' over her actions. She was conscious of both parts of her personality. It may be significant that her double was dressed in white, exactly how our Guardian Angels often choose to appear. Can it be that angels are in fact external projections of our inner partner, our Daemon?

The day of the doppelgängers

What Heywood experienced in her bedroom that night is not, as one might expect, an event that is only to be found in books on the occult. The perception of one's own double, or *doppelgänger*, is well documented in medical and psychiatric journals. The effect is found particularly among schizophrenics but is known to occur in individuals who do not suffer from this disorder. The effect is such that there is a rich mythology surrounding the subject, particularly in German literature and psychoanalysis. Sigmund Freud discusses the *doppelgänger* in an interesting essay, 'The Uncanny'[175]. Freud explains that the German word for 'uncanny' is *heimlich* which not only means frightening, but also its opposite, 'friendly', 'intimate' or 'familiar'. In English a 'familiar' is synonymous with *doppelgänger* and is seen as a mixture of the two elements: of being on the one hand frightening, and on the other being a protector.

The image of the double being a protector could be some form of suppressed memory that we all have a real double – albeit the being lives inside our head. However, sufferers of autoscopy actually 'see' their own double. It is as if the Daemon becomes visible to the eye. It is likely that this is some form of psychological projection that is more seen in the 'mind's eye' than in external reality, although individuals who experience this effect are quite convinced that the vision is real. Ian Wilson describes a case reported by Dr Lukianowicz, a psychiatrist based at Barrow Psychiatric Hospital near Bristol. Dr Lukianowicz observed that one of his patients, a depressive, not a schizophrenic, would see:

> ... an image of his own face 'as if looking in a mirror'. This phantom face would imitate all facial expressions and D. (the patient) would frequently 'play with it', forcing it to copy his mimicking. The patient's attitude toward his double was overtly sadistic ... For instance he would often strike the phantom on its head.[176]

To D the double was so real that he gained amusement from it. That the phenomenon is considered to be a real sensation is vindicated by the description of an 'autoscopic' experience given in *The Oxford Companion to the Mind*:

> The apparition takes the form of a 'mirror image' of the viewer, facing him and just beyond arm's reach. It is life-sized and may move. Indeed it usually replicates the viewer's posture, facial expressions, and movements as though it were his reflection. But beyond these features, reported experiences show several differences from the stereotype of popular imagination. First, the image is usually transparent; it has been described as being 'like jelly', or like a film projected on glass. (But not blurred or misty – its details are quite clear). Secondly, it is generally monochromatic; if colour is observed, it is described as dull or 'washed out'. And thirdly, although the apparition may be inferred to include the whole figure, only the face, or head or trunk, are commonly 'seen'.[177]

The article goes on to say, in effect, that psychiatry and psychology have no idea as to what is going on here; that this is one of those peculiar psychological manifestations for which science has no rational explanation. However, in the light of the evidence we have seen it may not be unreasonable to conclude that autoscopy is a visual manifestation of the Daemon in the same way as Jaynes' 'voices in the head' are an aural manifestation. Both can be categorized as 'hallucinations' in that they are not perceived by any other person, but this does not mean that they are any less real. At no time do we doubt that our thoughts are real and yet no other person perceives them either. As such thoughts can also be termed hallucinations.

Although Jaynes does not make this link, the 'gods' of our ancestors did not just speak to them but also manifested themselves in physical form. In view of what we now know about autoscopy it might be concluded that 'visions' of the gods were, in fact, *doppelgängers*. The difficulty with this is that *doppelgängers* manifest another curious habit which implies that the suggestion of the phenomenon being a projection of the Daemon is too simplistic. It seems that on occasions an encounter with one's double is an encounter with the future.

In 1863, at Sibberton in Northamptonshire, the double of a young married woman, Sarah Hall, appeared in front of her husband and two guests. The double wore totally different clothing to the 'real' Sarah – the phantom wore a 'spotted, light muslin summer dress' whereas Sarah wore a warm dress suitable for the chilly autumn season. She did not have such a dress at that time but it was reported that she 'wore one like it nearly two years afterwards'.[178] Again this appears to be evidence of a form of temporal confusion rather than an encounter with the Daemon. Could it be that there are two forms of *doppelgängers*: one that is perceived only by the observer, in which case it is a Daemonic projection, and a second sort that involves the double being seen by others? I am of the opinion that this second sort supports the argument that the world of conscious experience is a recording of events that once happened lifetimes ago. Occasionally there is the equivalent of a double exposure.

In his autobiography *Poetry & Truth*, German writer and poet Johann Wolfgang von Goethe described the following curious event:

> *I was riding on the footpath towards Drusenheim, and there one of the strangest presentiments occurred to me. I saw myself coming to meet myself on the same road on horseback, but in clothes such as I had never worn. They were light grey mixed with gold. As soon as I had aroused myself from the daydream the vision disappeared. Strange however, it is that eight years later I found myself on the identical spot, intending to visit Frederika once more, and in the same clothes which I had seen in my vision, and which I now wore, not from choice but by accident.*[179]

Goethe saw himself as he would be in eight years time. This incident suggests that Bohm's concept of enfoldment, Herman Weyl's explanation of Minkowski's *spacetime*[180] and my theory of a three-dimensional life projection may be correct. As far as my theory is concerned, this incident is a simple programming error. For a second Goethe slips out of his 'review' and perceives an event that to him is yet to happen but within the timeless zone of the life review has concurrent existence. As regards Bohm's theory, incidents like this are bound to occur as areas of enfolded reality touch upon each other.

Another explanation could be found within Everett's Many Worlds Interpretation. Goethe and his double inhabited parallel universes that just happened to overlap at that point. However, for Goethe this explanation would have been totally unnecessary because within his philosophy this was not his first time living his life – he believed he had followed the same life course many times before. In 1813 he attended the funeral of the fellow writer and philosopher Christoph Martin Wieland. The death of this respected man stimulated a fellow mourner, Johannes Falk, to ask Goethe where he thought Wieland's soul could be found. After some reflection the great man embarked upon a lengthy and detailed reply, during the course of which he commented:

> *I am certain that I have been here as I am now a thousand times before, and hope to return a thousand times.*

In this light, Goethe would not be at all surprised to meet his own future self because, as he says, he has been through his life many times and has become more subconsciously aware of what is really happening to him.[181] This idea was not unique to Goethe – in fact, this belief has a great historical pedigree and is to be found in many cultures around the world. It is known as the Eternal Return and it is not nearly as crazy as it sounds.

CHAPTER 10

Ouspensky's Roundabout

It's not true that life is one damn thing after another;
it is one damn thing over and over.

Edna St Vincent Millay

Return to sender

In September 1937 a play was to open at the Royalty Theatre in London that was to cause considerable confusion amongst critics and audience alike. The play *I Have Been Here Before* was written by one of the most successful playwrights of the 20th century, JB Priestley. The critics acknowledged that the work contained some of Priestley's best dialogues. The problem was nobody understood what he was trying to say. Priestley realized that he needed an easier vehicle to convey his philosophy and in doing so watered down the ideas and presented them in a much more approachable play, *Time And The Conways*. This was to become one of his most successful works. *I Have Been Here Before* still languishes in obscurity.

Priestley was trying to introduce the general public to the ideas and philosophy of an obscure Russian intellectual by the name of Petyr Ouspensky. A few years before, in 1931, Ouspensky had published a book called *A New Model Of The Universe*[182] in which he resurrected the long-held but little known philosophical concept of the Eternal Return.

Ouspensky argued that at death we return back to our own birth and live our life again. This is not a chance to live a new life but to live the same life and to do so not once but over and over again. Ouspensky realized that this suggested Calvinistic predestination at its most extreme and watered down his ideas by saying that it is only the most basic of people whose lives do not change from lifetime to lifetime. To describe these people he used a Russian word that does not translate well into English. The word *byt* means a life entrenched in mundane repetition. He writes that 'byt people' live:

> *... a life that is deeply rooted, petrified, and routine. Their lives succeed each other with the monotony that the clock hand goes round the dial. There is nothing unexpected, no adventures. They are born and die in the same house. National calamities wipe out hundreds of thousands of these people.*

Ouspensky considered these people to be a rarity in modern, particularly Western, society. For the rest of us, we can change the course of each subsequent life but only if we subconsciously realize the effects that our actions have on others. In *I Have Been Here Before*, the character Dr Gortler is one of those rare beings who has become aware that we are trapped in an ongoing cycle of death and rebirth. He realizes that something terrible will happen to some of the characters and he intends to assist them in avoiding their respective fates. In trying to explain Ouspensky's ideas, Priestley succeeds in showing the flaws in the Russian's philosophy. Ouspensky was neither a scientist nor a psychologist. He wrote purely from subjective experience and opinion. He offers no empirical evidence for his beliefs and in the end simply frustrates the open-minded but rational reader.

In the Prologue to this book I discussed in some detail the film *Groundhog Day*. The writer and director of this film, Harold Ramis, may or may not have been influenced by the philosophy of Ouspensky but it is clear that Ramis was applying the idea of the Eternal Return to a fictional context.

Both Petyr Ouspensky and Harold Ramis touch upon the truth, possibly the greatest truth of all. Advances in science, neurology and psychology and historiography have shown that life is not a one-off, a waste. It is part of a much greater reality.

It's all a matter of time

According to Minkowski the past, present and future all exist simultaneously within what he termed 'the Block Universe' (*see* page 118). It is human perception that gives the illusion of time's inexorable flow from future to past. As some scientists have jokingly stated, time is nature's way of stopping everything happening at once. But joking aside, there is a great degree of truth in this.

Earlier we looked at the curious perceptual anomalies brought about by the onset of schizophrenia. Schizophrenics seem to suffer from hypersensitivity, as if they are accidentally accessing the sensory inputs of their own Daemon. It may be that the Daemon can perceive a universe where time does not exist. Can this be the mental state described by these 1920s schizophrenics?

I stop still, I am being thrown back into the past by words that are being said in the hall. But this all is self-evident, it must be that way! There is no present anymore, there is only this stated being related to the past, which is more than a feeling, it goes through and through. There are all sorts of plans against me in the air of this hall. But I don't listen to them, I let my mind rest so that it doesn't corrode ... Is there any future at all? Before, the future existed for me but now it is shrinking more and more. The past is so very obtrusive ... it pulls me back ... By this I want to say that there is no future and I am thrown back ... Strange thoughts enter my mind and drive me off into the past ...[183]

It pulls me back, well, where to? To where it comes from, there, where it was before. It enters the past. It is that kind of a feeling as if you had to fall back. This is the disappearing, the vanishing of things. Time slips into the past, the walls are fallen apart. Everything was so solid before. It is as if it were so close to be grabbed, as if you had to pull it back again: Is that time? Shifted way back![184]

This falling out of time has been reported regularly in studies of acute schizophrenia. In 1961, the Swiss psychiatrist Luc Ciompi made the following crucial observation:

> *The patient elevates herself above normal boundaries of time*
> *without totally surmounting them. The distinction of the present*
> *and the future is not cancelled out as the patient still speaks*
> *about both dimensions, yet the line between the actual present*
> *and the only maybe-possible and unreal future becomes swaying*
> *and possible to cross. Both dimensions encapsulate and overlap*
> *each other without a steady transition. The future fuses with the*
> *present and vice versa and experiencing acquires a flickering*
> *twilight character which is radically distinguished from how a*
> *healthy person anticipates the future in day-dreams and the like*
> *... The edge between the present and the past is swaying as well.*
> *At the same time and in a totally different way, the past is*
> *included in and fuses with the events of the present as well as*
> *usually the present is part of the past. There is a kind of*
> *condensation of time; the present is not distinguished amidst the*
> *continuous, steady flow of the past any more, but at the same*
> *time the present is not filled with something past as it usually is*
> *with normal people; in this case it overlaps ...*
>
> *The three temporal levels of past, present and future therefore*
> *seemed to overlap in the psychotic experience of the patient in*
> *an extremely peculiar simultaneousness without really*
> *invalidating the distinction of past, present and future.*[185]

At this point it may be useful to recall Bleuler's schizophrenic patient who seemed to be able to predict the future (*see* page 227). Bleuler wrote:

> *Perceptions can also be transposed into voices without the*
> *patient being at all aware of it. In that event the voice becomes*

prophetic; a patient hears, 'Now someone is coming down the
hall with a bucket of water'; then the door opens and the
prophecy is fulfilled. [186]

If we are to accept the implications suggested by the reports from schizophrenics and the results of the experiments by Bierman and Radin, and Kolers and Von Grunau, then Minkowski's equations are vindicated. If the past exists as part of an eternal 'now' and the future occupies a similar position then everything that has ever happened still exists.

To go back to my train analogy, you are inside a compartment in a moving train. You see the lights of a station flash by the window. For a split second the station is visible through the window. The station appears from nowhere, is 'experienced' by your senses, and then moves out of your vision to become, for you, a memory. It becomes part of your personal past. However, the station existed before it appeared in the window and continued to exist after it had flashed by. It was you, or more accurately your mental processes, that were passing through an eternal and ongoing present. Indeed, you may pass through that station many times like a commuter who shoots past Clapham Junction every morning of the working week.

If this is true then time must run its course again and again, events must play through again and again. Hannibal is still crossing the Alps and Napoleon is on his way to Elba, guns are poised to shoot down the Russian royal family and the planes are still crashing into the World Trade Centre. What changes is the viewpoint of the conscious observer. Time, like matter in the Copenhagen Interpretation, becomes a product of consciousness.

Did that re-occur for Poincaré?

Is it really possible to conclude from the subjective opinions of those with a diagnosed mental illness that time, or human perception of time, is circular and not linear? For mathematicians and cosmologists, such a proposal is not at all irrational. The French mathematician Henri Poincaré proposed such a possibility when he presented to the world the mathematical theorem that has become known as Poincaré's Recurrence.

Poincaré showed that a finite collection of gas particles confined to a box and subject to Newton's laws of motion must always return to their initial state given a sufficiently long period of time. The state of the gas therefore undergoes 'recurrences'. This theory came about after the work of Ludwig Boltzman regarding the flow of time. The basic law of thermodynamics states that there is a flow from hot to cold, a one-way process as stated in Newton's second law. Boltzman showed that ultimately entropy occurs. Poincaré showed that whatever set of molecular motions increase the entropy, or chaos, of the gas, there must be another set that decreases it. In other words, there is a cycle at work. The popular science writer Paul Davies comments on this:

> The length of Poincaré's cycles are truly enormous – roughly 10^n seconds, where n is the number of molecules in the universe (about a trillion trillion in 40 litres of air). The age of the universe is a mere 10^{17} seconds, so the duration is huge even for a handful of molecules. Although these cycles dwarf any other time scale they are finite in duration, so the possibility of an entropy decrease at some stage in the far future cannot be denied.[187]

There is an analogy here to a pack of cards. If the pack is initially placed in suit and the number order then shuffled, it will be in a less ordered state than before the shuffling. However, because the pack has only a finite number of states, continued random shuffling must cause any given order to appear and reappear, infinitely often.

What Poincaré's theorem is saying is that given enough time any isolated system (such as the universe itself) will return to its initial state. Given an unlimited amount of time it will do so infinitely often.[188] We already know that within Everett's Multiverse there are trillions upon trillions of universes splitting millions of times a second into copies of each other. Within this Multiverse there are easily enough universes to have a number of Poincaré's Recurrences taking place at any time somewhere within its vastness. This idea may seem strange, but the proposal that we have all lived this very life before in exactly the same way is one of the oldest theological and philosophical beliefs.

The circle of life

The following words were written by the German philosopher Friedrich Nietzsche in 1882. Nietzsche asks us to imagine that a demon:

> ... crept after you one day or night in your loneliest solitude
> and said to you: 'This life, as you live it now and have lived it,
> you will have to live again and again, times without number,
> and there will be nothing new in it, but every pain and every
> joy and every thought and sigh and all the unspeakably small
> and great in your life must return to you, and everything in the
> same series and sequence – and in the same way this spider
> and this moonlight among the trees, and in the same way this
> moment and I myself. The eternal hourglass of existence will be
> turned again and again – and you with it, you dust of dust!' –
> Would you not throw yourself down and gnash your teeth and
> curse the demon who thus spoke? Or have you experienced a
> tremendous moment in which you would have answered him:
> 'You are a god and never did I hear anything more divine!' If
> this thought gained power over you it would, as you are now,
> transform and perhaps crush you; the question in all and
> everything: 'Do you want this again and again, times without

number?' would lie as the heaviest burden upon all your
actions. Or how well disposed towards yourself and towards life
would you have to become to have no greater desire than for
this ultimate eternal sanction and seal?[189]

As we have seen, the idea of linear time, that is time progressing from the past to the future, is a creation of Western culture, specifically a creation of the Judeo-Christian West. In order to believe that the world was created at some point in the past and will end at some point in the future there has to be a progression from one point to the other. As time flows inexorably towards the future it seems that nothing can stop it. However, this may not fully be the case. What can we possibly make of this peculiar section of the *Protoevangelium* (The Book of James)? Joseph, Mary's spouse, has gone to a cave in which Jesus will be born, and goes out to fetch a midwife:

> *Now I Joseph was walking, and I walked not. And I looked*
> *up to the air and saw the air in amazement. And I looked*
> *up unto the pole of the heaven and saw it standing still, and*
> *the fowls of the heaven without motion. And I looked upon*
> *the earth and saw a dish set, and workmen lying by it, and*
> *their hands were in the dish; and they that were chewing*
> *chewed not, and they that were lifting the food lifted it not,*
> *and they that put it to their mouth put it not thereto, but the*
> *faces of all of them were looking upward.*[190] *And behold*
> *there were sheep being driven, and they went not forward*
> *but stood still; and the shepherd lifted his hand to smite*
> *them with his staff, and his hand remained up. And I looked*
> *upon the stream of the river and saw the mouths of the kids*
> *upon the water and they drank not. And of a sudden all*
> *things moved onward in their course.*[191]

This little-known document was written prior to the 3rd century CE and is found in one early document (Papyrus Bodmer V).[192] But for a decision made by the early Church Fathers as to what was and was not to be included in the authorized books of the Bible, this uncanny event would have been part of the Christian Canon. The event would have been, within certain fundamental sects, considered the word of God and therefore 'Gospel' truth. One cannot help but wonder what effect this would have had on the philosophy and ultimate world-view of Christendom.

What was happening to Joseph? Taken at face value, it seems as if the world around him had stopped, or more accurately he had somehow stepped outside of time. Although with 21st-century eyes this description is not difficult for us to visualize, living as we do in a culture where frozen images of reality – photographs –are common, it would be difficult to understand the scene with no pre-conception of a world that was not moving. To someone living in the 3rd century CE perhaps the only comparison would have been the icons found in churches and these were so lacking in perspective or depth that they were very poor copies of reality. In this light it is not unreasonable to suggest that the writer of this particular narrative was describing a real experience that he had had at some time.[193] And if we look again at the descriptions of time confusion given by Fischer's schizophrenics (*see* page 254), it becomes possible that 'Joseph' and the schizophrenics are describing the same mental state.

It is unsurprising that the *Protoevangelium* was not included in the final version of the Bible because this description runs counter to the linear time beliefs of orthodox Christianity. If time is seen to stand still, then by inference it can also flow backwards as well as forwards. That Christianity had such an issue with time can be understood when one realizes that for time to move in any other way would cause profound theological problems. St Augustine summed these up when he said:

God forbid that we should believe in this for Christ died once
for us for our sins and rising again dies no more.

The belief caused much controversy within the early Christian Church. To suggest that time can flow in any direction, become static or repeat itself was to agree with the most pernicious of all pagan heresies: that of a belief in the concept of Eternal Return. In reference to these beliefs, another early Christian writer, Nemesius, Bishop of Emesa commented:

> *Socrates and Plato and each individual man will live again,*
> *with the same friends and fellow citizens. They will go through*
> *the same experiences and the same activities. Each city, village*
> *and field will be restored, just as it was. And this restoration of*
> *the universe takes place not once, but over and over again –*
> *indeed all eternity without end. Those of the gods who are not*
> *subject to destruction, having observed the course of one period,*
> *know from this everything which is going to happen in all*
> *subsequent periods, for there will never be any new thing other*
> *than that which has been before, but everything is repeated*
> *down to the minutest detail.*[194]

The belief in the Eternal Return was central to many of the pagan myths that originated during the classical Greek period. The individual that is considered to be the founder of this belief was the philosopher and mathematician, Pythagoras of Samos, who settled in Croton in southern Italy about 525 BCE.

In a historical sense it is difficult to come to any precise understanding of exactly what Pythagoras taught. The only information we have is through a small number of fragments from the time before Plato and from discussions by authors who wrote much later – most of whom were either Aristotelians or Neoplatonists. We are told that he taught by cryptic *akousmata* (something heard) or *symbola* (symbolic statements). His pupils collected these together and handed them on in various versions. These 'Sacred Discourses', or *Hieroi Logoi*, were current by the 4th century BCE and became the basis of Pythagorean teachings. In terms of life after death it is generally accepted that the Pythagoreans believed in the transmigration of souls. The basis for the suspicion that transmigration was the overt doctrine is a comment by the philosopher Simplicius of Cilicia (*fl. c.* 530 BCE), whose commentaries on pre-Socratic beliefs are held in high esteem by classical scholars. He is quite specific when he says:

> *... the Pythagoreans said that the same things are repeated again and again.*

This is quite contrary to a belief in reincarnation. In order for transmigration of souls to take place time must be linear. A person dies and is then immediately reborn in another body. This rebirth is always either straight away or some time in the future. Re-birth does not involve being born again in the past. This way of seeing reincarnation could cause profound philosophical problems because the same soul could be co-existing at the same time in two bodies. As Pythagoreanism, and all religions that teach this concept, believe in the indivisibility and immortality of the soul, this set of circumstances is logically untenable. It seems clear that Simplicius is saying that for Pythagoreans the same events occur over and over again, in the same order, and to the same people.

In this connection it is interesting to note the words of Eudemus of Rhodes, Aristotle's disciple:

> *Some people accept and some people deny that time repeats itself. Repetition is understood in different senses. One kind of repetition may be in the natural order of things, like repetitions of summers and winters and other seasons, when a new one comes after another has disappeared; to this order of things*

*belong the movements of the heavenly bodies and the
phenomena produced by them such as the solstices and
equinoxes which are produced by movements of the sun. But if
we are to believe the Pythagoreans there is another kind of
repetition. That means that I shall talk to you and sit exactly
like this and I shall have in my hand the same stick, and
everything shall be the same as it is now and time, as it is
supposed, will be the same. This applies also to repetition,
which is always the same. Everything is the same and therefore
time is the same.*

Time simply repeats itself, or to put it another way, we all exist in a universe of 'eternal returns'. The Pythagoreans, and all the schools that followed his teachings, considered that man was caught in a universe that simply repeats itself over and over again and man is also caught within this wheel of death and re-birth. The Stoics also believed that when the planets returned to the same relative positions as at the beginning of time, the cosmos would be renewed again and again.

Stoic belief was to continue flourishing within the educated sectors of Roman society. A famous passage in Virgil's 'Fourth Eclogue' shows just how strongly the concept of the eternal return was still believed:

*Now comes the last age of the song of Cumae: the great line of
the centuries begins anew ... A second Tiphys shall then arise,
and a second Argo to carry chosen heroes; a second warfare too,
there shall be, and again shall a great Achilles be sent to
Troy.*[195]

Although the advent of Christianity saw the decline of the concept of the Eternal Return, it may be of some significance that St Augustine himself had been a Manichee and then a Neo-platonist and he would have been well aware of the concept. His hostility towards the idea was to be found in all his writings. In *The City of God*, he wrote:

> *The Pagan philosophers have introduced cycles of time in which the same things are in the order of nature being restored and repeated, and having asserted that these whirlings of past and future ages will go on unceasingly ... From this mockery they are unable to set free the immortal soul, even after it has attained wisdom, and believe it to be proceeding unceasingly to false blessedness and returning to true misery ... It is only through the sound doctrine of a rectilinear course that we can escape from I know not what false cycles discovered by false and deceitful sages.*

Augustine was obviously a man of deep thought and he was aware that a non-cyclical concept of time implies that there was a time when God existed and the universe did not. In order to get round this difficulty he argued that in order for time to exist things must be taking place. In his *Confessions*, he attempts to answer the question in a curiously modern fashion:

> *I answer not, as one is said to have done merrily (alluding to the pressure of the question), 'He was preparing hell (saith he) for pryers into mysteries.'*

By use of subtle humour he avoids the answer, but it is evident that Augustine is aware of the power of the cyclical argument. One cannot help but wonder why this towering intellect is so pre-occupied with disproving the idea of Eternal Return. The reason for this may lie in the fact that he had been, as a younger man, a follower of Mani. As a well-educated and urbane individual, it is fair to conclude that he would have been that religion's equivalent of the Cathari *parfait* and would have been acquainted with the concept of the Daemon and the real meaning of the Eternal Return.

So why was the Eternal Return so compelling a belief? That we must repeat the same situations over and over again is not as irrational as it first seems. Nature itself is cyclical. The tides, solstices, seasons and the movements of the heavenly bodies are all cyclical in their nature. Early societies thought that since time was inseparable from the circular movement of the heavens time itself reflected this quality. The Maya of Central America believed that history repeated itself every 260 years. This period was termed the *lamat*. According to the Romanian anthropologist Mircea Eliade[196] there is a deep-rooted reason why the concept of the Eternal Return held such sway with early societies. It was a symbol of the unchanging nature of things. It was of great comfort to believe that the past is also the future because it means that there is no real history. Mankind, both as an individual, and as a society, is caught in a great, unchanging cycle of rebirth and death.

The propositions of Eternal Return are impossible to prove or disprove, but when we move away from received wisdom into areas of scientific and philosophical thought we find that the impossible can become plausible. So it is with the Eternal Return.

In order to demonstrate temporal circularity we must rely on anecdotal information. This is simply because we are dealing with subjective perceptions. The subject matter is perception, which in turn is only ever perceived by a perceiver. With this in mind, let us look at some interesting incidents that imply that time is a far more complex phenomenon than it seems at first sight.

The significance of coincidence

That human beings in some way know what is about to happen to them during their lives is supported by literally thousands of cases of premonitions and prophecies. This evidence has been recognized by researchers as proof that each person's lifetime is somehow already out there, just waiting to be experienced. In 1923, the director of the French Institut Métapsychique, Dr Eugene Osty[197] wrote:

> *Every human being knows his own entire life according to laws*
> *that are still to be discovered, and metagnomic subjects*
> *(sensitives) are psychic instruments of variable quality that*
> *reveal what each human being knows concerning himself*
> *without being aware consciously, or even subconsciously, that*
> *he has this knowledge.*[198]

In some cases precognition is the wrong term to use. Knowledge of previous incarnations can be seen in the far subtler, but nevertheless common synchronicities that occur in most people's lives. A synchronicity is a significant coincidence and involves a series of coincidental events that culminate in a feeling that something is behind the scenes manipulating events.

Synchronicities take place because the perceiver of these synchronicities is living not only within their own phaneron but also within a re-run of their original life. After multiple re-runs, synchronicities are bound to take place because the Daemon is 'setting up' changes in that life re-run. Time after time these subtle changes bring about large changes (as happens to Phil Conners in *Groundhog Day*). The writer Colin Wilson writes that synchronicities are a 'nudge in the ribs from some benevolent entity, telling us not to take our problems too seriously.'[199] He then goes on to sum up his feelings about these curious coincidences:

> *We are all at our best when the imagination is awake and we*
> *can sense the presence of that 'other self', the intuitive part of*
> *us. When we are tired or discouraged we feel 'stranded' in left-*
> *brain consciousness ... We can be jarred out of this state by*
> *sudden crisis, or by any pleasant stimulus, but more often than*
> *not these fail to present themselves. It must be irritating for the*
> *'other self' to find its partner so dull and sluggish, allowing*
> *valuable time and opportunity to leak away by default. A*

'synchronicity' can snap us into a sudden state of alertness and awareness. And if 'the other self' can, by the use of its peculiar powers, bring about a synchronicity, then there is still time to prevent us from wasting yet another day of our brief lives.

Synchronicities are subtle nudges given by the Daemon to move the respective Eidolon down a particular path. Sometimes these are heeded and sometimes not. In those cases the Daemon seems to take a more direct role in the life of its Eidolon.

The analytical psychologist Karl Gustav Jung was fascinated by synchronicity and, in response to the ideas of Paul Kammerer, proposed his own theory on the subject. For Jung synchronicity was part of a greater cosmic plan that human beings cannot really understand, but merely observe. When searching through his own consciousness Jung claimed that he had encountered another personality. This being, another older man, was called Philemon, and seemed to have an independent existence:[200]

Philemon and other figures of my fantasies brought home to me the crucial insight that there are things in the psyche which I do not produce, but which produce themselves and have their own life. Philemon represented a force which was not myself. In my fantasies I held conversations with him, and he said things which I had not consciously thought. For I observed clearly that it was he who spoke, not I. He said I treated thoughts as if I generated them myself, but in his view thoughts were like animals in a forest, or people in a room, or birds in the air ... It was he who taught me psychic objectivity, the reality of the psyche.[201]

This inner voice seems to be psychic in that it warns Jung about future events. Jung had a vision of Europe covered with blood and after this vision an inner voice (not directly identified as

Philemon) said: 'Look at it well: it is wholly real and will be so. You cannot doubt it.' In August 1914 it was to become real.

Self-evidently, Jung's Philemon is a manifestation of his Daemon. He finds this being deep within his own psyche and then discovers that it has not only independent motivations but also an ability to know what is about to happen.

That Jung's Philemon was aware of the outbreak of the First World War is interesting evidence of precognitive abilities on the part of the Daemon but to the cynical mind it is hardly convincing. It is reasonable to say that most Europeans were expecting a European conflict and had been for the previous 30 years or so, but if a Daemon could show knowledge of a subject that at the time of the prediction was totally unknown now that would be proof.

In his book *The Occult*, Colin Wilson describes an incident when Jim Corbett, author of *The Man-eaters of Kumaon*, was saved by what Wilson calls Corbett's 'sixth sense' but which I believe was his Daemon. In his book *Jungle Lore*, Corbett describes how one evening when he was about to take a bath he noticed that his feet were covered in red dust. He had no idea how this had come to pass. He was aware that on his walk home there was a place that had this form of dust but he could not recall walking there. Corbett then recalled that for some curious and unconscious reason he had crossed the road at a certain point where there was a culvert. He then re-crossed the road back to join up with his usual route. This baffled him, so the next day he re-traced his steps. In the sandy bed of the culvert he noticed the pugmarks of a tiger that had been lying there. He says:

> *The tiger had no intention of killing me; but if at the moment*
> *of passing him I had stopped to listen to any jungle sound, or*
> *had coughed or sneezed or blown my nose, or had thrown my*
> *rifle from one shoulder to the other, there was a chance that*
> *the tiger would have got nervous and attacked me. My*

subconscious being was not prepared to take this risk and
jungle sensitiveness came to my assistance and guided me away
from the potential danger.[202]

In this example the Eidolon was not even aware of the actions it had taken to avoid danger. In a classic example of what psychologists term 'dual consciousness' Corbett's Daemon had taken over bodily control and in some way 'switched off' the awareness of its Eidolon. In this way the Hidden Observer can act without the knowledge of its lower self and in doing so can remain in the shadows.

For reasons so far unclear, some Daemons take a much more active role in avoiding danger or giving advice. It may be that after a certain number of life-runs the Daemon can become more immanent in the life of its Eidolon. There could be stages that start with subconscious 'hunches', move on to dreams and then, as in Corbett's case, to physical control of the body. The final stage may be a visible manifestation in the guise of a doppelgänger or double. Before the physical manifestation phase there is an intermediate step where the Daemon vocalizes its concerns or instructions. Indeed, it was such a manifestation that led to Julian Jaynes constructing his thesis on bicameralism and the 'voices' that plague schizophrenics. But what about the everyday average person? What evidence do we have that the 'friend in the shadows' speaks to them as well?

The case for angelic assistance

In 1961, a Mrs Joyce Donoghue was prescribed new sedative pills for her 3-year-old son. These had just come on the market. She was assured by her GP that they were safe. The pills did not work for him, so she left them in the cupboard. A few months later, when she was pregnant, she looked in the cupboard during a sleepless night. She saw the sedatives and decided that if they were safe for her son they would be safe for her. She explained what happened:

> I filled a glass of water and was about to swallow two when a voice – from within, I felt, said clearly as could be, 'They were not prescribed for you so don't take them'. It was a voice of authority. I threw them away and made a hot drink.[203]

Three months later the news broke about thalidomide and how babies were being born without arms and legs. The bottle in her cupboard contained one of the trade brands of thalidomide. The baby she gave birth to grew up to be an artist. As she said later:

> I could have destroyed his gift and sentenced him to a handless existence.

How was it possible that this 'voice', if merely a projection of her own subconscious, knew something that even research scientists were not aware of? If you accept the application of Everett's Many Worlds Interpretation to this case then this particular intervention was to change one young man's life totally. In one universe he would have had great difficulty in becoming an artist, whereas in this one he had his hands to pursue his calling. One particular Daemon knew exactly what it was doing.[204]

In rare cases the Daemon seems to be able to communicate on a regular basis. A gentleman by the name of Albert Tanner, discussed in Colin Parson's book *Encounters With The Unknown*,[205] describes how for 30 years he could hear a voice whispering messages in his left ear. These communications were of such a mundane nature that Tanner naturally assumed that they were part of his own subconscious. However, on 28 April 1960 he came to the realisation that the source of the voice was definitely not part of his mind. On that day Tanner was in the process of boarding a plane to go on a business trip to North Africa. As he did so, the 'voice' said, 'Do not go to Morocco'. The voice was so insistent in its tone that Tanner decided to put off his journey. On the 1 May, an earthquake hit the city where he was to stay and a tidal wave destroyed much of what was left. This incident, very reminiscent of Jaynes' experience in Boston, made him aware of his hidden friend.

From then on Tanner's Daemon became positively chatty. In 1961, he met a girl at a dance. He was on the point of proposing to the girl when the voice said, 'Do not marry her, she is ill'. She appeared to be in good health but even if she was to be ill he still wished to marry her. The pre-marriage medical was to show that she was terminally ill with leukaemia. In what must have been a very sad meeting, she refused to marry him and died soon afterwards. The voice was to comfort him during this difficult time by informing him that:

All life is immortal – only her body is dead – you will meet again if that is what you want.

Tanner interprets this as meaning they will meet again in heaven or whatever, but I think the Daemon's words should be taken literally. The voice was informing Tanner that they will meet again as they met in that life, in exactly the same circumstance. Next time round, it is possible that circumstances will conspire that the leukaemia will be avoided.

The voice continued with its predictions. It told Tanner that he would marry a woman called Elaine. Tanner did work with a woman with that name, but at that time they seemed to really dislike each other. However, after the firm's annual visit to the theatre her car broke down and he had to drive her home to Surrey. They found that they had a lot in common. Six months later they married.

In this case it may be that the Daemon was deliberately

influencing the life of its less perceptive Eidolon. It is possible that in his previous 'return' Tanner had taken his and Elaine's mutual dislike seriously and not agreed to drive her home after the work's outing. If this were the case then a totally different train of events would have taken place. By pre-warning Tanner of his potential future with Elaine, the Daemon changed the pre-ordained future of two people.

Or alternatively, since we all exist in our own personal phaneron, our own Everett universe that we bring about by the act of observation, it may be that in Elaine's phaneron she turned down the offer of a lift and married somebody else. It was only in Tanner's world – or even more confusingly, your world (because after all these words only exist in your phaneron) – that he and Elaine marry. It is certainly confusing, but if the Eternal Return, Copenhagen Interpretation and Everett's Many Worlds are actually true reflections of conscious existence then that is simply the way it is.

If you and I, and, one assumes, the rest of humanity are all re-living our lives over and over again then there has to be a vague inkling that tells us that this is the case. We must have the occasional flashback to the last revolution of the roundabout, a fleeting recognition of a location, a set of circumstances or a strong emotion. On 17 February 1828, Sir Walter Scott made the following entry into his diary:

> *I cannot, I am sure, tell if it is worth marking down, that yesterday, at dinner time, I was strangely haunted by what I would call the sense of pre-existence, viz.; a confused idea that nothing that passed was said for the first time; that the same topics had been discussed and the same persons had stated the same opinions on them ... the sensation was so strong as to resemble what is called a mirage in the desert and a calenture on board ship ... it was very distressing yesterday and brought to my mind the fancies of Bishop Berkeley about an ideal world. There was a vile sense of unreality in all I said and did.*

In a crucial sequence in *The Matrix*, the hero, Neo, sees a cat walk in front of him only to see the cat do it again a second later. What was actually taking place was that the program that runs the reality illusion, the Matrix itself, was being re-loaded. In a curious agreement across over 150 years, the writers of *The Matrix* and the writer of *Ivanhoe* both refer to Berklian idealism – that reality is an illusion generated by the mind. Scott was far from alone in describing this curious sensation. In 1850, Charles Dickens wrote:

> *We have all some experience of a feeling that comes over us*
> *occasionally.*
> *Of what we are saying or doing have been said and done*
> *before, in a remote time – of our having been surrounded, dim*
> *ages ago, by the same faces, objects and circumstances – of our*
> *knowing perfectly what will be said next, as if we suddenly*
> *remembered it.*[206]

This sensation supports three of the cornerstones of my thesis on reality. Firstly, it implies that reality is an inwardly generated illusion; secondly, it agrees with my belief that memories are recorded by the mind in a process analogous to DVD or videotape, and an occasional 'jumping' of the tape can bring about a momentary confusion for the observer. The third support is the most important of all and that is that for most of us this life is being experienced again, at least once and possibly a thousand times. An eternal return is a fact not a theological speculation.

These ideas have the support of empirical research. In the early 1980s, a researcher asked a group of randomly selected subjects if they had ever had the feeling of familiarity with a place or set of circumstances that have never been visited before. Of the 76 non-selected subjects, 71 percent reported experiencing this sensation at some time in their life, with 47 percent in the previous six months.[207] This sensation is the most common inexplicable psychic phenomenon known to mankind.

CHAPTER 11

The Strangest of Feelings

I have been here before

But when or how I cannot tell;

I know the grass beyond the door,

The sweet keen smell,

The sight, the sound, the lights around the shore.

Dante Gabriel Rossetti – 'First Light'

The French have a word for it

The term *déjà vu* was first used in 1876. In that year a professor of philosophy at a high school in Poitiers had a letter published in the prestigious journal *Revue Philosophique*. The professor in question, Emile Boriac, spoke of a particular form of memory. He described these memories as *'le sentiment du déjà vu'*. However, it was not until 1896 that the term *déjà vu* was officially proposed by a M. Arnoud at a meeting of the Société Médico-Psychologique. Even at this early stage concern was echoed that *déjà vu* (literally 'already seen') was an inadequate term and that *déjà vecu* ('already lived') was a more accurate description of how it was perceived by those who experienced it.

In the English-speaking world the phenomenon was termed 'paramnesia' but slowly this has become replaced in layman-speak by the more romantic sounding *déjà vu*. Frederick Myers, who recorded the curious events surrounding the woman's encounter with a monkey (*see* page 169), suggested that the term *promnesia* was more accurate but this did not catch the imagination and in the same article in which he described the monkey encounter he was to write:

... a suddenly evoked reminiscence of a past dream may give rise to the feeling of 'déjà vu', of having witnessed the actual scene at some indefinite time before ... The really important question ... is whether the connection may be other than casual, whether the dreamer may in some super-normal way have visited the scene, or anticipated the experience, which he was destined afterwards to behold or undergo.[208]

What is actually taking place during a *déjà vu* experience is still an area of controversy – usually another way of saying that orthodox science has no idea what is happening. A popular suggestion is termed the 'dream hypothesis' of *déjà vu*. This is the belief that the events have been dreamed prior to the actual experience. This opinion is held by a number of 'serious writers', as *The Oxford Companion to the Mind* calls them. Technically, the feeling of having dreamed the event is called a 'pseudo-presentiment', so termed because the belief is held only at the moment that the observer witnesses the event. Therefore although the events had been dreamed they were located in the subconscious and only recalled as the actual events took place. This explains why an individual who experiences a *déjà vu* does not have the ability to predict the event before it actually occurs.

Because *déjà vu* is considered to be a 'remembering' of an event, some psychiatric and psychological authorities consider it to be an example of paramnesia. *The Oxford Companion to the Mind* states:

It is therefore not a question of how an individual could remember something he has not experienced but why he should think that he has not experienced the event before.[209]

But this is not the question at all. The introduction from nowhere of the phenomenon of paramnesia is interesting in that it seems to be a circular reference. It is only referred to once in the 800 pages of this book and that is in the article in question. An attempt to gain a definition from elsewhere also was cyclical; if one looks up the word in *The Oxford Concise English Dictionary* one will find a reference but no definition. Indeed it refers the reader directly to another entry; that entry being for *déjà vu*! So it seems that having a *déjà vu* is, by definition, an example of paramnesia, which is, by definition, an example of *déjà vu*. It seems that the original memory event has been 'suppressed' because it aroused such distress in the individual that they have simply erased it from conscious recall.

> *Any repetition of the experience cannot elicit conscious recall of the original occurrence. But it does constitute a 'reminder' to the ego, and it is this which is reflected in the déjà vu feeling.*[210]

One significant problem remains with regard to this psychoanalytical explanation. No cases cited in literature appear to involve trauma of any kind. Indeed, one of the major peculiarities of the whole *déjà vu* phenomenon is how 'ordinary' the events being pre-seen are. If this explanation is to be valid it would be thought that in a vast majority of cases the subject would remember with rising distress the original experience, but this does not seem to be the case.

A far more prosaic explanation, and one that has a semblance of objective credibility, is that the events have not actually been experienced before but they are very similar to an actual event. The question then arises as to why the person does not recognize the recognition – 'this place really reminds me of ...'. The subject of the *déjà vu* is suffering from another variation of paramnesia, this time termed 'restrictive paramnesia'. It appears that this refined version of paramnesia is something that occurs regularly to us; it is that frustrating experience of not being able to identify a person whom one knows in some other context. The most obvious problem with this solution is that when we fail to remember somebody's name we are well aware of the fact that we know the person – the problem is our ability to recall the totality of the previous meeting. In *déjà vu* the whole experience is new, not parts of it.

Simply a breakdown in communication?

In 1817, the great and the good had assembled at St George's Chapel at Windsor. The occasion was the funeral of Princess Charlotte. In the congregation was Dr AL Wigan (*see* page 205). As all the local eating-houses were closed as a mark of respect, Wigan had had little to eat and had spent a sleepless night in uncomfortable lodgings. He was therefore in a fairly weakened state by the time he arrived at the service. He subsequently had to stand for nearly four hours. Suddenly, as the coffin was being lowered into its place of rest he:

> *... felt not merely an impression, but a conviction, that I had seen the whole scene before on some former occasion, and had heard even the very words addressed to myself by Sir George Naylor.* [211]

Wigan was fascinated by this whole event and decided to attempt an explanation. He came to the conclusion that *déjà vu* is caused by faulty communication between the two hemispheres of the brain. He argued that one hemisphere is simply not following what it is receiving from the senses. The attentive hemisphere thus processes the information a short time before the ineffective side; consciousness receives two identical messages with a slight delay between them. As Wigan believed, the mind will only be aware of the delayed input and that the earlier data are not fully realized. Therefore the person has a vague feeling of familiarity as the later message is received.

Wigan's theory of double consciousness, although crude by modern standards, has become the generally accepted explanation for *déjà vu*. Many years later it was to be updated and given a more solid scientific base by the work of Robert Efron.[212] Since the non-dominant hemisphere does not have the power of speech, if this side of the brain receives the external signal first it is unable to verbalize the sensation. According to Efron, Wigan's time delay is brought about by the few milliseconds it takes for the signal to transfer across the corpus callosum from the receiving non-verbal hemisphere to the talkative dominant hemisphere. It is only when the message reaches the dominant hemisphere that the perception is received by the conscious mind. However, the other side of the brain has already 'seen' the event, so the whole brain receives the message twice, like an instant replay. In support of his theory, and an idea that is crucial to later sections of this book, Efron proposed that lesions brought about by epilepsy could slow this transfer even more. It is interesting to realize that central to Efron's theory is that the concept of 'now' is different for each hemisphere. Not only is it likely that your concept of the present moment differs from somebody else's, but also that there are two concurrent perceptions of when and now within your own head.

Although Efron's idea has a good deal to commend it, it fails to explain the wider sensations that accompany the *déjà vu* experience. Marilyn Ferguson, the American writer on 'new age' philosophies, summed this up well:

> *This explanation falls far short of accounting for the subjective feeling that one is recalling the distant past. Also the déjà vu phenomenon is sometimes accompanied by a wave of ineffable poignance; the 'memory' seems to be in an emotional context.*[213]

In this light, Efron's suggestion is unsatisfactory. How much information can be processed in a fraction of a second? It takes longer than that to realize that a *déjà vu* is taking place, and it is the totality of the experience, not a tiny split second of perception, which causes the feeling of strangeness. It can be added that, neurologically speaking, the right and left hemispheres process information from the outside world in totally different ways, so it is unlikely that confusion would occur.

In defending the work of Efron, British psychiatrist and writer Oliver Sacks widens the explanation to include Freudian and other psychoanalytical explanations for *déjà vu*. In his book *Migraine*, he explains that:

> A variety of psychological and physiological theories have been advanced to explain *déjà vu* and the symptoms with which it is commonly linked. Thus Freud ascribes the uncanniness of the experience to a sudden return of repressed material, while Efron sees *déjà vu*, aphasia, and subjective time distortions, when linked together, as representing an alteration of 'time labelling' in the nervous system. These two theories are in different dimensions of explanation, and are perfectly compatible with each other.[214]

The first writer to approach the phenomenon of *déjà vu* from the personality rather than the physiological aspects was Pierre Janet[215]. It is of relevance here that *déjà vu* was also an area of human psychology that was to catch his attention. As was typical of the man, he took a totally different approach to the phenomenon. In order to explain *déjà vu*, Janet invented the term *fausse reconnaissance* (false recognition). He considered that the question to be asked was not 'Why is the observer unable to remember the previous situation?' but 'Why does the observer feel that he recognizes the present situation?'. *The Oxford Companion of the Mind* answers the question in this way:

> He (Janet) considered *déjà vu* to be one outcome of the obsessional incapacity for active and adequate responses to the pressures of reality. The essence of *déjà vu*, he suggested, is not the 'affirmation of the past'; it is the 'negation of the present'. It is not a question of how the observer remembers a present event but how he perceives the present one.[216]

While earlier in the article it was stated with some certitude that the phenomenon is 'experienced occasionally by the majority of normal people', here we see Janet saying that 'the majority of normal people' have an 'obsessional incapacity for active and adequate responses to the pressures of reality'. If the majority of normal people cannot cope with reality then the collective mental state of human beings should be a cause for great concern.

Janet was followed by many who saw *déjà vu* as simply a form of psychic self-defence. Classic psychoanalytic theory regards *déjà vu* as an attempt by the ego to handle anxieties. The id and superego are said to play decisive roles in this process. Sigmund Freud, the founder of psychoanalysis, felt the need to split the human psyche into separate, individualized, components and this has interesting similarities with the concept of the Eidolon/Daemon dichotomy. Together with his associate Josef Breuer, Freud suggested that certain memories were buried deep in the subconscious mind where they became diseased, producing 'pathogenic ideas' as he termed them. Although Freud was aware that these memories could not be accessed by the everyday consciousness, nevertheless he said they were being perceived by *somebody* within the mind. It is from this initial suspicion that Freud developed his *perception-consciousness system* – usually abbreviated to 'pcpt.-cs'.

Freud and his slip at the Acropolis

For Freud, the psychic structure of all human beings consisted of three elements: the *id*, the *ego* and the *superego*.[217] The id represents the instincts and the basic needs. This is the most primitive part of the personality. The superego is the most developed element, the conscience; through the superego we receive our ingrained feelings of shame and guilt. Although functioning at a higher level of consciousness it is the superego that is the most vulnerable. It is active and open to influence soon after birth and it internalizes any bad experiences at that vulnerable time. The ego is the part of the id that interacts with the outside world. In order to do this it has to adapt to the pressures that this interaction brings about. Rather like a conductor in an orchestra, the ego has to reconcile the forces of the id and the superego in such a way as to maximize pleasure and minimize displeasure.

Freud's idea of the 'higher self' or superego may have been stimulated by an incident that took place in 1904. As part of a holiday in Greece he visited the Acropolis in Athens with his brother Alexander. There he had a profound *déjà vu*. Many years later, on the occasion of his seventieth birthday, Freud wrote of his feelings on that day to his friend Romain Rolland. As he had stood overlooking the ancient edifice a surprising thought entered his mind: 'So all this really does exist, just as we learned at school!' Freud was surprised because the thought was not generated by his conscious mind; it was more an observation made by a deeper presence. It was as if the view had, in some deep way, been seen before. This curious event has fascinated psychiatrists since Freud described it in 1936. Some have proposed that what Freud actually experienced was, in effect, the process of psychic self-defence as proposed by Janet. This little understood psychological state is termed 'derealization'. In this the subject has a sudden feeling that what they are actually seeing is not real; it is some form of projection in the mind. There are two general characteristics of this phenomenon. The first, as described by Janet, is a form of psychological defence with the aim of keeping something away from the ego, of disavowing it. The second is the subject's dependence on the past, on the ego's store of memories and on earlier distressing experiences which have since, perhaps, fallen victim to repression. In other words, Freud had experienced the circumstances on the Acropolis at some other time, possibly under unpleasant circumstances, and his mind had suppressed the memory. However, it is clear from Freud's biography that this was his first visit to Athens. How could he have a memory of a place he had never been to? Obviously he had seen photographs but this event was a memory of the overall, not just visual, experience.

He ended the letter with the comment:

And now you will no longer be surprised that the memory of the experience on the Acropolis haunts me so often since I have become old myself and require nursing and can no longer travel.

As we have already seen, Janet explained *déjà vu* as a form of derealization. Could it be that what Freud really experienced on that day in 1904 was both an encounter with his Daemon and also a powerful *déjà vu*?

In his book *Remembering*,[218] Sir Frederic Bartlett suggested that memory is a dynamic and constructive, rather than passive process. We do not remember an event from our past: we reconstruct it, taking into account the experiences and sensations we have had since the recalled event took place. We remember a subconsciously revised version of events and each time we recall the event additional changes are made. In this way what we remember is not the original event but our recollection of the last time we recalled it. Some psychologists argue that the more often an original event has been recalled the more modifications will have been introduced, and the weaker the subjective fit between our current recollection and any re-presentation of the actual original material. When we do see the original material there is a cognitive mismatch between our 'memory' of something and its reality. This confusion brings about the disassociation that categorizes *déjà vu*. The conscious mind fails to recognize the circumstances as a genuine memory but there remains a subliminal recognition.

The technical term for this confusion involves, yet again, the 'cover-all' word paramnesia, more specifically 'restricted paramnesia'. It is therefore due to forgetting, not remembering.

Psychologists Banister and Zangwill[219] argued that this interpretation was incorrect. For them *déjà vu* was different from paramnesia in that it involved reliving an event in its entirety and was not obviously initiated by an isolated feature. In addition, *déjà vu* may have no parallel in the history of the subject whereas restricted paramnesiac experience always turned out to have a genuine foundation in past experiences. Banister and Zangwill were not alone in this opinion. In a later paper, RW Pickford was to give his support.[220]

A further weakness of restricted paramnesia as an explanation of *déjà vu* is that if this is a regular construct of memory then why are we not experiencing *déjà vu* all the time? *Déjà vu* is noticed by the experiencer because it is so strange and unusual – not because it is a regular occurrence. It seems from all this that the majority of psychologists and psychiatrists are tying themselves in knots trying to avoid facing what is patently obvious: *déjà vu* is what it is claimed to be by those who experience it. They are remembering an event or place that they have experienced or been to before.

Vernon pools his resources

Vernon Neppe is not one of these. Originally senior lecturer and consultant psychiatrist at the University of the Witwatersrand, he is recognized as the leading expert on *déjà vu*. Determined to view the phenomenon in an objective and rational way, he felt that a simple definition of the subject was needed. After many years research he suggested the following definition of *déjà vu*:

> *Any subjectively inappropriate impression of familiarity of the present with an undefined past.*

For Neppe, it is important to understand precisely what we mean when we use the term *déjà vu*. He argues that it is not a *feeling* but an impression; a cognition rather than an effect. He also thinks that it is equally important to differentiate *déjà vu* from other similar phenomena such as flashbacks, cryptomnesia and actualized precognition. He explains:

> *Initially, let us consider the phrase in the déjà vu definition 'present experience with ... past'. For familiarity to occur there must be a comparison. Déjà vu experience is firmly rooted in the PRESENT; and the comparison is made with the PAST. By stressing the present, one is able to differentiate the interpretative component of déjà vu with the purely experiential flashback.[222] In the flashback experience, one may see facets of one's past life passing before one's eyes. One may for that brief period conceive of oneself as not in the present but actually back in the past. Flashbacks (also called 'playbacks') are different from conventional vivid memory: in a vivid memory, the imagery and percepts of the past come into focus but the subject is firmly rooted in the present. Both differ from déjà vu: for déjà vu to occur there needs to be an experience which is happening at that moment and it is that experience which seems familiar. Déjà vu also differs from cryptomnesia[223] (literally: hidden memories): for in the latter the person will have a memory of something which did not happen to him but there is no comparison with the present, just a sense of past ideas which are familiar yet should not be because they apparently do not exist.[224]*

We have already encountered cryptomnesia in our review of past-life recall. As Neppe points out, this is a very different phenomenon from *déjà vu*, as are flashbacks. It is important that this distinction is made. *Déjà vu* is not a memory of a previous life in an earlier time. It is a memory of that actual moment in time: a re-living of the actual event.

Neppe feels that it is important that the sensation involves an *undefined* period in the past. If the subject could define where the original event had taken place then the mystery would be of a totally different nature. In this case the past would be, as Neppe says, 'actualizing itself' in the present or pseudo-presentiment.[225] This is the sensation that the present situation has been foretold. This is different from precognition, which is the foretelling of some future event, an event by its very nature that is yet to take place. To experience pseudo-presentiment one must be at that point in time when the precognized event actually comes to pass. In the case of *déjà vu* the subject cannot recall the prediction; only a sensation that it has now come to pass. Neppe considers this to be a particular form of the déjà vu phenomenon and terms it *déjà pressenti*.[226]

This is not an easy concept to understand. It involves various points of view, temporal locations and subjective opinions. Neppe gives an example, reported by Carroll B Nash, of a subject who described the following experience:

> *In 1948 I had a most interesting experience in a sixteenth-century hacienda in Bolivia. While going through the building with the owner I suddenly found myself in an area I had seen in a dream which had recurred many times over a period of twenty years. To the astonishment of the owner I accurately described the layout and appearance of an entire wing before he had opened the door leading into it. Since that time I have not had this dream.*[227]

This is somebody re-living a dream sequence in real life. What makes this a *déjà vu* for Neppe is the fact that the scene is recognized as it takes place. Up until the point of recognition the location in time and space of the original dream is unknown. Indeed, it is important that the circumstances of the dream are only recalled at the point of recognition.

Earlier we touched on the work of the Switzerland-based American psychotherapist Arthur Funkhouser. Funkhouser is of the opinion that many *déjà vu* experiences can be attributed to dreams. The issue is that dreams are nearly always forgotten on waking and when foreseen circumstances come to pass they come as a surprise to the observer. This sensation is reflected in the following description found in Neppe's book on *déjà vu*. The narrator was a 56-year-old pension clerk who attributed all his *déjà vu* experiences to dreams. However, it was only after the event took place that he acknowledged it as being from a dream. He claimed he never remembered his dreams for more than a short time after waking. This was his chosen *déjà vu* case:

> *It happened in connection with my work recently. It signified*
> *something I had done. It proved what you had mentioned*
> *about déjà vu and déjà entendu. I had a sense of familiarity*
> *about the whole thing because I had dreamt it. But I couldn't*
> *remember the actual dream or when I dreamt it. Each thing*
> *that came up was familiar. I felt like a prophet because I knew*
> *what was coming up. I could have proved I was a prophet if I*
> *had mentioned it to someone before it happened, but I hadn't*
> *done so. It started off when the name of one of my clients was*
> *mentioned. I had to go through the file (as part of my work)*
> *and felt I knew what was coming next. I've had several*
> *instances like this – all dreams coming true but I can only*
> *remember this one well.*

This experience seems to vindicate both Funkhouser's 'dream theory' and the work of Dunne, although Funkhouser is still puzzled by one aspect of the phenomenon:

> *... why are déjà vu experiences so banal? Why am I given a*
> *preview of just this everyday situation, and not something more*
> *striking, or at least more meaningful? Is this just some random*
> *event, like radioactive decay, or is there some hidden, meta-*
> *purpose involved?*[228]

This question is crucial. The sheer ordinariness of the circumstances of *déjà vu* is by far one of its most outstanding characteristics. It is useful at this stage to review a few of these experiences, some experienced by the very famous and some by the not so famous, but all marked by the prosaic nature of the circumstances.

Time after time

In his book *Our Old Home*, the 19th-century American novelist Nathaniel Hawthorne wrote of an event that occurred when he was living in England. While he was visiting the manor house at Stanton Harcourt in Oxfordshire he describes the following curious sensation:

> *Now – the place being without a parallel in England, and therefore necessarily beyond the experience of an American – it is somewhat remarkable that, while we stood gazing at the kitchen, I was haunted and perplexed by an idea that somewhere or other I had seen just this strange spectacle before. The height, the blackness, the dismal void, before my eyes, seemed so familiar as the decorous neatness of my grandmother's kitchen ... I had never before had so pertinacious an attack, as I could but suppose it, of that odd state of mind wherein we fitfully and teasingly remember some previous scene or incident, of which the one now passing appears to be but an echo and the reduplication.*

It is important to note that Hawthorne's *déjà vu* is not a remembering of being in that place in the distant past, nor is it a recollection of living a life many centuries ago in that house. It is a remembering of standing, as Nathaniel Hawthorne, at that particular point in time. It was a 'memory' from his own past recalling an event in his present. This is a classic case of pseudo-presentiment.

The recognition of a place, usually a house, is particularly common. It is as if certain objects within a room can re-stimulate long-lost memories from deep in the subconscious. In relation to memory we reviewed in some detail the phenomenon of charged memories; the recollection of a seemingly unimportant event in one's past that seems to stay as a vivid image in the mind. This image never fades with time and, on occasions, can become more focused and powerful as we become older. These memories are usually tied to places rather than events. In this category falls the following account by one of Neppe's respondents, a 43-year-old accountant:

> In 1951, I was 15 years old and my mother, myself, and a younger sister were shifting house. I had not previously seen or inspected the new home until the day that we actually moved into it and it was therefore very strange for me to enter the house and suddenly realise that I knew the place, that I felt that I had been there before. This was, of course, not so. I had not seen the place in my life before. As I entered the front door everything seemed familiar. I stepped through the front door directly into the lounge and it seemed that everything became lighter. There was no gloom, every detail stood out brightly and I felt surrounded by a strange glow, all my senses felt sharpened. I knew that I knew the place from some other time, or that is what I felt. All sounds were clearer; I knew what the rest of the house looked like before I actually had been through it: I went from room to room with a growing sense of excitement, coupled with a feeling of exhilaration and curiosity, and as quickly as it came, so the sensation left me. It could not have lasted for more than three minutes or the time it took me to move through the whole house.

This case is of importance because it invalidates virtually all the psychoanalytic explanations of *déjà vu*. The person in question does not perceive the incident in 'sections' of half a second as would be expected if Efron and Wigan's explanations are to be believed. On the contrary, the subject recognized the next room and its contents before even going through the door. It is impossible for his non-dominant hemisphere to have already seen the room. If this description is to be accepted at face value then either *déjà vu* is a recollection of a past life or it is a form of precognition. No other explanation is feasible. The next case is also from Neppe:

> *It was in Nyanga in Rhodesia. I was twelve or thirteen. We were driving up the mountains. We had never been there before. The feeling started when we passed a particular tree - it was at a peculiar angle and had a stump next to it. Everything then looked familiar – the trees, I knew every tree. We were going up the straight and a corner was ahead. I knew that when we turned the corner there would be a decline onto a bridge. It was as though I had driven along it before.*

The psychoanalysts would have us believe that the young woman's mind followed the following inductive process as she experienced her *déjà vu*:

1 'Look, there is a strange looking tree'.
2 'That tree reminds me of something but I cannot quite recall it' [classical paramnesia].
3 'Now what does it remind me of? – oh yes, I remember seeing it before'.
4 'Yes, and now I remember all the other trees'.
5 'I remember that there will be a corner and a decline to a bridge'.

There is, however one more explanation of *déjà vu* that touches on what I believe actually to be taking place. Eli Marcowitz[229] argued that *déjà vu* was simply a wish for a second chance to correct unresolved guilts. He believed that *déjà vu* involved transient psychotic episodes, and was motivated by an extreme wish to turn back time. As such, *déjà vu* is really *encore vu* because the unsatisfactory had been repeated as the satisfactory.

The structures of transcendence

So far we have reviewed what is perceived during a *déjà vu* experience, but perception is only one side of a two-sided coin. Neurologists, unlike psychologists, are interested in the other side – the physical evidence of consciousness. For many anatomists and neurologists this is to be found in the limbic system (*see* page 207).

As well as discovering the area of the brain which was to be named after him, Paul Broca was also responsible for the term 'the limbic lobe'. In 1878, he used this to describe the part of the human brain surrounding the brain stem. If the brain is sliced in half so that the two hemispheres fall apart, the limbic system is seen as a complex conglomeration of modules, lumps, tubes and chambers lying beneath the cortex. These structures include the hippocampus, thalamus, hypothalamus and amygdala. With the exception of the pineal gland, each of these modules is duplicated in each hemisphere. Broca had no idea what functions these structures performed. It was only in 1935 that they were found to be the area where the non-physical world of emotions is processed and turned into physical action.

One of the most terrifying illnesses known to man is rabies. Within hours it can turn a healthy, rational human being into a raving mass of raw emotions. Caused by a bite from a rabid animal, usually a dog, it triggers such psychological changes that it was believed that those unfortunates who contracted the dread disease were possessed by demons or turning into werewolves. It was only in the mid-1930s that the anatomist James Papez suspected that something in the dog's saliva travelled from the site of the bite and infected the brain. He discovered that this something was a virus and that it travelled along the nerves around the bite and on to the spinal cord. From there it was a straight journey to the victim's brain. Papez was keen to know which part of the brain was attacked by the virus. On dissecting the brains of victims he discovered that the virus was quite specific in the region that it attacked – the limbic system. Because rabies manifested itself in fits of rage and terror it became clear to Papez that the limbic structures must be intimately involved in human emotional behaviour. A century after Broca had discovered the limbic system its function had been found.[230]

It has been subsequently found that the limbic system is a form of junction box. It receives input from all the sensory systems – vision, touch, hearing, taste and smell – and then transfers these data to other parts of the brain. It also processes this input in some way and produces an output of pure, irrational emotion. Orchestrating this output is the hypothalamus. This small mass of cells sends hormonal and neural signals to the pituitary gland. Acting on these instructions, the gland can change the actions of many bodily processes such as the production of tears, saliva, sweat, heart rate, body temperature and respiration – all those functions that are not controlled by the conscious mind. In this way the hypothalamus can be seen as a vestige of the original, unthinking brain of our animal and plant ancestors. Its four main functions are fighting, fleeing, feeding and sexual behaviour.

Our understanding of the limbic system was widened by the pioneering work of RG Heath. Operating on conscious, psychotic patients, using a process similar to that pioneered by Wilder Penfield, Heath stimulated an area of the hippocampus by means of an electrode and also by dripping a solution containing neurotransmitter chemicals onto the exposed surface. In some patients:

> ... *expressions of anguish and despair changed precipitously to*
> *expressions of optimism and elaborations of pleasant*
> *experiences, past and anticipated. Patients could calculate more*

rapidly than before stimulation.[231] *Memory and recall were*
enhanced.[232]

In 1969, Dr Jose Delgado of Yale University also applied the methods pioneered by Penfield to the limbic system, specifically the hippocampus and amygdala.[233] He had similar results to Heath but his had the additional factor that actual *déjà vu* experiences were directly stimulated by the electrodes. Delgado was amazed to discover that in certain cases the stimulation only needed half a second to cause a slip in the subject's perception of what constitutes 'now'. Delgado noticed that patients would listen to the subsequent exchange between themselves and the doctor with amusement and bewilderment:

> *But this has all happened before. I know what you were going to say before you said it.*[234]

This bears stunning similarity to the words uttered by the young lady affected by Penfield's electrodes over 30 years before:

> *... [I have the] feeling that I knew everything that was going to happen in the near future.*[235]

Nine years later, another group of researchers, lead by Dr E Halgren, carried on the work of Delgado. Unlike Delgado, they worked directly with individuals who suffered from the illness temporal lobe epilepsy (for more on this, *see* Chapter 12). Halgren and his associates worked with 36 epileptic subjects. Out of 3,495 stimulations they managed to evoke 267 mental experiences. Of these 19 were of a *déjà vu* nature in content. Halgren suggested that *déjà vu* is personality rather than physiology based since 18 of the 19 subjects who experienced 'dreamy states' had previously had *déjà vu* as part of their pre-seizure aura.

The results of the work by Delgado and Halgren vindicate the suggestion made by Karl Pribram that the limbic system is the point at which consciousness interfaces with the transcendent. Earlier we discussed in some detail Pribram's holographic theory of memory (*see* page 88). For him the brain holds memories across the cortex rather than in one specific location. In a paper published in 1969, Pribram wrote:

> *Epileptogenic lesions of the medial part of the pole of the*
> *temporal lobe of the brain near the amygdala episodically*
> *disrupt self-awareness. Patients with such lesions experience*
> *inappropriate déjà vu and jamais vu feelings of familiarity and*
> *unfamiliarity and fail to incorporate into memory experiences*
> *occurring during an episode of electrical seizure activity in*
> *their brains. In a sense, therefore, these clinical episodes point*
> *to a transcendence of content, a phenomenon of consciousness*
> *without content, a phenomenon also experienced in mystical*
> *states, and as a result of Yoga and Zen procedures-a*
> *transcendence of the dichotomy between 'self' and 'other'*
> *awareness.*[236]

In recent years, Pribram's application of Bohmian holography to memory has been given new life by the theories and writings of Herman Sno, a psychiatrist at De Heel Hospital outside Amsterdam. Sno has made an intensive study of the scientific literature on *déjà vu* and has come to a similar conclusion to Pribram – that the answer lies in holograms. We have seen that the image contained in a hologram is to be found in all parts of the photographic plate. If the plate is smashed each piece contains a fuzzy version of the original image rather than a part of the full image. Pribram, and now Sno, believe that memory works on the same principle. Memory is located all over the brain, not in one spot, and each part contains the image of the whole.

Sno argues that if memories are indeed stored in the brain as holograms, each part of the memory contains all the sensory and emotional data needed to recall the entire original experience. A single detail – the sound of a lover's voice or the smell of a child's clothing – can evoke the complete remembered scene. According to this model, *déjà vu* occurs when a detail from a current experience so strongly resembles a detail from a previous experience that a full-blown memory of the past event is conjured up. 'As a result of the mismatching,' says Sno, 'the brain mistakes the present for the past. You feel certain you've seen the picture before.'

Sno has a further refinement and it involves the theory that memories are recorded in a similar process to a DVD. As we have seen, there is strong evidence to suppose that the brain records all incoming sensory data and then replays the 'images' to consciousness as and when the information is needed. A record can be played once, twice or a million times and if the process of short-term recall is over-ridden this 'replay' may be perceived as being the first time by the observer, and for Sno a similar process is responsible for a *déjà vu* sensation. He proposes that sensory impressions of a current experience get detoured in the brain and are not immediately perceived, although the information is stored as a memory. This split-second delay in cognition creates the unsettling impression that the event is, as Sno explains, 'being experienced and recalled simultaneously.'[237]

Sno considers that what I call the Bohmian IMAX is the source of *déjà vu* experience and Karl Pribram implies that the temporal lobes are, like the limbic structures, a peculiar part of the brain where mind and matter overlap. But it does not stop there. In a similar way to that in which David Bohm believes that reality itself is a holographic image, the latest theories of the universe have curious echoes of what he termed the 'Holomovement'. The following is taken from the cover story of the August 2003 edition of *Scientific American*:

*An astonishing theory called the holographic principle holds
that the universe is like a hologram: just as a trick of light
allows a fully three-dimensional image to be recorded on a flat
piece of film, a seemingly three-dimensional universe could be
completely equivalent to alternative quantum fields and
physical laws 'painted' on a distant, vast surface ... Physicists
hope that this surprising finding is a clue to the ultimate theory
of reality.*[238]

To paraphrase what the writer, Jacob Beckstein, actually means by this statement: the universe is a hologram and therefore everything contained in that universe is also a hologram. This includes you, your brain and everything you perceive.

The aura of infinity

In 1870 a short paper appeared in the physicians' journal *The Practitioner*. The article was written by a young medical doctor using the pseudonym 'Quaerens'. This mysterious person explained that he had many times experienced *déjà vu* but the intensity and frequency had increased when he discovered that he had a new illness. He added that the attacks of this illness were always preceded by strong sensations of *déjà vu* and presentiment. The illness was a particular form of seizure termed temporal lobe epilepsy.

Ten years later, Hughlings Jackson, the pioneer in the study of epilepsy, was to show particular interest in the case of 'Quaerens'. For Jackson this case supported his belief that what he termed 'dreamy state' was identical to *déjà vu* and was directly linked to epileptic seizures.

Another patient of Jackson, also a medical doctor, identified simply by the letter 'Z', suffered from what Jackson termed 'reminiscence'. By this Jackson meant the peculiar pre-seizure feeling that epileptics have that augurs an attack. Z described this sensation:

What is occupying the attention is what occupied it before, and
indeed has been familiar, but has been for time forgotten, and
now is recovered with a slight sense of satisfaction as if it had
been sought for ... At the same time, or ... more accurately in
immediate sequence, I am dimly aware that the recollection is
fictitious and my state abnormal. The recollection is always
started by another person's voice[239], or by my own verbalised
thought, or by what I am reading and mentally verbalise; and I
think that during the abnormal state I generally verbalise some
such phrase of simple recognition as 'Oh yes. I see', 'Of course',
'I remember', etc, but a minute or two later I can recollect
neither the words nor the verbalised thought which gave rise to
the recollection. I only find strongly that they resemble what I
have felt before under similar abnormal conditions.[240]

For Hughlings Jackson, his 'dreamy state' was not uncommon and
could be found in non-epileptic individuals as well as those who
suffered seizures. In 1876, he wrote:

It is well known that such sensations of 'reminiscence' are not
uncommon in healthy people, or in trivial disorders of health.[241]

He considered that 'reminiscence' was a phenomenon of a
normally functioning brain. Unfortunately, this was not to
become the generally accepted position. To many physicians and
neurologists, from Victorian times to the present day, *déjà vu*,
reminiscence and dreamy states are all linked in some way to
pathological states in the brain. It is believed that any individual
who reports such a sensation should be observed carefully for
future brain disease.

In his 1895 Cavendish lecture before the West London Medico-
Surgical Society, Sir James Chrichton-Browne took as his major
topic Hughlings Jackson's 'dream states'. He made particular

reference to the effect that these sensations have on creative individuals. In particular he discussed the works of Rossetti, Scott and Dickens.[242] He then also pointed out that all three died of brain disease. For Chrichton-Browne and many of those present, this was evidence that any similar sensations reported by patients should be carefully observed and further tests made. His opinion is a reasonable and sensible approach. Abnormal psychological effects of any nature may be symptoms of something far more dangerous. For a physician to ignore such symptoms would be reckless in the extreme. It is therefore unsurprising that most psychiatrists and neurologists see *déjà vu*, dream states and reminiscences as evidence of physiological disturbances in the brain. However, if anecdotal evidence is to be believed *déjà vu* is experienced by far more people than those who have, or will develop, epilepsy or brain disease. Although there is an assumption that the likelihood of experiencing a *déjà vu* sensation is far greater in those who are diagnosed as suffering from epilepsy, how does this suspicion actually stand up to empirical analysis?

Crossing the frontier

The culmination of Dr Neppe's life-long study of the phenomenon of *déjà vu*, his major work, *The Psychology of Déjà vu*,[243] is the only extensive work available on the subject. In 1979, he carried out the first of his studies of the phenomenon when he took the opportunity to question 84 women who were attending one of his lectures in South Africa. Neppe found that 96 percent claimed to have had *déjà vu* at some time in their lives, 30 percent in the previous six months and 19 percent in the previous month.[244] However, one cannot escape the fact that an individual who chooses to attend a lecture by an expert on the subject will have personal motivations drawn from personal experience. In view of this the high incidence may not be surprising as the subjects had, in effect, self-selected. Neppe was particularly interested in the fact that over 90 percent of the respondents were over 40 years of age and that one of the few 'known facts' about *déjà vu* was that it has an inverse relation with age:[245] the younger the subject the more likely it is that they will experience it. However, it is reasonable to conclude that Neppe's subjects' positive responses were in a unique set of circumstances and therefore can only be analyzed in isolation.

Neppe was involved in a later study in the early 1980s. This was a structured and objective exercise which involved both an interview and the use of a questionnaire devised by Neppe himself. His aim was not only to isolate the incidence of *déjà vu* but also who experienced it and in what way. He had one group of non-selected subjects and a second group who had been selected because of their psychiatric condition. Of the 76 non-selected subjects, 71 percent reported experiencing *déjà vu* at some time in their life, with 47 percent in the previous six months.[246] However, it was the responses of those who had the form of epilepsy suffered by Hughlings Jackson's 'Quaerens' that demanded further analysis. For these individuals the source of the seizure lies in the temporal lobes of the brain, the same area that Karl Pribram located as the interface between mind and matter, the part of the brain where 'you' interfaces with 'reality'. Neppe found that 86 percent of the 'temporal lobe' epileptics (TLE) reported *déjà vu* experiences, as opposed to 71 percent of the control group. It is likely that there is something significant happening here.

Neppe was concerned that *déjà vu* was an inadequate and misleading term for certain forms of the sensation. The words literally mean 'already seen' but Neppe argues that in many cases the subject is experiencing a much wider sensation. In order to reflect this, Neppe suggested the term *déjà vécu* (already lived) as being far more accurate. While this leaves Efron's explanation of *déjà vu* as a valid proposal, he is unable to explain *déjà vécu*. It comes as no surprise that the TLE group showed a much higher incidence of this experience than of ordinary *déjà vu*. Out of the 12, 3 felt that they were 'reliving the whole'. The fact that *déjà vécu* is in some way an essential part of the whole TLE illness is echoed by the American psychiatrist Strauss. For Strauss, *déjà vécu* is a special kind of *déjà vu* with a deep qualitative component, going far beyond familiarity with an intensity sometimes so great that the impression of reliving exactly the same situation resulted.[247] Strauss considers that this special type of *déjà vu* occurs significantly more often in TLE than with the general population.[248]

For those with TLE the *déjà vu* experience has one other side-effect. Out of the 12, 9 reported that during the sensation they experienced a higher awareness of their environment, with their senses becoming far more acute, and 6 stated that this awareness was greatly enhanced. In a manner reminiscent of the experiences described by schizophrenics, this implies that they had more time available to process incoming sensory signals – in other words time was dilating for them.

From Neppe's findings it is clear that the incidence of TLE and *déjà vu* have a strong correlation. As he writes:

> *When frequency in individuals is considered, temporal lobe epileptics (TLEs) generally have déjà vu far more frequently than other groups …*[249]

In addition to time dilation, a heightened sensory awareness and a form of psychological transcendentalism seem central to the *déjà vu* experience of individuals with TLE. It is as if they are more attuned to the phenomenon than non-TLE subjects. The work of William Grey Walter implied as much. Working at the Maudsley Hospital in London, the noted Anglo-American physiologist developed a series of tests to isolate susceptibility to these curious storms in the brain. It had been believed for many years that the flickering of a light source could bring on an attack.

Working on this assumption, Grey Walter attuned a strobe light to reflect exactly the rhythm as the subject's brain wave patterns. The subject would then stare at the flashing light and would be asked to describe how they felt. Much to Walter's surprise, it was not just epileptic seizures that the experiment engendered. Many subjects experienced disruptions in the way they perceived time. In one memorable case the subject described the sensation as if:

> *... yesterday was at one side, instead of behind, and tomorrow was off the port bow.*[250]

The Russian writer Feydr Dostoevsky describes a similar situation in his book *The Possessed*. Two of the central characters, Stavrogin and Kirilov, are having one of those heated discussions on life and death that so permeate Dostoevsky's work. Stavrogin is asking Kirilov whether he believes in a future eternal life:

> *'No, not in a future eternal life, but in this present eternal life. There are moments – you can reach moments – when time suddenly stops and becomes eternal.'*

> *'And you hope to reach such a moment?'*

> *'I do'*

> *'It is hardly likely in our time', Stavrogin said slowly and thoughtfully, also without any irony. 'In the Apocalypse, the angel promises that there will be no more time'.*

> *'I know. There is a lot of truth in it; it is clear and precise. When man attains bliss, there will be no more time because there will be no need for it. It's a very true thought'.*

'Where will they hide time?'

'Nowhere. Time is not a thing, it's an idea. It will vanish from the mind.'

Dostoevsky is describing a similar sensation to that described by the writer of the apocryphal Book of James. Could it be that the vision of the unknown man in the Book of James was part of an epileptic seizure, or more accurately part of the pre-seizure *aura*? Does, in fact, epilepsy allow access to the temporal world of our Daemon?

The evidence that *déjà vu* is more than a simple confusion in the brain is overpowering. It is a phenomenon whereby ordinary individuals can perceive the greater picture. It seems that one group of individuals have an even wider perception of transcendence – those who suffer from TLE. Whatever they see and feel both prior to and during a seizure is indescribable, like somebody with sight trying to explain the sky to a blind person. It was Dostoevsky who tried to put this sensation into words in his book *The Idiot* when he described the sensations felt by Prince Myshkin:

> *That in his epileptic condition there was one phase before the attack itself (provided the attack came in waking hours) when suddenly in the midst of sadness, mental darkness, oppression, his brain momentarily was as if set on fire, and all his vital forces strained themselves at once, in an unusual outburst. His consciousness and feeling of being alive became almost tenfold during these moments, which repeated themselves like lightning. His mind, his heart were illuminated with an unusual light; all excitement, all doubts, all troubles, were at once as if at peace, solved in some higher calm full of clear harmonious joy and hope, full of intelligence and final reason.*

Yet these moments, these flashes, were nothing but the
presentiment of that final second (never more than a second)
with which the attack started. This second was unbearable.

In these few words we have it all: transcendence, illumination, harmony and, most importantly, time dilation. Whatever happens to temporal lobe epileptics, it seems that they are tuning into a different version of reality to the rest of us, possibly the reality of the Daemon itself.

CHAPTER 12

The Falling Sickness

Reality is that which, when you stop believing in it,
does not go away.

Philip K Dick

Peering over the precipice

Epilepsy is the price that some have to pay for having the most amazing object in the universe sitting a few inches behind our eyes. As with all complex systems, the more elaborate they are the more chances there are for small things to go wrong. In the case of epilepsy, the culprits are the group of chemicals called neurotransmitters.

The existence of neurotransmitters, although long suspected, was confirmed in the 1930s but it was only in the 1960s that their role was fully understood. To date, 50 or so have been isolated, the most important being serotonin, noradrenaline, glutamate and a group of pain-killing opiates called endorphins. These chemicals can have a marked effect upon mood and temperament. By stimulating the internal creation of neurotransmitters an individual's whole personality can be changed. For example, the much discussed 'feel-good' drug Prozac works by enhancing the production of serotonin within the axons.

The major cause of epileptic seizures could be said to be the design of the neurons within the brain. In general, speed of transmission is of great importance as regards nerve impulses. To facilitate this, most of the large neurons in the central nervous system are encapsulated by a multi-layered white-segmented sheath called myelin. This not only insulates and protects the axon but also increases the speed of nerve impulse conduction.

However, many of the axons that provide intercellular communication within the brain's grey matter do not have myelin. It appears that in order for the mammalian brain to function correctly the signals should travel more slowly than elsewhere. This allows information to be transmitted with stability and it helps the integration of the information onto the specialized receptors located in dendrites. It seems that messages need to 'overlap' in some way. As long as the messages remain at a certain level, the unmyelinated neurons can cope with ease, but damage to these areas, specifically scar material, can cause an overload. This precipitates a storm of over-excited neuronal activity to surge across the brain, resulting in uncoordinated spasmodic movements, collapse and possible loss of consciousness. For most people this is epilepsy. However, grand mal, or 'tonic-clonic' as it is now known, is just one form of epilepsy. For sufferers of tonic-clonic epilepsy the seizure always ends in a collapse and loss of consciousness with few, if any, recollections of the seizure itself. TLE, the form of epilepsy suffered by Dostoevsky and all the epileptics described in this book, is brought about by damage to the areas of the brain that use one particular neurotransmitter, glutamate. The areas damaged are the limbic system, particularly the hippocampus, and the temporal lobes.

It will be recalled that each hemisphere has its own series of small structures that sit underneath the respective cortex and that these organs – the hippocampus, amygdala, septum, thalamus, fornix, cingulate gyrus and reticular formation – are the location of man's basic instincts. It is this part of the brain that governs automatic responses such as fear, anger, parenting behaviour and aggression. It is also the seat of deep-rooted emotional reactions such as tears and laughter. This does not mean that it is 'primitive' in the accepted sense of the term, because some of man's most noble attributes such as love and the creative process may also be rooted here, but it is important to recognize that this area is unconscious and acts without the will and control of the conscious mind.

The reticular formation is also believed to be the part of the brain that is responsible for the general state of attention and awareness. Some neurophysiologists have, in an apparent contradiction, argued that this could be the seat of consciousness. It is argued that if this area is damaged then unconsciousness will result. When the brain is awake the reticular formation is active. During sleep the reticular formation ceases its activity and remains so during dreaming and thus cannot be involved in this crucial activity.

The temporal lobes sit just behind each ear and seem to be a common source of focal epileptic seizures. Unlike the frontal, parietal and occipital lobes, which have single clearly defined functions in terms of moving, feeling or seeing, the temporal lobe has many functions. Therefore, when seizures arise in this part of the brain, the experience is varied and powerful. What makes TLE so interesting is that many neurologists consider that this area is involved in some basic way with the storage of memories. This is not to say that memories are actually located within the temporal lobes but simply that they act as a librarian does in a library. They do not have the books with them but they know exactly where to find them when asked. We have seen that researchers such as Lashley and Pribram have evidence that memory is stored within the brain as a hologram stores an image – that is to say, that memories are everywhere and nowhere. In this context it is believed that the temporal lobes work closely with a particular structure within the nearby limbic system, the amygdala. The amygdala is a strange and interesting structure. Earlier we learned how Jose Delgado stimulated the exposed amygdala of conscious subjects and discovered that he could engender an immediate *déjà vu* sensation. From this he concluded that the amygdala was somehow directly responsible for the processing of short-term memory. Consequently, it is of no surprise to discover that when a partial seizure moves from one part of the brain to another and becomes what is termed a 'complex partial seizure', the most dramatic effects are seen when the storm moves from the temporal lobes into the limbic system, specifically the amygdala.

This transfer is used to explain the frequency of *déjà vu* sensations in those individuals who suffer from temporal lobe epilepsy (TLE). It is also reasonable to conclude that the electrical disturbance can stimulate long-dormant instincts within the limbic system. These sensations are nearly always manifested in the period prior to a full seizure, during the phenomenon termed 'the aura'.

The early warning system

Although now identified as an integral part of the seizure, the aura is still something of a mystery to neurologists and physicians. *The Oxford Companion to the Mind* attempts to convey the extraordinary sensations reported by epileptics by describing it as:

> ... *a feeling of familiarity as if everything has happened before. There may be a feeling of intense unreality, sensations of perceptual illusion such as micropsia or macropsia (seeing things as really big or really small), and occasionally, a complex visual or auditory hallucination is experienced.*[251]

All epileptics agree that words are simply inadequate to describe what they see and feel. Indeed the word *aura* was an Ancient Greek attempt to convey the otherworldliness engendered by its tender mercies. For the Greeks an aura was a slight breeze of wind, something invisible and yet perceptible.[252]

To the epileptic the aura can involve a definite feeling such as itching or tingling or something that is simply impossible for the sufferer to describe to anybody else. If the attack is a simple partial seizure it will consist of an aura and in some cases a temporary weakness in a limb or an inability to find words (dysphasia).

Alternatively, the complex partial seizure also starts with an aura but then moves on to disturbances of consciousness itself, the aura of TLE.

From the physiological angle, an attack of TLE commences with a localized (focal) electrical discharge in the temporal lobe. The discharge may cross into the limbic system and in doing so stimulate a massive release of neurotransmitters into this area of the brain. These internally generated chemicals flood the temporal lobes and in doing so cause a change in the level of consciousness of the subject. It is these chemicals that cause the specific aura unique to TLE. For the temporal lobe epileptic the aura involves a radical change in how reality is perceived. There can be an intense feeling of imminent death, together with feelings of *déjà vu*, time seems to slow down, or speed up, objects become either very large or very small and vivid memory recall can occur. These sensations, together with an overall feeling of transcendence and mysticism, involve some of the most curious perception changes known. For a few minutes the person perceives an alternative reality, an alternative denied to others. In an attempt to describe this sensation, Dostoevsky had one of his characters say:

> *You all, healthy people, can't imagine the happiness which we*
> *epileptics feel during the seconds before the attack. In His*
> *Koran, Mohammed assures us that he saw Paradise and was*
> *inside. All clever fools are convinced that he is simply a liar*
> *and a fraud. Oh no! He is not lying! He really was in Paradise*
> *during an attack of epilepsy, from which he suffered as I do. I*
> *do not know whether this bliss lasts for seconds, hours or*
> *months, but believe me I would not exchange it for all the joy*
> *that life may bring.*

As with all epileptics, the aura is usually the start of a full seizure. The 'electrical storm' within the neurons jumps from synapse to synapse and rapidly spreads across the brain. In doing so it triggers a full grand mal attack, particularly if it jumps across the corpus callosum and disrupts the other hemisphere. It is at this point that consciousness is lost. A radical solution to stopping this is to sever the callosum and in doing so restrict the abnormal firing to one hemisphere, but this can cause severe side effects such as the splitting of the personality into two beings. An alternative method is to isolate the focus of the attack by either surgically removing it or by placing incisions around it in the same way that firemen restrict a forest fire by digging trenches. In attempting this solution, Wilder Penfield was to discover that memory, *déjà vu* and epilepsy are all related.

Penfield had the idea that auras might result from early activation at the focus of the attack before it spread so far as to cause convulsions and seizure. From this he concluded that the content of an aura may identify the location of the focus; an aura or tingling in the left arm, for example, might be associated with a focus in the part of the brain responsible for movement in that area. Once isolated, an incision could be made around the area of focus in such a way that the abnormal synaptic firing would remain localized.

Penfield had already discovered not only that the brain holds a three-dimensional record of all that happens to the person but also that those memories can be stimulated by artificial means. In other words, we all have in our brain a full record of every perception, sensation and incident that we experience and these records can be switched on and off like a tape recording. In addition, temporal lobe epileptics report that during an aura they can access these memories without external stimulation. In a psychic state similar to an 'involuntary memory' these images flood the mind of the epileptic, giving them a sensation of actually revisiting their own past. In making his link between TLE and Jackson's Dreamy States, Penfield also showed that *déjà vu*, full memory recall and transcendental states are all directly linked to TLE.

Where God may be found

It has been long recognized that epileptics seem to see the world in a totally different way from the rest of the population. In 1875, the German psychologist P- Samt reported that some of his epileptic patients believed not only that they were already in heaven but that they were surrounded by divine beings. In some cases the patients even confused these divine beings with the physicians that were treating them. Samt termed this psychological state 'god nomenclature'.[253]

A related phenomenon was noted by Harvard-based neurologist Norman Geschwind. For over 20 years from the early 1950s onwards, Geschwind had been treating people with a variety of neurological problems. During this period he had noted that sufferers of TLE share a tendency to write or draw vast amounts of material of a religious or philosophical nature, as well as having a compulsive interest in recording the minutiae of their lives. He termed this tendency 'hypergraphia' and he suggested that this might be brought about by the abnormal stimulation of the temporal lobes by epileptic scar tissue. He believed that the normal functions of emotion and memory in the temporal lobes were being attenuated and heightened by this stimulation.

What Geschwind, together with his associate Stephen Waxman, discovered was that much of this religious and mystical interest was generated by the belief of the TLE patients that they were being controlled 'from outside'. They felt that another being, or beings, were responsible for their thoughts and actions. Some interpreted these as being God, others as creatures from outer space. For Geschwind the problem was that the patients had 'hyperconnectivity' – too many and too rapid connections in the emotional parts of the brain. In this way the patients saw emotional significance in everything they perceived and experienced. In many this was manifested in hyperreligiosity. On Geschwind's death in 1984 these personality traits were termed 'Geschwind's Syndrome' in his honour.

In recent years, the Anglo-Indian neuroscientist Dr VS Ramachandran has written a great deal on this subject. He terms this TLE-generated mysticism the 'God Spot'. In his book *Phantoms in the Brain*,[254] he describes a classical case of Geschwind's Syndrome involving a 32-year-old called Paul. In describing his first attack of TLE, Paul informed Ramachandran:

> *Suddenly it was all crystal clear to me, doctor. There was no longer any doubt anymore.*

Paul explained that this feeling was a rapturous sensation of oneness with the Supreme Being, God or the Creator. His frustration on failing to explain the feelings that welled up inside him had echoes of Dostoevsky's Prince Myshkin:

> *Well, it's not easy doctor. It's like trying to explain the rapture of sex to a child who has not yet reached puberty. Does that make any sense to you?*

The next day Paul returned to the laboratory office carrying a huge bound manuscript. In a classic example of hypergraphia, he explained to a startled Ramachandran that this was a project that he had been working on for several months. He explained that within its green bindings the document contained his views on philosophy, mysticism and religion. During this meeting Paul was to add a few comments about memory flashbacks. He explained:

> *The other day, during a seizure, I could remember every little detail from a book I read many years ago. Line after line, page after page, word for word.*

Here we have an example of a Penfield-like memory recall during a seizure. It is fair to conclude that Paul, and other temporal lobe epileptics, can access areas of memory normally denied to the average Eidolon. It will be recalled that there is another phenomenon that involves total memory recall, and that is cryptomnesia.

We have seen that cryptomnesia is not restricted to epileptics. Under certain hypnotic conditions the subconscious mind can call up images from memory and then 'read' those images in the 'mind's eye'. Again it seems that TLE is simply a channel whereby an Eidolon can access the data available to a Daemon.

If the TLE sufferer can access this information then it is possible to conclude that they may in some way sense their duality. As Geschwind reported, many patients consider that their mind is being controlled by another entity, but some temporal lobe epileptics report a far more tangible feeling of being more than one consciousness. The writer Margiad Evans describes the sensations she experienced during the aura:

> *I have tried to explain how time has come to mean nothing to me. In certain moods it seems I slip in and out of its meshes like a sardine through a herring net*[255] *... Time has become as rotten as worm-eaten wood.*[256]

This awareness of a greater depth to reality than normal perception allows, and the feeling of extreme religiosity has led some commentators to suggest that the writings of one particular mystic stand as evidence to his TLE. The writer, poet, painter and mystic William Blake was a particularly attuned individual, one who seems to have perceived the world of sub-atomic particles a century before modern science. A few lines of his poetry are worth repeating:

> *Every space larger than a red globule of man's blood*

> *Is visionary, and is created by the hammer of Los.*

And every space smaller than a globule of man's blood opens

Into eternity, of which the vegetable earth is but a shadow[257]

Through his possibly undiagnosed TLE, Blake was able to perceive reality as Bohm was to describe it many years later with the advantage of modern scientific knowledge. Could it be that Blake's Daemon was speaking through him? The implication is that the Eidolon of the TLE sufferer accidentally accesses the thoughts and memories of the Daemon. In practice this gives knowledge ordinarily denied to those who do not have seizures. In less sophisticated times this could be understood as a form of possession.

Those who prophet from possession

There is a clue in the very word 'epilepsy'. It is Greek in origin and has its root in the verb *epilambanein*, which means 'to seize' or 'to attack'. This demonstrates that even then it was recognized that epilepsy involved in some way another entity in the mind of the sufferer. A 'seizure', in its literal sense, involves an attack by taking over another. In the same way that captives are 'seized' by an enemy, epilepsy involved the body and mind being seized by another. This 'other' was readily identified as a discarnate spirit or demon. The person became 'possessed'.

Early Western civilization found epilepsy a difficult phenomenon to deal with. On the one hand, the rational, analytical philosophers saw the illness as something that could be treated and cured by medical intervention; on the other hand, the symptoms of the illness, and how it was sometimes interpreted by those who suffered from it, led others to see it as a form of possession, divine or demonic. These two positions inevitably led to very different interpretations of cause and it was inevitable that the more populist possession interpretation was to become accepted. Manipulated by others, epileptics became the voice-pieces of the gods; soothsayers, prophets and shamans.

The reason for this was that during a seizure some individuals seemed to make predictions about the future. At a time where prophetic abilities were in great demand, it was unsurprising that these individuals were recruited into the priesthood of the mystery religions. One group that showed particular epileptic tendencies were the *Sibyls*. These women were to be found at numerous times and locations across the Classical world. All seeming to use the same process to predict future events, the greatest Sibyl was known as the Cumaean. She lived in a cave at Cumae near Naples. Legend has it that she made her prophecies during a form of possession:

> *Her countenance and her colour changed and her hair fell in disarray.*

> *Her breast heaved and her bursting heart was wild and mad;*
> *she appeared taller and spoke in no mortal tones, for the god*
> *was nearer and the breath of his power was upon her.*

The 17th-century historian of epilepsy, Jean Taxil, was sure that the Cumaean was typical of her sort. He wrote:

> *The Sibyls who were convulsed, fell down, frothed and were tormented when possessed by the devil.*[258]

This opinion echoed Plato who ascribed the prophetic powers of the Sibyls to divine inspiration.[259, 260] It was evident to Taxil that the prophetic process involved some form of spectacular seizure. The Sibyls had one particular skill that kept them gainfully employed for many hundreds of years: their predictions, although couched in obscure wording, had a habit of coming to pass. Although the more rational observers such as Hippocrates saw epilepsy as a simple illness, the evidence seemingly pointed to a more divine origin.

The idea that epilepsy gave prophetic abilities to its sufferers was not confined to the Classical Greek and Roman civilizations. At the beginning of the 11th century BCE, a tale was told of Wenamon from Byblos in Phoenicia. One of the nobleman's pages went into a trance:

> *Now while he was making offerings to one of his gods, the god*
> *seized one of his youths and made him possessed.*[261]

This wild behaviour was also seen in the priests of Cybele, whose worship was celebrated with orgiastic dances and loud, wild music. In their efforts to reach a higher plane of consciousness and thus commune with the gods, these priests, termed *Corybantes*, imitated the symptoms of epilepsy.

However, it is to the Biblical basis of prophecy that most European commentators gravitate. The Old Testament prophets had much in common with their heathen counterparts. The process involved them suddenly feeling themselves in intimate communion with Yahweh (God) and they believed that his 'life-soul' (*nephesh*) had somehow extended itself into their lives. A particular example of this was the way in which Saul discovered his prophetic powers:

> *So he went there to Naioth in Ramah. Then the Spirit of God*
> *was upon him also, and he went on and prophesied until he*
> *came to Naioth in Ramah. And he also stripped off his clothes*
> *and prophesied before Samuel in like manner, and lay down*
> *naked all that day and all that night. Therefore they say, '[Is]*
> *Saul also among the prophets?'*[262]

Many commentators interpret this behaviour of Saul's at Ramah as being a typical sign of epilepsy, similar in many ways to the Corybantes. Later he was to have another 'seizure' after David's slaying of Goliath. The Bible describes that an evil spirit from God rushed into him and he 'prophesied' within his house.[263, 264] From then on Saul was given to ecstatic behaviour. In these trance-like states Saul, and one assumes other Old Testament prophets, had his consciousness taken over by another entity. This entity was identified either as Yahweh himself or as a spirit sent by Yahweh. In an article on Old Testament prophecy, the biblical scholar J Muilenberg makes the following observation as regards the OT prophets:

> *The one thing that remains constant is that he (the prophet) is*
> *possessed of a power not himself that invades his nephesh,[265]*
> *masters it, and makes it a vehicle for the accomplishment of*
> *Yahweh's will.*

Sometimes the prophet is totally overcome by the sensations of the 'ecstatic state'. Jeremiah feels the touch of Yahweh's fingers on his lips (Jer. 1:9) and then goes on to describe a sensation that he struggles to convey within the limitations of human language:

> *My anguish, my anguish! I writhe in pain!*
>
> *Oh, the walls of my heart!*
>
> *My heart is beating wildly:*
>
> *I cannot keep silent:*
>
> *For I hear the sound of the trumpet,*
>
> *The alarm of war.[266]*

The word 'ecstatic' comes from the Greek *ekstasis* and means 'standing outside oneself'. For these prophets, what they are experiencing is so out of the ordinary that their feelings cannot be conveyed. It is reasonable to conclude that many, if not all these Old Testament prophets, were epileptic.

This suspicion is reinforced by the fact that the Arabs of pre-Islamic times also had a tradition of prophetic epileptics. At the time of Mohammed, the *kāhan*, the soothsayer, was expected to foretell the future. Like the *shā'ir*, the poet of pre-Islamic times, he was influenced by the jinn, the demons who caused madness and epilepsy. The Arabs were so aware that epilepsy was directly related to prophetic abilities that they called it 'the diviner's disease'. This was reflected in the writings of the time. The Arab author Ali b' Rabban at-Tabari (c. 850 CE) wrote of 'the falling sickness' (*sar'un*) saying that:

> The people call it the diviner's disease because some of them
> prophesy and have visions of wondrous things.[267]

Here again we see the pattern of prophetic ability, out of the body experiences and the possession by another entity; for the Hebrew *demon* read the Arabic *jinn*. It will be recalled how that Nostradamus came upon his predictions. He explained in Centuries 1, quatrain 2 that he fell into a trance state. During this 'absence', as experts on epilepsy would describe it, Nostradamus claimed he was 'possessed' by an entity that he called his Divine Splendour. As he describes it:

> *A voice: Fear: he trembles in his robes.*

> *Divine Splendour.*

> *The God sits beside him.*

Nostradamus' use of words is also telling. He says that the 'god' sits beside him and as we saw the meaning of the word 'ecstasy' is literally being 'beside oneself'. This is exactly how Nostradamus portrays himself in relation to his Divine Splendour. The entity sits next to him and tells him of future events. This is a Daemonic rather than demonic possession.

The ability to foresee the future is not restricted to the famous prophets of the past. There is strong evidence that modern-day epileptics have a similar ability. These following are the words of a lady who responded to a radio request for examples of strange coincidences. She describes a particularly powerful intuition she had one morning, as her husband was getting ready for work:

> I was in the habit of getting up to get his breakfast and see him off before I dressed. As I was in my dressing gown, I did not go into the garden to see him off, as I should have done had I been dressed. On this occasion, I suddenly felt the compulsion to go down the path and watch the car until it was out of sight, as I knew that I should never see it again.

> On the M1, my husband drove over a nail, which punctured one of the tyres. The car, out of control, crossed two lanes and rolled down a 13-foot bank, just missing a railway line. Fortunately he suffered only a broken collar-bone, a cut right ear and slight concussion, but the car was written off.[268]

This is yet another anecdote from Brian Inglis's book *Coincidence*. After discussing the case Inglis mentions, purely as an aside, that the lady in question was an epileptic. Indeed in a curiously unperceptive comment he states surprise that her petit mal did not impair her precognitive skills!

The eliptoid nature of genius

Religious ecstasy and prophecy are but two of the Daemon-inspired skills to be found in the depths of a TLE aura because within its hallucinations and transcendentalism can be found the mark of genius. This belief flourished particularly during the Renaissance. Guillaume Rondelet, the French naturalist and physician, believed that Florence was such a successful city because of the genius of its inhabitants. This genius was directly related to the fact that epileptics were to be found in greater numbers within its walls than in any other Italian city. The Italian writer Tommaso Campanella took this to extremes in his novel *City of the Sun*. The inhabitants of this Utopia were described as employing various remedies against 'the sacred disease, from which they often suffer'. And then he added: 'This is a sign of great talent, therefore Hercules, Socrates, Mohammed, Scotus and Callimachus suffered from it.'[269]

It is likely that Campanella's novel was influenced by a book that had been published 13 years before, Cesare Lombroso's *Man of Genius*. In this work Lombroso cites example after example of historical figures of great genius that had suffered from suspected epilepsy. His list was impressive, including such luminaries as Napoleon, Molière, Julius Caesar, Petrach, Peter The Great, Mohammed, Handel, Swift, Richelieu, Charles V, Flaubert, Dostoevsky and St Paul.[270] He termed this powerful aspect of human psychology the 'Eliptoid Nature of Genius'.[271]

One of Lombroso's men of genius was Georges Louis de Buffon. Buffon was a true Renaissance man in that he not only suggested that the Earth had had successive geological stages, but he also anticipated the theories of Darwin and Lamarck. He is also remembered for his vivid, eloquent and majestic writing style. His concern with such matters was reflected in his inaugural address to the French Academy in 1753 when he said, 'style is the man himself'. Buffon had absolutely no doubt where his drive for knowledge was generated – within his epilepsy. He wrote:

It gradually unfolds and develops itself; you feel a slight electric
shock strike your head and at the same time seize you at the
heart; that is the moment of genius.[272]

The similarities between how Buffon describes his 'moment of genius' and the earlier quotations of Jeremiah and Dostoevsky present us with one self-evident conclusion: all three are describing the same sensation. This 'moment of genius' is brought about by a direct intervention, during a seizure, of the Daemon. Indeed, a common term used to describe intense artistic endeavour is to be touched by 'the daemon of creativity'. It is as if a seizure is the opportunity that our Hidden Observer uses to manifest itself directly into the consciousness of its Eidolon. Edmond de Goncourt and his younger brother Jules are classic examples of how a Daemon (or possibly two) can take over the creative processes of epileptics to the extent that they feel totally controlled.

The Goncourt brothers were the founding fathers of the literary style that was to become known as 'Realism'. To them the only way that any author can write is by experiencing the emotions and conditions that they are attempting to convey. They were particularly interested in the pathological or degenerate behaviour of their subjects. To them the human condition was both god-like and devil-inspired. This inspiration, demonic or divine, was also to be found in the source of their own ideas, because they claimed that their work was not theirs:

There is a fatality in the first chance which suggests your
idea. Then there is an unknown force, a superior will, a sort
of necessity of writing which command your work and guide
your pen; so much so, that sometimes the book which leaves
your hands does not seem to have come from yourself; it
astonishes you, like something which was in you, and of
which you were unconscious. That is the impression which

Soeur Philomène gives me.[273]

The novel in question was something that was within them but of which they were unconscious.[274] To their fellow writers it was their severe epilepsy that was their most noticeable characteristic: their seizures were of such intensity that Edmond de Goncourt was once quoted as describing life itself as 'an epileptic fit between two nothings'. In other words, he only felt really alive when he was sharing the consciousness of his Daemon.

Dostoevsky was of the same opinion. Using his central characters as his mouthpiece, his descriptions of time dilation, *déjà vu* and doppelgängers are not just literary devices but are all products of his epilepsy. This is shown well in the following extract taken from *The Possessed*. It must be read in its entirety for its message to be fully understood:

> *There are seconds, occurring five or six at a time, you suddenly*
> *feel you have fully attained the presence of eternal harmony.*
> *This is nothing worldly; I do not mean that it is something*
> *heavenly, but something which a man, in a worldly sense,*
> *cannot bear. One must either change physically or die. It is a*
> *clear indisputable sensation – as if you suddenly became aware*
> *of all nature and suddenly said; yes, this is true. When God*
> *created the world he said at the end of every day of creation,*
> *'Yes, this is true, this is good.' This is not a tender emotion but*
> *simply a joy. You forgive nothing because there is nothing to*
> *forgive. It is not that you love, oh – this is higher than love.*
> *What is most awful is that it is so terribly clear and such a joy.*
> *If it lasts more than five seconds, the soul will not endure it*
> *and must vanish. In these five seconds I live a lifetime, and for*
> *them I shall give away my whole life because it is worth it. To*
> *endure ten seconds one must change physically.*

Again we have not only the sensation of transcendence but also Dostoevsky's fascination with time dilation. Earlier in this book we saw how time is a totally subjective phenomenon, that it exists as its own reality for each of us. For epileptics it seems that this subjectivity is even more marked. During the early warning signs of an attack time loses all meaning. It slows down and for some actually stops. The epileptic steps outside of the temporal flow and perceives an alternative, deeper reality.

Dostoevsky's reference to Mohammed (*see* page 307) is of interest because the incident in question illustrates in beautiful poetic form how the epileptic perceives time dilation. Dostoevsky tells of the legend of how, as he left to embark upon a journey to Paradise, the Prophet accidentally knocked over the jug of water that was placed on his bedside table. His journey saw him fly above Mecca to arrive at the gates of Paradise. There he saw many incredible things and spent a deal of time observing the wonders awaiting those who submit to Islam. He then travelled back to Earth to discover that the last drops of water were dripping out of the overturned jug. His whole time in Paradise had been the time it had taken for his jug to empty of water.[275]

This dropping out of time is a common aspect of pre-seizure symptoms. In 1993, Dr Steven Schachter published a collection of descriptions of the epileptic experience from the viewpoint of the epileptics themselves.[276] The book is a fascinating insight into a world that is alien to most of us. The temporal confusion brought about by the onset of a seizure is described many times. One particular quote stands out:

> *The seizures I have when my mind races I find difficult to describe. It gets in the way. I believe the mind and memory work with time. I have experienced flashes of memory and highlight events that have occurred since then to the present. When it comes to the present my mind will 'ping' again and my memory will go back a bit further and race forward again*

to the present. At each stage I am thinking that each 'ping' is
going to be my death as each ping takes me back in time to a
point that I felt I got knocked out of the 'now' and therefore
my whole metabolism is working at a different time zone than
other people's.[277]

Earlier we learned how August Strindberg[278] described how, when talking to his friend, he found himself living part of his past again. What is of particular interest is his use of words. He said:

I made an effort to raise my eyes – I don't know if they were
closed – and I saw a cloud, a background of indistinct colour,
and from the ceiling descended something like a theatre
curtain; it was the dividing wall with shelves
and bottles.

'Oh yes!' I said, after feeling a pang pass through me. 'I am in
F's wine shop.'

The officer's face was distorted with alarm, and he wept.

'What is the matter?' I said to him.

'That was dreadful,' he answered.[279]

What does he mean by 'a pang' passing through him? This is not like a 'pang' of conscience because the circumstances are totally wrong. He is using the term to describe a jolt of realization, a sudden recognition of what was taking place in front of his eyes. I believe that with Strindberg's 'pang' and Schachter's correspondent's 'ping' they are trying to convey in inadequate language exactly the same sensation which suggests that whatever epileptics experience it is not unique to them: it is just that they are in some way more 'attuned' to these peculiarities of human consciousness.

In a less dramatic, but still telling way, another of Schachter's respondents wrote:

> *Seizure makes me feel as if everything is slowing down.*[280]

In a similar vein, another respondent describes a peculiar event that took place while he was affected by an aura:

> *It was late afternoon and I was winding along a country road*
> *on my motorbike. An extraordinary sense of stillness came upon*
> *me, a feeling that I had lived that moment before, in the same*
> *place – although I had never travelled on this road before. I felt*
> *that this summer afternoon had always existed, and that I was*
> *arrested in an endless moment.*

It is the observer who moves through time and not that time flows around the observer. The 'space-time' concept of Minkowski is curiously echoed in this quote – 'I felt that this summer afternoon had always existed'. Strangely, this aura was of another kind – the person in question was not a sufferer of TLE but somebody about to experience a physical sensation that is much more common: migraine.

The accidental tourist

Although a good deal more common, migraine is just as mysterious as epilepsy. Sufferers have a similar 'early warning' system that mirrors all the psychic phenomena reported by epileptics. In his book on the subject, Dr Oliver Sacks cites many examples of curious auras, some of which involve increased perception and spontaneous memories. One of his patients attempts to explain this sensation:

> *There is a greater depth and speed and acuity of thought. I*
> *keep recalling things long forgotten, visions of early years will*
> *spring to my mind.*[281]

Here the migraine aura heightens sensory awareness, but for some individuals the aura can involve a full hallucination. For example, this man describes how after the usual flashing lights and zigzag patterns he simply fell out of time:

> *A very strange thing happened. Shortly after my vision came*
> *back. First I couldn't think where I was, and then suddenly*
> *realised that I was back in California … it was a hot summer*
> *day. I saw my wife on the veranda, and*
> *I called her to bring me a coke. She turned to me with an odd*
> *look on her face and said, 'Are you sick or something?' I*
> *suddenly seemed to wake up, and realised it was a winter's day*
> *in New York, that there was no veranda, and that it was not*
> *my wife but my secretary who was standing in the office*
> *looking strangely at me.*[282]

This man was experiencing an hallucination involving all five senses. He knew that it was a hot summer's day and so presumably he could actually feel the heat around him. In fact, the heat was of such intensity that it engendered in him a feeling of thirst, a curious thing to happen when 'reality' was a winter's day in New York. He then 'sees' his wife outside on the veranda and calls to her. He goes on to describe that she 'turned to me' implying that the woman was facing away from him before he requests the coke. As she turns round he notices an odd look on her face and she asks if he is ill. It is only at this moment that 'reality' melts back into his mind and he sees his secretary. I think that it is fair to assume from his description that she (the secretary) was facing him and so it is unlikely that he confused her for his wife in the first instance because he recalled her (his wife) turning to him whereas his secretary would most likely have been facing him, at all times.

This man's consciousness had perceived an alternative reality. The nature of his description implies that it was not a memory and so it may have been an event yet to happen. There are immediate similarities between this incident and the one described by Strindberg. In both cases the protagonists lost contact with one reality and for a few seconds sensed another.

There is evidence that the Daemon can communicate 'hunches' through the medium of a migraine aura and in doing so change potential future events. Brian Inglis quotes one of the respondents to the Koestler Institute's report on coincidences. The lady in question was a migraine sufferer called Mary Farquhar. She describes how during a migraine aura she had the overpowering urge to visit a friend:

> *I had not seen this person for several months, and had no particular reason to think of her. The thoughts became so strong that I decided to cycle up to her home (some three miles away) despite a throbbing, painful head. When I arrived I found that she had taken an overdose of pills in a suicide attempt. I called the ambulance; her life was saved and I was there to care for her three small children.*[283]

If Mrs Farquhar had not had her Daemon-induced 'urge', it is likely that the woman would have died and three children's lives would have been totally changed. Clearly, profound changes were made to the future by this intervention.

The link between migraine and TLE seems to be the generation of particular neurotransmitters in the brain. While experiencing a migraine attack, subjects have had their neuronal activity monitored. Specific changes in neurotransmitter generation were discovered, particularly with regard to serotonin. It was concluded that a group of these chemicals facilitated the overall migraine experience. As we have seen, TLE is also brought about by the over-production of neurotransmitters, and so it is clear that although migraine and TLE are totally different illnesses, they both cause certain neurotransmitters to heighten awareness within the brain.

This phenomenon of heightened awareness can, in certain cases, drive the person involved to insanity and worse. Some neurologists are of the opinion that many schizophrenics are really TLE sufferers who simply cannot handle the way in which their senses become overpowering. Psychiatrist John Kuehnle argues that in many cases TLE is misdiagnosed as schizophrenia. He writes:

> *Fifteen to twenty percent of so-called schizophrenics, including many of the 'chronic residual schizophrenics' on the back wards of state hospitals who don't respond to traditional treatments for psychoses, are actually temporal lobe epileptics.*[284]

The similarities are so great that psychiatrist David Bear suggests that certain forms of extreme TLE should be termed 'schizophreniform'. Bear is of the opinion that many artists and writers who show signs of insanity are really suffering an extreme version of TLE. Vincent Van Gogh is often cited as an example of this intensely creative form of epilepsy.

The towering inferno

In the opening chapter of her book on TLE, the writer Eve LaPlante discusses in great detail the case of Van Gogh and draws a clear conclusion that his madness was brought about by TLE. Earlier we discussed the extreme religiosity of individuals with the complaint and saw how the opening up of certain channels of perception allows access to a wider understanding of the nature of reality. All react in different ways depending on their social and educational background. For some, like Ramachandran's 'Paul', it is proof of their own semi-divinity. To other sufferers, such as the science fiction writer Philip K Dick, of whom we will hear more later, it was evidence of a higher reality of perception. However for those of an already religious mind it can add to a feeling of failure and unworthiness. Both Van Gogh and Dostoevsky can be found in this last category. Within all his self-mutilation, both physical and mental, Van Gogh discovered that reality was far sharper and his senses more finely attuned to the inner meaning of what he saw.

It is well known that in a fit of insanity Van Gogh cut off his own ear and tried to give it to a prostitute as a 'keepsake'. What is less known is that after this he was to have one of his most creative periods. In an outburst of activity that would now be diagnosed as hypergraphia, Vincent executed many paintings, including a number of strange self-portraits. He also wrote two or three letters a day to his brother Theo. At the end of this month of frenzied creativity 'the storms within', as he termed them, returned. These unbidden emotions and hallucinations rose from deep within him. Some involved hyper-detailed charged memories that are reminiscent of both Penfield's patients' descriptions and those of examples of cryptomnesia. In one such seizure Van Gogh said he:

> *Saw again every room in the house in Zundert, every path,*
> *every plant in the garden, the views in the fields roundabout ...*
> *down to a magpie's nest in a tall acacia in the graveyard.*[285]

During these seizures he found that he could hear distant voices as if they were being spoken next to him and he had attacks of micropsia where everyday objects, in an echo of the world of another TLE sufferer, Lewis Carroll, shrank before his eyes. Paranoia also took him over. Like Philip K Dick he suspected a plot against him and saw enemies at every corner. In one of his many letters to his brother he tried in vain to convey this hypersensitivity:

The cypress (I am painting) is always occupying my thoughts.
It is as beautiful in line and proportion as an Egyptian obelisk,
and the green has a quality of high distinction. It is a splash of
black in a sunny landscape, but it is one of the most interesting
of the black notes, and the most difficult to strike exactly what
I can imagine. But then you must see the cypress against the
blue, in the blue rather. To paint nature here, as everywhere,
you must have lived a long time ... Sometimes I draw sketches
almost against my will. Is it not emotion, the sincerity of one's
feeling for nature, that draws us?

Not only does he describe the colours and depth of the sensory world of the Daemon, but also in an echo of the Goncourt brothers and their *Philomène*, his sketches are drawn almost 'against his will'. For a time his sensitivity was to have a positive effect but within two years he had committed suicide, unable to control or understand the sensations assaulting his unprepared brain. In the end it simply became too much to bear.

For some temporal lobe epileptics this ability to sense everything in super clarity is always of extreme discomfort. In 1857, the French novelist Gustave Flaubert wrote that his seizures:

Arrived like a whirlpool of ideas and images in my poor brain
during which it seemed that my consciousness, that my me
sank like a vessel in a storm.

But the most graphic description of this sensory overload was written by Arthur Crew Inman, an eccentric Bostonian who, after a breakdown at the age of 21, retired to a darkened, soundproof suite of apartments. He lived in these rooms from 1916 until his death by suicide in 1963. During this period he completed a 17-million-word diary.[286] In a classic case of hypergraphia, Inman wrote in great detail about the minutiae of his life. For him every sense was attenuated. In 1949 he attempted to describe this with an interesting analogy:

> *I live in a box where the camera shutter is out of order and the*
> *filter doesn't work and the film is oversensitive, and whatever*
> *that is beautiful or lovely registers painfully or askew[287] ... The*
> *simplest factors of existence, sunlight and sound, uneven*
> *surfaces, moderate distances, transgress my ineffective barriers*
> *and raid the very inner keep of my broken fortifications so that*
> *there exists no sanctuary or fastness to which I can withdraw*
> *my sensitivity, neither awake*
> *or asleep.[288]*

At the time it was believed that Inman suffered from a severe form of migraine. It is only in recent years that it has been suggested that the culprit was TLE. In a sad echo of Van Gogh, his sensory overload drove him to suicide when the soundproofing of his rooms could not protect him from the noise of the building of Boston's first skyscraper.

We have learned that TLE, schizophrenia and migraine, although not related in themselves, all seem to open up the neuronal pathways to allow otherwise normal human beings to glimpse another level of reality. That we all have these neuronal networks and can all generate the neurotransmitters needed to facilitate this super-consciousness leads to the conclusion that at some stage in our lives we too can perceive the universe of the Daemon. The question is: when? The answer may lie in a quotation found in Dr Steven Schachter's collection of personal descriptions of epileptic auras. This respondent describes an aura that involves sensations not previously discussed:

> *If the seizure begins during the period just prior to sleep*
> *(minutes before),*
> *I usually notice a feeling of being removed from my position; I*

can only describe it as feeling I'm being sucked into a constantly narrowing tunnel. During this period, sounds and voices in my surrounding environment become distorted in a fashion very similar to a record being played at a speed too slow for its design.

More recently, my pattern of seizures has changed somewhat, and has grown to include seizures which occur during the waking period. On many occasions, I experience only the distortion of sound described above and disorientation, often momentary, as to space and time. However this feeling can be followed by what I can only describe as being a rising or surging sensation, similar to what one might experience when going rapidly downhill and then uphill on an amusement park ride.[289]

Here we see the standard descriptions of sensory acuity and distortion, together with time losing its meaning. What is particularly unusual is this respondent's sensation of being sucked into a narrowing tunnel. It is something different in relation to epileptic auras but very common as regards another phenomenon; a phenomenon that has become known as the Near Death Experience (NDE).

CHAPTER 13

Ferry Across the Acheron

Death borders our birth,

And our cradle stands on the grave.

Joseph Hall

The unknown country

On 15 December 2001, an unusual article appeared in the medical journal *The Lancet*. Written by Pim van Lommel, a cardiologist at the Rijnstate hospital in Arnhem, it described the results and findings of a series of interviews that took place over a period of eight years. Its subjects were 344 patients who had been successfully resuscitated after suffering a cardiac arrest. The article reported that 18 percent of the patients told interviewers that they experienced what is commonly termed a 'near death experience' (NDE), with 12 percent having what Lommel termed a 'core experience' – an elaborate perception of the beginning of an afterlife. This result mystified both Lommel and his associates. Lommel argued that if there is a purely physiological or medical reason for the experience then 'most patients who have been clinically dead should report one'.

This article is interesting for two reasons. The first is that it shows that the NDE phenomenon is not only real but also something that is taken seriously by the medical profession. The second is confirmation that whatever is taking place in an NDE is not experienced by all. So what do we know about NDE and what is its history?

Crossing the threshold

The concept of NDE was introduced to the public in the early

1970s with the publication of Dr Raymond Moody's book *Life after Life*.[290] Moody's interest had been stimulated by two separate stories that he had been told regarding individuals who had 'died' and returned to tell the tale. The first case took place in Abilene, Texas, in 1943. It involved a 21-year-old army private, George Ritchie, who had been pronounced dead by a duty officer after a severe case of double pneumonia. As they were wheeling the 'corpse' to the mortuary, one of the orderlies noticed Ritchie's hand move. Adrenaline was then administered directly into his heart and this, it seems, brought Ritchie back to life. The experience engendered in him a fascination for both medicine and psychiatry and subsequently he trained as a doctor; by the late 1960s he had become a successful psychiatrist. He became frustrated that during his time 'dead' he had experienced many elements of the classic NDE but failed to convince his professional colleagues that it was anything other than a hallucination. Moody, as a young University of Virginia philosophy undergraduate, met Ritchie and was a ready listener, willing to take Ritchie's story at face value. It was only later when, as a teacher at a university in North Carolina, one of his students was to tell him of an amazing occurrence his grandmother had experienced when she also 'died' during an operation that Moody began to see a pattern.

The lady's descriptions were so similar to that of Dr Ritchie that Moody decided to collect together all the anecdotal evidence that he could find. Published in 1973, the book was a sensation. Although Moody never claimed that his research 'proved' survival after death – after all, these were descriptions of 'near' not 'actual' death – many people took it to be the case. What was needed was a more scientific analysis – one that attempted to answer some of the questions raised by Moody's book.

In the late 1970s, Kenneth Ring, a psychologist from the University of Connecticut, attempted to do just this.[291] He interviewed 102 people who had come close to death and what he found confirmed many of Moody's results. In 1980, Ring published his results and listed the most common features that occurred in the reports. He also discovered that in the majority of cases these features took place in the same order. In 60 percent of the cases the person experienced a feeling of inner peace. This was followed by the curious sensation of lifting out of the body. This phenomenon, termed out-of-the-body, occurred in 37 percent of the reports. They then felt themselves float off into darkness until they saw a bright light (16 percent), with 10 percent stating that they actually entered this area of light. Ring found that some people had more complex experiences, including a full past-life review and encountering a 'being of light'.

However, strong statistical analysis was still lacking. This was soon available through the work of Russell Noyes and Donald Slyman.[292] The 186 people interviewed were to confirm many of Ring's findings, but Noyes and Slyman also found three underlying factors. The most common was what they termed 'hyper-alertness'. This involved the speeding up of thought processes and super-sensitivity to visual and auditory stimulation. The second factor was a loss of the concept of self; a detachment from the body and a loss of emotion. Most interesting was that there was also an altered perception of time. The final factor, which was not experienced by all the respondents, was a feeling of mysticism which involved an awareness and understanding of the meaning of life. Memories came flooding back and there was a sensation of unity with all things.

With interest widely aroused, the Gallop organization published a national survey, 'Adventures in Immortality' (1982). This set out to discover what adult Americans believed about life after death. The questionnaire had many questions but perhaps the most significant one asked: 'Have you yourself ever been on the verge of death or had a "close call" which involved any unusual experiences at the time?' Surprisingly, 15 percent of the respondents answered in the affirmative. From this it seems that something extraordinary does take place at the moment of death. In order to make an informed judgement as to whether this phenomenon is the final psychochemical reaction heralding the end of a life, or the birth trauma of a new one, we need to look in detail at what these reports say, and examine the history of NDE.

The idea of life after death is a human universal. It is to be found in every society and in all areas of the globe. Perhaps surprisingly, the myths tend to deal with the 'arrival' after death rather than the journey itself. The process of dying is considered a taboo subject. Those that are fortunate enough to die and then return are often shunned or considered to be in league with the forces of evil. Although few, occasional descriptions have come down to us from the past. As a pupil of Socrates, what Plato has to say about life after death is relevant to the overall theme of this book. Plato describes how Socrates' Daemon, his Divine Sign, had been a central part of the philosopher's life. Consequently, one can reasonably conclude that any esoteric knowledge that Plato may have had regarding not only the concept of the Daemon, but also what happened to the Eidolon after death, would have been conveyed to his readers in some way. We know from other sources that the ancient Greek mystery cults, such as the Orphic Mysteries, were the major source of Gnostic, and therefore Manichean and Albigensian, theology. In the *Republic*, Plato describes one of the oldest surviving explicit reports of an NDE. When he tells of what happened to the soldier Er, he is not only informing his more sophisticated readers of a philosophical 'truth' but he is also giving a clue as to what was taught to the 'elect' groups within Gnosticism, such as the Cathari *parfaits*. This knowledge was not for the masses.

Plato relates the tale of Er, the son of Armenius, who was slain in battle, but when the corpses were taken from the battlefield he was:

... found intact, and having been brought home, at the
moment of his funeral, on the twelfth day as he lay upon the
pyre, revived, and after coming to life related what, he said, he
had seen in the world beyond. He said that when his soul went
forth from his body he journeyed with a great company and
that they came to a mysterious region where there were two
openings side by side in the earth, and above and over against
them in the heaven two others, and the judges were sitting
between these, and that after every judgement they bade the
righteous journey to the right and upward through the heaven
with tokens attached to them in front of the judgement passed
upon them, and the unjust to take the road to the left and
downward, they too wearing behind signs of all that had
befallen them, and that when he himself drew near they told
him that he must be the messenger to mankind to tell of that
other world, and they charged him to give ear and to observe
everything in the place.[293]

Plato is clear that the soul survives after death. He describes, through the experiences of Er, that some form of judgement takes place. This is made by celestial beings who, although it is not stated explicitly, seem to review the life of the soul in question. A decision is then made as to whether the soul is reborn again ('to the left and downward') or is allowed to move on to a higher plane of existence. This image we will see described again and again. Whatever happened to Er, he did experience a classical NDE, and without the opportunity to be influenced by received wisdom.

Plato mentions two of the three areas of the NDE that are of particular importance to this book. These are the mysterious 'Being(s) of Light' and the 'Past-life review'. Plato does not mention the third area – the peculiar way in which time becomes elastic at this crisis point – but this does not necessarily mean that Er did not experience it.

Your life on DVD

The past-life review is seen as an important, but not universal part of NDE. Indeed, the first written record of the concept is even older than the *Republic* and is found in the ancient Egyptian *Book of the Dead*. According to this manuscript, every soul had to give an account of their life to the god Osiris. It says:

> Hail to you great god, Lord of justice ... I have not done falsehood ... I have not deprived the orphan of his property, I have not done what the gods detest ... I have not caused pain, I have not made hungry, I have not made to weep, I have not killed, I have not made suffering for anyone ... I am pure, pure, pure![294]

Again we have the theme of a judgement about the soul's life, the judgement being made, on this occasion, by a single celestial being in the guise of Osiris.

The past-life review is the most interesting of the reported effects during an NDE. Researchers have found that between a quarter and a third of all reports include some form of life review.[295] What is particularly enlightening is that past-life reviews tend to occur when the individual knows that they are about to die and they are given a short period to reflect upon the circumstance. In an almost contradictory fashion, the death threat has to be unexpected. In a paper that reported on 200 interviews of persons who had been close to death, Noyes and his assistant authors (Kletti and Hoenk) stated that 44 percent of respondents who believed they were about to die from a life-threatening situation recalled life review whereas only 12 percent of those who did not believe they were about to die had the experience.

These circumstances may arise, for instance, when somebody falls a great distance, or is in the process of drowning. Thomas De Quincey, in the original version of *Confessions of an Opium Eater*, tells of a relative who, as a child, fell into a river. As she was on the verge of death:

She saw in a moment her whole life, in its minutest incidents,
arrayed before her simultaneously as in a mirror.

De Quincey was to add a footnote about the incident 35 years later.[296] He explained that the child was nine at the time, and having survived the incident, lived to a great age. In this later report he revealed that the woman in question was, in fact, his own mother. De Quincey goes on to give many more details of the accident, adding that from her account it seemed that at first she experienced a struggle and a deadly suffocation, and then there was a moment of no pain or conflict. This was followed by a 'dazzling rush of light', in which there came a rush of memories. Particularly interesting are the words that De Quincey uses to describe how she perceived this rush of memories. He says that she had the ability to:

> *... simultaneously comprehend the whole as every part.*[297]

or, as David Bohm would have termed it, have an 'enfolded' perception.

In terms of NDEs involving climbing accidents, the first to collect data was the Swiss geologist Albert Heim.[298] In an account of more than 30 incidents involving mountaineers who had fallen, he noted how most of them experienced panoramic memories, or life review. Heim's interest in the subject was stimulated when he himself experienced an NDE in 1871 when he fell 70 feet from a cliff face in the Alps. As soon as he realized what was happening a strange thing took place: time began to slow down and he slipped into a new mental state. He describes this sensation:

> *Mental activity became enormous, rising to a hundredfold*
> *velocity ... I saw my whole past life take place in many images,*
> *as though on a stage at some distance from me ... Everything*

was transfigured as though by a heavenly light, without anxiety
and without pain ... Elevated and harmonious thoughts
dominated and united individual images, and like magnificent
music a divine calm swept through my soul ...[299]

The 'flashbacks' were in great detail, although taking place in a microsecond of real time:

I saw myself as a seven-year-old boy going to school, then in
the fourth grade classroom with my beloved teacher Weisz. I
acted out my life as though I were on a stage upon which I
looked down from the highest gallery of the theatre.[300]

All this took place in a fall that took under three seconds!

Lyall Watson, the British biologist, described an incident involving a young skydiver. In 1972, the 19-year-old cadet had an amazing escape from almost certain death when his parachute failed to open. He fell over 3,000 feet but walked away with nothing worse than a broken nose. On leaving the plane he soon realized that he had a real problem. He started screaming as he fell, and then:

I knew I was dead and that my life was ended. All my past life
flashed before my eyes, it really did. I saw my mother's face, all
the houses I have lived in, the military academy I attended, the
faces of friends, everything.[301]

It seems from this description that time itself also becomes transformed. Although the events 'flash' they are seen, and experienced in great detail. It is as if time seems to cease being a factor. This belief is reinforced by a similar incident when an American parachutist fell over 3,500 feet. He described what happened in this way:

It is like a picture runs in front of your eyes, from the time you
can remember up to the time, you know, what is happening
(this is the present) ... It seems like pictures of your life just
flow in front of your eyes, the things you used to do when you
were small and stuff; stupid things. Like, you see your parents'
faces – it was everything. And things I didn't remember that I
did. Things that I can remember now, but I remember two
years ago or something. It all came back to me, like it refreshed
my mind of everything I used to do when I was little. It was
like a picture, it was like a movie camera running across your
eyes. In a matter of a second or two. Just boom, boom [snaps
his fingers]! It was clear as day, clear as day. Very fast and you
can see everything. It was like, wow, like someone was feeding
a computer or something. Like putting a computer in your head
and programming you, that's what it was like ... It was like
starting in the beginning and working its way to the end, what
was happening. Like clockwise, just going clockwise. One right
after another.[302]

This sounds like a video recording of the subject's life. He is quite specific in this. He feels that the events were running in sequence but somehow outside of him, as if he was watching it all on television. And this description is not unusual – another person reported the experience was:

Like climbing into a movie of your life. Every moment from
every year of your life is played back in complete sensory detail.
Total, total recall. And it all happened in an instant.[303]

And yet another:

The whole thing was really odd. I was there; I was actually
seeing these flashbacks; I was actually walking through

them, and it was so fast. Yet it was slow enough for me to take
it all in.[304]

It is unclear from these stories as to how the actual time was perceived, although in many cases it is stressed that the review takes place in a 'few seconds'. The question is how long are those few seconds in psychological time. We have already seen that time duration is a totally subjective experience, but it is important to understand exactly what 'time' is being perceived. A very rare case of a subject commenting directly on duration was described by the French astronomer Camille Flammarion. He tells of a French cavalry officer in Africa:

> *My friend Alphonse Bué was on horseback in Algeria, and*
> *following the edge of a very steep ravine. For some reason his*
> *horse made a mis-step and fell with him into the ravine, from*
> *which he was picked up unconscious. During his fall, which*
> *could hardly have lasted two or three seconds, his entire life,*
> *from his childhood up to his career in the army unrolled clearly*
> *and slowly in his mind, his games as a boy, his classes, his first*
> *communion, his vacations, his different studies, his*
> *examinations, his entry into Saint-Cyr in 1848, his life with*
> *the dragoons, in the war in Italy, with the lancers of the*
> *Imperial Guard, with the spahls, with the riflemen, at the*
> *Château of Fontainebleau, the balls of the Empress at the*
> *Tuileries, etc. All this slow panorama was unrolled before his*
> *eyes in less than four seconds, for he recovered consciousness*
> *immediately.*[305]

Bué recalls the slowness by which the memories were experienced, as if they were a second by second reliving of a past life. This dilation of time is a significant aspect of the whole phenomenon. What can be made of this description by a professional mountain guide by the name of Eugen Guido Lammer who, in August 1887, was carried away by an avalanche on the Massif du Cervin in the Alps? He says:

> *During this deadly fall my senses remained alert. And I can assure you, my friends, that it is a fine way to die! One does not suffer! A pinprick hurts more than a fall like this. And there is no thought of dying either – or only to start with. From the moment I realised that anything I could do to save myself would be useless, it was for me a great liberation. This person who was being swept across the path of the avalanche, thrown over the body of his companion, hurled into space by the tug of a rope – this was a stranger, more like a block of wood; my real self floated over the scene with the relaxed curiosity of a spectator at the circus. A wave of images and thoughts invaded my brain; memories of childhood, my birthplace, my mother. I could fill hundreds of pages with them! Yet during all this time I was coldly calculating the remaining distance before I would be thrown down dead at the bottom ... all this without agitation, without sorrow, I was totally freed from the chains of Self. Years, centuries passed during that fall.*[306]

It is useful to compare these quotes with a comment made by the journalist Dean Woolridge in relation to the Penfield experiments. Woolridge said that the stimulated memory came into mind as if:

> *... it were stored on a film or tape which automatically rewinds each time it is interrupted.*[307]

Here again is that curiously vivid focus on long-forgotten minutiae rather than important or life-defining events. It is as if the awareness of approaching death acts in the same way as Penfield's electrode.

The Sam Peckinpah effect

The sensation of time slowing down as potential death approaches and the past-life review that takes place is also described by the war correspondent René Cutforth. He was covering the conflict in Korea when his helicopter was hit by hostile fire. At the point that the lieutenant announced to all on board the helicopter that they were in trouble:

> *I was so frightened I had a kind of paralysis. My mind was going so fast that all action seemed to be in slow motion. The lieutenant's speech had seemed to last for twenty minutes. I had lived half a dozen lives while they were buckling my parachute.* [308]

Car accidents are, by their very nature, unexpected and sudden. There is not the amount of time available to the subject as there is in drowning or falling, so any life review has to be accommodated in a much shorter time period. Even so, it seems from the reported cases that time dilation occurs to allow for the hallucination. One of Dr Ring's patients was involved in a potentially fatal road accident. He described his review:

> *It was like I got to view my whole life as a movie, and see it and get to view different things that happened, different things that took place...somehow it's very hard on words describing ... basically it was like a movie ... although speeded up, probably to show you it all.* [309]

Again here is the analogy of a movie, but more importantly the crash victim felt that time was short and all the record of his life had to be rushed. There is a suspicion that this haste takes place because in some way the potential death situation has caught the 'projection crew' unawares. It was not expected and, in panic, the videotape or DVD is shown running on 'fast-forward'. Indeed, this is exactly how another of Ring's patients was to describe it:

> *It was like watching my life from start to finish on an editing machine stuck in fast forward. The review took me from my conception, which felt like the blackness I experienced after my out-of-body experience, through my childhood, to adolescence, into my teens, and through my near-death experience over again. I saw my life. I relived my life. I felt everything I ever felt before. When I say 'everything' I mean every cut, pain, emotion and sense associated with that particular time in my life.*[310]

Note that in this case the NDE itself became part of the past-life review, implying that the exercise could be repeated again and again in smaller segments of time – but more of that later.

Sometimes accidents are so sudden that time itself seems to go in reverse in order to accommodate the review. It seems that the projection crew has powers over the direction of the temporal flow. Peter and Elizabeth Fenwick describe a case that might suggest this.[311] Dr Peter Fenwick is President of the British Branch of the International Association for Near Death Studies and has spent many years collating cases of NDEs. The case in question involved a woman who had a serious car accident in June 1986. She describes the events:

> *I was driving in the central lane of a motorway, it was raining and although only just past midday, very dark. I realised a car in front of me had slowed down sharply, and I didn't want to brake for fear of skidding, so I steered right to the fast lane, and my car aquaplaned and went into a spin. I was struggling to control it, when suddenly I was not in the car anymore.*[312]

She then found herself travelling down a dark tunnel at an incredible speed. As the darkness lifted she could sense a presence, or presences, near to her. She knew, in some profound way that she found difficult to explain, that a great debate was going on about her. These entities were trying to decide if she should go back or not. It was as if she had arrived too soon for them. Everything then went blank. She opened her eyes and found herself back in the car, which had come to a standstill across the fast lane with the driver's side facing the oncoming traffic. She saw a white car approaching her at speed and knew that in a split second she would be hit, but she was not concerned. It is possible that her encounter with the world beyond had made her less fearful of death, but in realistic terms she also remembered that her car had a steel-reinforced bar in the door. She knew this would save her. The beings had decided that this was not her time. In actual fact, it was not the white car but the one behind that collided with her. She was knocked deeply unconscious but lived to tell the tale.

What is unusual about this case is that she had her out-of-the-body experience and NDE *before* the other car hit her. In fact, the NDE had come to an end and she was back in her body. There can have only been a few seconds between the spin and the impact and yet she had had the whole experience in that short amount of time. Indeed, it could be argued that her experience of the NDE was only 'before' the impact in 'real' time. Is it possible that for a few seconds time actually reversed for this lady and in celestial or inner time the NDE did come before the impact?

That time becomes meaningless while experiencing an NDE is extremely common. According to a study by Dr Michael Sabom on the subject – a study stimulated by his initial disbelief of the events outlined in Moody's *Life After Life* – over 90 percent of those who experienced an NDE said there was an absence of 'normal time'[313] An example of this involved one of Ring's patients, who said:

> My sense of time was way off. Time didn't seem to mean anything
> … It was just, well, I don't know how to explain it even.[314]

Time seems to go completely haywire under certain circumstances, particularly in those reports not of a past-life recall but a future-life recall. This is termed the 'personal flashforward' by Ring. In one striking case a child experiencing an NDE was shown certain events in his future. These included the fact that he would be married at 28 and would have two children. He was shown his adult self and his future children sitting in a room of the house he would eventually live in. As he looked around the room he noticed an object on one of the walls that he simply could not understand. Many years later he was to find himself in that very room and on looking round he recognized the object that caused such confusion to his younger self. On the wall was a 'forced-air heater', a kind of heater that had not been invented at the time of his NDE.[315]

These peculiar precognitions can bring about bizarre events that might seem unbelievable in any science fiction anthology. One of these involved a female NDEr who, during her experience, became aware of another being. This 'presence' informed her that a person called Raymond Moody would, sometime in the future, ask her questions about what occurred during her brush with death. This 'being' then showed her a photograph of Moody. This was in 1971 and Moody had not yet published *Life after Life*. The person in the picture and his name meant nothing to her. Four years later, Moody and his family moved into the same street as this woman. In a scene that would fit well in any of Stephen Spielberg's films, Moody's son, while 'trick-or-treating', called at the woman's house. In making conversation with her young visitor, she asked him his name. When he told her she immediately recalled what the mysterious entity had said during her NDE. With mounting excitement she requested that the boy inform his father that she needed to speak to him urgently. Of course, Moody was intrigued and on meeting her recorded her strange mixture of NDE and precognition.[316]

The white being at the right time

Who or what are these mysterious beings that accompany those experiencing an NDE through the event? In both the above case and that involving the motorway crash, the subjects reported that they sensed a presence close to them. This presence, or presences, seem to be a very important aspect of the whole NDE.

This 'Being in White', as this entity has become known, seems to be waiting at the 'other side' to guide the discarnate soul, to take it through the past-life review, and decide what happens next. One of Dr Ring's subjects, a woman who suffered cardiac arrest during a tonsillectomy, described her encounter with this presence:

> I was above – and there was a presence. It's the only way I can explain it – because I didn't see anything. But there was a presence and it may not have been talking to me but it was like, like I knew what was going on between our minds. [317]

The Being in White seems to be directly responsible for the past-life review. It is as if he (or she) is the chief projectionist and decides what is, and what is not, shown. Particularly interesting is the intimate knowledge that the Being shows in relation to the subject's life and personal motivations. According to one of Dr Moody's subjects:

> When the light appeared, the first thing he said to me was 'What do you have to show me that you have done with your life?' or something to this effect. And that's when these flashbacks started. I thought, 'Gee, what is going on?' because all of a sudden I was back in early childhood. And from then on, it was like I was walking from the time of my early life, on through each year of my life, right up to the present ... the things that flashed back came in the order of my life and they were so vivid. The scenes were just like you walked outside and saw them. Completely three dimensional, adding colour. And

they moved. For instance when I saw myself breaking the toy
(an incident from her kindergarten days in which she smashed
a toy that she had liked), I could see all the movements. It
wasn't like I was watching it all from my perspective all the
time. It was like the little girl I saw was somebody else, in a
movie, one little girl among all the other children out there
playing in the playground. Yet it was me. I saw myself doing
these things as a child, and they were the exact same things I
had done, because I remember them.[318]

The idea of being met at death by a mystic being might be seen as a form of Jungian archetype, a culturally inherited image that the brain fabricates at times of crisis. Those individuals of a religious persuasion readily identify this figure with that of Christ. Our natural suspicions are raised when we discover that in most cases this 'Christ' figure is described as if he just stepped out of a Renaissance painting complete with beard and long hair. In fact, the earliest known Roman pictures of Christ, painted in the 2nd century CE, show a clean-shaven man with short hair and many historians of fashion argue that Jesus would have probably looked more like this than the Christ of Giotto and Massaccio. Either way, this does not invalidate the objective experience of this being. It is reasonable to suppose that if it is some form of discarnate entity it will manifest itself in whatever cultural guise is needed to put the dying person at ease. The Being also appears to non-believers as well. An agnostic described his experience in this way:

I was stopped by this brilliantly lighted person. He knew my
thoughts and reviewed my life. He told me to go back – that
my time would come later.[319]

Evidence that this phenomenon is neither influenced by modern books on the subject nor is it interpreted as a Christian vision of

Christ is evidenced by the tale told by the Venerable Bede, an 8th-century Northumbrian monk. As a Christian and the author of *History of the English Church and People*, it is to be expected that he would take any opportunity to show God's involvement in the lives of the faithful. However, in this book he tells of a man by the name of Drychthelm who 'died' in the early hours of the night only to suddenly sit up alive again later in the day. He claimed that he left his body and found himself in a heavenly realm. Here he was met by what Bede described as 'A handsome man in a shining robe'.

Even though this classic NDE was experienced many centuries before the work of Moody and Ring, it follows the pattern. Unusually, Bede makes no religious points about it. Again we have a description of the Being in White.

Although a good deal has been written about these entities, researchers have come up with no idea of who or what they are. One of the most famous of those individuals who claim to be able to leave their body at will is a former American radio and television executive by the name of Robert Monroe. He claims that he has travelled hundreds of times into the alternative reality usually reserved for those who have NDEs. Along with his own experiences he has interviewed dozens of other individuals who all claim the same ability. He is particularly interested in these Beings In White but he is no nearer an answer. He says:

> *Whatever they may be (these beings) have the ability to radiate a warmth of friendliness that evokes complete trust. Perceiving our thoughts is absurdly easy (for them).*[320]

It is my opinion that out-of-body experiences and NDEs are related and that there is sufficient corroborative evidence that they do actually take place. It may be a good deal harder to accept that individuals can, at will, leave their bodies and go 'Astral Travelling' as it is termed. The evidence is simply not available. Objective tests have proved, at best, inconclusive, and at worst that these individuals are deluding themselves. Monroe's comments as regards the Beings in White are supported by reports made by NDErs. On balance, it is fair to conclude that this phenomenon is a part of NDE, but it may be that the researchers trying to identify these entities are looking in totally the wrong direction. In reality, they are not external to the human mind, but an integral part of it.

There is evidence that the Daemon/Being in White knows more about your life than you do. In fact, he knows not only what has happened to you, but also what will happen to you. How else can we explain the following incident described by DA Bak of Leicester, when he was under anaesthetic:

> *I heard a voice call my name, and while above my body I turned towards the voice and found myself facing another person who spoke to me and extended a hand to me ... I was aware of moving through a golden light, and there met a group of other beings who explained to me the reasons for this experience, and proceeded to show me the major events in the future of my life, which at the time I could never see happening. But all the events revealed at the time happened and fell into place.*[321]

This experience seems to imply many of the phenomena that we have discussed in earlier chapters. When Mr Bak hears the voice, he turns round and finds himself facing another person. In an earlier chapter we discussed autoscopy, the seeing of one's own double and a psychological state that is usually found in sufferers of schizophrenia. This was described in one case as:

> *... an image of his own face 'as if looking in a mirror'.*[322]

The moving through a golden light and then meeting a group of beings has echoes of the case of Billy Milligan in which all his multiple personalities existed in a room and the 'person' that 'stood in the light' was the one that controlled the consciousness. The strangest comment made by Mr Bak was that his Daemon also seemed to know what was going to happen to his Eidolon. As we have already seen, there is strong evidence that the Daemon is clairvoyant.

Take, for example, the case of Allan Pring. In 1979, Pring 'died' during an operation. What occurred to him during his NDE not only presents more information on past-life reviews but also gives a tantalizing glimpse of what may be going on as regards the Daemon's ability to foretell future events. He describes what happened:

On Monday 6 August the preparation for surgery was routine and I lost consciousness within seconds of being injected with anaesthetic. All perfectly normal. But the manner in which I regained consciousness was anything but normal. Instead of slowly coming round in a drowsy and somewhat befuddled state in a hospital ward I awoke as if from a deep and refreshing sleep and was instantly and acutely aware of my situation. Without any anxiety or distress I knew I was dead, or rather I had gone through the process of dying and was now in a different state of reality. The place that I was in cannot be described because it was a state of nothingness. There was nothing to see because there was no light; there was nothing to feel because there was no substance. Although I no longer considered that I had a physical body, nevertheless I felt as if I was floating in a vast, empty space, very relaxed and waiting. Then I experienced the review of my life which extended from early childhood and included many occurrences that I had completely forgotten. My life passed before me in a momentary flash but it was entire, even my thoughts were included. Some of the contents caused me to be ashamed but there were one or two I had forgotten about of which I felt quite pleased. All in all, I knew that I could have lived a much better life but it

could have been a lot worse. Be that as it may, I knew that it
was all over and there was no going back. There was a most
peculiar feature of this life review that was difficult to describe,
let alone explain. Although it took but a moment to complete,
literally a flash, there was still time to stop and wonder over
separate incidents. This was the first instance of distortion of
time that I experienced but it was the beginning of my belief
that the answers to many of the questions that are posed by
NDEs lie in a better understanding of the nature of time and
what we term reality.[323]

Pring gives an excellent description of a life review, but without the involvement of a 'Being in White', and his comments about the curious distortion of time are of great interest. His experience is qualitatively different from other reports in that Pring believes that the event had antecedents in his own past. When he was eight years old he had been so ill that his parents had been called to his bed. The doctors were of the opinion that the child was in danger of dying. Although deeply unconscious, Pring claims to have 'seen' the event. He describes how screens surrounded the bed. His mother and father stood at the foot of the bed while the hospital matron stood at the right-hand side. His viewpoint was looking down from above the screens – he was high enough to be able to see the rest of the ward. At a later time, when his illness had abated, he could recall this experience with extreme clarity. He believes that he was given panoramic knowledge of his own life, information about his own future that sat just below normal conscious awareness. He explains:

From time to time, perhaps once or twice a year over a period
of many years, I would have a most peculiar feeling, deliciously
pleasant but lasting only a moment. Most people have
experienced déjà vu, and everyone knows what it is like to have

a name on the tip of the tongue but not quite able to recall it.
The fleeting feeling that I would have was like a combination
of the two. But the oddity was that I felt that if I could only
think in a slightly different way, or somehow see in a different
way, then I would gain or remember this tremendous
knowledge. In fact, I used to describe the feeling to my wife by
saying that I felt in some magical way that I would know
everything that there was to know.[324]

The relationship between *déjà vu*, precognition and NDE is shown in yet another report by the Fenwicks. This time the individual in question was involved in a motorcycle accident when he was 17. After the accident he experienced a classic out-of-body sensation and became aware of a 'person in white clothing'. He found himself standing in front of two doors and he knew that he had to decide which one to go through. It is reasonable to suppose that this was a mental fabrication of his own, but the reason for having to make the choice is obvious. He made his decision and found himself back in his injured body lying in the road. Self-evidently, he survived to tell the tale. From then on he has had strong *déjà vu* experiences. He finds these to be extremely vivid and together with an ability to 'anticipate' major future events in his life, he believes that something else occurred during his NDE. He explains it as:

It is almost as if, during my near-death experience I saw a
speeded-up video of my future life in order to select it, or the
other. It seems that the odd video frame has been remembered.
Similarly, I can foresee some people's destiny, but not everyone's
just people who have a say in my own.[325]

In both cases the individuals in question had somehow become aware of the information available to their Daemons, the alternative self that resides in the mind. I suspect that this was the

Daemon in its role as Guardian Angel giving subtle clues as to actions to be taken. In the light of our knowledge of *déjà vu*, Pring's comments are fascinating. *Déjà vu* is simply an accidental leakage of data from the memory store of the non-dominant (Daemon) hemisphere of the brain into the dominant (Eidolon) hemisphere. The experiments by Penfield have suggested that all memories are stored somewhere in the brain, and this belief is reinforced by evidence for cryptomnesia. The Fenwicks come to a similar conclusion:

> *People who are given these glimpses of the future often find that they subsequently experience various psychic phenomena such as feelings of déjà vu, almost as though they have been shown a speeded-up video of their future life, and later recognise and remember odd frames from it.*[326]

There is counter-evidence in that the ability to see the future as an individual approaches death is not directly related to the classic NDE but is part of the actual death experience itself. Of the many examples collected by JB Priestley of time not behaving as it should, one of the strangest was of a young man approaching death whose perception of time seemed to 'slip' in that he was perceiving events a second or two before they actually took place. It was as if part of him was actually living a few seconds ahead of everybody else. Colin Wilson, citing Priestley, describes what took place:

> *[The mother] said that during her son's illness he suddenly remarked, 'a dog is going to bark a long way off'. A few seconds later she heard the faint bark of a dog. He then said 'Something is going to be dropped in the kitchen and the middle door is going to slam'. Within seconds both things had happened. When she told the doctor about it he said that he had known of this happening before and that her son's brain was working 'just ahead of time'.*[327]

Priestley was not in the position to speak to the doctor about this, but the physician's cryptic comment that he had known this to happen before implies that it was, in his opinion, unusual, but not unknown. This is the only example so far in this book of somebody who actually died. The young man was experiencing the real thing – not a 'false alarm'. In this event his case is not an NDE but evidence of what really takes place, the NDE being a watered down version triggered early by a stressed subconscious.

We have seen many examples of NDEs, but the major drawback is, with the exception of the case above, that all of them are, by their very nature, inner experiences. Their subjectivity means that conclusive proof of the reality of the event cannot be found. Each person went through an extremely stressful experience and the whole event could have been simply one of an overactive imagination. A cynic could be less generous and say that fabrication was the order of the day.

The article from *The Lancet* (*see* page 331) is not the only time that this publication has reported near-death peculiarities. It also published the case of an elderly Englishwoman who, in 1902, very nearly died from bronchial pneumonia. Fortunately for her, a physician, Dr Henry Freeborn, was on hand and her life was saved. What took place before and during his ministrations was of such interest to Dr Freeborn that he wrote up the case. He describes that as the woman lapsed into the 'crisis' of pneumonia she began to speak in a totally strange language. Although her ramblings confused most of those present there was one individual who had knowledge of Indian languages. This visitor immediately identified the language as Hindustani. Much to the surprise of him and all present, her ramblings described going to the bazaar to buy sweets. Events then took an even stranger turn as she began to recite Hindustani poems. This went on for 24 hours, after which she began to talk in English, mixed with some French and German.[328]

A week later she had recovered and was able to explain the mystery. Although she could only recall a few words of Hindustani she had spent her first three years in India and, after the death of her mother, was brought up by native Indian *ayas* or nursemaids. These women spoke no English and therefore could only communicate with the child in Hindustani. As she grew older she was shipped back to England where she spoke only English, subsequently learning French and German as she spent time living on the Continent. It seems that during the 24-hour period of her near-death crisis she had been taken though her life, from birth, working on a 'slow forward' until she arrived at the present time. All through this she was continually accessing long-lost language skills that had lain dormant in the deepest recesses of her mind. This was a classic case of cryptomnesia and it provides objective proof that the memory store is accessed at the approach of death. We therefore know that at least one of the symptoms of NDE has an objective reality.

We can only presume that these people are not liars. Time dilation, *déjà vu* and out-of-the-body experiences all do seem to occur during NDEs, but they are not unique to this phenomenon. Exactly the same sensations also occur on a regular basis to other, far more studied groups of individuals – temporal lobe epileptics, schizophrenics and, slightly more surprisingly, migraine sufferers.

The first clues

For the temporal lobe epileptic, those that suffer migraine, and certain schizophrenics, time dilation and out-of-body experiences are part of everyday reality. It may be that in some way NDE and TLE are related phenomena? If so, there should be evidence of past-life review for epileptics. Dostoevsky, whose role is so crucial to this, was a sufferer (if that is the correct term in his case) of TLE. His descriptions of his epilepsy and his wonderful evocations of the pre-seizure aura are central to his writing. However, he also had an amazing NDE involving both time dilation and a past-life review. At the age of 27, he was arrested with a number of others for belonging to a group called the Petrashevsky Circle. After a trial lasting many months he was condemned to be shot. Tsar Nicholas I decided to not go through with the full sentence but to stage a mock execution. When the prisoners were taken to the Semyonovsky Parade Ground they expected death. They were made to wear white shirts (death garments) and then to be shot in threes. Dostoevsky was in the second group. At the last possible moment they were told that they had been reprieved and that they would all get hard labour instead. Dostoevsky was given four years. Eighteen years later he used the images and events in *The Idiot*. In this book, Prince Myshkin tells his friends of a story told to him by a man he had met. This man had suffered circumstances similar to those experienced by the writer. Myshkin says:

> *He told me that these five minutes seemed to him like an*
> *endless term, vast riches, it seemed to him that in those five*
> *minutes he would live so many lives that it was unnecessary at*
> *present to think of the last moment.*

He worked out how he would spend the five minutes; two to take leave of his comrades, two for thinking for the last time, and one to have a last look around. The first two minutes he spent as he had planned. Now came the two minutes in which he knew beforehand what he was going to think about:

> *He wanted to imagine as quickly and as vividly as possible how*
> *was it: now he is here and is alive, but in three minutes he will*
> *be something – somebody or something – but who? And*
> *where? All this he thought he could solve in those two minutes!*

At this point all his attention was taken by the gilded roof of a church, not far off, that was shining in the sunshine.

> *He remembered that he kept staring intently at the roof and*

the rays that it reflected; he could not tear himself away from
those rays; it seemed that the rays were his new nature, that
after three minutes he would slowly merge with them.

Myshkin ends this long-term reflection with the statement:

What if one does not have to die! What if life is returned –
what an infinity in time ... then I would turn every minute
into an age.

While it can be argued that this may have nothing to do with Dostoevsky's epilepsy and everything to do with the fact that he was about to die, the description is unique in literature and for it to be written by an individual who was a known TLE sufferer is surely something more than a fortuitous coincidence. I believe that Myshkin's experience was related to Dostoevsky's epilepsy, and that recent research supports this position.

In order to investigate any potential link between TLE and NDE it is necessary to understand the role of the neurotransmitter glutamate. Glutamate is the only amino acid that can readily cross the barrier between blood and brain and, with glutamic acid, is thought to account for about 80 percent of the amino nitrogen of brain tissue. The majority of large neurons in the cerebral cortex use glutamate as their neurotransmitter. It is the key chemical messenger in the temporal and frontal lobes, and is central to the function of the hippocampus. Glutamate plays a vital role in the cognitive processes involving the cerebral cortex, including thinking and the formation of memories and recall, and is vital in perception. Glutamate is excitatory. When present in excess, it causes neurons to die due to excitotoxicity. This is the mechanism of neuronal cell death in hypoxia (deficiency of oxygen), ischaemia (reduction in blood supply), and epilepsy – all conditions that have been proven to lead to excessive release of glutamate.[329, 330, 331]

Research carried out by Karl Jansen at the Maudsley Hospital in London[332] and his subsequent summation[333] supports his contention that the hallucinogenic anaesthetic ketamine can reproduce all the features of the NDE. These include rapid trips down dark tunnels into light, seeing a being or beings, out-of-body experiences, mystic states and memory recall. In a monograph written on the general effects of psychedelic drugs, the effects of ketamine were reported to be:

> ... becoming a disembodied mind or soul, dying and going to
> another world. Childhood events may also be relived. The loss
> of contact with ordinary reality and the sense of participation
> in another reality are more pronounced and less easily resisted
> than is usually the case with LSD. The dissociative experiences
> often seem so genuine that users are not sure that they have
> not actually left their bodies.[334]

This is where the link between TLE and NDE can be made. There is a fair degree of evidence that the similarities between the two are brought about in some way by glutamate.[335, 336] As the key neurotransmitter in the temporal lobes it plays a crucial role in epilepsy. Therefore it is not surprising that TLE sufferers report very similar experiences to NDE.

In a study from the early 1960s, a full review was made of the neurological reasons for particular psychological phenomena experienced by people afflicted with TLE. The researchers suggested the existence of a neural or brain mechanism that helps the individual to cope with the psychological stress involved in epileptic seizures and possibly in other situations as well. When a person is faced with danger, a mechanism enables us to become either unusually vigilant or unusually distant. Most useful of all is the response that makes a person both highly vigilant *and* emotionally distant. This represents:

... an adaptive mechanism that combines opposing reaction
tendencies, the one serving to intensify alertness, the other to
dampen potentially disorganising emotion.[337]

In turn this dissociation is part of the NDE. It is an attempt to
cheat death by mimicking death itself. The psychiatrists Russell
Noyes and his associate Donald Slymen say:

> *The depersonalised state is one that mimics death. In it a*
> *person experiences himself as empty, lifeless and unfamiliar. In*
> *a sense, he creates psychologically the very situation that*
> *environmental circumstances threaten to impose.*[338]

The psychological outcome of this manoeuvre can be highly
successful:

> *In so doing he escapes death, for what has already happened*
> *cannot happen again; he cannot die because he is already dead.*

The 'tunnel' effect has also been shown to be part of basic brain
functioning. This has always been one section of the overall NDE
experience that has been open to a Freudian interpretation. This
popular theory says that dying is analogous with being born. The
out-of-body experience is literally just that – you re-live the
moment when you came out of your mother's body. This theory
was initially proposed by Stanislov Grof and Joan Halifax[339] and
then popularized by the astronomer Carl Sagan.[340]

This surely cannot be the full explanation. Any person with even
a basic grasp of female anatomy would not consider the vagina to
be a tunnel. The birth canal is stretched and compressed and the
baby is forced through headfirst. All the NDE descriptions involve
flying at great speed down a tunnel, with walls either side. Even a
forceps delivery cannot seem that fast to a newborn infant. The

final death knell for this proposal was research by Dr Susan Blackmore who questioned a group of people who had experienced NDEs. The percentages of those who experienced the tunnel effect was almost equal between those born by Caesarean section and those born normally.[341] It was this work which stimulated Blackmore to come up with her own explanation for the tunnel.[342] She has created computer simulations of the tunnel experience as well as examined the psycho-physiological effects. Blackmore notes that people do have an experience of a tunnel, but not a real tunnel. The brain constructs its version of reality from the available stimuli or signals. Specifically, the perception of random movements on the periphery of the visual field is interpreted by the brain as outward movements. From this interpretation the brain then infers that it has also moved. What presents itself to the brain as an apparently enlarging patch of flickering white light is then interpreted as a tunnel through which the person is moving. As an explanation this makes a good deal of sense.

The evidence seems to support the position that the brain is programmed to react in a certain way as the senses perceive that death is a possibility. This in itself is not evidence of survival after death, but what it does prove is that some form of higher awareness takes over. The perceptions experienced by TLE sufferers and those individuals who have NDEs are just as real; it is just that they take place in the here and now. They do not interact with discarnate beings and they do not float off somewhere else. When your heart stops beating, and when your brain dies of oxygen starvation, that is it. You cease to exist in the universe of an observer. Death is the end, it is final and there is no coming back – there is no life after death. However, this does not mean that you cease to exist within your own universe, phaneron or whatever we wish to call your own part of Everett's multiverse. You do this by, quite simply, falling out of time.

CHAPTER 14

The Friend in the Shadows

Life is an epileptic fit between two nothings.

Edmond Goncourt

The crying game

I exist. Are these not the two most amazing words possible? For all your life you have perceived that fact as a given. Cognitive scientists may argue that consciousness is an illusion but you know that this is simply untrue. Knowing that you exist is what makes you human. However, within existence lies a mystery – we exist only to die. This is the greatest truth and also the greatest horror and the greatest fear. Life is but a symptom of encroaching oblivion. One day you will die and all your vanities and achievements will be for naught. This feeling of impermanence has been reflected in every society throughout the ages. The Chinese poet Li Po spoke for Everyman when he wrote:

Life passes like a flash of lightning

Whose blaze barely lasts long enough to see

While the earth and the sky stand still forever.

How swiftly changing time flies across man's face.

O, you who sit over your full cup and do not drink.

Tell me what you are still waiting for?

It all appears such a waste of time and effort. On occasions it can seem that life is a process of learning and growing, of becoming something or someone more advanced. Life gives us many lessons and many opportunities, but if we have only one life in order to get things right what is the point? In order to answer this question, we need to review the evidence that man is not at the periphery of the universe but at its very centre.

That we exist at all is simply amazing. We can look back over time at a series of fortuitous events that brought about a universe that was perfect for beings such as ourselves. Had conditions in the first few milliseconds of the Big Bang been even slightly different we would not be around to tell the tale. The chance survival of carbon in those first few moments was so unlikely as virtually to be a miracle. If the oxygen energy level at that crucial moment had been 1 percent lower, then virtually all the carbon made inside stars would have been processed into oxygen and then much of it into heavier elements still. Consequently, carbon-based life forms like you would not exist. If we disregard Everett's Many Worlds Interpretation then this universe is the only one that has ever been. This fortuitous event took place at the first, and only, time of asking, and this was but the first of many chance events that fine-tuned the universe for your consciousness to evolve. This may make some of us feel that it was planned, but if the Copenhagen Interpretation is to be accepted the universe was looking out for itself, for without the evolution of your consciousness your universe could not exist.

You will recall that the matter that surrounds you is not what it seems. It may appear solid but its basic constituents are fuzzy waves of probability. You are reading these words in a book. The book is made of paper, which in turn owes its solidity to billions upon billions of molecules bunched so closely together that they make up a physical mass. These molecules are, in turn, made up of atoms – small, indivisible 'lumps' of matter, and these little lumps not only consist mostly of empty space but also the particles that make up the small percentage of 'solidity' are themselves mere 'waves of probability'. Not only that, but these 'wave functions', as physicists term them, need an 'observer' to collapse them into a solid point of matter. Without an observer they cannot become real. Therefore a universe with no observer is an impossibility because without observers to collapse the wave function matter cannot exist!

This model of reality works, however illogical it may seem at first. Time and again those who simply cannot accept its implications have tried to prove it wrong and have failed. This theory, termed the Copenhagen Interpretation, or Statistical Interpretation of Quantum Physics, has given us, among other things, the atomic bomb and pocket calculators. It has been the accepted model of reality for over 70 years and seems unassailable.

The implications of Copenhagen have a good deal to say about the human condition. We are the conscious observers that bring matter into reality – without mind there is no matter. However, mind is located in matter. Consciousness comes about through electrical impulses in the brain. There is no evidence that consciousness exists outside of the brain, so how can consciousness bring forth matter if consciousness cannot exist outside of matter? It is like the story of the little boy lifting himself into the air by pulling on his bootstraps.

This concern stimulated Erwin Schrödinger to propose his cat in a box experiment, in which the cat is both alive and dead at the same time. It is only when an observer, in the guise of the experimenter, looks into the box that the wave function collapses and allows the cat to be either alive or dead. Contrary to Schrödinger's intentions, explanations of the seemingly impossibility of having an alive and dead cat brought forth an even more peculiar alternative, Hugh Everett's Many Worlds Interpretation.

Everett stated that the cat can be both alive and dead at the same time, since there is more than one version of the cat. At the point that the cat became either alive or dead, the universe split into two copies, one containing a dead feline and the other an alive version of the same animal. Everett proposed that the universe splits at every such quantum event, in which case all possible events can and will happen in one of these alternative realities. This idea, initially ridiculed as pure science fiction, is accepted by many theoretical physicists. The recent work by the Israeli physicist David Deutsch has shown that we can actually measure the effect that these alternative universes have on our version of the 'Macroverse'.

Many Worlds is an alternative to the Copenhagen Interpretation. There are two options – either the universe splits into copies of itself or matter depends on consciousness for its physical existence. But what if they were both right and each consciousness brought about its own version of reality, its own universe based on its particular viewpoint?

Max Tegmark proposed that the concept of both Many Worlds and Schrödinger's Cat could be brought together as a final proof of immortality. As related earlier, he imagined a hypothetical experiment in which a machine gun is attached to a device that measures the z-spin of a sub-atomic particle.

Tegmark's logic is simple. In the universe where the bullet was fired the observer would be killed and therefore that person's world line could only go one way, into a universe where the bullet was a blank and they continue to live. This takes Wheeler's 'participatory universe' to its logical conclusion. If this universe is your universe then its existence both now and back to the first rumblings of the 'Big Bang' need you to be observing it. If you die you cease to observe and your universe also ceases. But also all historical record of its existence will similarly dissolve. In a startling paradox your death ensures that your universe never happened.

In order for your universe to continue you must continue to observe, therefore you cannot die and the Many Worlds Interpretation ensures that this is the case. In your own personal Minkowskian time line, you always avoid the accidents, become immune to the illnesses and seem to live a charmed life. I stress 'in your own universe' because in many others you do die, or at least from the viewpoint of the 'observer' responsible for that universe. And that is how you experience the death of others. They only die in your universe, whereas in their own they go on.

Although you may find this very comforting, it is likely your mind reacts strongly against such an idea. And so it should because you are programmed not to see the obvious. Everything presented to you in this book is fact, in that either it has been objective science or subjective experience. While one can never ultimately prove the truth of a subjective experience, since these reports are consistent both in content and circumstances it is reasonable to conclude that something significant is taking place. And so it is.

Life, death and all the places in-between

It is clear from the survivor reports that something unusual does take place in the brain as death approaches. The brain is literally flooded with neurotransmitters, the same neurotransmitters that bring about the world of delusion and illusion of schizophrenics and the otherworldly perceptions of pre-seizure temporal lobe epileptics. They are different aspects of the same phenomenon. There are three significant events that are consistently described by those who survive a brush with death: a slowing down of time, a meeting with an entity described as The Being In White, and a past-life review.

Firstly let's look at the perceived slowing down of time. Dr Michael Sabom found that over 90 percent of those who experienced an NDE reported an absence of 'normal time'.[344] We now know that time within the world of the Daemon does not exist in the way that we understand it. The NDE experiencers were, by virtue of the chemical releases in the brain, slipping out of time in exactly the same way that schizophrenics and epileptics do.

However, this slipping out of time is no accident. They enter the temporal world of the Daemon for a good reason – they are about to meet the Daemon – The Being in White.

As with the changes in time perception, those who report NDEs regularly say that either they sense or actually see another presence. This being, usually bathed in such bright white light that it cannot be identified as anybody in particular, seems to have uncanny knowledge about the dying person. What is interesting about this being is that it seems to fulfil a religious role for whoever encounters it in that it can be identified as Jesus, Allah, Buddha or Brahman depending upon the persuasion of the dying person. As it is unlikely that it can be a personification of all these deities it is logical to conclude that it is simply playing a role to ease the shock for the person in question. In this way can be explained the occasional report when the subject is met by a relative, friend or even, in some cases, a pet. In fact, the Being in White is none of these. It is a projection of the self because it is part of the self. It is the Daemon which knows everything about the subject – it should do, having just shared a whole lifetime with him or her. The subject, or Eidolon, naturally fails to recognize its own alter ego because it is simply not prepared for such a reality.

The role of the Daemon is far more than just a 'meeter and greeter'. Its purpose is to prepare the Eidolon for the third consistently reported event of the NDE – the past-life review. The past-life review is generated from all those memories and experiences recorded on the internal Bohmian IMAX. As NDErs report, the Being in White takes them through an incredibly detailed but super-fast review of their past life and in doing so points out the effects that certain actions or decisions had upon others. At this point it is usual for the dying person to be informed that their time has not yet come and that they must go back. They then find themselves back in their body, usually racked with pain and with a feeling of profound disappointment.

But this is because these reports are of NDEs, not actual death. Nobody has ever come back from actual death. In this way, the phenomenon known as the NDE must be seen as an error, a glitch in the system. Put simply, an NDE is when somebody, specifically the Daemon, makes a mistake, a large but understandable mistake.

So what really happens at the point of death? We have some knowledge from NDEs but these, it could be argued, are trauma brought about by the potential reality of the real thing. The body prepares itself for death by giving the person positive feelings rather than negative fears. The proliferation of supportive evidence since the publication of Moody's *Life After Life* might be because each person who reports the similarities experiences them in that way because that is what is expected. While nobody has ever actually come back from beyond the point of death, we are still left with supposition, but I am of the opinion that the NDE is not only a real phenomenon but is closely related to what actually happens.

Each report we have of an NDE involves a potentially fatal situation that was not foreseen in any way – car crashes, plane crashes, accidents and potential murders. What we do not have is an example from someone who knew, with absolute certainty that death was about to take place at some time. Indeed, with the exception of an execution – and even then errors can be made – the moment of death can never be predicted. Those with terminal illnesses approach death with foreknowledge but in all cases death actually takes place and it is usual that the approach to that death is made in a cloud of painkilling drugs. In terms of the classic NDEs, there is foreknowledge of imminent death but with a very short lead-time. The classic examples are car crashes where the victim sees the potential collision a second or two before actual impact. In these cases many of the classic symptoms are reported; the time dilation, the meeting with the Being In White, the Tunnel and the past-life review. And the longer the victim has to face certain death, the more likely it is that a past-life review is experienced.

In support of my interpretation of these events I should point again to the first real research into NDE which was stimulated by a climbing accident in which the Swiss geologist Albert Heim[345] fell 70 feet while climbing in the Alps. The duration of the fall was long enough for him to experience a full past-life review. After surviving the experience he went about collecting reports from his fellow climbers. Of the 30 cases that he reviewed the vast majority had experienced past or 'panoramic' life reviews.

The likelihood of experiencing an NDE is even greater when the time available for reflection is longer. This is particularly the case when it comes to survival of sky-diving accidents. In these cases life reviews are extremely common. The reason for this is because the mechanism that stimulates the NDE is panicked into thinking that actual death is about to take place. Then, on realizing that it was not to be, the memories of the event become confused and clouded. As with other traumatic episodes in one's life, memory places a comfort blanket around it. The question is: who is responsible for this mistake and why do they make it?

You will not be surprised to hear that this is the Daemon – and a Daemon of a particular sort. I believe this to be a trainee. While the Daemon shares our life with us, in many cases the Daemon itself is unaware that it is different from its Eidolon. The Daemon shares every thought and feeling of its Eidolon and cannot perceive itself as an independent entity. Indeed, it may be that a human being at this stage of its existence is, to all intents and purposes, a single entity. That is why most of us are not aware that 'I' constitutes a 'We'. Life goes on and both potentialities coexist in ignorance. It is only at the moment that death seems imminent that the split occurs and the Daemon suddenly realizes that it is independent. This self-awareness may be brought about by an initial flood of chemicals in the brain but either way it comes as a shock. Although there can be no proof of this, at the point of death the whole self is only aware of its Daemon personality and the Eidolon is an unthinking *tabula rasa*. The Daemon understands what its purpose is – it sees death approaching and instinctively sets a past-life review in train.

For reasons that will become clear shortly, the Daemon has misunderstood the clues. It realizes quickly – as part of its sudden self-awareness – that the time is wrong. To anthropomorphize briefly, imagine the Daemon with its finger on the start button of the 'Life Review DVD-IMAX' machine. It sees death approaching and starts the review. It suddenly then realizes it has got it all wrong, panics, and presses the 'fast-forward' button. The life review then rushes past the senses of the Eidolon in its entirety but, in respect of the temporal perception of the Eidolon, at phenomenal speed. The Daemon may then show itself to its Eidolon and make some form of excuse such as 'It is not yet your time' or some such anodyne comment. The Eidolon then blacks out and wakes up in a hospital bed or in pain at the roadside. In this way the past-life review is perceived by the Eidolon as taking place in a split second. It is simply a fast-forward.

So much for the NDE, but what then happens when the real thing takes place? Well, the run-up is identical. The Daemon realizes who it is and what it should do but on realizing that death will take place it keeps its metaphorical finger on the metaphorical 'play' button. The real past-life review begins. And something else happens as well. Throughout this book I have made play on the fact that time is an illusion of the senses and that we all travel through that illusion at different speeds.

At the moment that death becomes unavoidable, chemicals are released into the brain. These influence how the Eidolon perceives time. The temporal flow begins to slow down. As we have seen, the human brain is flexible in its perception of temporal flow: drugs, mood and metabolism all contribute to time's perceived duration. It is an acknowledged fact that massive chemical changes take place in the body at the point of death. What is also recognized – but less known – is that these chemicals are virtually identical to those released during an epileptic seizure.

Two researchers, Juan Saavadra-Anguiler and Juan Gomez-Jeria, originally made the link between NDE and TLE in 1989. They suggested that the stress brought about by a close brush with death leads to a release of a particular class of chemical called neuropeptides and specific neurotransmitters such as endogenous endomorphins, dopamine and glutamate. These chemicals become particularly active in the limbic and temporal lobe areas of the brain and cause psychological effects during near-death trauma identical to those experienced by epileptics during a pre-seizure aura.[346] From this it is possible to conclude that all the changes in perception, particularly in terms of the time perception reported by epileptics, are experienced at much greater intensity, at the point of death.

In this way, psychological time begins to slow down for the dying person. In effect, they fall out of the time perspective of any observers who may be witnessing the death. For the dying person each second may take twice as long to pass as the previous second. Their consciousness moves away from the observer's, whose seconds continue to be seconds.

To understand how this mechanism works it helps to look at the mystery of Zeno's paradox. Zeno of Elia (*c.* 450 BCE) was trying to prove that motion was impossible. In his paradox of Achilles and the Tortoise he gave humanity one of its most enduring puzzles. Zeno suggests that a race was proposed between the fleet-footed hero Achilles and a tortoise. As Achilles can run ten times faster than his reptilian opponent, he agrees to give him a ten-metre start. The starter's flag comes down and Achilles swiftly runs the ten metres. However, because we know that he can run ten times faster than the tortoise the tortoise will have walked one metre. Achilles moves on to run the next metre but the tortoise will have walked a further decimetre. Achilles runs that decimetre in the time that the tortoise progresses a further centimetre towards the finishing line. Rushing along the centimetre, Achilles discovers that he is still a millimetre behind. One can go on *ad infinitum* but Achilles will never overtake the tortoise.

Clearly this is ridiculous. Simple empirical observation shows that this situation does not occur in the 'real' world, but there is a curious logic to Zeno's argument and for hundreds of years philosophers argued over its implications. In 1954, James Thomson, later Professor of Philosophy at the Massachusetts Institute of Technology, suggested an alternative version that cannot be dismissed so easily. Called the 'Thomson Lamp', this paradox shows exactly how my proposal of survival after death may be understood.[347]

In his book *Travels In Four Dimensions*, Robin Le Poidevin, Professor of Metaphysics at the University of Leeds, takes Thomson's original proposition to its logical conclusion.[348] He asks us to imagine a lamp on which the switch is controlled by a sophisticated timer. The lamp is switched on and remains on for exactly one minute. At the end of that minute it is switched off. The lamp remains off for exactly 30 seconds and is then turned on again for 15 seconds. Again it is switched off for 7.5 seconds and on again for 3.75 seconds. The timer is so sophisticated that it can be programmed to continue this 50 percent time decrease alternating between on and off forever. Expressed mathematically, the lamp is on (off) for n seconds then it is off (on) for $n/2$ seconds. Thomson asked us to consider two questions concerning the state of the lamp after exactly two minutes: firstly, how many times has the lamp been switched on and off and, secondly, is the lamp now on or off?

The answers are really strange but totally logical. The timer will continue switching the lamp on and off in ever decreasing time segments but these time segments will never add up to two minutes because in order to do so the lamp will have been switched on and off an infinite number of times. As regards the series of on and off switchings, the two-minute point is *never reached*. By the same logic, an observer can never know the state of the lamp (on or off) at the two-minute point.[349]

And so it is with human consciousness at the point of death, but what if the moment of death, like the lamp's two-minute point, is never reached? We all die at a specific point in time. That is an absolutely irrefutable fact. Let us imagine that a lady called Zoë Eternus will die at exactly 12:59 and 59 seconds on 31 December 2006. She has a car crash – she falls asleep and drives her car, at a speed of 60 kilometres per hour, into a wall head on and dies instantly. The second before impact she wakes up to see a wall rushing towards her and believes she is about to die. In that final second she is 16.6 metres from the wall. As death approaches Zoë's brain is flooded by ketamine and glutamate chemicals. These endorphins immediately start to affect how Zoë perceives the passage of time. As far as she is concerned, she begins to live in a real-time version of Zeno's bisection paradox. You will recall the concept of 'the chronon' suggested by the physicist David Finklestein – an indivisible 'bit' of time that can be objectively measured; in the case of Zoë, the endogenous chemicals ensure that each 'chronon' is subjectively perceived by Zoë as twice the length of the one before. An infinite series of finite chronons of time must be experienced by Zoë in order for her to arrive at her actual moment of death. In fact, Zoë never manages to travel the full 16.6 metres that is needed for her, and the car, to hit the wall.

In the same way that Thomson's sequence of ons and offs never reaches the two-minute point, so it is that Zoë's consciousness never reaches her actual point of death – in space or time. She slips out of time and into an alternative and subjectively based Everett Universe. Meanwhile, in the universe of an observer, Zoë dies. Just as with Max Tegmark's 'quantum gun' experiment in which the experimenter never finds a live bullet in the gun in her world, so it is that Zoë never dies in hers. In both cases the individuals in question follow a Minkowski time line into a personal universe.

As we have seen from the theories of Julian Barbour and Henri

Bergson, it is possible that time is totally relative and to inhabit our own version of psychological time is perfectly logical. Without it how could Maury have created his dream of the French Revolution in the split second it took the message of the headboard hitting his neck to reach his brain?

While experience has shown me that this is the most difficult concept to get across, in fact the proposition is in keeping with basic science. It is a literal interpretation of the scientific concept of half-life, only in this case we are dealing with a real life. Radioactive substances decay in such a way that they lose half of their radioactivity in a given period of time. For example, the radioactive isotope cobalt-60, used in radiotherapy, has a half-life of 5.26 years. Thus after that interval a sample that originally contained eight grams of cobalt-60 would contain only four grams of cobalt-60 and would emit only half as much radiation. After another interval of 5.26 years, the same sample would contain only two grams. However, in a real example of Zeno's paradox, the amount of cobalt-60 never reaches zero, it just halves every 5.26 years from now to eternity. And so it is with our life force. We also have a real half-life that within our own phaneron is a full-life. As with Einstein's realization that it is time that must give in terms of relativity theory, so it is that time must also give in the world of near-death.

Although this is simply an analogy and analogies by themselves prove nothing, it may be possible to demonstrate exactly how this mechanism of falling out of time takes place. The François-Hoagland theory states that the higher the temperature or metabolic rate of the observer, the slower time seems to pass for them. It has also been shown by experimentation that during periods of high stress, individuals sense a slowing down of time. What can be more stressful than dying, or more importantly, knowing that you are about to die? The increase in metabolic rate that takes place is brought about by the brain of the dying person being flooded by the neurotransmitter glutamate. In large doses, glutamate can over-excite the synapses and cause a massive increase in electrical activity. Once started, this process rapidly gets out of control and an epileptic seizure takes place.

Might this be the mechanism by which both reality is brought into existence and temporal perception is slowed down? Within each cell, including the brain's neurons, is a structural network, the cytoskeleton. The structural scaffolding of the cytoskeleton is made up of tiny hollow cylinders – microtubules. For some scientists (including Roger Penrose and Stuart Hameroff) there is evidence that something inside these microtubules may initiate the wave-function collapse that brings about one version of reality rather than another. If this is the case then the universe 'out there' really is your own version, generated by electrical discharges across your synapses. But there is more.

Thought and consciousness are generated by electrical discharges across the brain. It is the neurotransmitters that bring about the transfer of calcium ions across the synaptic gaps. The distances involved are so small that quantum events may be affected by quantum decoherence. And since electricity travels at the same speed as light, the electrical discharges across the brain travel at that speed as well.

One major question fascinated Albert Einstein: what would he perceive if he was to find himself travelling on a light wave? It was his answer to this question that was to change the world. Einstein realized that time would cease to exist at light speed. Not only that, but the closer an observer came to light speed, the slower time would 'flow'. For an observer not on the light beam, time would continue at its normal pace. In other words, if one person is on a light beam and the other is not they will cease to be existing in the same Minkowskian 'time line'.

So as Zoë and her car approach the wall, her metabolism rate increases and her brain is flooded by neurotransmitters. Her synapses chatter with hyperactivity and a massive discharge of electricity – travelling at the speed of light. This 'glutamate flood' only takes place once in a lifetime, at the approach of death. Could it be that such a deluge pushes consciousness itself towards the speed of light and therefore 'out of time'?

And what of the viewpoint of a witness to Zoë's crash? For the observer, Zoë and her car impact at speed and Zoë is killed. However, Zoë is already existing in another time line in which the impact has yet to take place – and may never actually take place. In the universe of the observer Zoë dies, and in Zoë's universe she goes on living in smaller and smaller chronons.

For a small sector of humanity these 'little deaths' take place on a regular basis. From the descriptions of epileptics we know that large amounts of glutamate brings about huge change in consciousness and a slowing down of time. An associate of mine, a sufferer of TLE, described how in her first experience of the 'aura' she literally fell out of time. She described an incident strikingly similar to that of the Tom Cruise character, David Aames, in *Vanilla Sky*. In the film, Aames has time 'freeze' when he is in a bar. A 'guide' brings this about as a way of illustrating to Aames that the world he perceives is an inwardly generated illusion.

My associate was having lunch in a crowded company restaurant. She suddenly felt a click in her head and everything and everybody around her froze. She stared in horror at her friend who had been in the process of pouring a cup of tea. As she focused on the tea hitting the bottom of the cup she noticed that time was not frozen but was passing very slowly. She watched as the cup took minutes to fill. She then noticed that everybody else was moving in super-slow motion. She spent hours trapped in this temporal flux and then, just as suddenly as it had begun, the aura ended and normal time began again. Her friend looked at her strangely and asked if she was okay. As far as her friend was concerned, the subsequently diagnosed TLE sufferer had stared at her for, at most, two or three seconds.

It is probable that what she experienced was the subjective effect of a glutamate flood as part of a pre-seizure aura. If this is the case then the perception of time duration does slow down for those approaching death. In a similar way, our young woman, Zoë, has moved out of time and, it must be said, space, and is inhabiting a world within her own mind. She has, in effect, unlimited time – but what is this time for? In answering this question we must return to the Daemon.

The Daemon is now aware of what its task is to be. It is responsible for ensuring that the past-life review takes place – but not as it is known from the reports of NDE experiencers. The standard description is always similar to 'my life passed before my eyes in a split second'. In the real run that is stimulated by an actual death situation, the review takes place at normal speed, in a minute-by-minute equality. Each minute of the life record is perceived by the Eidolon as an actual minute. Put another way, the Eidolon lives its life again in real time.

Ring in the changes

At a few microseconds before actual death the dying person's consciousness is flooded with new images, images of re-birth. The Eidolon finds itself coming into a virtual reality world as a newly born baby. Its memory banks wiped clean, it remembers nothing of its previous life. It begins afresh in a world created from recovered memories. As described by Penfield's patients, every sound, feeling and emotion is reproduced in perfect fidelity. As far as the Eidolon is concerned, this is all new. However, this second life has one major difference. It has a conscious and aware Daemon who has a knowledge of everything that is about to take place. As the child grows, so the Daemon keeps a watchful eye over its progress. It experiences everything and in dreams may communicate subtle changes to the progress of this second life.

As the Eidolon-child becomes older, circumstances may occur in which either by accident or design the Daemon causes a 'glitch' in the programme. The Eidolon will be confused at these strange sensations, and will experience a feeling that it has lived these events before, that it *remembers* what will happen next. On reading up or commenting to others, it will discover that these curious sensations are termed *déjà vu*.

There may be occasions when the Daemon wishes to change the course of action followed by its Eidolon. The Daemon may manifest itself in many ways: as a voice in the head, a dream or possibly a doppelgänger. In this way it can manoeuvre its 'lower self' into a better position or into a situation where it may learn from experience. These situations I term 'temporal mutations' and they work in exactly the same way that Darwinian mutations take place in nature.

A classic 'temporal mutation' was posted on the web site of Dr Samuel K Spitzner.[350] While reading this account, it will be useful to bear in mind both Julian Jaynes' bicameralism and Everett's Many Worlds:

> *It was just before Christmas in 1987, and I was living in Bethlehem, Israel. I shared a small flat with my fiancé and young son. The time of year was extremely cold with icy winds and snow constantly blowing through the town. This one particular night, we had all decided to go to bed early, for the only heating we had was a small gas burner. Our flat had only one bedroom, so my fiancé and I slept in the bedroom, whilst my young son, slept on a sofa bed in the family room. Sometime during the night, I found myself standing about mid way up a very large white stoned staircase. A realisation came to me, that if I continued to walk further up the staircase, that there would be no turning back. I stood for a moment pondering my situation, when thoughts came into my mind, of the decision I had to make. If I went up, lives would be lost, and a new life would never get the chance to be born. I realized my responsibilities and began to walk back down the steps. The next thing I became aware of, was an audible voice*

saying Rosalyn get up and go to the bathroom. I replied No! to the voice as I did not want to go to the bathroom. The voice became louder and more insistent. Finally on the third call, I said ok! Climbing out of bed in the pitch darkness, I stumbled for the bedroom door, but was unable to open it as my body began to shake and spasm. As I hit the ground my fiancé woke up and leapt out of bed in a mad panic and ran to the bedroom door and then to the front door opening it up, screaming at the top of his lungs. I on the other hand was still convulsing on the floor and saying Please God, don't let me be sick! As the fresh air began to filter in, I stopped convulsing and instead went into fits of laughter as I heard all the commotion outside as neighbours came rushing into the flat. They too were dropping like flies. When I had managed to regain control of myself. I checked on my young son, who was blissfully unaware and unaffected by what I suspected to be a gas leak. We were all slowly being gassed to death. I tried to explain to my Arab neighbours that it was nothing more than a gas leak, but by this time they were all firmly convinced a demon was in the room, making people fall down. It took a fair bit of convincing on my part, that some one must have either left the gas stove on, or the gas burner had a leak. But to this day, they still think it was an evil force bent on destroying us. Anyway thank you God! for saving our lives and helping me to make the right decision for life. As I now have 3 wonderful children and a lovely husband. And a hard working guardian angel.

There are striking similarities between this case and that of the pregnant lady and thalidomide (*see* page 270). On both occasions a nocturnal 'voice' warns against certain actions or circumstances and in doing so totally changes the lives of both the subject and those they love.

With regard to 'temporal mutations', it might be asked if the second life is little more than a virtual reality projection, how can it be changed? After all, we cannot change the ending of a film if we do not like the plot. The difference lies in Many Worlds and Bohm's concept of enfoldment. While the dying person has moved outside of time and space and exists in his own phaneron, this phaneron consists of a universe of his own making. Real people with real motivations populate each universe. Actions taken by one person bring about another universe. In this way, all possible events can and will take place. Added to this is the idea that each universe enfolds and is contained within every other universe. Changes made in one lifetime can and will affect the lives of others within their own phanerons – one can make right any wrongdoings of the previous life!

And so the human 'soul' evolves in the same way that an animal species evolves. Equivalent to each Darwinian generation is a life, each one subtly changed from the last one. As with Phil Conners in the film *Groundhog Day*, we each have endless lives to get things right. The mechanism is simply a repeat of the end of the first life. Death again approaches and is again denied by the person's consciousness dipping out of time. Psychological time again slows down in an exponential way, leaving Charon yet again with an empty boat.

Preparing for the worst

For both the Daemon and the Eidolon, the approach of death is a stressful time. It is the time that the interaction between the two should be at its most intense. The evidence to support this contention is that the Daemon seems to become visible to the dying Eidolon. The following example is taken from the work of Osis and Haraldsson,[351] two renowned writers on the subject of NDEs. They relate:

A college-educated Indian man in his twenties was recovering
from mastoiditis. He was doing very well. He was going to be
discharged that day. Suddenly at 5 am he shouted 'someone is
standing here dressed in white clothes. I will not go with you!'
He was dead in ten minutes. Both the patient and the doctor
expected a definite recovery.

This is a genuine NDE in that the patient did actually die and it
demonstrates that the Being in White is seen as part of the real
thing as well as 'near misses'. The chemicals released in the brain
prior to death create a level of awareness in normal consciousness
that allows perception of our higher self. In this case the Daemon
decided to be seen as a being that cannot be recognized as another
version of the self. There has been a long-held belief that to see
one's double is a portent of death. Might this have come about
when the dying person reported that he could see his own
doppelgänger?

In 1918, Wellesley Tudor Pole reported a double being seen at
the point of death of a French foreign legionnaire:

When seemingly beyond speech, he half rose from the pillow in
the sand where he had tried to take refuge from the sun, and
cried out in broken French 'Why, there is myself coming to
meet me. How wonderful!' Then he fell back and died and we
reported the incident on reaching Bou Saada the next day.[352]

It is reasonable to conclude that some Daemons are happy to
show themselves at this point. Others take on the appearance of
whatever person or religious archetype will instil in the dying
person a feeling of happiness and joy. It is usually reported that
the Daemon spontaneously appears and that there is no
perception of the bifurcation of the mind, but this must take place
in order for the Daemon to be perceived as being 'out there' as

opposed to a voice in the head or a hunch. It fact, we can sometimes actually sense this splitting process, as suggested by this report by the world-renowned anatomist Sir Auckland Geddes:

CHAPTER 14 The Friend in the Shadows

I realised that I was very ill ... thereafter at no time did my consciousness appear to be in any way dimmed, but I suddenly realised that my consciousness was also separating from another consciousness, which was also me. These, for purposes of description, we could call A and B consciousness, and throughout what follows (my awareness was attached) to the A consciousness, which was now me, seemed altogether outside my body, which I could see. Gradually I realised that I could see, not only my body and the bed on which I was lying, but everything in the whole house and garden.[353]

Thus, for a few seconds, Geddes found himself astride the two elements of his being. Like Rosalind Heywood with her 'white and pink me', he perceived reality as both a Daemon and an Eidolon.

The Gnostics considered that at the point of death the human soul splits into two separate entities. In the Gnostic *Gospel of Thomas*, the scribe has Jesus make this cryptic comment:

Two will rest in a bed, but one shall die and another will live.

To end this section, here is a little-known historical anecdote. During the final three days of her life, 21–24 March 1603, Queen Elizabeth I claimed that her double watched over her at all times. A manuscript entitled 'The Relation of the Lady Southwell of the late Q(ueen's) death', written in April 1607, reads:

She fell downright ill, and the cause being wondered at by my lady Scroope, with whom she was very private and confidential, being her near kinswoman, her Majesty told her (commanding

her to conceal the same), 'that she saw one night her own body
exceedingly lean and fearful in a light of fire'. This vision was
at Whitehall, a little before she departed for Richmond, and
was testified by another lady, of whom the Queen demanded
'Whether she was not wont to see sights in the night?' telling
*her of the bright flame she had seen.*354

The nexus of eternity

At the moment of death the Eidolon is transported back to the
point where the embryo becomes a person. If my theory is
correct, this can take place as soon as the neurons have
developed sufficiently for the Eidolon to attach itself. At this
point the brain 'wakes up' and becomes, if not fully conscious,
at least aware in some basic way. At this point dreaming begins.
The Eidolon has the opportunity to review and reflect on what
took place in its previous life, possibly under the guidance of the
Daemon. This form of pre-natal dreaming is a form of 'active
sleep'. According to the biologist Lyall Watson, the developing
foetus spends most of its time doing this.355 The question is:
what can a being who has had absolutely no experience possibly
dream about?

At birth, the density of neurons within the brain is relatively
small. It is only after birth that the cortical dendrites grow and the
glia cells multiply. Any mental activity that takes place will be very
basic. The newly born child has no concept of self or identity. It
has no real consciousness, just an ability to react to external
stimuli in an autonomic way. But if this is the case, how is it that
certain people claim that they remember being born and some
even remember events in the womb?

Stanislav Grof (*see* page 359) came across anecdotal evidence
that implied that our ability to perceive our environment and lay
down memories starts very early. Patients accurately described
characteristics of the heartbeat of their mother, the nature of

acoustic phenomena in the peritoneal cavity, specific details of blood circulation in the placenta, and even details about the various cellular and biochemical processes taking place. They could also describe the thoughts their mother had during pregnancy and events such as the physical traumas she had experienced.[356]

Grof's results were given massive support when, in 1986, an example of a child remembering his own birth by Caesarean section was reported.[357] The child in question was extremely precocious in terms of his general development. On day one he was able to lift his head, focus, and follow an object with his eyes. At three months he was speaking recognizable words, and sentences at five months. It was at age two, while sitting in the bath, that he asked a startling question of his parents. He wanted to know why the lights were so bright 'when I was new'. On being asked what he meant by 'new' he explained that he meant 'being born' and said there were many things he did not understand about this. He did not stop there.

He went on to ask why it was that the light was circular and intense where he was but dim elsewhere; why the bottom half of faces were missing, with a green patch there instead; why someone had felt his anus with their finger; why he was put in a plastic box and taken somewhere; why liquid was put in his eyes so that he could not see; and what was inserted in his nose that made a loud sucking sound. Indeed, he went on to describe not only other experiences of his birth but also experiences he had in the womb. The article's writer, Laibow, states that the child had never seen a surgical unit, or surgical green masks; he did not know that silver nitrate solution is routinely used in the eyes of the newly born, and he had not seen or heard a suctioning device used in the nostrils except on the occasion of his own birth.[358]

This appears to demonstrate that, contrary to general belief, memories of birth are available to certain individuals. The curious thing about this case is that the baby not only had the verbal ability to recall the events but also to be able to take in all the incoming external stimuli around him. How could he focus in such detail on the objects and people around him? Here we have a newly born baby who seems to recognize everything around him. Could it be that it is the newly born, but much older in actual lifetime(s), Eidolon that recalls these images? It may take a few days for the lower self to forget how to process information as its Daemon does, so the memories are fully available for 'eidolonic' recall.[359]

And so it is that very young babies can dream, a reality that fascinated, among others, Jung. Jung used this in support of his belief that human consciousness is outside of the brain and therefore was not affected by neuronal development. In reply to a question by his friend Michael Serrano, he wrote:

> *There are other phenomena which can support this hypothesis.*
> *You know of course that a small child has no clearly defined*
> *sense of ego. Nevertheless it has been proven that small*
> *children have dreams in which the ego is clearly defined just as*
> *it is with mature people. In these dreams the child has a clear*
> *sense of the persona, but if, from a psychological point of view,*
> *the child has no ego, what is it in the child that produces these*
> *dreams, dreams which, I may add, affect him for the rest of his*
> *life? And another question; if the physical ego disappears at*
> *death, does the other ego also disappear, that other which has*
> *sent him dreams as a child?*

We now know that Jung's 'other ego' is, in fact, the Daemon.

For those who suffer from TLE much of what I have suggested will come as no surprise. It may be the case that this book may help explain some of the most bizarre cases known to psychiatrists and neurologists, particularly one reported in the journal *Psychopathology* in 2003. Written by two Japanese psychiatrists, the article described how a male patient with TLE was convinced that he had repeatedly lived the part of his life between the ages of 21 to 25. As the patient reported:

> *Up until the age of 25, my life was unremarkable. I was employed, and often enjoyed going for drives or to karaoke with my friends on weekends. I cannot remember the details. At the age of 25 I married a girl from Hiroshima, and lived safely. Nothing particular happened after my marriage. However, soon after, I happened to notice that I was again 21 years old and unmarried ... Then I lived again between the ages of 21 to 25. Once again I held the same job, and again at the age of 25, I married the same girl. This endless cycle has already repeated itself five or six times. Now I am sure I will continue forever. I attempted suicide to escape from this endless repetition.*[360]

This is a real-life equivalent of *Groundhog Day*, consisting of not one day but four years. For this individual the temporal fugue was so real that he committed suicide at the (externally observed) age of 28. If my theory is correct then this unfortunate person really was living his life over and over again. The endogenous chemicals that flood all our brains at the point of death had, for some reason, repeated their effect over and over again. This was directly related to his TLE and brought about a personal version of Nietzsche's demon-evoked Eternal Return.

I believe that there is sufficient evidence to conclude that during the last few seconds of our previous life we will all experience a full TLE seizure. A cocktail of endogenous drugs that stimulate the brain into its final activities brings about this seizure. A slowing down of time and a past-life review is then stimulated and we start again. And as we emerge into our new life the neurological echoes of the old are still reverberating around our brain. How do I know? Well what do you make of this?

If electrodes are attached to the stomach of a woman in late
pregnancy, the brain waves of the foetus can be recorded.
Usually these prove to be slow delta waves at a frequency of
less than three cycles per second, but sometimes this regular
pattern is interrupted by larger discharges similar to the spiky
recordings obtained from adults in an epileptic attack. As the
baby approaches full term, these convulsions become more
frequent, until at birth they are almost continuous as the child
thrashes its way into the world. We are all born in something
like epilepsy, and if we survive the experience, it seems likely
that this could be just the sort of positive conditioning
necessary to produce the same response again in a later
comparable crisis.

In other words, we die in an epileptic fit and we are born in one.
On that point, we may be reminded of the epileptic writer
Edmond Goncourt, who described life as:

... an epileptic fit between two nothings.

In fact, this book has shown it to be:

... nothing between two epileptic fits.

Epilogue – The Enfolding Dream

> So the Platonic year
> Whirls out new right and wrong,
> Whirls in the old instead;
> All men are dancers and their tread
> Goes to the barbarous clangour of a gong.
>
> *W B Yeats*

As I have already mentioned, Philip K Dick was a modern writer and mystic who touched upon the underlying structure of what we term reality. Careful reading of his books and stories present the reader with a cosmology that looks back, not forward. Dick's stories are full of ideas based upon Bohm's Implicate Order, Everett's Many Worlds and Wheeler's Participatory Universe and yet his inspiration was not these modern theorists – he looked back to the writings of the great Gnostic philosophers. Dick created a theoretically possible universe by applying ideas many hundreds of years old. Stimulated by his own duality, he looked for explanations in philosophy and theology, not quantum physics and neurology and in doing so created a universe that accurately reflected how the deep structures of matter were revealing themselves to science. As he described in his book *Valis*, it was his Daemon 'Sophia' that was to point the way.

And it was a very specific direction that Sophia wished Dick to take. Of all his books *Ubik* implies that Dick may have been aware, consciously or subconsciously, of the proposals made by this book. In this curious tale, science has discovered that when people die their consciousness slips into what Dick terms half-life. What he means by this is that their life force dwindles in the same way that radioactivity does. In this way Dick fictionalizes the reality proposed in my book. Within his story he also, possibly unknowingly, applies Everett's Many Worlds Interpretation and Borges' *Garden of The Forking Paths,* in that he has people who can change the present by causing an alternative bifurcation in the past. We have to conclude that it was his interest in Gnosticism that brought about this idea.

You will, I hope, agree that the evidence for human duality is not only very strong, but can be supported by personal, subjective experience. However, it seems that no human culture has incorporated my theory of consciousness and reality into their own theology and world-view. None except one, and they are probably the most inwardly attuned members of the human race: the Australian aborigines. Existing in their own metaphysic, the philosophy and cosmology of the indigenous Australians is totally at odds with our Western world-view. For these people reality is, as Dick and Blake argued, an illusion. However, for the aborigine that is not all. For them existence itself is a duality similar to my Eidolon/Daemon dichotomy.

As far as the aborigines are concerned, 'reality' consists of not one, but two space/time continuums. These alternative states co-exist and overlap, the nexus point being human consciousness. Everyday waking existence is simply that, 'wake-time'. During sleep, man accesses the other form of temporal flow, *altjiranga* or 'Dreamtime'. Dreamtime is a curious psychological state in which time itself flows differently. In echoes of Minkowski, the aborigines consider that the two versions of time are different, in that Dreamtime runs ahead of Waketime. In this way the future can be experienced whilst in a Dreamtime psychological state. This can be achieved by sleep, drugs or, more usually, by ritualistic dancing and music.

During this state the individual ceases to be an individual, they merge into the greater being of nature. They perceive Bohm's 'enfolded order' and like the two particles in the Paris Experiment, in this state they can exist everywhere and everywhen. This 'at-one-ment' with all of nature is evident in the curious fact that indigenous Australians seem to have an awareness of events that are occurring hundreds of miles away. In the 1940s anthropologist AP Elkin made an extensive study of Aborigine culture and was surprised to find that this perception at a distance was a common and accepted part of aborigine life. He wrote:

> *A man will suddenly announce one day that his father is dead,*
> *that his wife has given birth to a child or that there is some*
> *trouble in his country. He is so sure of his facts that he would*
> *return at once if he could.*

Elkin took the opportunity to check out some of these 'hunches' and found them often to be correct and therefore in his opinion to be more than pure coincidence.

Dreamtime contains all memories and experiences and in this way the past can be relived as if it were the present. This has startling similarities with what Penfield discovered with his electric probe. This is not all. Everett's Many Worlds Interpretation would be greeted with nods of agreement to those sitting in the shadows of Mount Ziel. All possible outcomes of actions can be found somewhere in the vast expanses of Dreamtime.

And what of my final moments of life when the dying person slips, Zeno-like, out of both time and space? Again, these supposedly 'primitive' people have a single word – 'Inbetween' – which accurately describes what has taken me many pages to attempt to convey.

In this book I have attempted to bridge the gap between serious science and subjective experience. Clearly, I can never 'prove' that the evidence I have presented is true – but then again how can anyone prove the existence of his or her own subjective consciousness to another person? All I can present is a way of interpreting the evidence in such a way that a reasonable person may at the least appreciate my conclusions.

To finish, here is one final NDE, one that was posted on the web without an e-mail address and so I was unable to contact the person in question.[361] Why not read this report while bearing in mind the major issues highlighted in this book – which are:

1 The DVD/movie re-run;

2 Escaping the Gnostic's 'Realm of the Demiurge'/'Philip K Dick's 'Black-Eyed Prison';

3 Bohm's 'Enfolded Universe';

4 Bohm's 'Holomovement';

5 The Daemon;

6 The idea that the Daemon exists right through one's life;

7 The idea that the Daemon is like a 'guardian angel', and that the Daemon is another aspect of the self;

8 Julian Jaynes' voices;

9 Daemon assistance via hunches and intuition;

10 Time Dilation.

This is my NDE. Even though I've talked to several people about this experience, I didn't realize how hard it would be to put it into written words. Oh well, here goes …

It happened in May 1992. I was driving a '68 Spitfire convertible and a friend was riding as a passenger. We were driving on a narrow country road and as we entered a 90-

degree turn one of the back tyres separated from the rim (i.e. blew out). The car spun around and slid off the road backwards while still spinning. A 3–4 foot drop off at the edge of the road gave the car enough momentum to flip endwise.

I clearly remember most of the events leading up to the car leaving the road. I remember I was lying on my back in the grass as the car pushed me down the hill. It felt like I was under a bulldozer. As I looked up, I saw the car as it was hovering above me, balanced on the back fender. I watched it as it fell upon me. An instant before the impact, I had a very lucid memory of a conversation between me and my friend (who was riding with me) about convertibles. I had casually made the comment, 'Convertibles are nice, but if you rolled one, you'd be dead for sure!' Talk about irony …

As the car hit me, I heard a loud crunch, then everything changed instantly. It was like sitting in a movie theatre watching a crash scene and then the film breaks **[1]**. *You suddenly realize that you are in a theatre and the crash (and the associated stress, excitement, etc.) are just an illusion* **[2]**.

There was no discontinuity of consciousness. My first thought was 'Well, I guess this is what it's like to be dead'. There was no fear or anxiety. I wondered what had happened to my friend. Was he dead, too? I thought that I should look for him, but realized that I had no body. Actually, there was no physical reality whatsoever. Physical movement had no meaning.

On the other hand, I knew that this new place had some type of dimension. I just didn't know what it was. It seemed like I was in an area of 'lesser concentration' surrounded by an area of 'greater concentration' located at a 'distance' **[3]**. *The 'area of greater concentration' felt like it might be a 'city' of some* *kind. I sensed that there were many entities there. I also had a feeling that I would also eventually go there as well.*

I decided to wait for someone or something to make contact with me. I assumed that whoever or whatever entities existed in this new reality knew I had arrived. There was no worry whatsoever and I felt very comfortable just waiting.

While I waited I become aware of how good I felt. I'd go so far as to say it was a feeling of peaceful bliss. That's an understatement, but it's hard to describe the actual feeling. It seemed that my efforts in life were like mowing the lawn on a very hot, very humid summer day. This place was like coming inside to air conditioning and drinking cold lemonade while sitting in big cushy chair.

I was thinking about these feelings when I felt something 'move' near me. At that point, I realized the meaning of 'movement' in this place. I was in an emotional space. The movement was the movement of emotions [4]. I realize now that we all are aware of this type of movement and use related phrases in our everyday language. For example, we say 'I feel close to her', 'He seems distant', or 'We are drifting apart'. Since my NDE, I realize that I exist in this 'other place' at the same time as I exist in this physical space. This was true before the NDE as well, but I didn't realize it. (Yes, I know it sounds strange.)

I recognized the 'movement' as being the movement of an entity. I 'recognized' that this entity [5] had been with me all my life [6]. I don't know if it was what people call a guardian angel [7] or if it was just another disassociated aspect of my psyche [8]. However, I suddenly remembered that this entity had 'spoken' to me many times earlier in my life. I had always

labelled the communication as 'intuition' [9]. *The 'speaking'*
was clear, yet didn't really involve words (although I
'remember' the conversation as words).

The entity then asked me a series of questions. It asked, 'Do
you like where you are?' I said I thought it was fantastic – I
felt better than I ever had before. It then asked, 'Do you want
to stay here?' My first thought was that this was a silly
question given my first answer, but I said, 'Yeah, sure! I want
to stay'. The entity then 'reminded' me that I had not fulfilled
my purpose yet. Suddenly, I remembered events that had
happened before I was conceived. I had chosen to come to this
physical existence for a particular reason. I wasn't supposed to
know what that reason was until it was time to fulfil my
purpose. I also knew that I could stay in this other place
without fulfilling the purpose and it wouldn't be held against
me. However, I felt it was better to go back ('to' Earth), fulfil
my purpose, and then return.

As I had this thought, I started to have a spinning and falling
sensation. It was like I was being poured through a funnel. As
I spun, I slowly felt the sensation of weight and solidity. When
the spinning stopped, I opened my eyes. I was standing next to
the car at the bottom of a ravine. I observed, more with
curiosity than terror, large amounts of blood flowing from my
face. I again wondered what had happened to my friend. I
called his name and, out of the corner of my eye, I saw him
still rolling in the grass as the result of being thrown from the
car. The whole experience had happened in a fraction of a
second [10].

I felt the presence of 'grace' throughout the aftermath of the
accident (and I still do). My injuries required 200 stitches'
worth of plastic surgery in my face and 40 stitches in my arm.

*However, I was able to leave the hospital after three days
instead of the estimated three weeks. Although several doctors
thought that my nose was damaged beyond repair, today my
nose looks completely normal. You have to look closely to see
any scars at all.*

*This experience changed my outlook on life and reality in more
ways that I can describe in this message. I hesitated to post it
since it didn't actually involve clinical death, but I thought
somebody might find it meaningful (or at least interesting).'*

My 'discovery' of this particular e-mail was portentous in the
extreme. In attempting to explain how interwoven this is, I am
reminded of a painting by the Dutch artist MC Escher. Entitled
Drawing Hands, it shows exactly that, two hands drawing each
other. In over a year's writing and research I had found many
examples to support my theory but none that incorporated all of
the crucial elements. I was surfing the Internet when quite by
chance I discovered a relevant web site and on this web site I
found exactly what I needed. In doing so my own Daemon proved
to me not only that all my research was correct but also that he
himself was guiding me to find the right information at the right
time. As Escher's hands draw each other so my Daemon drew me
to proof of his existence.

A request

Anthony Peake is planning to continue his research into all the
areas discussed in this book and is keen to hear from any readers
who have had experiences similar to those described. Please
contact him via his website: www.anthonypeake.com

He will try to respond personally to all communications.

Notes

1 For an interesting discussion on this subject see the magazine *Discover*, June 2005.

2 Baierlein R, *Newton to Einstein*

3 *New Scientist*, October 1999, p27

4 *Nature*, 406 43, 2000

5 The SUNY experiment used superconducting quantum interference devices (SQUIDs). These are ring-shaped devices in which persistent currents, made of billions of pairs of electrons, circulate in either a clockwise or an anti-clockwise direction without decaying. The SUNY team wanted to see if the system remembered its quantum state as it tunnelled. The results were exactly as predicted by assuming the system is in a macroscopic superposition of states.

6 Tegmark, 'The Interpretation of Quantum Mechanics: Many Worlds or Many Words'

7 Myers FWH, 'The Subliminal Self', p497

8 Funkhouser AT, 'The Dream Theory of Déjà vu', p115

9 Pais A, *Subtle is The Lord*, p443

10 Bohr N, *Phys. Rev 48*, p696-702

11 For an interesting variation on this popular quotation see http://myridedownfeynmansdrain.netfirms.com/main.html

12 Feynman R, *The Character of Physical Law*, p29

13 Aspect A & Grangier P, 'Experiments on EPR type correlations with pairs of visible photons'

14 A remark was reported at an American Physical Society seminar on the history of theories in science, by a scientist who participated in the Oppenheimer seminars.

15 Bohm D, *Hidden Variables In The Implicate Order*, p38

16 Ibid p48,

17 Ibid p172

18 Ibid p23

19 Bohm D & Peat D, *Science, Order and Creativity* , p185-186,

20 Bradley FE, *Appearance & Reality*, p248

21 'Does The Universe Exist If We Are Not Looking?' *Discover*, vol 23, no 6

22 Maury A, *Sleep And Dreams*, p133-4

23 Maury was also greatly influenced by his dreams. Elsewhere in his book on sleep and dreams he describes how a mystical dream person helped him to learn English.

24 Inglis B, *Coincidence*, p167

25 http://www.consciousness.arizona.edu/quantum-mind2/Qmind1_Abs/index.htm

26 Anderson MK, *Wired News*

27 Geldard F & Sherrick C, 'The Cutaneous Rabbit: A Perceptual Illusion', *Science* 178

28 Dennett D C, *Consciousness Explained*, p143

29 Deeke L, Grötzinger B, & Kornhuber H, 'Voluntary Finger Movements in Man: Cerebral Potentials and Theory'

30 Penrose R, *The Emperor's New Mind*, p569

31 Ibid p569

32 Goodman N, *Ways of Worldmaking*, p73

33 Dennett D C, *Consciousness Explained*, p115

34 Ryle G, *The Concept of Mind*, p17

35 Pribram K, 'Problems Concerning The Structure Of Consciousness', p297-313

36 This term refers to the writings of French philosopher René Descartes, who argued that the brain and the mind are two separate things. The belief that the being called 'I' exists outside of the brain was considered self-evident by Descartes.

37 Priestley JB, *Man & Time*, p207

38 Strindberg A, *Legends*, p56-57

39 Ibid p92-93

40 Poundstone W, *Labyrinths Of Reason*, p3-4

41 Penfield W & Roberts L, *Speech & Brain Mechanisms*, p45-47

42 Penfield W, *The Mystery of Mind; A Critical Study of Consciousness and the Human Brain*, p21

43 Professor Pribram was at pains to point out that Penfield's experiments have never been repeated with non-epileptic patients. For Pribram the crucial factor was the scar tissue on the surface of the brain which focused the holographic potential for recollection. Pribram managed to get Penfield to acknowledge this towards the end of his life.

44 Pribram K, 'Problems Concerning The Structure Of Consciousness', p297-313

45 Pribam K, 'Some Comments on the Nature of the Perceived Universe', p83-101

46 Ramachandran VS, *Phantoms in the Brain*, p72

47 A later chapter discusses the theories of time of Julian Barbour. This case supports his idea that time does not exist and that motion is an illusion. This woman sees reality 'correctly'. It is the rest of us that are in error.

48 Sacks O, *An Anthropologist on Mars*, p153-156

49 Poulet G, *Studies In Human Time*,

50 Pinker S, *How The Mind Works*, p306

51 Bergson H, 'Le souvenir du présent et la fausse reconnaissance', p561-593

52 Known in the USA as *hypermnesia*, evidence elicited by hypnosis has been accepted in US courts of law. However, in an important US case (People v Kempinski, 1980) the defence successfully challenged a positive identification of their client from hypnotic regression.

53 Hunt M, *The Universe Within*, p91-92

54 Gindes BC, *New Concepts in Hypnosis*

55 Luria AS, *The Mind of a Mnemonist*

56 For an interesting discussion on synaesthesia see 'Art and Synesthesia' by Dr Hugo Heyrman presented at the First International Conference on Art and Synesthesia 25-28 July 2005, Universidad de Almeria, Spain.

57 Huxley A, *The Doors of Perception*, p11

58 Huxley A, *Heaven and Hell*, p98

59 Sèchehaye MA, *Autobiography Of A Schizophrenic Girl*

60 Huxley A, *Heaven and Hell*, p98-99

61 Bergson H, *Time And Free Will: An Essay on the Immediate Data of Consciousness*, p98

62 Ibid, p107-108

63 Priestley JB *Man and Time*, p67

64 Graham Greene was profoundly influenced by precognitive dreams. In his autobiography *A Sort of Life*, Greene comments that his dreams often gave him awareness of disasters to come,

most notably that involving the Titanic.

65 Cornwall J, *Powers of Darkness, Powers of Light,* p4

66 Roy A, 'World Enough and Time', p1653

67 Later in the book, there's an example given of a lady who, as part of a near-death experience, began to talk in fluent Hindustani, a language she had not spoken for 70 years.

68 Orme JE, *Time, Experience And Behaviour,* p13

69 Koehler W, *The Mentality of Apes*

70 Walker S, *Animal Thought,* p190

71 Whorf BL, *Language, Thought and Reality*

72 Pais A, *Subtle is The Lord,* p152

73 Of course, this is a theoretical statement. In order to do this one would need a very powerful light source and an almost unachievable low trajectory.

74 Weyl H, *Space-Time-Matter*

75 'Proceedings of the 33rd Annual Symposium on Frequency Control', p4

76 Davies P, *About Time – Einstein's Unfinished Revolution,* p55,

77 Ibid p69

78 Clay R & Crouch P, 'Evidence of Tachyons', *Nature,* vol 248, p28

79 Bilaniuk OM & Sudershan G, 'More about Tachyons', *Physics Today,* Dec 1980

80 Sarfatti J, *Implications of Meta-Physics for Psychoenergetic Systems,*

81 Parmenides was an Italiote Greek (Eleatic) philosopher of the 6th–5th centuries BCE. He argued that time and motion were illusions. For him 'Being', as in subjective existence of the self, is the only fact that a conscious creature can truly prove.

82 Godel K, 'Relationship between Relativity Theory and Idealistic Philosophy'

83 Barbour J, 'Timeless', *New Scientist,* 16 Oct 1999

84 Ibid

85 To show that our movement is subjective try placing yourself in a totally darkened room with a small dim light display at the far end. If you look at the light for a few seconds it will start to move around, although in reality it stays in one place. This effect, known as 'autokinetic phenomenon', has never been properly explained.

86 It should be recalled that this phenomenon is far more complex than stated by Barbour. The brain not only transmits the data backwards and forwards in the brain but also in *time*. The experiments by Kolers and von Grunau imply that Barbour's theory is correct.

87 If this does come to pass Nixon was certain where was the safest place to be, namely 'In God's holy acre/Twixt Mersey and Dee', otherwise known as the Wirral Peninsula.

88 Barbour J, *The End of Time,* p28-29,

89 Ramachandran VS, *Phantoms in the Brain,* p72

90 Hoagland H, 'The Physiological Control of Judgements of Duration', p267

91 François M, 'Contribution à L'Étude du Sens du Temps', p186

92 Cooper LF, reported in *Science Newsletter,* May 1948

93 Holden C, 'Altered States of Consciousness: Mind Researchers Meet to Discuss Exploration and Mapping of Inner Space', p983

94 Smythies JR, 'Aspects of Consciousness', p248

95 Erickson MH, 'Special Enquiry with Aldous Huxley', p88

96 Ashe G, *The Book Of Prophecy,* p222-226

97 Tyrell J, *Past Present and To Come*

98 Wilson C & Grant J, *The Directory of Possibilities*, p133

99 Ashe G, *The Book Of Prophecy*, p140-141

100 Cheetham E, *The Further Prophecies of Nostradamus*, p205

101 Ibid p99

102 Randi J, *The Supernatural A–Z*, p213-214,

103 Dunne JW, *An Experiment With Time*, p49

104 Ibid p57

105 Talbot M, *The Holographic Universe*, p206

106 Dalton G F, 'Serialism and the unconscious', p225-35

107 Kooey JMJ, 'Space, time and consciousness', p259-272

108 Sondow N, 'The decline of precognized events with the passage of time: Evidence from spontaneous dreams', p33-51

109 Orme JE, 'Precognition and time', p351-365

110 Radin D, *The Conscious Universe: The Scientific Truth of Psychic Phenomena*, p116-124

111 Funkhouser A T, *Dreams and Déjà vu*

112 Barker JC, *Journal of the Society for Psychical Research*, 44, 1967, p196-180

113 Priestley JB, *Man & Time*, p225-226

114 Ibid p208

115 Ibid p258

116 Myers FWH, 'The Subliminal Self', p488

117 Randles J, *Beyond Explanation*

118 Hilgard E, *Divided Consciousness: Multiple Controls in Human Thought and Action*

119 Wilkes KV, 'Fuges, Hypnosis and Multiple Personalitities',

120 Ibid

121 Hilgard E, 'The Hypnotic State'

122 Talbot M, *The Holographic Universe*, p210

123 Erickson MH, 'Special Enquiry with Aldous Huxley', p88

124 The word *aura* was also used by the Ancient Greeks to describe the curious perceptual changes that are experienced by an epileptic just before a seizure.

125 The Greek word that Homer uses to denote Aeneas's double was not *daemon* but *eidolon*. In Homer's time this word also meant a 'representation' or image. In time it was used to describe any man-made image of a god.

126 Homer, *The Iliad*, Book V

127 Guthrie WKC, *History of Greek Philosophy*, p318

128 *Apology* 31d, *Phaedrus* 242 and *Republic* 496c

129 Epictetus, *The Teachings of Epictetus*, p145

130 Lane-Fox R, *Pagans and Christians*, p129

131 Codex II

132 Mayer M (Ed), *The Nag Hammadi Library in English*,

133 The full English text of not only all the Nag Hammadi documents but also of many other Gnostic texts can be found at: www.webcom.com/~gnosis/search_form.html

134 Exodus 20 verse 5

135 Pagels E, *The Gnostic Gospels*, p62

136 Hollroyd S, *Gnosticism*, p69

137 Freke T & Gandy P, *Wisdom of the Pagan Philosophers*, p40

138 Segal RA, *The Gnostic Jung*,

139 Lane-Fox R, *Pagans and Christians*, p565

140 Jeans J, *The Mysterious Universe*,

141 Lane-Fox R, *Pagans and Christians*, p565

142 Hollroyd S, *Gnosticism*, p69

143 Robinson JM, *The Nag Hammadi Library*, p201

144 Globus GG, *Consciousness & The Brain*, p170

145 Puccetti R, 'Brain Bisection and Personal Identity', Br J Philos Sci 1973,24, p339-355

146 LeDoux J, Wilson DH and Gazzaniga M, 'A Divided Mind'

147 Penrose R, *The Emperor's New Mind*, Vintage, London, 1990

148 Gazzaniga M, 'The Split Brain in Man,' p24-29

149 Crabtree A, *Multiple Man*

150 Binet A, *On Double Consciousness*

151 Talbot M, *The Holographic Universe*, p141

152 McDonald N, 'Living With Schizophrenia', in Goleman & Davidson 1979

153 Bleuler E, *Dementia Praecox or The Group of Schizophrenias*

154 Gregory RL (ed.), *The Oxford Companion to the Mind*, p697

155 Raines et al, 'Phenomenology of Hallucinations in the Deaf'

156 Bleuler E, *Dementia Praecox or The Group of Schizophrenias,*, p98

157 Kirshner LA, 'The mechanism of déjà vu', *Diseases of the Nervous System*, p246-249

158 Ferguson M, *The Brain Revolution*, p226

159 Jaynes J, *The Origin of Consciousness and the Breakdown of the Bicameral Mind*, p86

160 Homer, *The Iliad*, p197

161 Ibid Book 4, 437ff

162 Ibid Book 3, 164ff

163 Ibid Book 2, 56ff

164 Jaynes J, *The Origin of Consciousness and the Breakdown of the Bicameral Mind*, p86

165 Lane-Fox R, *Pagans and Christians*, p129

166 Inglis B, *Coincidence*, p85

167 Heywood R, *The Infinite Hive*, p106

168 Ibid p125-6

169 Keyes D, *The Mind of Billy Milligan*

170 From *The Catholic Encyclopaedia* http://www. newadvent.org/cathen/07049

171 St Thomas Aquinas *Summa Theologica* 1:113:4

172 Ibid 1:111:4

173 Ibid 1:111:3

174 Heywood R, *The Infinite Hive*, p105-06

175 Freud S, *The Uncanny*

176 Wilson I, *The After Death Experience*, p143

177 Gregory RL (ed.), *The Oxford Companion to the Mind*, p200

178 Gurney E, Myers F & Podmore F, *Phantasms of the Living*, vol 2, p217

179 Davies R, *Doubles, The Enigma of the Second Self*, p121

180 Weyl, title, page ref

181 Goethe was convinced that the vast majority of his writing came from a spiritual source outside of himself, namely his Daemon, his 'invisible genius'. It is therefore surprising that he met his own *doppelgänger* which made him believe he had lived his life many times before.

183 Fischer F, 'Zeitstruktur und Schizophrenie', p563

184 Ibid p561

185 Ciompi L, 'Uber abnormes Zeiterleben bei einer Schizophrenen', p104

186 Bleuler E, *Dementia Praecox or The Group of Schizophrenias*

187 Davies P, *About Time – Einstein's Unfinished Revolution*, p37

188 Poincaré H, 'Compte Rendus de l'Académie des Sciences', p550

189 Nietzsche F, 'A Nietzsche Reader',p249-50

190 Borges wrote a short story that mirrors both the freezing of time outlined in the 'Protoevangelium' and in Dostoevsky. Entitled 'The Secret Miracle', it tells of the final few seconds of a fictional Jewish dramatist.

191 Cohen & Phipps, *The Common Experience*, p175

192 Brown E, Fitzmayer J & Murphy R (eds.), *The New Jerome Biblical Commentary*, 67:64 (III)

193 I suspect that the narrator was a sufferer of TLE, causing the chemicals released into his temporal lobes and hippocampus to affect his perception of time.

194 Whitrow GW, *Time in History*, p43

195 Ibid p59

196 Eliade M, *The Myth of the Eternal Return*

197 Vaughan A, *Patterns Of Prophesy*

198 Osty E, *Supernatural Facilities in Man*

199 Wilson C, *Beyond The Occult*, p150

200 Ibid p141

201 Jung CG, *Memories, Dreams, Reflections*

202 Wilson C, *The Occult*, p41-42

203 Inglis B, *Coincidence*, p85

204 One of the main objections made to time travel is known as the 'Grandfather Paradox'. This states that if the hero went back in time and while in the past brought about the death of his own grandfather he would cease to exist in the future. However, if he has never existed he is not able to go back in time and his grandfather remains alive. Everett's Many Worlds Interpretation solves this paradox - the grandfather lives in one universe and dies in another.

205 Parson C, *Encounters With The Unknown*

206 Dickens C, *David Copperfield*, ch 39

207 Neppe VM, *The Psychology of Déjà Vu – Have I Been Here Before?*

208 Myers FWH, 'The Subliminal Self', page 341

209 Gregory RL (ed.), *The Oxford Companion to the Mind*, p182

210 Ibid p183

211 Wigan AL, *The Duality of Mind*

212 Efron R, 'Temporal perception, aphasia and déjà vu', p403-424

213 Ferguson M, *The Brain Revolution*, p69

214 Sacks O, *Migraine*, p78

215 Janet P, *Les obsessions et la psychasthénie*

216 Gregory RL (ed.), *The Oxford Companion to the Mind*, p183

217 Freud S, *The Ego and the Id*

218 Bartlett FC, *Remembering: A Study of Experimental and Social Psychology*

219 Banister H & Zangwill OL, 'Experimentally induced visual paramnesia', p30-51

220 Pickford RW, 'A restricted paramnesia of complex origin', p186-191

221 Neppe VM, 'The Concept of Déjà vu', p4-5

222 Mullan S & Penfield W, 'Illusions of comparative interpretation and emotion', p269-284

223 McHarg J, 'Personation: cryptomnesic and paranormal – two contrasting cases', p36-50

224 Neppe VM, 'The Concept of Déjà vu', p4-5

225 Neppe VM, *The Psychology of Déjà Vu – Have I Been Here Before?*

226 Ibid

227 Nash CB, *Science of PSI: ESP and PK*, p124

228 Funkhouser A T, 'The 'Dream' Theory of Déjà vu', p121

229 Marcowitz E, 'The meaning of déjà vu', p481-489

230 Papez JW, 'A proposed mechanism of emotion', p725-39

231 This may perhaps explain how those cruelly termed idiot savants can, although mentally challenged, perform feats of mathematical genius. There is very strong evidence that these 'skills', together with phenomenal powers of recall seen in those with 'savant's syndrome' are brought about by a failure of a crucial process that takes place just before birth.

232 Gregory RL (ed.), *The Oxford Companion to the Mind*, p529

233 Delgado JMR, *Physical Control of the Mind*

234 Ferguson M, *The Brain Revolution*, p69

235 Penfield W & Roberts L, *Speech & Brain Mechanisms*, p45-47

236 Pribram K, 'The neurobehavioral analysis of limbic forebrain mechanisms; revision and progress report', p297-332

237 Geary J, 'Been There, Done That', *Time*, vol 149, no 18,

238 Beckstein JB, 'Information In The Holographic Universe', p49-55

239 Note his words 'always started by *another person's voice*'. Could this be the voice of the Daemon as experienced by such people as Julian Jaynes?

240 Jackson JH, 'On a particular variety of epilepsy', *Brain*, 11, p202

241 Ibid p702

242 Chrichton-Browne J, 'Dreamy Mental States', *Lancet*, July 6, p1–5, July 13, p73-75,

243 Neppe VM, *The Psychology of Déjà Vu – Have I Been Here Before?*

244 Neppe VM, 'A Study in the incidence of subjective paranormal experience', p15-37

245 Stanford R, 'Is scientific parapsychology possible?' p231-271

246 Neppe VM, *The Psychology of Déjà Vu – Have I Been Here Before?*

247 Strauss H, 'Epileptic disorder', p109

248 It is important to note that 3 of the 13 schizophrenics also reported strong déjà vécu experiences.

249 Neppe VM, 'The incidence of déjà vu', *Parapsychology Journal of South Africa*. 4:2, p103

250 Walter WG, *The Living Brain*

251 It has long been suspected that Lewis Carroll, the writer of *Alice In Wonderland* suffered from TLE. Many of the images found in both *Wonderland* and *Through The Looking Glass* have aura undertones, specifically Alice growing very big and very small.

252 The term *aura* was also applied by the Ancient Greeks to the disembodied aspect of the human personality that manifested itself as a *double* - another intriguing link between human duality and epilepsy.

253 Samt P, 'Epileptische Irreseinsformen' p339-344

254 Ramachandran VS, *Phantoms in the Brain,*p180-181

255 Evans M, *A Ray of Darkness*, p182

256 Ibid 122

257 Taken from Blake's poem 'Milton: The Sky is an Immortal Tent Built By The Sons of Los'.

258 Taxil J, *Traicté de l' épilepsie,*p155

259 Plato, *Phaedrus*

260 Pollard J, *Seers, Shrines and Sirens*

261 Muilenberg J, *Old TestamentProphecy*, in Peake's Commentary p411d

262 1 Samuel, 10 verses 23-24

263 This is translated as 'raved' in the Revised Standard Version.

264 I Samuel, 18:10

265 *Nephesh* is a concept within OT Judaism translated as 'being' or 'soul'. In this particular case it implies that the day-to-day consciousness is taken over by a higher being. Within the context of this book it can be freely interpreted as being the Hebrew term for *Eidolon*, with the *Daemon* manifesting itself as a 'demon sent by God'.

266 Jeremiah 1:9

267 Rabban at-Taban A, *Paradise of Wisdom*, p138

268 Inglis B, *Coincidence*, p177

269 Campanella T, *La Città del Sole*, p31-32

270 Lombroso C, *The Man of Genius*, p338-352

271 Ibid p336

272 Ibid p339

273 Ibid p339

274 Jung called his Daemon guide 'Philemon' in the same way that the Goncourt brothers called their Daemon-inspired novel *Soeur Philomène*. In taking this name both the Goncourt brothers and Jung seem to imply that at a higher level all people have two distinct, but united, personalities.

275 Temkin O, *The Falling Sickness*, p374

276 Schachter SC, *Brainstorms: Epilepsy in Our Words*

277 Ibid quotation 8

278 The neurologist William Gordon Lennox considers that Strindberg himself was an epileptic. This incident can be explained as a part of his illness. In *Epilepsy and Related Disorders* (Little, Brown, 1960) he also lists Petrarch, Tasso, Dickens, Socrates, Pascal, Swedenborg, Pythagoras, Richelieu, and Newton as epileptics, many of whom are in this book.

279 Strindberg A, *Legends*, p92-93

280 Schachter SC, *Brainstorms: Epilepsy in Our Words*, quotation 27

281 Sacks O, *Migraine*, p84

282 Ibid p83

283 Inglis B, *Coincidence*, p117

284 LaPlante E, *Seized*, p111

285 Ibid p5-6

286 Inman AC, *The Inman Diary*

287 LaPlante E, *Seized*, p235

288 Ibid p235

289 Schachter SC, *Brainstorms: Epilepsy in Our Words*, quotation 34

290 Moody R, *Life After Life*

291 Ring K, *Life At Death*

292 Noyes R & Slyman D, 'The Subjective Response to Life Threatening Danger', p312-21

293 Plato, *Republic X*, 614b,c,d

294 Faulkner RO (ed.), *The Ancient Egyptian Book of the Dead*, p29-31

295 Noyes R & Kletti R, 'Panoramic Memory: A Response to the Threat of Death', p181-194

296 De Quincey T, *Opium Eater and Sequels*

297 Ibid p511-512

298 Heim A, 'Notizen über den Tod durch Absturz', p45-52

299 Ibid p45-52

300 Watson L, *The Romeo Error*, p63

301 Ibid

302 Ring K, *Life At Death*, p116

303 Whitton J & Fisher J, *Life Between Life*, p39

304 Moody R, *Life After Life*, p68

305 Flammarion C, *Death And Its Mysteries*, p142 footnote

306 Hulin M, *Sur La Chute En Montagne*, Bulletin IANDS

307 Woolridge D, *The Machinery Of The Brain*

308 Cutforth R, *Reporting The War In Korea*

309 Ring K, *Life At Death*, p71-72

310 Ring K & Valarino EE, *Lessons From The Light*, p22

311 Fenwick P & E, *The Truth in The Light*

312 Ibid p47

313 Sabom M, *Recollections of Death; A Medical Investigation*

314 Ring K, *Life at Death*, p97

315 Ring K, *Heading Towards Omega*, p186-187

316 Moody R & Perry P, *The Light Beyond*, p22

317 Ring K, *Life at Death*, p76

318 Moody R, *Life After Life*, p56 & 66

319 Rawlings M, *Beyond Death's Door*, p88

320 Monroe RA, *Journeys Out of the Body*, p51

321 Fenwick P & E, *The Truth in The Light*, p120

322 Wilson I, *The After Death Experience*, p143

323 Fenwick P & E, *The Truth in The Light*, p113

324 Ibid p121

325 Ibid p143

326 Ibid p121

327 Wilson C, *Beyond the Occult*

328 Freeborn H, 'Temporary Reminiscence of a Long Forgotten Language during Delirium of

Broncho-Pneumonia', p1685-6

329   Olney et al, 'Excito-toxic mechanisms of epileptic brain damage', p857-877

330   Mody I & Heinemann U, 'NMDA receptors of dentate gyrus cells participate in synaptic transmission "following kindling"

331   Cotman et al, 'Anatomical organisation of excitatory amino acid receptors and their pathways', p273-279

332   Jansen K L R 'Neuroscience and the near-death experience' p25-29

333   Jansen K L R 'Neuroscience, Ketamine and the Near-Death Experience'

334   Grinspoon L & Bakalar S 'Psychedelic Drugs Reconsidered', p34

335   Persinger M & Makarec K 'Temporal lobe epileptic signs and correlative behaviours displayed by normal populations', p179-95

336   Saavedra-Aguilar J & Gomez-Jeria J 'A neurobiological model of near-death experiences', p205-222

337   Roth M & Harper M 'Temporal Lobe Epilepsy and the Phobic Anxiety-Depersonalisation Syndrome', p 215-226

338   Noyes R & Slyman D 'The Subjective Response to Life Threatening Danger' p313-321

339   Grof S & Halifax J, *The Human Encounter With Death*

340   Sagan C, *Broca's Brain*

341   Blackmore S J, 'Birth and the OBE; an unhelpful analogy' p229-238

342   Blackmore S J, *Dying To Live,*

343   Tegmark M, 'The Interpretation of Quantum Mechanics: Many Worlds or Many Words'

344   Sabom M, 'Recollections of Death; A Medical Investigation'

345   Heim A, 'Notizen über den Tod durch Absturz', p45-52

346   Saavadra-Anguiler J & Gomez-Jeria J 'A Neurobiological Model Of Near Death Experiences' p205-222

347   Thomson J, 'Tasks and Super-Tasks', p94-95

348   Ibid

349   LePoidevin R, *Travels In Four Dimensions*

350   www.ArchiveX/stories.html

351   Osis K & Haraldsson E, *At The Hour Of Death*, p44

352   Davies R Doubles, *The Enigma of the Second Self* p126

353   Ibid p129

354   Ibid p114

355   Watson L, *Lifetide*, p222

356   Grof S, *Realms of the Human Unconscious*, p20

357   Laibow R, *Birth Recall: A clinical report*, p78-81

358   Mollon P, *Multiple Selves, Multiple Voices*

359   A work colleague told me a curious story about the reaction of their 2-year-old when told she was going to have a new brother or sister. She claimed to know all about it and asked if the baby would be 'swimming in the dark' as she did - a concept not previously discussed with her.

360   Murrai T & Fukao K 'Paramnesic Multiplication of Autobiographical Memory as a Manifestation of Interictal Psychosis' p49-51

361   The e-mail can be seen at : www.mindspring .com/~scottr/nde/anon2.html

Bibliography

Books

Arieti S (ed.), *American Handbook of Psychiatry*, Basic Books, New York, 1959

Ashe G, *The Book Of Prophecy*, Blandford, London, 1999

Baierlein R, *Newton to Einstein*, Cambridge University Press, Cambridge, 1992

Bailey L & Yates J, *The Near Death Experience*, Routledge, London, 1996

Barbour J, *The End of Time*, Phoenix, London, 1999

Bartlett FC, *Remembering: A Study of Experimental and Social Psychology*, Cambridge University Press, Cambridge, 1995

Bergson H, *Time And Free Will: An Essay on the Immediate Data of Consciousness*, George Allen & Unwin, London, 1988

Binet A, *On Double Consciousness*, Open Court, Chicago, 1980

Blackmore SJ, *Dying To Live*, Grafton, London, 1993

Bleuler E, *Dementia Praecox or The Group of Schizophrenias*, (trans. Zinkin J), International Universities Press, New York, 1950

Bohm D, *Wholeness and the Implicate Order*, Routledge & Kegan Paul, London, 1980

Bohm D & Peat D, *Science, Order, and Creativity*, Bantam, New York, 1987

Bradley FE, *Appearance and Reality*, Oxford University Press, Oxford, 1897

Brown E, Fitzmayer J & Murphy R (eds.), *The New Jerome Biblical Commentary*, Cassell, London, 1988

Campanella T, *La Città del Sole*, University of California Press, Los Angeles, 1982

Cheetham E, *The Further Prophecies of Nostradamus*, Corgi Books, London, 1985

Cohen & Phipps, *The Common Experience*, Rider, London, 1979

Cornwall J, *Powers of Darkness, Powers of Light*, Penguin, London, 1992

Crabtree A, *Multiple Man*, Praeger, New York, 1985

Davies P, *About Time – Einstein's Unfinished Revolution*, Viking, London, 1995

Davies R, *Doubles, The Enigma of the Second Self*, Robert Hale, London, 1998

De Quincey T, *Confessions of an English Opium Eater*, Macdonald & Co, London, 1956

Delgado JMR, *Physical Control of the Mind*, Harper Row, New York, 1969

Dennett D C, *Consciousness Explained*, Penguin, London, 1993

Dunne JW, *An Experiment With Time*, Faber, London, 1927

Eliade M, *The Myth of the Eternal Return*, Routledge & Kegan Paul, London, 1955

Evans M, *A Ray of Darkness*, John Calder, London, 1978

Faulkner RO (ed.), *The Ancient Egyptian Book of the Dead*, British Museum, London, 1985

Fenwick P & E, *The Truth in The Light*, Headline, London, 1995

Ferguson M, *The Brain Revolution*, Taplinger, New York, 1973

Feynman R, *The Character of Physical Law*, Penguin, London, 1992

Flammarion C, *Death And Its Mysteries*, The Century Co, New York, 1921

Freke T & Gandy P, *Wisdom of the Pagan Philosophers*, Journey Editions, London, 1998

Freud S, *The Uncanny*, Penguin Classics, London, 2003

— *The Ego and the Id*, Norton, New York, 1962

Gindes BC, *New Concepts in Hypnosis*, George Allen & Unwin, London, 1953

Globus GG, *Consciousness & The Brain*, Plenum Press, New York, 1976

Goleman D & Davidson RJ, *Consciousness, Brain, States of Awareness and Mysticism*, Harper Row, New York, 1979

Goodman N, *Ways of Worldmaking*, Harvester Press, Sussex, 1978

Gregory RL (ed.), *The Oxford Companion to the Mind*, Oxford University Press, Oxford, 1998

Greyson B & Flynn C (eds.), *The Near-Death Experience, Problems, Prospects, Perspectives*, CC Thomas, Springfield, 1984

Grinspoon L & Bakalar S, *Psychedelic Drugs Reconsidered*, Basic Books, New York, 1981

Grof S, *Realms of the Human Unconscious*, EP Dutton, New York, 1976

Grof S & Halifax J, *The Human Encounter With Death*, Souvenir Press, London, 1977

Gurney E, Myers F & Podmore F, *Phantasms of the Living*, (abridged edition), Kegan Paul Trench Tubner & Co, London, 1918

Guthrie WKC, *History of Greek Philosophy*, Cambridge University Press, Cambridge, 1962

Heywood R, *The Infinite Hive*, Chatto & Windus, London, 1964

Hiley BJ & Peat FD, *Quantum Implications*, Routledge & Kegan Paul, London, 1987

Hilgard E, *Divided Consciousness: Multiple Controls in Human Thought and Action*, John Wiley and Sons, New York, 1986

Hollroyd S, *Gnosticism*, Element Books, London, 1994

Hunt M, *The Universe Within*, Corgi Books, London, 1984

Huxley A, *The Doors of Perception*, Flamingo, London, 1994

— *Heaven and Hell*, Flamingo, London, 1994

Inglis B, *Coincidence*, Hutchinson, London, 1990

Inman AC, *The Inman Diary – A Public and Private Confession*, Harvard University Press, Boston, 1985

Janet P, *Les obsessions et la psychasthénie*, Alcan, Paris, 1903

Jaynes J, *The Origin of Consciousness and the Breakdown of the Bicameral Mind*, Houghton Mifflin, Boston, 1976

Jeans J, *The Mysterious Universe*, Cambridge University Press, Cambridge, 1931

Jung CG, *Memories, Dreams, Reflections*, Routledge & Kegan Paul, London, 1963

Keup W, *Origins and Mechanisms of Hallucinations*, Plenum Press, New York, 1970

Keyes D, *The Mind of Billy Milligan*, Random House, New York, 1981

Koehler W, *The Mentality of Apes*, Penguin, London, 1957

Lane-Fox R, *Pagans And Christians*, Penguin, London, 1986

LaPlante E, *Seized*, Harper Collins, New York, 1993

Lehrman DS, Hinde RA and Shaw E (eds.), *Advances in the Study of Behaviour*, Academic Press, New York, 1969

LePoidevin R, *Travels In Four Dimensions*, Oxford University Press, Oxford, 2003

Lombroso C, *The Man of Genius*, Walton Scott, London, 1905

Luria AS, *The Mind of a Mnemonist*, Jonathan Cape, New York, 1969

Maury A, *Sleep And Dreams*, Paris, 1878

Mollon P, *Multiple Selves, Multiple Voices*, Wiley, New York, 1995

Monroe RA, *Journeys Out of the Body*, Anchor Press, New York, 1985

Moody R, *Life After Life*, Corgi Books, London, 1977

Moody R & Perry P, *The Light Beyond*, Bantam Books, New York, 1988

Nash CB, *Science of PSI: ESP and PK*, CC Thomas, Springfield, 1978

Neppe VM, *The Psychology of Déjà Vu – Have I Been Here Before?*, Witwatersrand University Press, Johannesburg, 1983

Orme JE, *Time, Experience And Behaviour*, Illife, London, 1969

Osborn A, *The Future is Now: The Significance of Precognition*, Theosophical University Press, Wheaton, 1973

Osis K & Haraldsson E, *At The Hour Of Death*, Avon Books, New York, 1977

Osty E, *Supernatural Facilities in Man*, Methuen, London, 1923

Ouspensky P, *A New Model Of The Universe*, Arkana, London, 1931

Pagels E, *The Gnostic Gospels*, Penguin, London, 1979

Pais A, *Subtle is The Lord*, Clarendon Press, Oxford, 1982

Parson C, *Encounters With The Unknown*, Robert Hale, London, 1991

Penfield W, *The Mystery of Mind; A Critical Study of Consciousness and the Human Brain*, Princeton University Press, Princeton, New Jersey, 1975

Penfield W & Roberts L, *Speech & Brain Mechanisms*, Princeton University Press, Princeton, New Jersey, 1959

Penrose R, *The Emperor's New Mind*, Vintage, London, 1990

Penrose R & Isham CJ, *Quantum Concepts in Space & Time*, Oxford University Press, Oxford, 1986

Pinker S, *How The Mind Works*, Penguin, London, 1997

Pollard J, *Seers, Shrines and Sirens*, Allen & Unwin, London, 1965

Poulet G, *Studies In Human Time*, Harper, New York, 1959

Poundstone W, *Labyrinths Of Reason*, Doubleday, New York, 1988

Priestley JB, *Man & Time*, Aldus, London, 1964

Radin D, *The Conscious Universe: The Scientific Truth of Psychic Phenomena*, Harper Collins, New York, 1997

Ramachandran VS, *Phantoms in the Brain*, Fourth Estate, London, 1998

Randi J, *The Supernatural A–Z*, Headline, London, 1995

Randles J, *Beyond Explanation*, Hale, London, 1985

Rawlings M, *Beyond Death's Door*, Sheldon Press, London, 1978

Ring K, *Life At Death*, Coward McCann, New York, 1980

— *Heading Toward Omega*, Morrow, New York, 1984

Ring K & Valarino EE, *Lessons From The Light: What Can we Learn from NDE?*, Plenum/Insight, New York, 1998

Robinson J (ed.), *The Nag Hammadi Library in English*, Harper, San Francisco, 1990

Robinson JM, *The Nag Hammadi Library*, Harper Collins, New York, 1978

Rubin MH & Shih YH, *Fundamental Problems In Quantum Theory*, Wiley, New York, 1997

Ryle G, *The Concept of Mind*, Penguin, London, 1990

Sabom M, *Recollections of Death; A Medical Investigation*, Harper Row, New York, 1982

Sacks O, *Migraine*, Picador, London, 1995

— *An Anthropologist on Mars*, Picador, London, 1995

Sagan C, *Broca's Brain*, Random House, New York, 1979

Sarfatti J, *Implications of Meta-Physics for Psychoenergetic Systems*, Gordon & Breach, New York, 1974

Schachter SC, *Brainstorms: Epilepsy in Our Words*, Raven Press, New York, 1993

Schlipp PA, *Albert Einstein: Philosopher-Scientist*, Open Court, Chicago, 1970

Sèchehaye MA, *Autobiography Of A Schizophrenic Girl*, Signet, New York, 1970

Segal RA, *The Gnostic Jung*, Routledge, London, 1992

Shaw RE & Bransford, *Perceiving, Acting, and Knowing*, Erlbaum Associates, New Jersey, 1977

Siffre M, *Beyond Time*, McGraw Hill, New York, 1964

Smythies JR & Koestler A, *Beyond Reductionism*, Hutchinson, London, 1969

Strindberg A, *Legends*, 1912

Talbot M, *The Holographic Universe*, Grafton, London, 1991

Tart C, *Altered States of Consciousness*, Harper Collins, New York, 1990

Taxil J, *Traicté de l' épilepsie*, Tournon, 1602

Temkin O, *The Falling Sickness*, John Hopkins University Press, Baltimore, 1945

Ullman M, Krippner S & Vaughan A, *Dream Telepathy*, Macmillan, New York, 1973

Vaughan A, *Patterns Of Prophesy*, Turnstone, London, 1973

Walker S, *Animal Thought*, Routledge & Kegan Paul, London, 1983

Walter WG, *The Living Brain*, Penguin, London, 1968

Watson L, *Lifetide*, Hodder & Stoughton, London, 1979

Weyl H, *Space-Time-Matter*, Methuen, London, 1922

Whitrow GW, *Time in History*, Oxford University Press, Oxford, 1989

Whitton J & Fisher J, *Life Between Life*, Doubleday, New York, 1986

Whorf BL, *Language, Thought and Reality*, MIT Press, Boston, 1956

Wigan AL, *A New View Of Insanity: The Duality of Mind*, Longman Brown Green & Longmans, London, 1844

Wilkes KV, *Self & Identity: Contemporary Philosophical Issues*, MacMillan, New York, 1991

Wilson C, *Beyond The Occult*, Bantam Press, London, 1988

— *The Occult*, Hodder & Stoughton, London, 1971

Wilson C & Grant J, *The Directory of Possibilities*, Corgi Books, London, 1982

Wilson I, *The After Death Experience*, Sidgwick & Jackson, London, 1987

Woolridge D, *The Machinery Of The Brain*, McGraw Hill, New York, 1963

Articles

Aspect A & Grangier P, 'Experiments on EPR type correlations with pairs of visible photons', in Penrose R & Isham CJ, *Quantum Concepts in Space & Time*, Oxford University Press, 1986

Banister H & Zangwill OL, 'Experimentally induced visual paramnesia', *British Journal of Medical Psychology*, 32, 1942

Barbour J, 'Timeless', *New Scientist*, October 1999

Beckstein JB, 'Information In The Holographic Universe', *Scientific American*, August 2003

Bergson H, 'Le souvenir du présent et la fausse reconnaissance', *Revue Philosophique*, 66, 1908

Bilaniuk OM & Sudershan G, 'More about Tachyons', *Physics Today*, December 1980

Blackmore SJ, 'Birth and the OBE; an unhelpful analogy', *Journal of the American Society for Psychical Research*, 77, 1982

Bohm D, 'Hidden Variables In The Implicate Order', in Hiley BJ & Peat FD, *Quantum Implications*, Routledge & Kegan Paul, London, 1987

Chrichton-Browne J, 'Dreamy Mental States', *Lancet*, July 6, 1–5, July 13, 1895

Ciompi L, 'Uber abnormes Zeiterleben bei einer Schizophrenen', *Psychiatrie und Neurologie*, 1961

Clay R & Crouch P, 'Evidence of Tachyons', *Nature*, vol 248, 1974

Cotman et al, 'Anatomical organisation of excitatory amino acid receptors and their pathways', *Trends in Neurosciences*, 10, 1987

Dalton G F, 'Serialism and the unconscious', *Journal of the Society for Psychic Research* 37, 1954

Deeke L, Grötzinger B, & Kornhuber H, 'Voluntary Finger Movements in Man: Cerebral Potentials and Theory', *Biological Cybernetics*, 23:99, 1976

Efron R, 'Temporal perception, aphasia and déjà vu', *Brain*, 86, 1963

Erickson MH, 'Special Enquiry with Aldous Huxley', in Tart C, *Altered States of Consciousness*, Harper Collins, New York, 1990

Fischer F, 'Zeitstruktur und Schizophrenie', *Zeitschr. Ges. Neurol. Psychiat*, vol 121, 1929

Folger T, 'Does The Universe Exist If We Are Not Looking?', *Discover*, vol 23, no 6, June 2002

François M, 'Contribution à L'Étude du Sens du Temps', *Année Psychologie.*, 28, 186, 1948

Freeborn H, 'Temporary Reminiscence of a Long Forgotten Language during Delirium of Broncho-Pneumonia', *The Lancet*, 14 June, 1902

Funkhouser A T, 'The 'Dream' Theory of Déjà vu', *Parapsychology Journal of South Africa.*, 4:2, 1983

Geary J, 'Been There, Done That', *Time*, vol 149, no 18, 1997

Geldard F & Sherrick C, 'The Cutaneous Rabbit: A Perceptual Illusion', *Science*, 178, 1972

Godel K, 'A Remark about the relationship between Relativity Theory and Idealistic Philosophy', in Schlipp PA, *Albert Einstein: Philosopher-Scientist*, Open Court, Chicago, 1970

Heim A, 'Notizen über den Tod durch Absturz', *Omega Journal Of Death & Dying*, 3: 45–52, 1972

Hilgard E, 'The Hypnotic State', Goleman D & Davidson RJ, *Consciousness, Brain, States of Awareness and Mysticism*, Harper Row, New York, 1979

Hoagland H, 'The Physiological Control of Judgements of Duration', *Journal of General Psychology*, 9. 267, 1933

Holden C, 'Altered States of Consciousness: Mind Researchers Meet to Discuss Exploration and Mapping of Inner Space', *Science*, 179, 1973

Hulin M, 'Sur La Chute En Montagne', *Bulletin IANDS*, 1983

Jackson JH, 'On a particular variety of epilepsy', *Brain*, 11, 1889

Jansen KLR, 'Neuroscience and the near-death experience: roles for the NMDA-PCP receptor, the sigma receptor and endopsychosins', *Medical Hypotheses*, 31, 1990

— 'Neuroscience, Ketamine and the Near-Death Experience', in Bailey L & Yates J, *The Near Death Experience*, Routledge, London, 1996

Kirshner LA, 'The mechanism of déjà vu', *Diseases of the Nervous System*, 34, 1970

Kooey JMJ, 'Space, time and consciousness', *Journal of Parapsychology*, 21, 1957

Laibow R, 'Birth Recall: A clinical report', *Pre- & Perinatal Psychology*, 1, 1986

LeDoux J, Wilson DH and Gazzaniga M, 'A Divided Mind', *Annals of Neurology*,2 , 1977

Marcowitz E, 'The meaning of déjà vu', *Psychoanalytic Quarterly*, 2, 1962

McDonald N, 'Living With Schizophrenia', in Goleman D & Davidson RJ, *Consciousness, Brain, States of Awareness and Mysticism*, Harper Row, New York, 1979

McHarg J, 'Personation: cryptomnesic and paranormal – two contrasting cases', *Parapsychology Journal of South Africa.*, 4:1, 1983

Mody I & Heinemann U, 'NMDA receptors of dentate gyrus cells participate in synaptic transmission "following kindling"', *Nature*, 326, 1987

Mullan S & Penfield W, 'Illusions of comparative interpretation and emotion', *Archive of Neurological Psychiatry.*, 81, 1983

Myers FWH, 'The Subliminal Self', *Proceedings of the Society for Psychic Research*, 1895

Neppe VM, 'A Study in the incidence of subjective paranormal experience', *Parapsychology Journal of South Africa.*, 2:1, 1981

— 'The Concept of Déjà vu', *Parapsychology Journal of South Africa*, 4:1, 1983

— 'The incidence of déjà vu', *Parapsychology Journal of South Africa.* 4:2, 1983

Noyes R & Kletti R, 'Panoramic Memory: A Response to the Threat of Death', *Omega, Journal Of Death & Dying*, 8, 1977

Noyes R & Slyman D, 'The Subjective Response to Life Threatening Danger', in Greyson B & Flynn C (eds.), *The Near-Death Experience, Problems, Prospects, Perspectives*, CC Thomas, Springfield, 1984

Olney et al, 'Excito-toxic mechanisms of epileptic brain damage', *Advances in Neurology*, 44, 1986

Orme JE, 'Precognition and time', *Journal of the Society of Psychic Research*, 47, 1974

Papez JW, 'A proposed mechanism of emotion', *Archive of Neuralogical Psychiatry*, 38, 1937

Persinger M & Makarec K, 'Temporal lobe epileptic signs and correlative behaviours displayed by normal populations', *Journal of General Psychology*, 114, 1987

Pickford RW, 'A restricted paramnesia of complex origin', *British Journal of Medical Psychology*, 19, 1942

Pribram K, 'Problems Concerning The Structure Of Consciousness', in Globus GG, *Consciousness & The Brain*, Plenum Press, New York, 1976

— 'The neurobehavioral analysis of limbic forebrain mechanisms; revision and progress report', in Lehrman D S, Hindle R A & Shaw E (1969), 1969

— 'Some Comments on the Nature of the Perceived Universe', in Shaw RE & Bransford, *Perceiving, Acting, and Knowing*, Erlbaum Associates, New Jersey, 1977

Puccetti R, 'Brain Bisection and Personal Identity', *British Journal of the Philosophy of Science*, 1973

Raines et al, 'Phenomenology of Hallucinations in the Deaf', in Keup W, *Origins and Mechanisms of Hallucinations*, Plenum Press, New York, 1970

Roth M & Harper M, 'Temporal Lobe Epilepsy and the Phobic Anxiety-Depersonalisation Syndrome: Part II: Practical and Theoretical Considerations', *Comprehensive Psychiatry*, 1962

Roy A, 'World Enough and Time', *Unexplained Magazine*, (part-work), Orbis, London, 1982

Saavedra-Aguilar J & Gomez-Jeria J, 'A neurobiological model of near-death experiences', *Journal of Near-Death Studies*, 7, 1987

Samt P, 'Epileptische Irreseinsformen', *Archiv für Psychiatrie und Nervenkrankheiten*, 5, 1876

Smythies JR, 'Aspects of Consciousness', in Smythies JR & Koestler A, *Beyond Reductionism*, Hutchinson, London, 1969

Sondow N, 'The decline of precognized events with the passage of time: Evidence from spontaneous dreams', *Journal of the American Society of Psychical Research*, 82, 1988

Stanford R, 'Is scientific parapsychology possible?', *Journal of Parapsychology*, 46, 1982

Strauss H, 'Epileptic disorder', in Arieti S (ed.), *American Handbook of Psychiatry*, Basic Books, New York, 1959

Tegmark M, 'The Interpretation of Quantum Mechanics: Many Worlds or Many Words', in Rubin MH & Shih YH, *Fundamental Problems In Quantum Theory*, Wiley, New York, 1997

Thomson J, 'Tasks and Super-Tasks', *Analysis*, 15, 1954

Toshiya Murrai & Kenjiro Fukao, 'Paramnesic Multiplication of Autobiographical Memory as a Manifestation of Interictal Psychosis', *Psychopathology*, 36, 2003

Wheeler J.A, 'Does The Universe Exist If We Are Not Looking?', *Discover* 23, 6, 2002

About the author

Anthony Peake holds dual honours degrees in Sociology and History from the University of Warwick. He studied at postgraduate level at the London School of Economics, receiving a post-graduate diploma in Personnel Management and Labour Law. He also studied at Masters degree level at the University of Westminster. He is a qualified psychometrician and has applied this knowledge in various business sectors for over twenty years. He developed an interest in para-psychology whilst at Warwick, specializing in the sociology of religion and the sociology of language. He has continued his interest in the subject and has read widely over the last twenty-five years. He lives in the Wirral, England, with his wife Penny and is a member of the International Association of Near Death Studies and the Scientific and Medical Network.

Index